For those who have made it their business in life to speak truth to power, there is nothing left but to continue so to speak, less frequently perhaps than they used to and certainly with less confidence that it will in the short run make much of a difference in the affairs of men.

With that somber statement, Hans J. Morgenthau introduces the collection of his essays that comprise TRUTH AND POWER, a work of penetrating analysis whose scope covers the events of the most explosive and divisive decade in American history since the Civil War. Re-creating a period that began in hope and ended in despair and violence, he captures the commitment to reform that characterized the Kennedy years, and sees that mood turn to bitter frustration as America, still mired in Southeast Asia, moves into the 1970's. Thus emerges a picture of America facing more extreme manifestations of the problems it could not cope with in the previous decade.

With the boldness and originality of vision that have marked his widely acclaimed books on international politics, Professor Morgenthau cuts through the complexities and ambiguities of each issue to expose its essence. Whether he is discussing the Vietnam war, race conflicts, poverty, or the cold war, his analysis bears the stamp of a vigorous intelligence and a profound sense of history. His conclusion that these issues are today "not susceptible to rational solutions within the existing system of power relations" is as painful as it is honest. But despite the pessimism of this conclusion, TRUTH AND POWER offers the enlightening ideas that have come from one man's continuing efforts to inform the "powers-that-be" of the truth.

The book is organized around three broad themes, each relating to the ambivalence and contradictions of modern society. The first section—"The Philosophy"—includes an examination of the bitter conflicts between the intellectuals and the power-holders that marked the Johnson era and an important statement on the place of dissent in a democratic society. The second section—"The Men"—presents revealing profiles of the leading figures of the 1960's: De Gaulle confronting the Atlantic Alliance, Khrushchev challenging Marxist legitimacy, Johnson becoming ever more deeply enmeshed in the Vietnam war. The final section—"The Issues"—analyzes the critical problems that have dominated the past ten years: racial discontent and economic deprivation, the impact of technology and the military on the democratic process, the crisis in the Communist world, and, above all, the war in Southeast Asia.

In a moving epilogue, the author relates all these questions to the ferment in America today and sees this revolt as a "national manifestation of a world-wide revulsion against the world as it is." Arguing the meaninglessness of "challenging the establishment at its fringes," he contends that it is the larger society and its power centers that must be the targets of change. Yet, such radical action will undoubtedly bring repression. Articulating the fears and despair many feel today, he concludes:

Truth and Power

TRUTH

and

POWER

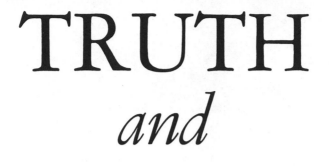

Essays of a Decade, 1960–70

HANS J. MORGENTHAU

PRAEGER PUBLISHERS
New York • Washington • London

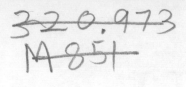
PRAEGER PUBLISHERS
111 Fourth Avenue, New York, N.Y. 10003, U.S.A.
5, Cromwell Place, London S.W.7, England

Published in the United States of America in 1970
by Praeger Publishers, Inc.

Library of Congress Catalog Card Number: 70–112983

Printed in the United States of America

To Hans Kelsen, who has taught us through
his example how to speak Truth to Power

Contents

Part III: The Issues

Preface

This book is a collection of essays written during the 1960's. It differs from my other collections published previously—*Dilemmas of Politics, Politics in the Twentieth Century* (3 vols.)—in that it is selective rather than inclusive. The principle underlying selection has been the likelihood of each essay's having more than transitory interest by virtue of intellectual substance rather than topical relevance.

I have, as far as possible, tried to eliminate duplication and have in a few instances combined articles dealing with the same subject matter. Early articles on Vietnam, starting with "Vietnam—Another Korea?" in May, 1962, and ending with "Vietnam: Shadow and Substance of Power" in September, 1965, were separately published in *Vietnam and the United States* and have not been reprinted here.

May, 1970

Acknowledgments

Grateful acknowledgment is made to the following, in whose pages these essays first appeared:

Book Week: "Understanding Military Strategy," June 20, 1965; "Fascism," February 13, 1966. Reprinted by permission from the Washington Post Company.

Business *International* Chief Executives Roundtable on Long-Range Corporate Planning: "Government and Private Enterprise," January 9–10, 1964.

The Christian Science Monitor: "How Totalitarianism Starts: The Domestic Involvement of the CIA," March 10, 1967. Reprinted by permission. © 1967 The Christian Science Publishing Society. All rights reserved.

Columbia Law Review: "Modern Science and Political Power," December, 1964.

Commentary: "Kennedy the Politician," January, 1962; "U Thant," January, 1963; "Charles de Gaulle: The Grand Design," March, 1963; "On Trying to Be Just," May, 1963; "The Impotence of American Power," November, 1963; "The Coming Test of American Democracy," January, 1964; "J. William Fulbright," May, 1964. Copyright © 1962–64 by the American Jewish Committee. Reprinted by permission.

Continuum: "*Pacem in Terris* and the World Community," Summer, 1963, and Autumn, 1965.

Council on Religion and International Affairs, "U.S. Policy in the Far East: Ideology, Religion, and Superstition" (*CRIA Special Studies* No. 205, 1968): "The Far East."

Democratic Advisory Council, Advisory Committee on Foreign Policy: "The Principles of Propaganda," May 31, 1960.

Encounter: "Arguing About the Cold War," May, 1967.

Norman A. Graebner, ed., *An Uncertain Tradition: American Secretaries of State in the Twentieth Century:* "John Foster Dulles." Copyright © 1961 by McGraw-Hill, Inc. Used by permission of McGraw-Hill Book Company.

Oscar Handlin *et al.*, "Dissent, Democracy and Foreign Policy—A Symposium," *Headline Series* No. 190 (New York: Foreign Policy Association): "The Right to Dissent," August, 1968.

Horace V. Harrison, ed., *The Role of Theory in International Relations*: "The Intellectual and Political Functions of Theory." Copyright © 1964 by Litton Educational Publishing, Inc., by permission of Van Nostrand Reinhold Company.

The Hudson Review: "The Writer's Duty and His Predicament," Summer, 1965. Copyright © 1965 The Hudson Review, Inc.

Illinois Democratic Forum: "Barry Goldwater: The Romantic Regression," Autumn, 1964.

International Organization: "The Police in Their Political Setting," February and April, 1963.

The *Journal of International Affairs*: "International Relations: Common Sense and Theories." Copyright by the Board of Editors of the *Journal of International Affairs*, reprinted from Volume XXI, No. 2, pp. 207–14, 1967. Permission to reprint is gratefully acknowledged to the Editors of the *Journal*.

Look Magazine: "What Should We Do Now?" Reprinted by courtesy of the editors from the August 9, 1966, issue of *Look* Magazine. Copyright 1966 by Cowles Communications, Inc.

The New Leader: "Kennedy and Foreign Policy," July 3, 1961; "The Kennedy Legacy," December 9, 1963; "Khrushchev: The Inner Contradictions of Communism," October 10, 1964; "Freedom and Freedom House," January 2, 1967; "The Middle East," June 19, 1967; "Thoughts on the October Revolution," November 6, 1967; "Czechoslovakia," September 9, 1968. Copyright © 1961, 1963–64, 1967–68 The American Labor Conference on International Affairs, Inc. Reprinted with permission.

The New Republic: "Adlai E. Stevenson: Tragedy and Greatness," August 7, 1965; Johnson's Dilemma: The Alternatives in Vietnam," May 28, 1966; "Truth and Power," November 26, 1966; "What Ails America?" October 28, 1967; parts of "The Doctrine of War Without End," November 2, 1968; "The Rhetoric of Nixon's Foreign Policy," March 21, 1970. © 1965–68, 1970 Harrison-Blaine of New Jersey, Inc.

The New York Review of Books: "Monuments to the Late President," January 6, 1966; "Lyndon B. Johnson: The Summit of Power," March 31, 1966; "Room at the Top," June 23, 1966; "The Inner Weakness," August 18, 1966; parts of "The Doctrine of War Without End," April 6, 1967; "Robert F. Kennedy," August 1, 1968; "Eugene McCarthy," August 22, 1968; "Nixon vs. Humphrey: The Choice," November 7, 1968; "The Limits of Historical Justice," July 10, 1969. Copyright © 1966–69 The New York Review. Reprinted with permission.

The New York Times Magazine: "The Problem of Germany," September 8, 1963; "The Future of Europe," May 17, 1964. © 1963–64 by The New York Times Company. Reprinted by permission.

Problems of Communism: parts of "The Crisis of Communism," September–October, 1966.

University of Cincinnati, Center for the Study of U.S. Foreign Policy, Paper No. 4 (1965): parts of "The Crisis of Communism."

Truth and Power

"The amount of superstition
is not much changed, but it
now attaches to politics,
not to religion"—WILLIAM GRAHAM SUMNER

Prologue

The decimal system is not particularly informative as a principle of organizing our historic experiences. The great events that can be said to have ended one, and ushered in a new, period of history have taken place without regard to our addiction to thinking in terms of decades and centuries. Nothing particularly memorable happened, to consider only modern history, in 1600, 1700, 1800, or 1900, or, for that matter, at the beginning or end of most of the decades into which we subdivide the centuries. Quite to the contrary, 1904 (the Russo-Japanese War), 1914 (the beginning of World War I), 1917 (the Bolshevist Revolution), 1933 (the Nazi seizure of power), 1939 (the outbreak of World War II), 1941 (the entry of Japan and the United States into World War II), 1945 (the first nuclear explosion), 1949 (the Communist seizure of power in China), 1965 (the open intervention of the United States in the Vietnam war) are some of the great historic turning points of the past century that our consciousness has marked as the beginnings and ends of historical periods. The sole exceptions I can think of are the Franco-German War of 1870 and the outbreak of the Korean War in 1950.

There is, then, something artificial and mechanical, something alien to the nature of history and, hence, misleading in our looking back upon the 1960's and forward to the 1970's as self-contained and distinct periods of history. Rereading at the beginning of the 1970's these essays, written during the 1960's, with the knowledge of what has happened since they were written, I am struck by the contemporary character of most of those dealing with current political issues. The issues that were acute then are still acute now. We reflect today on our "national priorities" as a decade ago we tried to rediscover our "national purpose." Race relations are today as precarious as they were ten years ago; the shift of the confrontations from the legislative assemblies and the courts of law to the several arenas where the races meet—schools, places of work, neighborhoods—continues. The war on poverty is being fought, very much like the phony war of 1939–41, through minor encounters, which leaves the positions of the contenders essentially intact. The same observation applies to the other major domestic issues that began to come to the surface in the 1960's, such as the decay of the cities, the destruction of a livable natural environment, and public responsibility for individual health. The closing of public health facilities and the discontinuation of publicly financed medical research, insignificant items in a $200 billion federal budget, amount, in the words of the editor of *Science*, to the "mindless dismantling of American science," illustrating the government's sense of priorities.

As concerns the Vietnam war, the military tactics with which it is being fought and the political tactics with which it is being made palatable to the American people have changed; the moral, political, and military issues to which it has given rise have not. The contradiction between a war fought at a cost of $30 billion a year and a peace economy, supposed to support that war without inflation, price and rent controls, and increases in taxes, persists in dislocating the economy. The economically ruinous and, in the end, biologically fatal nuclear arms race continues to move toward ever higher levels and ever greater insecurity. The government continues to govern through the politics of make-believe rather than by putting into operation the policies appropriate to the issues it faces. In consequence, the gap between what the government says it is doing and what it actually does is as wide as ever. Also in consequence, the people's mistrust of and indifference to the government are as great as ever. And so is the tendency of the government to discredit and stifle dissent.

Thus the substance of the issues we faced in the 1960's has not changed since these essays were written. Those issues are, by and large, as far from solution now as they were then. What has, however, changed—and in good measure because of the lack of solution—is the mood, the moral, intellectual, and political attitudes, with which many of us approach those issues today. Rereading particularly the essays dealing with current political problems, I am struck by the activistic, almost rationalistic mood that permeates them. One only needs to call the President's attention to the probable consequences of certain policies and show him the alternatives and their probable consequences, and he will choose a policy most likely to serve the national interest. I remember with wry amusement my strenuous and ultimately successful efforts in 1965 to bring my views on the Vietnam war to the attention of President Johnson—efforts undertaken in the naïve assumption that if power were only made to see the truth, it would follow that lead. President Johnson's political reaction to this kind of responsible criticism is a matter of public record. His personal reaction was a systematic attempt, making full use of the informal powers of his office, to discredit and silence the voice of the dissenter. In that latter undertaking, he had the voluntary and sometimes enthusiastic assistance of eminent academic and institutional (for instance, Freedom House) supporters of his policy.

I find my faith, suggested by some of these essays, in the power of truth to move men—and, more importantly, statesmen—to action the more curious since almost 25 years ago I launched, in *Scientific Man vs. Power Politics*, a frontal (and, as it turned out, premature) attack against these and other liberal illusions. The disavowal of that faith by political experience was absorbed by me and many, if not the great mass, of my contemporaries not as an isolated incident but as the definitive refutation of one of the main tenets of liberal philosophy. We came to realize now, through political experience, what some of us had concluded before by way of philosophic reflection, that power positions do not yield to arguments, however rationally and morally valid, but only to superior power. We also came to realize that the distribution of power in America favors the continuation of policies that we regard to be indefensible on rational and moral grounds.

That new mood of discouragement and foreboding was already present in qualified form in the 1963 introduction to the paperback edition of *The Purpose of American Politics*. I said then:

Looking back with a critical eye on this analysis of the contemporary crisis of the American purpose, I am impressed with the persistence with which the crisis continues to manifest itself at home and abroad. . . . The shortcomings of our social and political life, which were obvious when this book was written, have persisted. At best, some have been ameliorated; at worst, some have been aggravated.

And I concluded:

> The two great domestic changes testing again the purpose of America—equality in freedom for the American Negro and the restoration of a meaningful economic and social order—are interconnected. The former cannot be fully achieved, and might even be ultimately jeopardized, without the latter. For even if the Negro were to come into full possession of legal and social equality, he would still be exposed to the disabilities of a contracting labor market. As an unskilled laborer, discriminated against as a Negro, he is likely to be permanently unemployed. But as a skilled worker competing without discrimination for ever scarcer jobs, he would still be threatened with unemployment. The resentment of Negroes whose new equality reveals itself as meaningless in economic terms would be a source of alienation from America. The resentment of the ever swelling mass of white unemployed would be a source of alienation from the political and social *status quo*. And in all probability one resentment would be pitted against the other, fanning anew the enmity of races.
>
> Thus the domestic changes, actual and impending, which we have been witnessing since this book was written raise again in a novel and acute way the central issue of American existence: how can the purpose of America be achieved under novel conditions? That issue comprises, as it has always done, mortal dangers and unique opportunities. It puts into question the very existence of America.

While we then stressed the opportunities over the dangers, we now put the emphasis the other way around. For it has become obvious that the great issues of our day—the militarization of American life, the Vietnam war, race conflicts, poverty, the decay of the cities, the destruction of the natural environment—are not susceptible to rational solutions within the existing system of power relations.

The militarization of American life is rooted in three factors, of which only one, the first, is susceptible to rational argument: the assumption that the same modes of thought and action which since the beginning of history have been applied to conventional weapons are also applicable to nuclear ones; a demonological conception of the world in which the United States is pitted in ineluctable conflict against other nations of incalculable power and infinite cunning; and social interests that have economic and political stakes in the continuation of policies derived from these factors. Our involvement in the Vietnam war is similarly justified by this demonological conception of the world, which assigns to the United States the mission to defend the "Free World" against aggression and subversion from the Communist conspiracy. The strangeness to each other of the races is an existential psychological fact, transformed into acute antagonism and conflict by prejudice (which within limits is susceptible to rational refutation), concern for relative social status, and economic interests. Poverty on a large scale, like the decay of the cities and the ruination of the natural environment, is a result not of accidental misfortunes but of social and economic policies in whose continuation powerful social groups have a vested interest.

To the degree that these issues have been created and maintained in their unsolved state by powerful social groups, any approach toward reform that leaves the relative distribution of power intact will at best mitigate the social ills or at worst convey to the victims the soothing appearance of remedial action while confirming the *status quo*. In brief, the overriding single issue, of which all the others are but specific manifestations, is the distribution of power in American society, and that distribution has in its determining essentials survived all reform movements, from Populism, through the Progressive movement, Theodore Roosevelt's Square Deal, Woodrow Wilson's New Freedom, Franklin D. Roosevelt's New Deal, and Harry Truman's Fair Deal, to John F. Kennedy's New Frontier, Lyndon B. Johnson's Great Society, and the contemporary antiwar movement. These movements have achieved much by changing the relations of the government to different social groups as well as the conditions of the social groups themselves. But when it comes to the over-all distribution of power in American society, they all appear in retrospect as essentially futile attempts at accomplishing through rational and moderate reform what can be accomplished only as a result of a new distribution of power, either through the spontaneous disintegration of the existing power structure or through revolution.

Spontaneous disintegration is in the laps of the gods; rational argument and public pressure can at most support it, but they cannot bring it about. Popular revolution, on the other hand, is forestalled by the unprecedented concentration of power in the hands of the ruling groups, who possess a near-monopoly of the most effective technologies of communication, transportation, and welfare. What is still possible is the revolutionary tantrum, in both words and action, which both sides tend to take for the real thing and which the powers-that-be will suppress ruthlessly and with ease. This concentration of power, unchallengeable from without, calls forth the alienation, romantic eccentricities, and violent anarchy on the part of those groups, especially the young, who have been trying in vain to change the existing distribution of power. The same futility is attested to by the essays in this volume that are concerned with the succession of presidents and unsuccessful aspirants for that office. Each is an account of the failure, of different kind and degree, to govern or plan effectively on behalf of the issues to whose solution these men were rhetorically committed.

What is the likely outcome of this impasse? It can be taken for granted that the polarization between the defenders of the *status quo* and those opposed to or alienated from it will not last. It will be resolved in one of three ways. The main bulk of the opposition can make its peace with the "establishment," drawing the practical conclusions from the latter's invincibility; the remainder will either retreat to a private world of alienated culture, tolerated because it is harmless, or be eliminated in the name of "law and order." Or the opposition to and alienation from the *status quo* can become so widespread as to undermine confidence in its cause and the effective cohesion of the "establishment" itself; the "establishment" may then disintegrate without being willing and able to resist and make way for a new distribution of power. Or, finally, the powers-that-be will try to defend the *status quo* with all means at their disposal, using their economic, political, and technological monopolies for the purpose of reintegrating with totalitarian methods the democratic society whose spontaneous consensus had disintegrated under the impact of unsolved and seemingly insoluble issues.

Whichever of these alternatives materializes, it is likely to leave truth at the mercy of power. The first and third alternatives will simply make truth a function of power, the first through voluntary conformity, the third though totalitarian controls. It is only the second alternative that leaves open at least the possibility for truth to maintain itself against power. But then, that alternative is the least likely to materialize. Thus the trend toward the corruption of truth by power and the consequent disintegration of society, to which these essays testify, will continue, and in this respect at least, the 1970's will be an organic extension of the 1960's. For those who have made it their business in life to speak truth to power, there is nothing left but to continue so to speak, less frequently perhaps than they used to and certainly with less confidence that it will in the short run make much of a difference in the affairs of man.

In the long run, however, the voice of truth, so vulnerable to power, has proved more resilient than power. It has built empires of the mind and the spirit that have outlasted, and put their mark upon, the empires of power. On January 22, 1967, about thirty people demonstrated in Pushkin Square in Moscow against the arrest of four persons who had transcribed the court records in the trial against Andrei Sinyavsky and Yuli Daniel. One of the organizers of the protest, Khaustov, who was sentenced to three years at hard labor, admitted at his trial that he had read Kant and Hegel and that his reading of Kant "made me see a lot of things in a new light." The experience of the 1960's has dispelled the illusion that truth can show power the way in direct confrontation. But historical experience reassures us that truth can indeed make people "see a lot of things in a new light." And when people see things in a new light, they might act in a new way.

PART I

THE PHILOSOPHY

1

Truth and Power

[November, 1966]

It is commonplace to say that the relations between President Johnson and the intellectual community are not what they ought to be. President Johnson has bitterly complained in private about the alienation of the intellectuals and has attributed it, probably thinking of John F. Kennedy's better luck, to a snobbish contempt for his Texas style and upbringing. In public, he has gone out of his way to woo the intellectual community in word and deed. He has established in the White House what amounts to the position of an "intellectual-in-residence," who is supposed to keep the channels open between the President and the intellectual community. He has appointed eminent academics to important positions, and he has assigned to intellectuals a regular place in the social life of the White House. He has sent out a task force to scout the campuses for "new ideas," and he has asked the president of the Ford Foundation to perform the same task in the intellectual community of New York. He has dedicated two speeches, at Princeton on May 11, and in honor of the Brookings Institution on September 29, 1966, to paying his respects to the intellectuals. In order to show how much he respects them, he pointed with pride to the fact that "the major appointments I have made in the last two and one-half years collectively hold 758 advanced degrees," and quoted Macaulay, MacLeish, and Leonardo da Vinci.

Yet there has been no improvement in the relations between the President and the intellectuals. There could not have been, since the problem never has been correctly put, and, hence, what has been done to solve it has been irrelevant or has only served to aggravate it.

The intellectual lives in a world that is both separate from and potentially intertwined with that of the politician. The two worlds are separate because they are oriented toward different ultimate values: The intellectual seeks truth; the politician, power. These different orientations by no means imply the superiority of the intellectual over the politician. I argued against the intellectual's snobbish condescension toward the politician in July, 1961, addressing myself to the intellectuals of the Kennedy era. Nor does this different orientation imply that the intellectual has a monopoly of truth while the politician lives in the darkness of error. A highly intelligent and skillful politician such as President Johnson may be much closer to the practical truth in matters political than the intellectual who may be intelligent but is not wise in the ways of the world. The only point I want to make here is that the decisive distinction between the intellectual and the politician lies in their orientation toward different ultimate values. In his search for the truth, the ideal type of intellectual is oblivious to power; in his pursuit of power, the politician at best will use truth as a means to his ends. Yet the two worlds are also potentially intertwined; for truth has a message that is relevant to power, and the very existence of power has a bearing both upon the expression and the recognition of truth.

The two worlds are not only separate from and potentially intertwined with each other, they are also hostile to each other. Truth threatens power, and power threatens truth. Power, in order to be effective, must appear as something other than what it actually is. Deception—deception of others and of self—is inseparable from the exercise of power. As John Adams put it:

> Power always thinks it has a great soul and vast views beyond the comprehension of the weak and that it is doing God's service when it is violating all His laws. Our passions, ambitions, avarice, love and resentment, etc., possess so much metaphysical subtlety and so much overpowering eloquence that they insinuate themselves into the understanding and the conscience and convert both to their party.

Conversely, truth, by unmasking the pretensions of power, at the very least disturbs the power-that-be; for it puts power on the intellectual and moral defensive. Furthermore, it questions the purposes and processes of power, and thereby endangers the very framework within which power operates. Truth may even challenge the *status quo* of power on the level of practical politics if it is supported by sufficiently powerful interests. Once those interests have won the struggle for power, yesterday's truth becomes today's ideology, justifying, rationalizing, and covering up for the new powers-that-be. Then a new cycle begins, and truth again challenges power.

To this existential estrangement and potential interconnectedness between truth and power, between the intellectual and the political world, the intellectual can respond in four different ways: by retreat into the ivory tower, by prophetic confrontation, by expert advice, by surrender.

Repelled by the incompatibility of truth and power, the intellectual can separate himself from the political sphere altogether. He can tell the powers-that-be what Archimedes told the Roman soldier: "Do not disturb my circles." He can say, with Leonardo da Vinci, reproached by Michelangelo for his indifference to the fate of Florence, that the study of beauty occupies his whole heart. Finding, with Goethe, that "the political song is an ugly song," he can pursue the good, the true, and the beautiful within his own chosen sphere, as though the political sphere did not exist. Great works of the intellect have thus been achieved, as Archimedes's, Leonardo's, and Goethe's examples prove. But this retreat into the ivory tower disposes of the problem by evading it. It solves it for the intellectual as a private individual but it leaves it unsolved both in its philosophic dimensions and insofar as it bears upon the interests of the community.

Second, the intellectual can maintain the integrity of his position as an intellectual by remaining outside the political sphere, yet he can try to make the knowledge and insight peculiar to him count for the purposes and processes of politics. He is concerned with, but personally detached from, politics. He looks at the political sphere from without, judging it by, and admonishing it in the name of, the standards of truth accessible to him. He speaks, in the biblical phrase, truth to power. He tells power what it can do and what it ought to do, what is feasible and what is required. What he has to say about politics may have political consequences, which he may welcome or deplore as the case may be. But these consequences are a mere by-product, hoped for but not worked for, of his search for the truth.

These political consequences are particularly marked in a society that is pluralistic in both its organized political and its unorganized academic manifestations. Even after the President has made a policy decision, that decision may be contested on a lower level of government by way of interpretation and implementation (a former high official of the Department of State once confided to me with pride how he had, in the 1930's, sabotaged President Roosevelt's new policy toward the Soviet Union), and the dissensions within the government over Vietnam policy have now become a matter of public record. Government officials, split on policy, find support for their respective positions in an academic community equally split. That is to say, the academic community provides rational arguments for policy positions that within the government often must remain unacknowledged or at least inarticulate. He becomes the spokesman for the silent or whispering defense of, or opposition to, official policy.

The intellectual performs a function for the submerged opposition not only within the executive branch but also within Congress. The enormous weight of presidential power not only stifles opposition from within the executive branch, but also at the very least blunts the opposition of Congress. At times, the opposition from within these two branches of government has been so cowed that the critical intelligence of the intellectual, committed only to the truth, has been virtually the only audible voice of opposition.

Finally, the intellectual can enter the political sphere as an expert. As such, he does not question the purposes and processes of government but accepts as given the framework within which the government operates. He tells the powers-that-be what they need to know in order to achieve a particular result and how they must go about achieving it. Given a certain objective, of which he may or may not approve, he gives advice as to how to achieve it. The ultimate standard by which he orients himself is still the truth and not power, even though he puts his truth at the service of power.

What enables the intellectual to perform these vital roles for the democratic process and for the improvement of policy is his immunity from outside pressures, manifested in job security through tenure. This immunity provides the academic with opportunity as well as with temptation. He has the freedom to speak truth to power without needing to be afraid of more than irritating reprisals of the powers-that-be. The White House could threaten me with the FBI and make the Internal Revenue Service waste many man-hours in repeated audits of my income tax return; it could order the Secretary of Defense to fire me as consultant to the Department of Defense, banish me from the councils of government, and ostracize me socially. But it could not deprive me of my livelihood or of my freedom to speak and write, insofar as the media were willing to resist its pressure to deny me a hearing.

Immunity from serious interference by the powers-that-be allows the academic to perform his different important functions for the formation and the conduct of policy. But it also offers the academic two temptations: irresponsibility and corruption. The academic can speak but he cannot act, and from the words he utters no consequences follow directly in the world of action. Thus he is free to speak wisely or unwisely, rationally or with circumspection, as he sees fit, since what he says will make very little direct difference in the real world.

The words of the statesman, on the other hand, are themselves a form of action. What the statesman says and does forms an integral part of a dynamic field of pressures and counterpressures. His words and actions are both the result and the source of such pressures and counterpressures. Hence, they must be adapted carefully to the conditions from which they arise and which they are intended to influence, and they are bound to fall short of the logical consistency and theoretical purity that are the earmarks of the intellectual detached from action.

The intellectual oversteps the bounds of his competence if he holds the statesman to these standards, which he, but not the statesman, can afford to observe without compromise. Thus I could criticize the Kennedy Administration for its handling of the Cuban missile crisis because I had no decision to make, and I knew that what I was saying could have no direct influence upon the course of events. President Kennedy, on another occasion, commented upon my criticism of one of his policies by saying that I ought to sit where he did. President Kennedy had a point. While the intellectual must indeed speak truth to power, he must also be tolerant of the inability of power to live up to the truth without taking into account the contingencies of power.

Only a small step separates these independent positions from that in which the intellectual becomes an agent of the powers-that-be while maintaining his pretenses, and drawing upon his prestige, as an intellectual. The intellectual here ceases to be an intellectual, to be judged by the standards of truth, and becomes an ideologue, that is, a political agent, subject to the criteria of power. He invests popular passions with the dignity of reason and power with the appearance of truth. He justifies what politicians do in terms not only of necessity, as did Machiavelli, but also of truth and virtue. Here we are in the presence of what Julien Benda forty years ago called *La Trahison des Clercs* (The Betrayal of the Intellectuals). Their betrayal does not just consist in the exchange of one calling for another, which can be respectable and even worthwhile. It consists in the exploitation of one calling on behalf of another, in the false pretense of politicians, dedicated to the pursuit of power, who make it appear as though they were still intellectuals dedicated to the pursuit of truth.

The powers-that-be can concern themselves with the voice of truth, which questions their purposes and processes, in four different ways; they can heed, silence, discredit, or corrupt it. If they heed it they embark upon the most promising but also the most complicated and risky course of action available to them. It is the most promising because it maximizes the chances of political success, harmonizing political action with objective reality. It is the most complicated and risky course to take because the awareness of the truth, informing purpose and policy, must go hand in hand with the—now conscious—denial of the truth through the deception that makes political action acceptable to the electorate.

It is much simpler, and therefore also much more common, for the powers-that-be, if they are confronted with unpalatable truth, first to try to corrupt it and, if they do not succeed, to try to discredit it and, if they do not succeed in that, to silence it. The government's ability to corrupt derives from its power to reward those who are willing to be corrupted. Its ability to discredit stems from the authority of power with which it speaks and from the influence it is able to exert upon the mass media of communications. Its ability to silence results from its ability to corrupt—silence being a kind of passive corruption —and ultimately from the ability to make totalitarian use of the police and the criminal laws.

Reflecting, in the light of these theoretical considerations, upon the relations that exist at present between the intellectuals of America and the Government of the United States, one cannot escape, however much one would like to, two conclusions: The Administration has tried to discredit, silence, and corrupt, and it has in good measure succeeded, with the support of the intellectuals themselves.

The Johnson Administration tried to discredit intellectual dissent on two grounds: pragmatic, in terms of competence, and philosophic, in terms of moral legitimacy.

President Johnson and his Secretary of State have consistently argued that private citizens are incompetent to challenge the policies of the government, since they are without the information, accessible only to the government, that is essential to the formation of good policy. The argument is specious. I have based my comments on public policy primarily on information in the public domain, but I have also had, over considerable periods of time, access to top-secret information. The difference between the two types of information is not in their content; I remember only a single item classified "top secret" that could not have been ascertained through the perusal of public sources. What is peculiar to classified information is the light it sheds upon the positions of public officials and their interplay in the political process, and it is the protection of the privacy of that process that justifies secrecy.

The information available to the government is quantatively but not qualitatively superior to that accessible to the general public. A case can even be made in support of the proposition that the enormous quantity of information to which the decision-makers of the government are exposed impedes sound judgment. The abundance of information that must daily be sifted and brought to the attention of competent officials makes virtually impossible demands upon the political judgment of officials who must decide on the spur of the moment what is important and for whom. To mention but two glaring examples: the information concerning the impending attack on Pearl Harbor in December, 1941, and the readiness of Japan to surrender in August, 1945, before the atomic bombs were dropped, had entered the channels of intelligence before the event but did not reach the desks of the highest authorities before they made their decisions.

The moral argument against intellectual dissent is equally untenable. President Johnson's attitude toward the intellectuals was determined by a basic philosophic defect: the confusion between consensus and the consent of the governed. The two must be sharply distinguished. Yet President Johnson assumed, and in good measure acted upon the assumption, that they are identical. Consensus is the general precondition for any civilized government; the consent of the governed is the precondition for a particular democratic government. All politically civilized societies owe their continuing existence to a consensus concerning the foundations of society. Thus, the citizens of a democratic society conclude among themselves, as it were, a social contract in which they agree upon their common purposes, the procedures by which these purposes are to be effectuated, and the institutions intended to serve them.

The consent of the governed concerns itself not with the fundamentals of the democratic polity, which it takes for granted as vouchsafed by the consensus, but with the specifics of a particular democratic government, at a particular point in time. Without consensus no civilized political society can survive; without the consent of the governed a democratic government cannot survive in power. The dissent of the governed, in turn, far from being tainted with the stigma of disloyalty, since it rises from the common foundation of consensus, is a prerequisite of democratic vitality. The vitality of democratic competition is predicated upon the chance, in principle open to all, that today's dissenters may carry the day tomorrow.

By equating the consent of the governed with consensus, President Johnson is compelled to equate dissent with disloyalty. Thus, in his Chicago speech of May 17, 1966, he could refer to the critics of his Vietnam policies as "some Nervous Nellies and some who will become frustrated and bothered and break ranks under the strain. And some will turn on their own leaders and their own country, and on our own fighting men." Commenting on Mr. Nixon's criticism of the Manila communiqué, the President in his press conference of November 4, 1966, charged "some of the politicians" with "not trying to clarify it but confuse it," and concluded: "And we oughtn't to have men killed because we try to fuzz up something." And he can say, according to Rowland Evans and Robert Novak in *The Washington Post* of August 17, 1966, that "Ambassador Dobrynin seems to have more votes in the Senate than the President." John D. Pomfret summed up the President's attitude in *The New York Times* of July 25, 1966:

> Before yesterday's whirlwind tour that took him into Indiana, Kentucky and Illinois, the President appeared to question the patriotism of his critics in public on only one major occasion. That was in Chicago in mid-May. . . . But yesterday, Mr. Johnson, in three speeches, aimed caustic, accusatory remarks at critics of American involvement in the war. He seemed almost to be asking which side they were on.

Time magazine of June 24, 1966, summarized the President's position in these terms:

> Johnson is not content to let history make its own judgments. In a sense, he may be a victim of what historian James MacGregor Burns calls the "corruption of consensus." In *The Crucible of Leadership* . . . Burns elaborates: "No matter how benign a government may be, it will be tempted to manipulate public opinion, to cover up mistakes, and to cast doubt on the patriotism or at least the honesty of outside critics. The more that government represents a consensus, or claims to, the more tempted it may be to succumb to . . . these tendencies."

I have taken a look at Woodrow Wilson's and Franklin D. Roosevelt's attitudes toward domestic dissent, and I have been struck not by the similarity but by the difference between their democratic ethos and the climate of opinion prevailing today. They were harsh and devastating in the criticism of their critics, but they did not question the legitimacy of their position. They remained bound by the ethos of free discussion, which the late Professor Zechariah Chafee, Jr., has thus defined:

> The First Amendment protects two kinds of interests in free speech. There is an individual interest, the need of many men to express their opinions on matters vital to them if life is to be worth living, and a social interest in the attainment of truth, so that the country may not only adopt the wisest course of action but carry it out in the wisest way. This social interest is especially important in war time. Even after war has been declared there is bound to be a confused mixture of good and bad arguments in its support, and a wide difference of opinion as to its objects. Truth can be sifted out from falsehood only if the government is vigorously and constantly cross-examined, so that the fundamental issues of the struggle may be clearly defined, and the war may not be diverted to improper ends, or conducted with an undue sacrifice of life and liberty, or prolonged after its just purposes are accomplished.*

It illuminates the problem that concerns us here that President Johnson is more tolerant of dissent coming from within the political sphere than he is of dissent from without. Being in an extraordinarily pervasive measure committed to the pursuit of power, he can understand dissent that is at the service of power and can try to handle it in accordance with the rules of the power game. Dissent that speaks in the name of truth, without regard for power, must sound to him as a voice both strange and threatening. It must sound strange, because it has nothing to contribute directly to what is the overriding purpose of his being—the pursuit of power—and it must sound threatening, for here is a realm of human existence that owes nothing to power, that is indifferent to power, that, given the restraints of the democratic ethos, is even immune to power. That power is limited by power, the men of power must take in their stride; that power should be limited by truth is an intolerable affront.

It is, therefore, not by accident that among the dissenting politicians Senator Fulbright has become the *bête noire* of the Johnson administration. For Senator Fulbright is in the ambivalent position of being both a politician and an intellectual. He acts within the framework of power but from time to time speaks with the voice of truth, regardless of power. That ambivalence impairs his effectiveness as a politician and as a purveyor of truth. Thus he has the worst of both worlds. Both

---

* Zechariah Chafee, Jr., *Free Speech in the United States* (Cambridge, Mass.: Harvard University Press, 1941), p. 33.

the intellectuals and the politicians suspect him. The former ask what might be his political purpose when he seems to speak the truth. To the latter he appears as a kind of Trojan horse, a horse, as it were, of a different, nonpolitical color. Since that voice of truth, speaking outrageously from within the political arena, could be neither silenced nor corrupted, it had to be discredited. Thus the President has never deigned to argue with the Senator but has ridiculed and mimicked him and treated him with contempt in public and to his face. White House–broken journalists have taken their cue and have treated a brilliant, knowledgeable, and high-minded public servant as though he were an ignorant, irresponsible fool.

The way Senator Fulbright has been treated is not an individual aberration. It is but a particularly spectacular and distressing example of a general policy. The White House "Project Morgenthau," which in 1965 had the task to disseminate "information" about me reflects the same general attitude. Unable to recognize the autonomy of the intellectual sphere and to accept the positive function the intellectual as an independent agent is able to perform for politics, the President has only two courses of action to choose from: He must either silence and corrupt the intellectuals by making them into his agents, or he must discredit those who cannot be silenced and corrupted. Wanting desperately to have the intellectuals' approval and support and thinking only in terms of power, the President either embraces those who are embraceable or tries to destroy those who resist his advances. Thus the intellectuals become either the tools or the victims of his power. This is his tragedy: By trying to overwhelm the intellectuals, he destroys them one way or another, and by doing this he destroys any independent contribution, except expertise, the intellectuals could make to the enlightenment and the greatness of his power.

How this tragic misunderstanding has the exactly opposite practical effects from those intended is clearly demonstrated by the approach of President Johnson's last "intellectual-in-residence." Professor John D. Roche expressed his philosophy after his appointment in an interview with Jimmy Breslin, according to the *Chicago Sun-Times* of September 18, 1966, as follows: "The term intellectual has been batted about too loosely. When you mention intellectuals today, who do you mean? There is a broad group. The ones we talk about when we mention the President's relations with them are only a small body of self-appointed people who live in affluent alienation on Cape Cod and fire off salvos against the vulgarity of the masses. But this is a well-orchestrated outfit with fine Madison Avenue techniques. Their way of criticizing makes the group seem bigger than it is. The main problem is that an awful lot of these guys prefer style to performance."

To the question "These alienated intellectuals, who are they?" Professor Roche gave this answer: "Mainly the New York artsy-craftsy set. They're in the *Partisan Review* and *The New York Review of Books* and publications like that. The West Side jackalbins, I call them. They intend to launch a revolution from Riverside Drive. Names, there are plenty of names who write for them. Alfred Kazin writes, then Irving Howe and Norman Mailer."

"He was talking about a small group of people," comments Mr. Breslin, "who number maybe 100 and who live on the West Side of New York. Their role in life is to be intellectuals. Their main publication is the *Partisan Review*. This is a small magazine with no picture on the cover and for which, at one time or another in his career, everybody in university life has written articles. The West Side intellectuals concerned with the magazine have no real academic connections. They live in those old, once highly fashionable apartment houses which tower over the Hudson River. And they send out a flow of words against the war in Vietnam and against Lyndon Johnson. Their out-of-town copy comes from Cambridge and Berkeley and, in the Midwest, from Prof. Hans Morgenthau of the University of Chicago." With the exception of Norman Mailer and Alfred Kazin, these intellectuals "are mainly high class illiterates. A story by Irving Howe, for example, should be edited with flea powder."

In *The New York Times Magazine* of October 14, 1965, Professor Roche summarizes my political position by referring to me as "a scholarly, urbane European intellectual: his major premise is that Americans cannot be trusted with power and since Johnson (like Kennedy, who got the same treatment) is an American, there is little more to say." It is not necessary to point out that this summary of my political position is pure fabrication, and it cannot be lost even on an obtuse reader that here an attempt is being made to exploit a residual American xenophobia in order to question my credentials.

In April, 1966, Professor John Kenneth Galbraith referred to Vietnam as "a country which has not the slightest strategic importance." Here is Professor Roche's answer according to *Time* magazine for May 6, 1966: "Galbraith reminds me of the Lord High Executioner in *The Mikado*. He's got them on his list, and they'll none of them be missed —Vietnam, Thailand, you name it. I guess what makes a country obscure is whether Ken Galbraith likes it or not." Professor Galbraith may be dead wrong, but Professor Roche has not advanced an argument to prove it.

These remarks are samples of a uniquely personal style which is characterized by three organically connected qualities: the refusal to deal with an argument on its own merits, a cavalier attitude toward ascertainable facts, and the attempt to discredit by invective. Those are the qualities not of the intellectual but of the demagogue. Professor Roche has himself denied that he has the task to provide a link between the intellectual community and the White House, making the voice of truth audible at the seat of power. His own pronouncements make clear by implication what he conceives as his official task: to be the hatchet man who will try to ruin the reputation of those intellectuals who dare openly to disagree with his master. This task reflects indeed, on the level of journalistic practice, the President's own philosophy. Given that philosophy, one must admit, not without a sense of embarrassment, that, by making Professor Roche his "intellectual-in-residence," the President has chosen well.

However, this frontal attack upon the reputation of the dissenting intellectuals is an act of desperation resorted to only against those whom the government has failed to silence or corrupt. And large segments of the intellectual world have indeed been silenced or corrupted. This is especially true of those segments which are professionally concerned with the activities of government. If one examines, for instance, the lists of intellectuals who have gone on record against the war in Vietnam, one is struck by the relative paucity of political scientists. One is also struck by the frequency with which those who remain silent in public express their opposition in private. It must also be noted that some intellectuals have attacked their dissenting colleagues with unaccustomed violence and with arguments so tortuous and inconsistent as to be inexplicable on purely intellectual grounds while, unknown to the public, they were working for the government part-time or accepted a government position shortly afterward. Finally, there is the type of intellectual who habitually moves from the intellectual into the political sphere and back again and whose overt political views change with these movements and with changes in the climate of political opinion.

Three factors account for this susceptibility of the intellectual community to remaining silent and being corrupted: the conformism of American society, personal ambition, and inducements that the government holds out to those who do not openly dissent.

American society, lacking in good measure in those historic, ethnic, and cultural values and institutions to which traditional societies owe their integration, has had to rely for its survival upon unorganized social pressures to keep its members in line. To be a "regular fellow" or a "member of the team," that is, not to deviate from what everybody thinks and does, thus has become a virtue in itself. As Mr. Justice Holmes put it: "I have no practical criticism [with regard to laws] except what the crowd wants."

This pressure to conform is powerfully reinforced by personal ambition. Academics in particular, that is, intellectuals, who are professionally committed to the pursuit of truth, are not immune from aspirations for power, academic and political. In order to avoid an open conflict between those potentially incompatible goals, in order to be able to pursue the truth without jeopardizing the satisfaction of personal ambition, the intellectual must concern himself with issues—and deal with them in ways—that are noncontroversial because they neither deviate from the standards of society nor invite dissent from the policies of the government. Thus, the intellectual deals with "safe" subjects in a "safe" manner. On the great issues of political life, which are controversial by definition, he must remain silent. He does not need to be silenced; he silences himself. Silence with regard to these issues is the passive manifestation of conformity.

Silence is the minimal compliance with the requirements of both conformity and ambition. Both requirements are consummated in the positive support of whatever policies the government pursues. This compliance is, in good measure, the intellectuals' spontaneous act; it is an act of protective mimicry. However, the government does not leave the silence and subservience of the intellectuals to chance. It has at its disposal a plethora of varied, subtle, and insidious instruments with which to forge reliable ties with large segments of the intellectual world. Thus the "military-industrial complex," to which President Eisenhower referred in his farewell address, is duplicated by an academic-political complex in which the interests of the government are inextricably intertwined with the interests of large groups of academics. These ties are both formal and informal, and the latter are the more dangerous to intellectual freedom, as they consist in the intellectuals' unconscious adaptation to imperceptible social and political pressures.

The intimate connection that research contracts have established between the government and the universities has recently been brought to public attention. It stands to reason that an academic who is working on such a contract or who expects to work on one is not likely to question the basic policies of the government, either within his contractual research or outside it. Thus the interests and expectations of the government not only determine the subject matter of contractual research but also influence ever so subtly its scope and in a certain measure its results. Beyond these specific limitations, the connection with the government cannot help but narrow the scope and and direction of the scholar's search for truth.

Aside from these formal contractual relations with which the government is able to keep large segments of the academic community silent or render them subservient, the government disposes of a whole gamut of professional and social rewards serving the same purpose, from appointments and consultantships to foreign travel and invitations to social functions at the White House. By adroitly promising, dispensing, and withholding them, it keeps a large segment of the academic community at bay. The academic, by accepting one or the other of these rewards, enters into a subtle and insidious relationship with the government, which imperceptibly transforms his position of independent judge to that of client and partisan. In consequence, his intellectual function is also transformed. In the measure that he values these social rewards and professional advantages more highly than his commitment to the truth, he becomes a political ideologue, justifying morally and rationalizing intellectually the policies of the government. Yet he performs this ideological function while he draws upon his prestige as a scholar. Thus his reputation as an independent searcher after the truth is put at the service of the government, and what is but the ideological defense of a partisan position, an intellectual gloss upon power, is made to appear as the objective truth.

Nor is subservience induced by subtle or sometimes not so subtle governmental pressure limited to the academic community. That subservience pervades the whole intellectual life of the nation, and it is particularly marked in the mass media. A future historian, one might hope, will write the story of the far-flung, systematic, and largely successful efforts embarked upon by the government to suppress the truth and to bend it to its political interests. Great newspapers have published articles written by reputable scholars purporting to be an objective account of the personnel and the processes of the government, while they were for all practical purposes commissioned by the White House. Correspondents stationed in Vietnam either transcribe the official briefings or hide the truth in an Aesopian language, requiring a special perspicacity to unravel. Some of them, after their return home, have reported facts of which no trace was to be found in their dispatches from the field. And some have attached to these factual accounts policy conclusions that have no logical connection with the former. Upon this larger intellectual sphere, as upon the academic community, direct governmental and imperceptible social pressures are brought to bear, and what social prudence and political opportunism will not achieve, direct government intervention will bring about: to silence and to corrupt the truth. The intellectuals of America have indeed been raped; but many of them have looked forward to the experience and are enjoying it.

But even those intellectuals who are most vociferous in their commitment to the powers-that-be are so committed only for the time being. They betrayed their calling as intellectuals in order to get power. But in truth they are only in the presence, not in the possession, of it. They are not in the seats of power but only at court. Thus they are ready at any time to cry: "The king is dead, long live the king." And it is amusing and saddening to witness the intellectual acrobatics of some of the intellectual courtiers of King John's court who entered cautiously the court of King Lyndon, only to move for the exit when the star of pretender Robert seemed to be on the rise. In other words, President Johnson has the support of the intellectual ideologues only because he has power and as long as he has it. Let power slip from his hands, and his intellectual servants will look for a new master.

Here is indeed the tragedy both of President Johnson and of the intellectuals of America as well. It results not so much from the arrogance as from the blindness of power. That blindness has deformed the relationship between the intellectuals and the powers-that-be, which, as we have seen, by its very nature cannot help being uneasy and precarious. The intellectuals of America who have preserved their independence are faced with a Presidential power of unprecedented magnitude. That power seeks not only their support, to which it is entitled, but also their submission. These intellectuals must maintain their own regard for the truth in the face of a massive official disregard for it, which goes far beyond the necessities of the political game. The official pronouncements on President Kennedy's assassination and the Vietnam war could perhaps still be justified in terms of reason of state, although they have made civilized public debate with public officials virtually impossible. But it is a different matter to habitually play fast and loose with the truth, regardless of the public ends that might justify such play and for the sole purpose of enjoying another dimension of power.

President Johnson can think of intellectuals only as holders of college degrees who bring prestige to his administration and purveyors of ideas who improve its policies. But that is not what defines the intellectuals' function for the political sphere. Intellectuals are not sitting in their offices producing ideas like so many items to be picked up and acted upon or filed away by the political authorities. The President does not need new ideas, except in the narrow technical sense; the ideas necessary for good government are part of the public record. What he needs is not ideas but wisdom, and to provide it is indeed the natural task of the independent intellectual. What Jakob Burckhardt has said of historians is indeed true of all intellectuals: They aim "to make us not clever for one day but wise forever." What the

President needs, then, is an intellectual father-confessor, who dares to remind him of the brittleness of power, of its arrogance and blindness, of its limits and pitfalls; who tells him how empires rise, decline, and fall, how power turns to folly, empires to ashes. He ought to listen to that voice and tremble.

It is indeed the privilege of power to close its ears to such reminders and ride roughshod over those who refuse to do its bidding. It is the privilege of power to deem itself omnipotent. It has been said of the British Parliment that it can do anything except make a man into a woman. The President of the United States, too, can do almost anything. He can play with truth, deform it, and discard it at his whim. But there is one thing he cannot do: He cannot still the voice of truth. As long as there are men in this country or anywhere else in the world who will speak truth to power, the voice of truth will be heard at least by some. If it should come to pass, which is technologically possible, that a worldwide totalitarianism were to silence the last voice of truth on earth, one could then say, modifying a famous statement of Kant, that it would make no sense for human beings to continue to exist.

What makes this deformation of the relationship between the intellectuals and the political sphere tragic for the intellectuals is that what is true in general is true with particular poignancy for Americans: that power needs truth to be wise and great. This nation owes its very existence, its institutions, and its ethos to a rare conjunction of intellectuality and power. *The Federalist* is not only a practical political document; it is also an unsurpassed compendium of political truth. Abraham Lincoln combined a commitment to power and a dedication to truth, crowned with political success, of which history knows no other instance. Thus the rejection of the independent intellectuals by the powers-that-be in contemporary America would be unwise and self-defeating in any case but is particularly so in the case of America; for it cuts off the political sphere from its vital historic roots of wisdom and ultimate success.

In the face of this misunderstanding and scorn for the function the intellectual can and must perform for the political sphere, the intellectuals of America can do only one thing: live by the standard of truth that is their peculiar responsibility as intellectuals and by which the men of power will ultimately be judged as well. Thus they will remain faithful not only to their calling but also to the spirit of their nation. For America was founded not upon power blindly and unrestrainedly pursued, but upon power informed and restrained by truth.

2

What Ails America?

[October, 1967]

Contemplating the American scene today—the disarray of foreign and domestic policies, the violence from above and below, the decline of the public institutions, the disengagement of the citizens from the purposes of the government, the decomposition of those ties of trust and loyalty that link citizen to citizen and the citizens to the government—one is reminded of the other two great crises that similarly put into question the very identity of America; the crisis of the 1860's and that of the 1930's. However, a comparison among these three crises puts the peculiar gravity of the present one into stark relief.

The Civil War was a conflict between the two geographically defined, incompatible conceptions of the nature of American government and society, strengthened within their respective geographic areas by the very fact of conflict. That conflict, manifesting itself in military terms, could be, and was, settled by force of arms. The victory of the North restored and strengthened beyond challenge the unitary character of American government and established in legal terms the equality and freedom of all American citizens. Yet it is the measure of the failure of Reconstruction that in actual terms the drastic inequality which it was one of the purposes of the Civil War to confine, if not

29

eliminate, was preserved and even accentuated in its aftermath. While Lincoln proclaimed that this nation could not endure half free and half slave, that is exactly as it has endured.

The crisis of the 1930's was similar to the present one in that it threatened to tear asunder the very fabric of American society. It was a crisis of the American purpose; it challenged the assumption of the uniqueness of America and suggested the failure of the American experiment. However, there were two escapes from the despair the crisis engendered: Marxism, which drew the logical conclusion from the denial of American uniqueness and the apparent failure of the American experiment by promoting the class struggle, which would transform the United States in the image of an equalitarian and libertarian utopia; and the New Deal, which affirmed the American promise through radical reform and creative reconstruction.

It is the distinctive and ominous mark of the present crisis that it has produced no remedy consonant with the ideals of America. It could not have produced one, for the inability to do so is an element of the crisis itself. The democratic state is in a blind alley, and so is American democracy. America, then, suffers from two types of ailments: those it has in common with the other major democracies, and those that are peculiarly its own.

The general crisis of democracy is the result of three factors: the shift of effective material power from the people to the government, the shift of the effective power of decision from the people to the government, and the ability of the government to destroy its citizens in the process of defending them.

Throughout history, the ultimate safeguard of the interests and rights of the people vis-à-vis the government has been the ability of the people to overthrow the government by force, that is, to make a revolution. This ability was a result of an approximately equal distribution of the means of physical violence between the government and the people. Before the beginning of the century, roughly speaking, the government met the people, barring superior organization and training, on a footing of approximate equality. Numbers, morale, and leadership then decided the issue.

This approximately equal distribution of military power between government and people has in our age been transformed into the unchallengeable superiority of the government. The government has today a monopoly of the most destructive weapons of warfare, and because of its centralization, the government can acquire instantly a monopoly of the most effective means of transportation and communications as well. Against such a monopolistic concentration of superior power, the people can demonstrate, protest, and petition, but they cannot overthrow it through revolution. Thus, as long as a democratic government can count upon the loyalty of the armed forces, it need not fear the wrath of the people, exploding in revolution. What it must guard against is to be voted out of office.

However, the voting process, both in the legislatures and in popular elections, has lost much of the bearing it formerly had upon the substantive decisions of the government. For the most important decisions the government must render today, in contrast to the past, are far removed both from the life experiences and the understanding of the man in the street. A century ago, the issue of slavery was susceptible to the judgment of all; today the issue of intergrating the descendants of the slaves into American society presents itself as an intricate complex of technical problems, to which the man in the street may react emotionally but with which only experts in education, housing, urban affairs, welfare, and so forth can competently deal. Thirty years ago, the American people and their elected representatives could still have a competent voice in determining the military policy of the United States; today, Congress passes the $70 billion budget of the Department of Defense with essentially ritualistic scrutiny, giving the experts the benefit of the doubt. The great issues of nuclear strategy, for instance, cannot even be the object of meaningful debate, whether in Congress or among the people at large, because there can be no competent judgment without meaningful knowledge. (The ABM debate of 1969 is the exception that proves the rule.) Thus, the great national decisions of life and death are rendered by technological elites, and both the Congress and the people at large retain little more than the illusion of making the decisions that the theory of democracy supposes them to make.

The great decisions democratic governments are called upon to make are always justified in terms of the common good—that is, of the benefits which, at least in the long run, will accrue to the great mass of the citizens. Even where that justification obviously masked special interests or served as an ideology for a particular class identifying its interests with those of the community, the claim had in the past a certain plausibility. For even a democratic government that only served the pursuit of the happiness of some of its citizens sought to preserve the life and liberty of most of them. In the last analysis, the performance of this elementary and vital function established in the eyes of the citizens the moral legitimacy of government. The government had a claim upon the citizens' obedience and allegiance because, at the very least, it made it possible for them to live.

It is the distinctive characteristic of the nuclear age that this moral foundation upon which the legitimacy of democratic government has rested in the past is no longer as firm as it used to be. A government armed with nuclear, biological, and chemical weapons of mass destruction still intends to protect the life of its citizens against a government similarly armed. But in truth it cannot defend its citizens, it can only deter the prospective enemy from attacking them. If deterrence fails and he attacks, the citizens are doomed. Such a government, then, bears the two faces of Janus: Insofar as it is able to deter, it is still its citizens' protector; if it fails to deter, it becomes the source of their destruction.

This new quality of modern government, precariously poised at the edge of the abyss of self-destruction, is vaguely felt, rather than clearly understood, by the man in the street. He beholds with awe and without confidence that gigantic machine of mass destruction which is anachronistically called the Department of Defense, and he wonders whether it will not cause his own destruction while destroying the enemy, and he also wonders whether a government so constituted still deserves the obedience and loyalty it claims and once deserved. If it is true that *ubi bene, ibi patria*, where is his fatherland?

These ailments, from which all major democratic governments suffer, are reinforced by the ailments peculiar to America. It is not just that the latter must be added to the former, but the peculiar ailments of America provide specific instances of the general crisis, they make that crisis relevant to specific issues facing America; and they give those issues a general poignancy. Three such issues call for our attention: racial violence, Vietnam, and the Presidency.

What the citizen suspects of the government's performance of its function as his protector against the foreign enemy, he has empirical proof of in his relations with his fellow citizens: The government is no longer able to perform its elementary function of protecting the lives of its citizens. It is unable to protect the black American and his white sympathizer against the violence to which they are subjected by white racists and arbitrary law enforcement, and it is unable to protect the citizens from the violence that has erupted in the black ghettos and is likely to erupt again and spread. And it is unable to put into practice the imposing body of legislation enacted by Congress for the purpose of integrating the blacks into American society and the poor into the productive economy. A government possessed of unprecedented power appears to be impotent in the face of the threat of social disintegration and the promise of social justice.

I shall not here repeat the arguments I have advanced since 1961 against our involvement in Vietnam, first by warning against it and then by pointing to its political aimlessness, military uselessness and risks, and moral liabilities. I want only to re-emphasize, and enlarge upon, two points.

The war is not only politically aimless and militarily unwinnable in terms of the Administration's professed aims, but it also violates the very principles upon which this nation was founded and for which it has stood both in the eyes of its own citizens and of the world. It is an antirevolutionary war fought by a revolutionary nation. It is Metternich's war fought by the nation of Jefferson and Lincoln. As the President and the Secretary of the General Synod of the Netherlands Reformed Church put it on July 24, 1967, in a letter addressed to the National Council of Churches of the United States:

Hostilities in Vietnam have reached such proportions that the United States government's professed aim, *viz.* to stop the advance of communist influence in South East Asia and to establish a democratic regime in Vietnam, seems remoter than ever before. This is all the more alarming since the nation in whose behalf the war is supposedly being fought is being slowly but surely brought to ruin by the subtlety of the chemical and conventional weapons used and by the complete social, cultural, and spiritual dissolution with which it is threatened. A nation's "liberation" is sealing its doom. If the United States really has the well-being of the people of Vietnam at heart, we are prompted to ask whether there is any point at all in continuing this war. . . .

We Dutchmen and Dutch Christians and Churches owe our liberation from the yoke of cruel, anti-Christian oppression partly to your nation's willingness to sacrifice lives and property. Since the war, too, the Dutch and other nations cherished great hopes of the United States' contribution to the organization of a new community of nations. In view of this it is all the more regrettable that we are compelled to point out to you that your nation is losing the confidence placed in it, since it is [casting doubt on] the sincerity of its pleas for freedom and justice. . . . For that reason alone the United States should stop the war in Vietnam without delay by taking new initiatives."

The United States is incapable of liquidating the war because of its faulty perception of reality and its unattainable goals. It acts upon the assumption that it is defending South Vietnam against aggression. If only North Vietnam left its neighbor alone, to quote Mr. Rusk's celebrated phrase, there would be no trouble in South Vietnam. However, fruitful negotiations with the government in Hanoi are impossible because we seek to gain at the conference table what we have been unable to achieve on the battlefield: the destruction of the Viet Cong as an organized political force. Even if the government of North Vietnam were willing to hand us that victory, it would be unable to do so without the cooperation of the Viet Cong. The test of our willingness to liquidate the war will be not the cessation of bombing but the establishment of a civilian government in Saigon that will inevitably negotiate a settlement of the war with the Viet Cong.

The waging of a war that runs counter to the national ethos and the inability of the most powerful nation on earth either to win or to liquidate it has had a deleterious effect upon the prestige of the government and of the political system through which we are governed. If we had a parliamentary system, this Administration would not govern us today, and its place would have been taken by an Administration not compelled by its psychological needs to prove itself through military victory. As it is, the opponents of the war, within and outside Congress, can only raise their voices in warning and protest, they can collect signatures and table and even pass resolutions; but they know that they have no power to change the course of events. The only resort left to them is to work for a change in Administration through the next elections, and they must hope, but can by no means be confident, that another Administration will pursue a wiser course.

Thus, they cannot help but ask themselves what kind of democracy it is in which the will of the people and of their elected representatives counts for so little and in which a President and a few advisers, having acquired a vested psychological interest in the perpetuation of error, are allowed to persist in involving the nation in a disastrous war. We thought that this was the way absolute monarchies were run in times past. Thus, Talleyrand could say in 1808 to Czar Alexander I: "The Rhine, the Alps, and the Pyrenees are the conquests of France; the rest, of the Emperor; they mean nothing to France." We could say with equal right today: The integrity of the American territory and institutions, the Monroe Doctrine, the balance of power in Europe and Asia—those are the interests of America; the war in Vietnam is the President's; it means nothing to America.

However, the Administration must make it appear that our involvement in Vietnam is not the result of the errors in which a succession of Presidents and their advisers have persisted, but that it serves the vital interests of the nation. The obvious implausibility of such a representation has opened up what has come to be known as the "credibility gap." The people refuse to believe what the government tells them it is doing and plans to do. As they once credited Washington with not being able to tell a lie, so they almost take it for granted that his contemporary successors will not tell the truth. This lack of trust is not limited to official statements on Vietnam; it extends to all matters of public concern. For deception is being practiced not occasionally as a painful necessity dictated by the reason of state, but consistently as a kind of lighthearted sport through which the deceiver enjoys his power.

This withering away of the public's trust in the government might matter little to a totalitarian regime, which can afford to govern through terror and the manipulation of the mass media of communications. Yet a democratic government cannot rule effectively, and in the long run it cannot rule at all, if it is not sustained by at least a modicum of the freely given support of the people and their elected representatives. In the American system of government, in particular, the President, by constitutional arrangement and political tradition, is the molder of the national will, the educator of the people, the guardian of its interests, and the protagonist of its ideals. The President is the incarnation of the nation-in-action; when the nation wants to know what it is about, it looks to the President to find out.

In that noble and vital mission, President Johnson has completely failed. For a time, he triumphed in that sphere of action in which he is a past master: the manipulation of Congress in support of legislation. Yet even these legislative triumphs have in large measure remained ineffectual; for President Johnson, seeking an unattainable consensus and bent upon avoiding inevitable conflict, has been unable to marshal the popular energies necessary to implement the legislative enactments. And his failure as a national leader and the decline of his personal prestige have made him ineffective even in his dealings with Congress.

This personal failure is not just an issue between this particular President and the American people. It affects the vitality of the democratic process itself. If his Administration could be neither influenced nor trusted, why should one hope to influence and trust another one? If this is what the democratic process leads to, how good is democracy?

The combined impact these two sets of critical issues—the general ones common to all major democratic nations and the peculiarly American ones—have had upon American society has resulted in the present crisis of American politics. In order to assess the nature of that crisis, it is first necessary to consider the uniqueness of the American body politic.

America is unique in that it owes its creation and continuing existence as a nation not to geographic proximity, ethnic identity, monarchical legitimacy, or a long historic tradition, but to an act of will repeated over and over again by successive waves of immigrants. It was not natural or historical necessity that created America or Americans, but a conscious choice. This voluntary element in the American nationality accounts for a peculiar looseness in the social fabric of America, whose texture is subject to continuous change. In consequence, American society is singularly adaptable to changing circumstances. But it is also singularly vulnerable to disruption and disintegration.

Since America owes its existence to a series of successive choices, those who have chosen America are free to choose otherwise. That availability of choice is strikingly revealed in the emphasis of the Declaration of Independence upon the right to revolution as a universal principle and, more concretely and personally, in what Abraham Lincoln wrote to Joshua Speed on August 24, 1855: "When it comes to this [the Know-Nothings' getting control], I should prefer emigrating to some country where they make no pretence of loving liberty—to Russia, for instance, where despotism can be taken pure, and without the base alloy of hypocrisy." No other Western nation, with the exception of Spain, has since the French Revolution had to reaffirm its very existence as a nation through a bloody civil war.

It is, then, not surprising that the combined impact the critical issues discussed above have had upon American society has been both disruptive and disintegrative. The refusal of large groups of politically conscious blacks to participate in the life of white Americans amounts to the disruption of American society into two separate and hostile societies. The alienation of many intellectuals and the retreat of the more sensitive and morally committed youth from political life are indices of disintegration.

What these different movements have in common is a negative attitude toward American society and the American purpose that that society is supposed to serve. They do not work within American society in order to improve or transform it, or even to revolt against it. They offer no viable alternatives to the *status quo*, but only different ways of escaping from it. They have given up on American society and opted out of it. Theirs is a politics of despair, that is, no politics at all, for America. "Black Power" is a self-defeating futility born of such despair. Advocacy of an Afro-American society within an indigenous social, economic, and paramilitary framework substitutes for the American purpose of equality in freedom for all citizens the very segregation, albeit with a positive content, that that purpose has been trying to overcome. The "New Left," the refusal to bear arms or pay taxes, the hippie movement, are protests against the political and social order, reassertions of individual choice outside the political order, or anarchism and return to nature à la Thoreau, albeit without any positive moral orientation toward a new social order.

Nobody will underestimate the seriousness of the disruption of American society through black separatism and hostility. But there is a strong tendency, officially inspired, to dismiss as inconsequential the apolitical and antipolitical attempts at escaping from American society and politics altogether. Most of the individuals who thus try to escape are not predestined for that role; they are not, as it were, the congenital nonconformists and eccentrics. Quite to the contrary, they would have been, if they had been given a chance, the pillars of society, the experts, the reformers, the politicians and statesmen, that is, the elite —small in numbers but irreplaceable in quality—from which a society receives its ability to grow, renew itself, live up to its purpose. That some of her best children have turned their backs upon America, that the powers-that-be have reacted to that desertion with either equanimity or derision and vilification is a measure of the gravity of the American crisis.

A society threatened with disruption or disintegration can maintain itself in two ways: through a creative effort at reconstruction or through violent repression. The former is the democratic way, of which America and modern England provide examples. The other is the fascist way through which Germany, Italy, and Spain maintained themselves as integrated societies. Yet these examples show that the two choices are available only in the initial stages of the crisis, that is, when the powers-that-be are tempted to close their eyes to the potential seriousness of the crisis. Once the destructive results of disruption and disintegration have become obvious, it is likely to be too late for democratic remedies. There is, then, an element of tragedy in such a crisis of democratic society: When it could still be saved by democratic measures of reconstruction, there appears to be no need for them, and when the need has become obvious, it is too late for them.

It would be rash indeed to try to predict the outcome of the present crisis of American society. Yet whatever the outcome, the present trend toward violence rather than creative reconstruction is unmistakable. The white man in the street appears to believe that too much has already been done for the blacks, and he is afraid and in an ugly mood. The politicians translate that mood into calls for war against "crime in the streets" and for the defense of "law and order," that is, violence in defense of the *status quo*. On a higher level of sophistication, we are lectured by Mr. Moynihan on the merits of "The Politics of Stability" for an existentially unstable society, and liberals are asked to make "much more effective alliances with political conservatives"—an echo of the *"union sacrée"* through which the societies of Western Europe tried to save themselves in the interwar period.

On the highest level of authority and power, the trend toward violent repression rather than creative reconstruction coincides with President Johnson's consensus philosophy. That philosophy, untenable on both theoretical and practical grounds, is readily available as ideological justification and rationalization for the formation of a phalanx of all law-abiding citizens, protecting the established order from troublemakers of all sorts. Among them, the powers-that-be count not only the black rioters but also the opponents of our involvement in Vietnam. President Johnson and his supporters time and again accused the dissenters of giving aid and comfort to the enemy, thereby strengthening from above, and giving an official sanction of sorts to, the trend toward disintegration operating on the individual level. If the powers-that-be have the courage of their convictions, they must sooner or later do openly what at times they have tried to do surreptitiously and what an organization ironically misnamed Freedom House has openly advocated: stifle the dissent which they equate with disloyalty or treason.

Finally, there exists indeed an organic relationship between the trend toward violence at home and our policies in Vietnam. For in Vietnam, too, we have had a choice between accepting as inevitable a national and social peasant revolution and destroying the revolutionaries through violent repression, and we have chosen to pound, thus far without decisive effect, an intractable problem into oblivion. In intellectual, moral, and practical terms, nothing is indeed easier and less ambiguous than to deal with a social problem by oppressing and getting rid of the human beings who pose it. It is not accidental that many congressional advocates of violent repression in Vietnam represent states whose societies could not exist without the violent oppression of large masses, sometimes the majority, of their populations. Nor is it by accident that a retired Air Force General was, according to the *Anaheim Bulletin* of August 12, 1967, loudly applauded when he told his audience of American Legionnaires: "Military takeover is a dirty word in this country, but if the professional politicians cannot keep law and order it is time we do so, by devious or direct means." The problems we are facing at home are infinitely more complex and resistant to creative manipulation than those we are facing in Vietnam. Thus *a fortiori* the powers-that-be must be tempted to deal with our domestic problems as they are dealing with the problem of Vietnam: through the violence of impotence.

This is an ominous prospect. It can be avoided only if it is faced in time. We cannot afford the policies of consensus and stability, which are the result, not the condition, of sound substantive policies and can be imposed upon an unstable and warring society only through violence. We need a supreme effort at radical reform creating unity and stability out of that dissension and unrest that are inseparable from radical reform. While I know that this is what we need, I have no idea how to bring it about. Could it be that we have exhausted our creativeness at solving social problems, or must we wait for history to afford us an opportunity at showing again what we can do?

3

The Right to Dissent

[August, 1968]

The right to dissent derives from the relativistic philosophy of democracy. That philosophy assumes that all members of society, being rational, have equal access to the truth, but none of them has a monopoly of it. Oliver Cromwell expressed the relativistic ethos of democracy when he said to the representatives of the Church of Scotland: "I beseech you, in the bowels of Christ, think it possible you may be mistaken." If, on the other hand, a political elite is convinced that it has a monopoly of the truth, it has then not only the right but even the duty to suppress dissent; for dissent is here tantamount to heresy and treason. Thus it is perfectly consistent for totalitarian governments, such as that of the Soviet Union, to pride themselves on their freedom of the press and to disparage ours, since, as they argue, ours lends itself to the dissemination of lies, thereby misleading the public, while their press only prints what the government tells them to, that is, the truth. If the totalitarian philosophic assumption be correct, it would indeed be pointless and even immoral to give dissent an opportunity to be heard.

What creates the tension between the consent of the majority and the dissent of the minority in a democracy is the tendency of both to

40

assume that they have discovered "the" truth and that they have therefore the right and duty to defend it and make it prevail. That tendency is rooted in the conviction, of which democratic relativism takes no account, that there exists one correct policy, however dimly discernible, to the exclusion of all others. In view of that tendency, to think it possible that one might be mistaken requires a moral restraint of a high order, which is hard to come by. To insure action in conformity with that restraint requires legal and institutional safeguards difficult to apply. It is much more convenient and satisfying to assume that one's own policy is right and the opponent's is wrong than to allow at least for a doubt in the matter. In consequence, dissenters are tempted to move outside the democratic framework and to attack the system rather than the majority within the system, and the majority is tempted to push the dissenters beyond the confines of that framework and treat them as heretics and traitors rather than legitimate dissenters.

This tension between the consenting majority and the dissenting minority is aggravated by the peculiar character of American democracy. For in contrast to the Jacobin type of democracy, American democratic philosophy and practice do not hold that the will of the majority is the ultimate source of truth in matters political. They assume the existence of a "higher law" with which the majority must conform in order to be obeyed as legitimate. Judicial review, presidential veto, and the original indirect method of electing senators—even the present method—testify to the limitations the American system of government has imposed upon the will of the majority. As a consequence, dissent is doubly legitimate in the United States. It is legitimate not only by virtue of the relativistic ethos that all types of democracy share but also by virtue of the fact that American democracy is founded upon certain absolute, objective principles, which legitimize majority rule but are not subject to change by it.

It is decisive for the argument presented here that these two kinds of dissent are qualitatively different and lead to different political consequences. The type of dissent born of democratic relativism is essentially pragmatic. The majority favors a certain policy, which the dissenting minority opposes as running counter to its interest or as unwise or unnecessary. From this confrontation ensues, to quote Mr. Justice Holmes, "the competition of the market," from which truth is supposed to emerge and in which the minority competes with the majority on the basis of equality with a chance of becoming the majority itself.

The other type of dissent, upholding the absolute, objective principles of American democracy against its alleged majoritarian violators, calls into question the very existence of the American political system. This kind of dissent raises the issue, not just of the pragmatic desirability of a particular measure supported by the majority, but of the very legitimacy of the will of that particular majority. It amounts to an implicit declaration of civil war. The forms it takes are different from those of the other type. They aim not at the transformation of a dissenting minority into the majority but at thwarting the will of the majority. They run the gamut from peaceful protest through civil disobedience to actual civil war.

It is hardly necessary to dwell upon the undesirability of this type of dissent and the dangers it carries for the domestic peace of society and, indeed, the very survival of democracy. That much is obvious. The absolute, objective principles upon which American democracy is founded require of both the majority and the minority a kind of implicit social contract in which both pledge that, however much they might disagree on specific policies, they will abide by those basic principles. If the majority or minority violates this undertaking, it places itself outside the legitimacy of the American political system. If the minority does so, it will be exposed to repression by the majority. If the majority does so, the minority will try to thwart it. But in reaction, the majority will then attempt to repress the minority, and democracy might well die.

What is important to note is that the main responsibility for this vicious circle generally lies with the majority or the government claiming to represent it. It is of course possible that an utterly misguided or treasonous minority puts forward a program or embarks upon actions that are incompatible with the terms of the silent compact. But the historical record shows that it is generally their predominant social and political power that induces the majority and its government to overstep the bounds of the compact.

Thus, the corruption or outright violation of the terms of that social contract by the majority or its government calls forth a reaction on the part of the minority that is not mere dissent within the framework of democracy, expressed according to its rules, but an attack upon the system itself, a system that permits the corruption and violation of the very principles from which it derives its moral sustenance. A government may, for instance, embark upon a war that has no intelligible bearing upon the national interest and is morally repulsive to large segments of the population. Such a government, then, exposes itself to a popular reaction that oversteps the bounds of legality in the name of the moral principles on which the commonwealth is founded. The government's policy is in this case as unwise as the popular reaction is undesirable. But one or the other or both may under certain conditions be inevitable.

The issues discussed here arise with particular force in the conduct of foreign policy in a democracy. For what happens in domestic politics only occasionally is virtually typical in foreign policy: The preferences of the majority are at odds with the rational requirements of good policy. Alexis de Tocqueville made this point with special emphasis upon the American experience:

> Foreign politics demand scarcely any of those qualities which are peculiar to a democracy; they require, on the contrary, the perfect use of almost all those in which it is deficient. Democracy is favorable to the increase of the internal resources of state; it diffuses wealth and comfort, promotes public spirit and fortifies the respect for law in all classes of society: all these are advantages which have only an indirect influence over the relations which one people bears to another. But a democracy can only with great difficulty regulate the details of an important undertaking, persevere in a fixed design and work out its execution in spite of serious obstacles. It cannot combine its measures with secrecy or await their consequences with patience. . . .
>
> The propensity that induces democracies to obey impulse rather than prudence, and to abandon a mature design for the gratification of a momentary passion, was clearly seen in America on the breaking out of the French Revolution. It was then as evident to the simplest capacity as it is at the present time that the interest of the Americans forbade them to take any part in the contest which was about to deluge Europe with blood, but which could not injure their own country. But the sympathies of the people declared themselves with so much violence in favor of France that nothing but the inflexible character of Washington and the immense popularity which he enjoyed could have prevented the Americans from declaring war against England. And even then the exertions which the austere reason of that great man made to repress the generous but imprudent passions of his fellow citizens nearly deprived him of the sole recompense which he ever claimed, that of his country's love. The majority reprobated his policy, but it was afterwards approved by the whole nation.

It requires the character of a Washington and the political intelligence of a Hamilton to pursue a sound foreign policy in the teeth of passionate opposition by the majority. It is much easier and, in the short run, much more rewarding politically to follow what we have come to call "public opinion" than to try to create through courageous leadership a new majority on behalf of sound foreign policies. Since the great innovations of 1947—the Truman Doctrine, containment, the Marshall Plan—American governments have almost consistently pursued that easy and in the long run disastrous course.

In this situation, a dissenting minority performs a vital function for the political and moral welfare of the Republic. By upholding the rational principles of sound foreign policy, it offers an alternative to the foreign policy pursued by the government with the support of the majority; at the same time it keeps open the possibility that the minority of today will become the majority of tomorrow and that the principles of sound foreign policy will then prevail. If the government should pursue a foreign policy that is not only unsound on rational grounds but also repugnant to the very principles upon which American democracy is based, the dissenting minority, by its very existence, would remind the government and its majority of the continuing vitality of those principles.

Neither the minority nor the majority is vouchsafed the correctness of its views. But both must argue and act on the conviction that they are right, a conviction tempered by the awareness of the possibility that they might be mistaken. If both the majority and the minority remain within this relativistic ethos of democracy, while at the same time respecting those absolute, objective principles that are beyond the ken of that relativism, the vitality of their contest will accrue to the vitality of democracy. Otherwise, they will strain the delicate ties that keep a democratic society together, and they will risk destroying it while trying to keep it alive.

4

Freedom and Freedom House

[January, 1967]

In *The New York Times* of November 30, 1966, an adver-
tisement covering seven full columns of a page appeared with the title
in boldface: LEADERS WARN THAT EXTREMISTS COULD
DELAY VIETNAM NEGOTIATIONS. The subheading continued:
"A Crucial Turning Point! A Freedom House statement signed by
145 distinguished Americans urges the responsible critics of the Vietnam war to dissociate themselves from wild charges being made against
the nation and its leaders." The statement was signed by a former
President of the United States, a former Secretary of State, and other
distinguished men. Some of them I have counted among my friends;
others have been students of mine.

This is indeed a remarkable document. It is remarkable for three
reasons: for its views on the prospects for peace in Vietnam, for its
views on what constitutes "responsible" criticism of our Vietnam
policy, and for its conception of freedom of speech.

The document declares that failure by the responsible critics of our
Vietnam policy "to draw the line between their positions and the
views expressed by irresponsible extremists could encourage our Communist adversaries to postpone serious negotiations, raising the cost

45

in lives and delaying the peace we earnestly seek." In other words, the blood of our men who must die in Vietnam is on the hands of the "irresponsible" opponents. This charge derives from the assumption that the policies of our Vietnamese adversaries are determined by what some Americans may or may not say about the policies of their government. This is an extraordinary view of the policy-making processes of any government, past or present. I would have thought—and there is some evidence in history for thinking so—that a government engaged in war will be influenced in its attitude toward peace by its estimate of the military situation and of the peace terms it thinks it can obtain. As long as it thinks it can win, or can get better peace terms by continuing the war, it will go on fighting; when it thinks it is likely to lose, or has nothing to gain from continuing the war, it will stop fighting.

It is of course true that Communist governments dogmatically believe that capitalistic governments govern without the consent of the governed, since a capitalistic society is by definition a class society ruled by an exploiting minority. Whatever dissent there is in a capitalistic society, "responsible" or "irresponsible," provides empirical support for that dogmatic assumption and is for that reason eagerly quoted. The dogmatic assumption stands on its own feet, however, being an integral part of the received Marxist-Leninist truth. The dogma would be believed even if there were no dissent at all. Thus Communist writers have for two decades berated the "warmongers of Wall Street," myself included, who drag an unwilling American people toward war, regardless of the evidence pro or con. But I have not deemed it proper in the past to adapt my expression of opinion to the changing winds of Marxist polemics, and I do not intend to do so in the future.

The Freedom House document presents a list of five criticisms, which it calls "fantasies" and obviously regards as "irresponsible." Let us quote and examine them in sequence.

1. "That this is 'Lyndon Johnson's War' or 'McNamara's War' or any other individual's war." While I have never used such terms, I have expressed the conviction that our involvement in this war is in good measure the result of the personal shortcomings of our policy-makers. Their personal prestige, as they see it, requires the perpetuation of error, because a liquidation of the war on terms acceptable to the other side would be tantamount to admitting they were consistently wrong in their calculations and forecasts. Indeed, the argument most frequently heard nowadays in Washington runs like this: "If we had known two years ago what we know now, we wouldn't be in that mess. But we are in it, and what can we do?"

2. "That the American leaders are committing 'war crimes' or in-dulging in 'genocide.' " A war fought against indigenous guerrillas, either supported by the population or to whom the population is indifferent, is bound to obliterate the traditional distinctions between combatants and noncombatants, soldiers and civilians. It cannot but degenerate into indiscriminate killing, and victory can be won only by incapacitating everybody, guerrilla and non-guerrilla alike. This is not what our policy-makers intend to do, but what they are forced to do by the inexorable logic of the enterprise upon which they have embarked.

3. "That military service in this country's Armed Forces is an option exercisable solely at the discretion of the individual." I know of no proposition of this kind put forward in connection with the war in Vietnam, and I can therefore only guess what the document is aiming at. If it is aiming at the draft card burners and those who refuse to be inducted into the armed services without claiming the status of con-scientious objectors, it is dealing with individuals who are breaking the law but not with criticism, "responsible" or "irresponsible." If it is referring to members of the Armed Forces who would rather be re-lieved of their command or court-martialed than be responsible for indiscriminately killing civilians, they are not engaging in "criticism" either. But they are the real moral heroes of this war, even though they will never get the Congressional Medal of Honor.

4. "That this is a 'race' war of white versus colored peoples." Statistically the document is of course right in claiming that our white soldiers are fighting side-by-side with soldiers who are not white. But what is decisive in moral and political terms is how the war is being experienced by the Vietnamese people. To the Vietnamese, we appear as the successors to the French—whose ranks, by the way, also included nonwhite soldiers. It is we, a predominantly white people, who tell the Vietnamese that they ought to be dead rather than red, and we are in the process of making that statement stick. We can argue that the Vietnamese ought not to hate us as the white destroyers of their country. But they have begun to hate us as such, and it is this fact that counts.

5. "That this nation's leaders are obsessed with some compulsion to play 'world policeman' or to conduct some 'holy war' against the legitimate aspirations of underdeveloped people." The President, the Vice President, the Secretary of State, and our military leaders have stated innumerable times that we are in Vietnam to "stop Commu-nism." That is another way of saying we are engaged in an ideological war, and we consider "legitimate" only those aspirations that are anti-Communist. Whether or not one calls such a war "holy" is a matter of terminology; it does not affect the substance of what we say we are

doing. Our leaders have also told us repeatedly that being the most powerful nation on earth, we have a special responsibility to preserve peace and order and to oppose aggression throughout the world. Secretary of State Dean Rusk, appearing on August 25, 1966, before a Senate subcommittee, put it this way: "No would-be aggressor should suppose that the absence of a defense treaty, Congressional declaration, or U.S. military presence grants immunity to aggression." Whether or not one describes this as playing the role of "world policeman" is again a matter of terminology, and has nothing to do with the case.

I must confess that, insofar as the statements cited refer to intelligible criticisms of our Vietnam policy, I and many other reputable citizens subscribe to them, and I have expressed them consistently at least since July, 1961. Thus, by the standards of this document we are indeed "extremist" and "irresponsible" critics. But perhaps this stigmatization is not so much a reflection upon the critics as upon the stigmatizers. This brings me to the last and most important point: the issue of free speech.

The Freedom House document, in spite of a ritualistic bow to free speech, effectively limits free speech. It distinguishes between the arguments against our policies in Vietnam that are legitimate and those that are not. The arguments just analyzed are declared to be illegitimate. But considering the comprehensive character of the strictures, it is clear that while the document pretends to distinguish between legitimate and illegitimate criticism, its purpose is really to put the stamp of illegitimacy upon most of the criticism—past, present or future—advanced against our Vietnam policies.

Technically, of course, the issue is not freedom of speech, since Freedom House has no power to prevent the expression of opinions it condemns. But morally this is indeed the issue. For, by condemning certain opinions as not only mistaken but as aiding the enemies of the United States and helping to destroy the lives of American soldiers, the document removes them from the sphere of the morally acceptable as assuredly as the courts would be removing them from the sphere of the legally permissible by punishing the holders of these opinions. Such removal of a body of substantive opinion from the sphere of legitimacy is abhorrent to the Anglo-American tradition of free speech.

Free speech is limited by certain specific statutory prohibitions—for example, those involving libel and slander, obscenity, blasphemy, and sedition; it is also limited by the concern for preventing a clear and present danger to public order. But beyond these specific legal limitations, speech is supposed to be free on both moral and legal grounds. Beyond these limitations, there can be no substantive limits to criticism in a free society. "No person or group," to quote James M. Landis, "is wise enough to be trusted to discriminate between valid and invalid ideas." And the legitimate concern for the effectiveness of the government in times of war does not override this consideration. As Judge Charles F. Amidon put it in legal terms:

> The framers of the first Amendment knew that the right to criticize might weaken the support of the government in a time of war. They appreciated the value of a united public opinion at such a time. They were men who had experienced all those things in the war of the Revolution, and yet they knew too that the republic which they were founding could not live unless the right of free speech, of freedom of the press was maintained at such a time.

The Freedom House document is trying to establish a political orthodoxy with regard to our policies in Vietnam. It tells us that we are morally entitled to criticize the government, but not with regard to the fundamental issues it enumerates. That is to say, we are not morally entitled to criticize the government in any meaningful way. It is both illuminating and disquieting to note that this is how the moral right to criticize is formulated by the enlightened totalitarianisims of the day. The governments of the Soviet Union and Eastern Europe, with the exception of East Germany, all make a distinction between "responsible" and "irresponsible" criticism, and "irresponsible" criticism is defined as that which attacks the foundations of government policies. That the immune foundations are much more broadly defined by totalitarianism than by Freedom House, addressing itself only to the issue of Vietnam, does not affect the principle, which violates the democratic ethos. It is ironic that an organization calling itself Freedom House should thus, unwittingly and misguidedly, attack the very foundations of American freedom. This is but one of the ironies of this document. There are two others.

The document condemns the holders of certain opinions as being responsible for the continuation of the war in Vietnam. I hold these opinions. And it is exactly because I hold them that I have consistently warned against the policies which first led to our involvement in this war, and then to our inability to extricate ourselves from it. If my advice had been followed there would be no war in Vietnam today, and our interests in Southeast Asia and throughout the world would be the better for it.

But aside from this perverse logic, which blames the opponents of the war for its continuation, the document does not raise the question of whether the responsibility for continuing the war might not at least be shared by those policy-makers who have been consistently wrong in their calculations and forecasts and have since 1963 repeatedly, and finally with success, urged upon the President the bombing of North Vietnam as a sure road to victory. Nor does the document raise the general question of whether those who make policy might not bear a greater share of responsibility than those who criticize that policy. It could dismiss the question only if it proved that the policies of the government could win the war quickly were it not for the irresponsibility of the critics.

The Freedom House document, so extraordinary in its implications, is the result of a misguided sense of patriotism. This patriotism deems it its duty to support the policies of the government in times of crisis, thus identifying the government with the nation, and in the process sacrifices the interests of the nation upon the altar of conformity. I am reminded of the famous manifesto which in the fall of 1914 was addressed "to the civilized world" by 93 luminaries of German scholarship, art, and literature, men such as Baeyer, Behring, Brentano, Ehrlich, Eucken, Haber, Haeckel, Harnack, Hauptmann, Laband, Lamprecht, Lenard, Liebermann, Neisser, Nernst, Ostwald, Planck, Reinhardt, Röntgen, Schmoller, Vossler, Wassermann, Weingartner, Wilamowitz-Moellendorf, Willstätter, Windelband, and Wundt. It declared that it was "not true" that Germany bore any responsibility for the war, that Germany had violated the neutrality of Belgium, that "the life and property of a single Belgian citizen had been injured" without military necessity, etc. That manifesto has gone down in history as a prime example of how wrong good and meritorious men can be when their patriotic passions are aroused. I think the Freedom House document will fare no better.

5

How Totalitarianism Starts: The Domestic Involvement of the CIA

[March, 1967]

Disclosure of the domestic involvements of the Central Intelligence Agency raises three fundamental issues: (1) the ability of American democracy to pursue an effective foreign policy without destroying at home what it promotes abroad; (2) the feasibility and morality of domestic clandestine operations; and (3) the relations between the federal government and the intellectual community

Foreign policy in our period of history has become total in that all the resources of a nation—political, military, economic, technological, psychological, and moral—are marshaled for the support of the nation's interests. In that competition, a democratic society is at an obvious disadvantage.

A totalitarian government by definition has society in all its manifestations at its beck and call, for it has absorbed what we call the "private" sphere. A democratic government, presiding over a pluralistic society, must somehow manage to mobilize private organizations on behalf of its policies. How can it do that without impairing, if not destroying, the "private" character of such organizations? This is the dilemma the Government of the United States faced 15 years ago when it decided to subsidize on a large scale and by clandestine methods a great number of private and ostensibly autonomous organizations, such as the National Student Association, to help wage the cold war.

By doing this, the government committed two interconnected errors: It allowed itself to be too impressed by the efficiency of totalitarian organization and tried to beat the enemy at his own game by countering his totalitarian controls with clandestine ones; on the other hand, it did not fully appreciate the roots of its own strength —the unquestionably spontaneous support it receives from free citizens and autonomous organizations.

Thus it subverted the substance of that autonomy while trying to preserve its appearance. It tried to compete with the enemy on his terms rather than its own. Such a policy could succeed only so long as the appearance of the autonomy of client organizations could be preserved. While a totalitarian government does not need to worry about appearances, a democratic government runs the risk that the scrutiny of public opinion will discover the reality of government control behind the appearances of private autonomy and thereby ruin the policy.

Had the CIA been able to conceal indefinitely the true state of affairs, it would have proved not only the correctness of its policies but also the weakness of democratic controls. It would have demonstrated that the methods of a surreptitious totalitarianism can escape democratic scrutiny. It testifies to the vitality of our democratic habits that the scrutiny of public opinion has been able to uncover governmental deception and that in consequence the CIA has been forced to retreat from it exposed domestic positions. But a heavy price has to be paid for this reassertion of democratic scrutiny both domestically and internationally. The pity of it is that, had the government had more confidence in the strength of a free democracy than in the efficiency of pseudo-totalitarian methods, it could have served the national interest without paying so heavy a price.

Internationally, all individuals and organizations, speaking on behalf of the United States, will from now on be suspect as secret agents of the government. Even if they speak the truth as free agents, they will risk not being believed. Thus the unique and precious asset of a free society, the intellectual and moral autonomy of its members *vis-à-vis* the government, will go to waste. Instead there will be the suspicion, but not the reality, of totalitarian control. Thus the government has impaired, if not lost, that unique quality which from the beginning of American history has served as a model for other nations to emulate and has gained nothing in return except a bad reputation, in good measure undeserved.

Domestically, the moral confidence of the people in their government has been shaken. This is not a political crisis affecting this particular Administration but a moral crisis affecting American democracy itself. An English diplomatist of the sixteenth century defined a diplomat as "an honest man sent abroad to lie for his country." More and more of our citizens have come to look upon a public official as (perhaps) an honest man staying at home to lie for the government.

The decline of confidence in our democratic institutions and the increase in cynicism about politics are unmistakeable. The "New Left," however aimless its politics may be, is alienated not only from this Administration but from all conceivable ones, and it is exactly for that reason that its politics is aimless in view of traditional American political institutions and practices. But the awareness on the part of tens of thousands of students, present and former, that they have been deceived by their leaders and used by the government for hidden purposes is bound to spread that disaffection beyond the relatively narrow limits of the "New Left."

It would be comforting if one could assume that this fiasco, comparable in its magnitude to the Bay of Pigs, were nothing more than the result of an isolated operation. If it were just that, appropriate reforms could prevent a repetition, and the books could be closed on yet another ephemeral incident, as they have been on the Bay of Pigs. But in truth the issue that confronts us here by far transcends the recently revealed activities of the CIA. Rather, these activities are but a special instance of a general attitude, which is in the process of transforming the relations that have traditionally existed in America between the government and the governed. In the traditional view, the private sphere was supposed to be independent of the government. That independence was jealously guarded as the mainspring of the vitality of democratic pluralism—which in turn would periodically revitalize the personnel and policies of the government. The new ideal is consensus, that is, the convergence of the public and private sphere on the terms of the former. In that view, private dissent from public policy is at best a nuisance and at worst akin to disloyalty.

The government's attempts at establishing a consensus in support of its policies are continuously frustrated by critical voices from the private sector. The government, quite logically from its point of view, calls them "irresponsible." These attempts are supported by the traditional conformism of American society and by the government's access to, and support by, the mass media of public opinion, which private dissent cannot even come close to matching. They are also supported by systematic deception, paralleling that practiced by the CIA. A high official of the government, charged with public information, has been quoted as having referred to the press as "handmaidens of government" and to have added: "Look, if you think any American official is going to tell you the truth, then you are stupid. Did you hear that?—stupid."

This is the philosophy not of democracy but of totalitarianism. And that philosophy is continuously put into practice. To take just one recent example: The Department of Defense has distributed to civic organizations and high schools a movie called "Why Vietnam?" which both in its technical cleverness and in its utter disregard for the truth is a typical example of totalitarian propaganda.

Under Secretary of State Nicholas deB. Katzenbach, speaking for President Johnson, put the CIA affair in the broader context it deserves when he declared on Feb. 15, 1967: "The President believes strongly that the integrity and independence of the educational community must be preserved. He has directed a careful review of any government activities that may endanger this integrity and independence." Such a review, if it is really careful and comprehensive, will discover that the integrity and independence of the educational community need to be not so much preserved as restored; for not only have that integrity and independence been compromised by the CIA, they are being compromised every day through what has become the normal relationship between the government and the educational community.

As the integrity and independence of the government have been subverted by the "military-industrial complex," so the integrity and independence of the educational community have been impaired by the academic-political complex. The educational community has in large measure become the handmaiden of government, while maintaining its pretense to independence. It is that contrast between pretense and actual dependence that is incompatible with intellectual integrity. There is nothing wrong with student leaders' or academics' serving the government as long as they do not pretend that they are serving their organizations or the truth.

The trust that the leaders of the National Student Association betrayed by working secretly for the CIA is being betrayed less blatantly by large number of academics. And that "treason of the intellectuals" is doing more damage to the nation than the transgressions of the student leaders. For by making it appear as though the voice of the government were of necessity the voice of truth, it powerfully supports the trend toward consensus politics and the concomitant destruction of an autonomous private sphere already referred to. It also tends to obliterate the confrontation between truth and power from which stems the vitality of democratic pluralism.

Thus, seen from the general perspective which President Johnson has suggested, what the CIA has done with the cooperation of private organizations—and it could not have done it without that cooperation—appears as nothing more than a particularly spectacular instance of a general trend. To stem that trend, it will not be sufficient to make the CIA stop what it has been doing. Both the government at large and the academic community will have to stop what they have been doing. To reverse this pervasive trend requires more than a review by a Presidential committee. It requires a radical moral reorientation of both the government and the academic community.

6

The Writer's Duty and His Predicament

[Summer, 1965]

The outlet open to a writer determines, at least in a certain measure, the kind of writing he can do. A writer who does not write, say, for *The New Yorker* is precluded from the kind of writing for which *The New Yorker* has a monopoly. On the other hand, a writer who specializes in writing for *Commentary* cannot help but adapt both substance and presentation to the character of that publication. Obviously, *Commentary* would not print what appears in *The New Yorker*, and vice versa. Thus, the kind of outlet open to a writer limits and molds his creative energies. The more limited these outlets are, the fewer and more precarious are his opportunities for self-expression. What he actually writes, then, tells only half the story. What he could have written if somebody had been willing to print it will never be known.

The editor has three choices: He can print the manuscript as it stands; he can suggest editorial changes, which the author is free to accept or reject; or he can reject the manuscript as being unsuitable for publication. What he cannot do is substitute his judgment for that of the author. He cannot force himself as a ghost writer on an unsuspecting and unwilling author. By taking the place of the author, the

56

editor makes it impossible for the latter to discharge his duties toward himself and toward society. What is at stake here is the issue of intellectual freedom in its most profound and personal sense, and insofar as the writer's inability to discharge his duties is concerned, it makes no difference if his intellectual freedom is abridged on purpose or through ignorance and obtuseness.

The editor would have the right to impose his judgment upon the author only if there existed one correct philosophy, one correct kind of argumentation, and one correct way of writing to the exception of all others. Societies indeed exist that believe in, and practice, these propositions; we call them totalitarian. There the writer must think, argue, and write as the editor tells him to, and generally the editor doesn't need to tell him, because a rigid system of political and social rewards and punishments will keep the writer in line without editorial prodding. In a free society such as ours, the writer is subject to the rules of logic, grammar, and syntax, and even those the editor has no right to force upon the writer. He may only suggest their observance to the writer, who risks not being published if he does not observe them.

The ease with which the editor imposes his judgment upon the writer is a symptom of a barbarization that threatens to smother creative expression of any kind. This barbarism is oblivious of the true nature of creativity, assimilating it to some kind of standardized repetitive production, and therefore is incapable of respecting its uniqueness. More particularly, it has no feeling for the organic and intimate relationship between thought and the language through which thought is expressed.

Thus it comes about that great works of literature, philosophy, and scholarship are edited, condensed, summarized, and fragmented by hacks who know better than the authors what is "important" and what is not and how to express the meaning the author intended to convey. Thus it comes about that, to give only one example among many, Hochhuth's *The Deputy* is "produced" in New York in virtually unrecognizable form insofar as the dramatic intentions of the author are concerned, with scenes transposed, sentences transferred from the mouth of one person into that of another, whole sentences written in by the producer. It does not matter that *The Deputy* is not a very good play and that it is in need of cutting. What matters is that the producer usurped the functions of the writer, taking the writer's work as raw material for what he thought the play should be like. This procedure would have been scandalous even if in the process the play had been improved, which, heaven knows, it was not. Mr. Hochhuth could have prevented the performance of the disfigured play by suing the producer. He did the least he could have done as a self-respecting author: He stayed away from the premiere.

It would, however, be unfair to blame the middlemen, the editors and producers, for this barbarization. The writers themselves are lacking in understanding of, and respect for, their mission. They don't mind, they even welcome, expressing their thoughts through the language of others. In consequence, the ghost writer has become an accepted literary institution. I remember how shocked I was a few years ago when I tried to engage a scholar of considerable repute in a conversation about a review of a book of mine, which had appeared under his signature. He referred me to a graduate student who he said had written the review. What shocked me was the complete naturalness of that reference, as though it was naïve to assume that a scholar had actually written what he pretended to have written. The collectivization of scholarly research inevitably blurs the identity of authorship. Yet the lack of scruple with which reputable scholars appropriate the work of research assistants and graduate students points to more than a moral deficiency in certain individuals. It points to that degeneration by which our culture, in losing respect for individual language, has lost respect for individual thought as well.

Language and thought are indeed inseparable; for it is only through language that thought becomes conscious of itself and makes itself heard. Standardized language is appropriate to standardized thought, and here is the proper domain of the ghost writer, the presumptuous editor, and the usurping producer. Yet creative thought, through which the intellectual and moral personality of an individual expresses itself as uniquely as his physical person does through his fingerprints, requires a language as uniquely his own. His language is not just a carrier on which his thoughts as well as other thoughts can be transported or for which another carrier could be substituted, performing the same mechanical function of transportation. His language *is* his thought. Change his language, and you have changed his thought.

The creative writer, faithful to his duty toward himself and society, searches for the language that reveals exactly what he wants to say. It is a painful task; for the language must be molded, like a piece of metal, to the thought. But it is also a rewarding task; for in that rare moment of perfect achievement, when meaning, rhythm, and sound have become one, the writer is enraptured by that aesthetic elation which poets and composers must feel when their work has been perfectly done. Language, then, becomes music, rhythmical and melodious, and the writer's ear measures its perfection by being reminded of the rhythm, melody, and structure of a familiar piece of great music.

Language and thought stand in an organic and intimate relation to each other. (Writing the preceding sentence, for instance, I pondered whether "Thought and language" was preferable to "Language and thought." I chose the latter version, for I felt that its sequence of vowels and its rhythm are aesthetically satisfying and that, since we are here dealing with the problem of language, we should start the paragraph with that word, thus setting its theme.) This relation, however, does not render the editor's task superfluous; it rather defines its nature and its limits. That perfect harmony between sound, rhythm, and meaning is but rarely attained. "Homer himself hath been observ'd to nod." In particular, no writer who must meet deadlines can write only perfect sentences. Thus, the civilized editor who knows what it means to write and is endowed with that chameleon-like ability to crawl into the skin of his author, simulating the creative process, is indeed a valued and, at certain occasions, indispensable participant in the creative process. Writers have gratefully acknowledged their debt to such editors, and I acknowledge mine to Alfred Knopf, to whom I owe more than to any other single man whatever ability I have to express my thoughts in a language appropriate to them.

The run-of-the-mill editor is a world apart from this civilized type. With clumsy fingers, he tears apart the carefully spun fabric of language, giving no heed to what the intentions of the author might have been. It does not occur to him that the complexity of language might be the result of a complexity of thought, which cannot be expressed otherwise, or that an unexpected subtlety of phrase might have a purpose. For these literary retailers, language is a standardized commodity, and language that differs from theirs must be "wrong" because it differs. In common with all that is mediocre, they resent excellence, which by its very existence indicates the limits of their gift. I have sometimes been tempted to offer one of Carlyle's essays for publication without revealing the author's name, just to see how Carlyle would sound in the standardized version of higher journalese.

The editorial attack upon the writer's workmanship is vulgar and barbaric; for it has no feeling for either thought or language or for the unbreakable relation between the two, and it substitutes for genuine literature, which by its very nature is peculiar and unique, a *lingua franca*, which the middlemen think is the only English there can be because it is theirs. Yet that onslaught is also immoral; it offends not only against thought and language but also against the inalienable rights of the human person. It not only breaks the ties between thought and language, disfiguring both; it also intrudes in the relation between the human person, on the one hand, and his thought and language, on the other. By doing so, it wounds and disfigures the human person. *"Le style c'est l'homme."* What you do to his language, you do to the man. Distort his language, and you have distorted the man who, as an intellect and a moral person, lives in his language. The writer is nothing without his language. Take his language away, and you have silenced him. Put words into his mouth, and you have made him speak in a voice not his own. Refuse him the right to say what he wants to say in his own words, and you have as thoroughly destroyed his freedom, nay, himself, as though you had sealed his lips and chained his hands. At best, he will have become a freak, a composite of his own thought and language, and somebody else's.

7

On Trying to Be Just

[May, 1963]

To do justice and to receive it is an elemental aspiration of man. It is as elemental as the aspiration to live on after one's physical death, to be free from the power of other men, to exert power over man and nature, to love and to be loved. Justice, immortality, freedom, power, and love—those are the poles that attract and thereby shape the thoughts and actions of men. They have one quality in common that constitutes the distinction of men from beasts and gods alike: Achievement falls short of aspiration. A beast does not seek to be more than it is by nature: A pig does not seek to be a lion. A god, being perfection by definition, cannot seek to be more than he is by nature, for he is already all that he, or anybody, can be.

Man alone is, as it were, suspended between heaven and earth: an ambitious beast and a frustrated god. For he alone is endowed with the faculty of rational imagination that outpaces his ability to achieve. His desire to live forever must be satisfied by an act of faith, which, insofar as it is empirically founded at all, rests upon the tenuous foundation of things preserved and deeds remembered. His freedom is marred by the power of others, as his power is by their freedom. His capacity to love and to be loved falls short of his desire. And so it is with justice, but in a peculiar way. Freedom, power, and love, man can have; what he cannot have is the kind and quantity of freedom, power, and love he would like to have. With justice, as with immortality, it is different: The question here is whether he can have it at all.

The school of thought that answers this question in the negative, without qualification, traces its ancestry to the very beginning of Western philosophy, when Plato's Callicles and Thracymachus defined justice as the interest of the stronger, that is, equated it with power. As Thracymachus put it in *The Republic*: ". . . in all states there is the same principle of justice which is the interest of the government; and as a government must be supposed to have power, the only reasonable conclusion is that everywhere there is one principle of justice which is the interest of the stronger." In this view, justice for the many who are lacking in power is an illusion. It is, as we would say today, an ideology with which the powerful conceal and legitimize their power, thereby making its exercise acceptable to the many who are weak. The invocation of justice, then, is an instrument of domination. In the measure that it succeeds, it makes the weak a voluntary subject of the power of others; it internalizes the power relation in the mind and will of the subject. In consequence, the invocation of justice serves the economy of power; for the more power is voluntarily accepted as just, the less will it be necessary for the holders of power to impose it from above.

This view of justice has been echoed in modern times from Machiavelli, Hobbes, and Spinoza to Marx and Kelsen, and history seems to bear it out. Powerful and weak alike tend to equate their interests with justice. The powerful defend the *status quo* as just and condemn those who oppose it as unjust. The opponents of the *status quo*, in turn, proclaim the justice of their cause and the iniquity of things as they are. Nations, religions, classes, parties, litigants, parents and children, husbands and wives—they all fight each other in the name of justice. Since they cannot all be right, is it not fair to conclude that they are all wrong, deceiving themselves and the world? Perhaps Mr. Justice Holmes has the last word with what he wrote to Sir Frederick Pollock about judging "the goodness or badness of laws": "I have no practical criticism except what the crowd wants." And perhaps we can do no better than Pontius Pilate, washing our hands and letting the majority decide what justice requires.

We are not concerned here with debating the view that justice does not exist and is a mere illusion. Rather, we want to show that, even if assuming the reality of justice, we are incapable of realizing it. The two positions are by no means identical. They are no more identical than the atheistic position denying the existence of God is identical with the view that man is incapable of knowing God, even if He does exist. The position we are taking here has the advantage, at least for cognitive purposes, that it coincides with the one men have always taken because they could not do otherwise. Men have always thought and acted *as though* justice were real.* We are proceeding here on the same assumption, trying to show that, even if justice is real, man cannot achieve it for reasons that are inherent in his nature. The reasons are three: Man is too ignorant, man is too selfish, and man is too poor.

Justice requires that men give to others, and receive from others, what is their due. In order to be just, man must give to others what they deserve in view of their desires, needs, and actions; and in order that justice be done to him, he must receive what he deserves. But where do we find the standards by which we can measure the adequacy of what a man receives and gives? How do we determine the point at which a man gives and receives neither more nor less but exactly what is required by justice?

We all, as a matter of course, pass judgments that assume certain knowledge of such standards. It is the common quality of such judgments that they derive from a particular view of the world, of its constitution and purpose, and of man's place within it. When we say that it is unjust for a man to have so much power or wealth or to use his power or wealth in such a manner, we assume to know how much power or wealth he ought to have and how he ought to use it. In our society, such knowledge typically derives from an equalitarian conception, which assumes that justice requires keeping disparities in the distribution of power and wealth to a minimum. An aristocratic philosophy, on the other hand, assuming the natural inequality of men, will find justice in the unequal distribution of power and wealth and injustice in leveling them off. A libertarian philosophy will identify justice with freedom and will be unconcerned with the issue of equality, at least in its economic manifestation. A theocratic conception of the world, in turn, may find the issues of both equality and freedom within secular society irrelevant for justice, since justice will be done in the other world by God. In sum, our knowledge of what justice demands is predicated upon our knowledge of what the world is like and what it is for, of a hierarchy of values reflecting the objective order of the world. Of such knowledge, only theology can be certain, and secular philosophies can but pretend to have it.

However, even theology can have that knowledge only in the ab-

---

* The famous discussion between the Athenians and the Melians reported by Thucydides, which is carried on in terms of naked power and explicitly stripped of all pretenses to justice, is not an account of historical fact but a literary device to bring out the core of the issue.

stract and is as much at a loss as are secular philosophies when it comes to applying abstract principles to concrete cases. The two great papal encyclicals that formulate the principles of social justice for modern Catholicism exemplify that insufficiency. In *De Rerum Novarum*, Leo XIII declared in 1891 that "among the most important duties of employers the principal one is to give every worker what is justly due him. Assuredly, to establish a rule of pay in accord with justice, many factors must be taken into account." Forty years later, Pius XI recognized in *Quadragesimo Anno* that "certain doubts have arisen concerning either the correct meaning of some parts of Leo's Encyclical or conclusions to be deduced therefrom, which doubts in turn have even among Catholics given rise to controversies that are not always peaceful. . . ." Quoting Leo's definition of just pay, Pius had nothing to add but this paraphrase: "The just amount of pay, however, must be calculated not on a single basis but on several." "Relations of one to the other [capital and labor]," said the Pope in another passage,

> must be made to conform to the laws of strictest justice—commutative justice, as it is called—with the support, however, of Christian charity. . . . The public institutions themselves, of peoples, moreover, ought to make all human society conform to the needs of the common good; that is, to the norm of social justice.

It is clear that nothing follows from these abstract pronouncements, in good measure tautological, for the decision of concrete cases. Was it just for the steel companies to try to raise the price of steel in 1961? Was there justice in the demands of the printers against the New York newspapers in 1963? The pronouncements of theology do not answer these questions or, rather, answer them whichever way one wants them answered. The substance of the answers derives not from the abstract pronouncements but from the concrete interests at stake. These interests fill the gap between abstract statements and concrete cases; they give concreteness to the abstractions.

All of us look at the world and judge it from the vantage point of our interests. We judge and act as though we were at the center of the universe, as though what we see everybody must see, and as though what we want is legitimate in the eyes of justice. Turning Kant's categorical imperative upside down, we take it for granted that the standards of judgment and action produced by the peculiarities of our perspective can serve as universal laws for all mankind. The great philosophers have pointed to man's capacity for self-deception, and modern psychology has systematically explored its unexpected all-persuasiveness.

This propensity for self-deception is mitigated by man's capacity for transcending himself, for trying to see himself as he might look to others. This capacity, however feeble and ephemeral it may be, is grounded in man's rational nature, which enables him to understand himself and the world around him with a measure of objectivity. Yet where rational, objective knowledge is precluded from the outset, as it is with justice, the propensity for self-deception has free rein. As knowledge restrains self-deception, so ignorance strengthens it. Since man cannot help but judge and act in terms of justice and since he cannot know what justice requires, but since he knows for sure what he wants, he equates with a vengeance his vantage point and justice. Empirically we find, then, as many conceptions of justice as there are vantage points, and the absolute majesty of justice dissolves· into the relativity of so many interests and points of view. "Why do you kill me?" asks Pascal. "But don't you live on the other side of the water? My friend, if you lived on this side I would be an assassin and it would be unjust to kill you thus; but since you live on the other side I am a hero, and that is just."

Even third parties not directly involved in the conflict of interests —judges, arbitrators, innocent bystanders—try as they may, cannot escape that relativity of justice. At worst, they will satisfy their interests vicariously by favoring the interests similar to their own. At best, they will bring their particular view of world and man to bear on the case; yet the justice they do is justice only within the limits of the perspective from which they view the world.

It is the saving grace of ignorance and egotism that they are easily concealed. For if they were not, they would be a deadly affront to our need to be just. Thus, with that biological wisdom that is a quality not only of our bodies but of our minds as well, the poison of ignorance and egotism creates illusion as its own antidote. In order to save ourselves, we are not only able, but compelled, to delude ourselves into believing that ignorance is knowledge, and egotism impartiality.

The predicament of poverty is a heavier burden because it is not so easily concealed. We think we know what justice requires, and we are resolved to act in accordance with it, but we do not have what it takes to do it. We know what we ought to do, and we want to do it, but we cannot. That is the tragedy of trying to be just.

In the economy of justice, demand exceeds supply. The freedom people claim from the government as their due cannot be granted without impairing the governmental power needed to maintain order.

So many people have in justice a claim on our love, but there is not enough love in us to satisfy them all. How does one in justice reconcile the demands of one's work with the claims of one's family, the claims of one's family with those of one's friends, the claims of the individual members of one's family with each other? How does one do justice to oneself and to others at the same time? After satisfying the demands of self, even if they were not inflated as they generally are, what is left over is not enough to go around. However one may try, the accounts of justice never square, because there is too much demanded and not enough to give.

Yet man cannot afford to let it go at that. He must see to it that justice is done, and he cannot admit that it cannot be done. Thus he calls to the aid of justice three remedies, which are expected either to compensate for the deficiencies of human nature or to transcend the problem of justice altogether. The remedies are equal distribution, power, and love.

The equal rationing of necessities of life that are in short supply appears to compensate for both ignorance and poverty. If we are not sure how much we owe, and if we have not enough of what we know we owe, the best we seem able to do is give each claimant an equal share of what we have. Yet what may appear to the giver to be the best he can do must leave the recipient dissatisfied. Since justice requires giving everyone his due, everyone has the right to have his case considered on its individual merits and not on a footing of mechanical equality with all others. That claim, inherent in the concept of justice, is strengthened and exaggerated by the egotism of the claimants, all of whom naturally are convinced that they deserve more than their equal share because they are superior in need or merit. King Solomon, proposing to cut the baby in half, showed up the fallacious and even self-defeating character of such a remedy, which would be a true remedy only if justice—as opposed to law—required nothing more than the mechanical distribution of equal shares.

King Solomon had one great asset, which enabled him to do justice in the case of the two women, each claiming the baby as her own: He had the power of a king. Those who think they know what justice requires but have no way of seeing it done either can resign themselves to the injustice of this world or can find in that combination of conviction and impotence the motive force for the acquisition of the power to make justice prevail. Men seek to acquire that power through movements of reform, revolution, and war. The more certain men are in their knowledge of what justice requires, the more ruthless they are in the search for, and the use of, power. The end of justice, clearly seen, justifies the means of power necessary to achieve it.

Yet men want power not only as a means for the ends of justice but also for its own sake. While the aspiration for justice aims at using power for its ends, it eggs on the lust that seeks power for power's sake. And in that dialectic between justice and power, power gets the better of justice. For the work of justice is never done and always dubious; the work of power, however ephemeral it may be, is clearly seen and simply enjoyed. "Justice," to quote Pascal again, "is subject to dispute; might is easily recognized and is not disputed. So we cannot give might to justice, because might has gainsaid justice and has declared that it is she herself who is just. And thus, being unable to make what is just strong, we have made what is strong just."

It is, then, the predicament of trying to be just that we are too ignorant, too selfish, and too poor to do what justice demands of us. Yet there is a mode of being and action for which knowledge is irrelevant, in which selfishness is overcome and poverty at the very least takes on the appearance of wealth, and that is the mode of love. Love, as the spontaneous surrender of two persons to each other, transcends the calculus of justice. The lover does not ask what is his and the beloved's due; he gives and receives all that can be given, even at the risk of the sacrifice of self.

But is it justice to give and receive all that can be given, rather than what one ought to give and receive? Love may be superior to justice in its denial of self, but it is not justice; for it is of the very essence of justice to require an objective standard of distribution or retribution that allows us to say: I have received what is my due, and I have given what is the other's due. Thus, love evades the problem of justice by transcending it; it does not answer the question justice asks. Trying to compensate for Hamlet's debilitating doubt with Lear's indiscriminate love, we only exchange one defect for another.

Thus, we are condemned by the nature of justice, and our own, to give and to receive either too little or too much, or at least to be ignorant of whether we have received and given too little or too much. In the eyes of man, the accounts of justice never square. Yet we must try to square them, even though, like Sisyphus, we cannot succeed.

8

The Limits of Historical Justice

[July, 1969]

Goethe remarked to Eckermann that the one who acts is always unjust and that nobody has justice but the one who observes. Twenty-five years ago, I quoted that epigram with approval. But having in the meantime read many writings of trained observers of past political events, that is, of professional historians, I conclude that the epigram, like most epigrams, is in need of considerable emendation. Most certainly, the act itself, impinging upon men and things on behalf of the actor's interests, is bound to be unjust. For it at best neglects and at worst impairs the interests of others. That is true even of the unselfish act. By supporting an old-age home, I withhold support for the hungry, who also have a claim on my charity. In short, the claims of justice by far exceed man's ability to satisfy them. Thus man establishes a hierarchy among the interests to be served, and his own interests and preferences take precedence over all others. Nobody but God knows what actions the "just" hierarchy would require, but it can safely be said that a hierarchy oriented toward the interests and preferences of one man among hundreds of millions can but have a negligible chance of coinciding with the "just" order of the universe.

But while the act cannot be just, save by remote coincidence, the act, to be successful, cannot afford to be without an element of justice.

That is particularly true of the political act. The requisite element of justice pertains to the intellectual sphere. The successful political act presupposes a respectful understanding of its object, its nature, its interests, its propensities and potentialities. The political actor may hate his opponent or despise the one whose support he seeks. But for the very sake of the satisfaction of his interests and preferences, that is, for the very sake of his own injustice, he must "do justice" to the other man. He must detach himself from his own emotions and aspirations and judge the other man with an objectivity similar to that with which a scientist tries to understand the phenomena of nature. He must put himself into the other man's shoes, look at the world and judge it as he does, anticipate in thought the way he will feel and act under certain circumstances. Seeking to deprive the other of his worth as a person by using, diminishing, or destroying him, the political actor must assess him exactly as a person in his own right. Paradoxically, he must be just in judgment in order to be effectively unjust in action.

If indeed the actor is always unjust in action while he must be just in judgment, what must we say of the corollary that nobody has justice but the one who observes? Mark that Goethe does not say that he who observes *is* always just, but that he is the only one who *can* be just. He can be just because he does not act and, hence, can allow free play to the detachment and objectivity of his mind. Detached and objective understanding—for the actor the means to the end of successful action —is for him an end in itself. Only the observer can be just, but in what measure is he? I am raising this question here not in its comprehensive meaning, but only in regard to the writing of political history.

Homer, the great poet-historian, and the other great historians of ancient Greece, Herodotus and Thucydides, have proved that a political historian can be just. Reading their accounts of the wars between the Greeks and the Trojans, the Greeks and the Persian "barbarians," and among the Greeks themselves, one finds it hard to determine "whose side they are on." They behold the contestants as different incarnations of the same species of man, endowed with the same virtues and vices, equally capable of great and mean deeds, of wisdom and folly, and sharing the same fate ordained by the same gods. They are all equally worthy of remembrance. Thus, Herodotus sets himself the task "of preventing the great and wonderful actions of the Greeks and the barbarians from losing their due meed of glory." And they are all equally deserving of compassion. Thus, Euripides can honor the grief of the Trojan women whose men were killed by the Greeks.

It was this ideal of impartiality, both an intellectual and a moral virtue, that Acton put before the contributors to the first *Cambridge Modern History* when he wrote in his letter of instructions that "our Waterloo must be one that satisfies French and English, German and Dutch alike; that nobody can tell, without examining the list of authors, where the Bishop of Oxford laid down the pen, and where Fairbairn or Gasquet, Liebermann or Harrison took it up." However, with perhaps the sole exception of Tolstoy in *War and Peace*, the Greek historians have had no successors. A deep chasm separates the modern historic sensibility from that of the Greeks. Imagine an American historian writing of the war against Japan—or against Spain or Mexico, for that matter—in order to preserve "the great and wonderful actions" of the enemies of the United States in their deserved glory! And imagine a Northern American playwright commemorating the sufferings of the Southern women during the Civil War!

The modern historians are partisans—partisans of nation, religion, class, and individual men. Let us take a look at some undoubtedly great modern historians. The greatest of them all, Ranke, assigned to history the task of finding out "how it really was." Yet his Prussian history is a panegyric to the virtues and greatness of Prussia, a testimony to the author's nationalism. Mommsen, the great historian of Rome, was also a disappointed liberal politician, longing for an effective leader of the liberal cause, and he judged Rome—praising the Republic and Caesar, condemning Caesar's enemies and Caesarism— by the standards of nineteenth-century liberalism. Froude, who revolutionized the historiography of the Tudor period, was ardently opposed to the Church of Rome, and his twelve volumes of *The History of England from the Fall of Wolsey to the Defeat of the Spanish Armada* read frequently like a learned anti-Catholic tract.

More recently, eminent German historians have given a qualitative weight, out of all proportion to its actual importance, to the German anti-Nazi resistance, being moved by their patriotism to exculpate the German people from responsibility for the Nazi regime. American history has been perceived by virtually all American historians from the vantage point of the white immigrants, and in consequence the actions and conditions of the blacks and Indians either have not been perceived at all or have been noticed only as reflections of white history. When I was a student, Austrian and Prussian historians debated passionately the question of who was responsible for the Seven Years War; no Prussian argued that it was Frederick the Great, and no Austrian that it was Maria Theresia.

These observations are called forth by the massive book * in which Professor Kolko of the State University of New York at Buffalo lays bare the politics behind the strategy of World War II. It is a book of major importance, the first revisionist book concerned with the origins of the Cold War that is also a work of first-rate scholarship. As such, it marks a turning point in the historiography of the war and postwar period. It must, however, be said in passing that it is marred by a great number of stylistic deficiencies and outright grammatical errors that could not have escaped the attention of a halfway alert editor.

It is also an unsettling book. The truth that emerges from it is radically different from what we have taken for granted to be the truth. What we had been but dimly aware of now occupies the center of the stage, and what we had been accustomed to think of as the decisive determinants fades into insignificance or disappears altogether. Professor Kolko convinces us of the injustice of his predecessors, but he fails to persuade us of his own justice. His picture of the political world is as one-sided as theirs, only in a different way. He emphasizes what they neglected, and he underplays what they laid stress on. He illuminates those parts of the scenery they left in the shadows or in complete darkness, and he does not care to shed light on those parts that stood out in their picture of the war and postwar world.

The received truth about the politics of World War II assigns to the Soviet Union the main responsibility for the breakup of the alliance and for the Cold War, in which the politics of World War II organically blend. The traditional imperialism of Russia, the world revolutionary aspirations of Bolshevism, the suspicions, deviousness, and brutality of Stalin—those were the elements of which the "Cold-War guilt" of the Soviet Union appears to be composed. In comparison with the Soviet Union, which knew what it wanted and how to get it, the United States appears well-meaning and bumbling, anxious to get the war over with as quickly, cheaply, and thoroughly as possible, devoid of clearly defined political objectives that could have given a political purpose to the military operations. Thus, the United States, virtuous but ineffective, faced the Soviet Union, vicious and ruthlessly effective. The conclusion, which became the rationale of the Cold War, was inevitable: The United States could not do business with the Soviet Union.

The picture that emerges from Professor Kolko's account bears hardly any resemblance to the received truth. In that picture, the

* Gabriel Kolko, *The Politics of War* (New York: Random House, 1968).

United States appears as the villain, and a politically astute and purposeful villain at that. Its aim, consistently pursued for ideological and economic reasons, is the restoration of the prewar *status quo*. This aim signifies the military and political disarmament of the antifascist resistance movements as the most urgent task in the liberated areas. It also signifies the containment of the Soviet Union long before that policy was officially inaugurated. And it finally signifies the restoration of the defeated Axis powers as guardians of the *status quo* and bulwarks against the Soviet Union. On the other hand, the Soviet Union, too, is cast in the role of a "conservative" power (Professor Kolko uses the adjective many times to characterize Soviet policies), which, for the sake of Allied unity, common victory, and national security, discourages revolution, keeps aloof from civil war, and promotes the Popular Front within a framework of democratic legality. Its resort to totalitarian exclusiveness in Eastern Europe is seen as a reaction either to the unreasonableness of the people it had to deal with, as in Poland, or to Western exclusiveness, as in the case of Rumania, where exclusion of the West is explained as a response to the exclusion of the Soviet Union from the administration of Italy.

The reader who has followed us thus far may well ask how a book that replaces the excesses of partisanship of its predecessors with excesses of its own can be a major contribution to historical understanding. The answer lies in the very nature of historical understanding. The historian is limited in his understanding of the past by the vantage point from which he beholds the past. That vantage point, in turn, is determined by the sum total of his "personal equation," that is, his personality, his interests, his philosophy, his attitude toward the issues of the present. That limitation we must take for granted in all historians. No historian can have the whole truth about the past; for he is able to see only what is visible from his particular vantage point, which is determined by his personal traits and tendencies and by his involvement in the present.

What distinguishes the mere partisan of a cause from the historian is not partisanship—Mommsen was as much a partisan of liberalism under strong national leadership as any politician supporting Bismarck's ascent to power, and Froude saw in the Church of Rome as much a threat to the national interests of England as any politician supporting disestablishment. What sets the historian apart from the politician is his relation to the factual evidence. The politician appeals to interest, prejudice, and emotion; the historian lets the evidence— carefully selected for his purpose, it is true—speak in support of his position. The professionalism of the historian flows from the competence with which he handles the factual material and the conclusiveness with which he marshals it in support of his position. His aim, by which his efforts must be judged, is the coherent reconstruction of the past, which illuminates the past, the present, and the human condition, regardless of time and place.

Professor Kolko's book achieves this aim in three significant respects. It demonstrates the unexpected extent to which the United States competed with Great Britain for control of the postwar world. It shows to what extent World War II was an international civil war in which the defeat of the Axis powers was sought by the West as a means to the end of the restoration of a pre-fascist *status quo*. Subsidiary to this end was the Western opposition to Communism in its Soviet manifestation, in the resistance movements throughout occupied Europe, and in the Communist parties and governments emerging from the war. One can now see to one's surprise that the ideological commitment of the West to the restoration of a pre-fascist *status quo* was much stronger and purer, that is, undiluted by considerations of national advantage, than was the Soviet ideological commitment to the Communization of the world. For the West, the destruction of fascism and the containment of Communism were ends in themselves; for fascism and Communism were evils to be contained if they could not be destroyed. For Stalin, the destruction of fascism and the spread of Communism were means to the end of the security of the Soviet state.

Thus, in the months before the outbreak of World War II, Great Britain, France, and Poland preferred risking defeat at the hands of the Nazis to a chance to contain them through an alliance with the Soviet Union. What the French Right proclaimed openly in the slogan "Rather Hitler than Blum" underlay, as a deep-seated ideological preference, the domestic and foreign policies of the West: Fascism was bad, but Communism was worse. On the other hand, Stalin, without so strong an ideological commitment, could choose between seeking an alliance with the West against Germany and, that failing, coming to an understanding with Germany—both for the purpose of containing German expansion, at least in the direction of the Soviet Union. Stalin chose the latter alternative and stuck with it even after it had become imprudent to do so. It was Hitler who forced both upon the West and the Soviet Union a course of action that they would have preferred not to take: The West, in order to save itself, had to allow the Red Army to advance into Central Europe, and the Soviet Union had to bear the main brunt of the German onslaught. It is not surprising that an alliance forged not by the free choice of its members but by the necessity imposed upon them by the common enemy began to dissolve when the weight of necessity began to lift. One can now see that alliance as a kind of interlude in an international civil war, which began in 1917 and has continued to this day. One can now also see that this international civil war was not so much interrupted by the alliance as glossed over and forced underground.

Professor Kolko's book is in good measure an account of how that civil war was waged by the United States. That account is persuasive and illuminating. But it suffers from two major deficiencies. They are interrelated, stemming as they do from the author's personal perspective mentioned above, which sees only the faults of the United States while shoving into the background the faults of others, if it does not pass them over altogether. Since Professor Kolko sees the United States as the villain and embraces the philosophy of economic determinism, he yields to the temptation of attributing to American policy a rational coherence and Machiavellian purpose that run counter to the historical evidence. The author himself shows clearly the weakness of Roosevelt's leadership, a weakness of knowledge, understanding, and will. Only Secretary of War Stimson and Assistant Secretary of War McCloy emerge from his account as statesmen who understood the interplay of interests and power, of ends and means, in the foreign policy of their own country as well as that of others; and they were, not by accident, I presume, the least ideologically motivated of American statesmen.

What his account does not reveal is the messiness of the political management of the war on the American side. This is particularly obvious in the disjunction between political objectives and military operations. Had American policy been endowed with the single-minded political purpose that Professor Kolko attributes to it, it would have made military strategy a servant of that purpose. That is to say, it would have followed Churchill's advice: It would have gone as far east as possible and stayed there until the Russians had fulfilled their part of the bargain. Instead, no clear-cut and consistently applied political purpose informed military strategy. That was as true in Asia as it was in Europe. The exchange of messages among Generals Marshall, Eisenhower, and Bradley concerning strategy during the last phase of the war against Germany provides a classic illustration of the political vacuum that existed at the top and made it inevitable for generals mindful of their subjection to the civilian authorities to fashion their strategy without regard to a political purpose. Had the government of the United States really been as politically acute as Professor Kolko makes it out to have been, it would have pursued a military strategy that could easily have kept Czechoslovakia out of the Soviet orbit and prevented Berlin from becoming an enclave in Soviet-controlled territory. What the author leaves out of account is the enormous and frequently decisive influence ignorance, absent-mindedness, and a naïve reliance upon the beneficial effects of good will have exerted upon American foreign policy. What he overstresses and misconstrues as a conscious, clear-cut, and consistent foreign policy is in essence a conservative mood, a fear of radical social change, especially in the form of Communism.

It is the same urge to pin the responsibility for the breakdown of the alliance and for the Cold War upon the United States that is responsible for Professor Kolko's neglect of certain objective factors that make international conflicts—as they do domestic ones—well-nigh inevitable. As orthodox and revisionist historians look at the world from different perspectives, forcing upon them different views of the world, so nations look upon the world and, more particularly, upon each other from different vantage points, misunderstanding each other and themselves in the process, seeking to realize incompatible types of world order, and opposing each other by dint of those different world views and misunderstandings. As concerns the relations between the United States and the Soviet Union, spheres of influence are a case in point.

Since World War II, the Soviet Union has been the foremost practitioner of a spheres-of-influence policy, while the United States has been opposed to spheres of influence as a matter of principle. The Soviet Union never made any bones about its desire to acquire a sphere of influence in Eastern Europe and to divide the world into spheres of influence as well. According to the "Secret Additional Protocol" to the Treaty of Nonaggression of August 23, 1939, better known as the Molotov-Ribbentrop Pact, the Soviet Union and Germany "discussed in strictly confidential conversations the question of the boundaries of their respective spheres of influence." During World War II, the Soviet Union persistently pressed Great Britain for a spheres-of-influence agreement dividing Europe, and while Great Britain appeared agreeable, the United States was as persistently opposed. It was in the face of that temporarily relenting opposition that Churchill and Stalin, on October 9, 1944, concluded personally and most informally an agreement dividing the Balkans into Soviet and non-Soviet spheres of influence. The agreement gave the Soviet

Union 90 percent dominance in Romania and 75 per cent in Bulgaria, divided Soviet and Western influence equally in Hungary and Yugoslavia, and allotted to Great Britain 90 per cent predominance in Greece. After the war, the Soviet Union made numerous proposals for the division of the world into two gigantic spheres of influence, dominated respectively by the Soviet Union and the United States. While these proposals were never officially acknowledged by the United States, they were occasionally referred to in the press. In *The New York Times* of March 13, 1950, for instance, James Reston reported such a proposal under the heading "Soviet Move Seen for Deal with U.S. to Divide World" and concluded that "there is no evidence that officials here are even slightly interested in such a deal."

This lack of interest was not limited to the officials of the day; rather it reflects a consistent opposition to spheres of influence of any kind. During World War II, Secretary of State Cordell Hull was in the forefront of that opposition. In his *Memoirs,* he declared himself not to be "a believer in the idea of balance of power or spheres of influence as a means of keeping the peace." When he reported on November 18, 1943, to Congress on the Moscow Conference, which had agreed on the establishment of the United Nations, he declared that "there will no longer be need for spheres of influence, for alliances, for balance of power, or any other of the special arrangements through which, in the unhappy past, the nations strove to safeguard their security or promote their interests." And Franklin D. Roosevelt stated as a matter of fact on March 1, 1945, in his report to Congress on the Yalta Conference: "The Crimean Conference . . . spells the end of the system of unilateral action and exclusive alliances and spheres of influence and balances of power and all the other expedients which have been tried for centuries—and have failed."

This opposition to spheres of influence is rooted in two tenets of American political philosophy: the availability of a viable alternative to "power politics" in the form of a universal international organization and the universal applicability of democratic procedures and institutions as a remedy for political ills. The first tenet is clearly and consistently expressed in Hull's utterances. Recalling in his *Memoirs* his opposition to a Soviet sphere of influence in Eastern Europe, he wrote:

I could sympathize fully with Stalin's desire to protect his Western borders from future attack. But I felt that this security could best be obtained through a strong postwar peace organization. . . . It seemed to me that any creation of zones of influence would inevitably sow the seeds of future conflict. I felt that zones of influence could not but derogate from the overall authority of the international security organizations which I expected would come into being.

In other words, nations have a choice between traditional "power politics," with all its moral liabilities and political risks, of which spheres of influence form an intrinsic part, and a new and different kind of foreign policy free of these liabilities and risks.

The other tenet was most eloquently formulated by Woodrow Wilson in his message to the Senate on January 22, 1917:

> No peace can last, or ought to last, which does not recognize and accept the principle that governments derive all their just powers from the consent of the governed and that no right anywhere exists to hand peoples about from potentate to potentate as if they were property. . . . I am proposing, as it were, that the nations should with one accord adopt the doctrine of President Monroe as the doctrine of the world: that no nation should seek to extend its policy over any other nation or people, but that every people should be left free to determine its own policy, its own way of development, unhindered, unthreatened, unafraid, the little along with the great and powerful.

At Yalta and at the conferences and in the diplomatic exchanges following it, our insistence upon democratic governments for the nations of Eastern Europe became the main ideological weapon with which we tried to nullify the transformation of Eastern Europe into a Soviet sphere of influence.

However, this opposition to spheres of influence as a matter of principle has been completely at odds not only with the Soviet conception of international order but also with two facets of our own foreign policy: the championship of a sphere of influence, when it has been supposed to serve our interests, and our acquiescence, as a matter of fact, in the Soviet sphere of influence in Eastern Europe.

The Monroe Doctrine, stipulating the exclusion of European political institutions and territorial acquisitions from the Western Hemisphere and thereby allowing the preponderance of the United States free play, is the most comprehensive unilateral proclamation of a sphere of influence of modern times. American statesmen have not hesitated to refer to the Western Hemisphere or part of it as an American sphere of influence. Secretary of State Robert Lansing, invoking the Monroe Doctrine as well as more specific American interests, wrote in a state paper addressed to President Wilson that "the Caribbean is within the peculiar sphere of influence of the United

States. . . ." It was none other than Woodrow Wilson who said that "in adopting the Monroe Doctrine the United States assumed the part of Big Brother to the rest of America" and who referred to the Western Hemisphere as an "implied and partial protectorate." The inconsistency of dealing, as a matter of course, with the Western Hemisphere as an American sphere of influence and opposing, as a matter of principle, all other spheres of influence moved Winston Churchill, defending his deal with Stalin on the Balkans against the American opposition, to write to the British Ambassador in Washington: "On the other hand, we follow the lead of the United States in South America as far as possible, as long as it is not a question of our beef and mutton. On this we naturally develop strong views on account of the little we get."

American opposition to spheres of influence *per se* is not only inconsistent with American practice in the Western Hemisphere; it is also inconsistent with American practice in regard to that sphere of influence which provoked our most strenuous opposition: the Soviet sphere in Eastern Europe. The conflict between ourselves and the Soviet Union, which is at the root of the Cold War, arose at Yalta from incompatible conceptions and aspirations concerning the shape of the postwar world. The Soviet Union, following in the footsteps of Tsarist Russia, wanted an exclusive sphere of influence in Eastern Europe. The West wanted to keep at least a measure of influence in the region through the instrumentality of democratic governments, which, however, were supposed to be friendly to the Soviet Union.

Yet Stalin saw the inner contradiction of that proposal and did not hesitate to resolve it in favor of the Soviet Union. "A freely elected government in any of these countries," he observed at Yalta, "would be anti-Soviet, and that we cannot allow." The Red Army, then already in control of Eastern Europe, provided the guarantee that what the Soviet Union could not allow would not come to pass. Thus, what the United States sought to achieve at Yalta was impossible of achievement as long as the Red Army was in control in Eastern Europe. When President Roosevelt reported to Congress that "The Crimean Conference . . . spells the end of the system of unilateral action . . . spheres of influence . . . and all the other expedients which have been tried for centuries," he intended to proclaim victory for the American conception of the postwar world. In truth, he ratified, without knowing it, the triumph of the Soviet conception. For it was exactly through this "system of unilateral action, spheres of influence, and all the other expedients" of traditional power politics that Stalin intended to, and actually did, secure the interests of the Soviet Union.

The briefing book that President Truman took with him to the Potsdam Conference in July, 1945, summarized the situation in these laconic terms: "Eastern Europe is, in fact, a Soviet sphere of influence."

American rhetoric refused to reconcile itself to this fact. As the Soviet Union has reproached us for refusing to recognize its sphere of influence, so we have reproached the Soviet Union for having acquired it. More than that, for about a decade following the end of the war, we intimated through slogans such as "liberation" and "rollback" that we were contemplating a policy to undo what Stalin had achieved. But, as the London *Economist* pointed out on August 30, 1952, "Unhappily, 'liberation' applied to Eastern Europe—and Asia— means either the risk of war or it means nothing. . . . 'Liberation' entails no risk of war only when it means nothing."

That this is what it meant became obvious when the United States remained inactive on the occasion of the German uprising of 1953, the Polish revolt and Hungarian Revolution of 1956, and the Soviet occupation of Czechoslovakia in 1968. The two latter events are particularly revealing in that the United States declared from the outset, in the case of the Hungarian Revolution through its President, that it would refrain from intervening on behalf of democracy and against exclusive Soviet control. We are here not concerned with the merits of this policy of abstention, but only with its bearing upon the American opposition to spheres of influence, especially to the Soviet sphere in Eastern Europe. Our policy of abstention, reducing "liberation" to nothing, by the same token amounted to the implicit recognition of the Soviet sphere of influence. What we had refused to do explicitly at Yalta and ever since, we have done implicitly through consistent inaction. Our inaction repudiated our policy at Yalta and our rhetoric following it, as well as the moral principles from which both stem.

Not only have American policies concerning spheres of influence been at odds in different periods of history, but the official opposition to spheres of influence has been challenged by the highest political authority, the President himself. One challenge remained without practical results. It was reported by the late Cardinal Spellman in a memorandum about a conversation the Cardinal had had with President Roosevelt on September 3, 1943, headed "Here are a few outstanding points of the conversation." Under the subheading "Collaboration of the 'Big Four,'" we read:

It is planned to make an agreement among the Big Four. Accordingly the world will be divided into spheres of influence: China gets the Far East;

the U.S. the Pacific; Britain and Russia, Europe and Africa. But as Britain has predominately colonial interests it might be assumed that Russia will predominate in Europe. Although Chiang Kai-shek will be called in on the great decisions concerning Europe, it is understood that he will have no influence on them. The same thing might become true—although to a lesser degree—for the U.S. He hoped, although it might be wishful thinking, that the Russian intervention in Europe would not be too harsh.

The other challenge, operating within President Roosevelt's mind as well as between himself, on the one hand, and Cordell Hull and Harry Hopkins, on the other, concerned the British-Soviet spheres-of-influence agreement with regard to the Balkans. Churchill informed Roosevelt of his plan, and Roosevelt ordered that an approving cable be sent to Churchill. Hopkins intercepted the cable and persuaded Roosevelt to send instead a cable to Stalin, reaffirming the American opposition to spheres of influence.

> There is in this global war literally no question, either military or political, . . . in which the United States is not interested. You will naturally understand this. It is my firm conviction that the solution to still unsolved questions can be found only by the three of us together. Therefore, while I appreciate the necessity for the present meeting, I choose to consider your forthcoming talks with Mr. Churchill merely as preliminary to a conference of the three of us.

However, Roosevelt approved the deal once it was made, while Hull remained strenuously opposed.

Spheres of influence, as Churchill and Stalin knew and Roosevelt recognized sporadically, have not been created by evil and benighted statesmen and, hence, cannot be abolished by an act of will on the part of good and enlightened ones. Like the balance of power, alliances, arms races, political and military rivalries and conflicts, and the rest of "power politics," spheres of influence are the ineluctable byproduct of the interplay of interests and power in a society of sovereign nations. If you want to rid the world of spheres of influence and the other "expedients" of "power politics," you must transform that society of sovereign nations into a supranational one, whose sovereign government can set effective limits to the expansionism of the nations composing it. Spheres of influence is one of the symptoms of the disease, if this is what you want to call "power politics," and it is at best futile and at worst mischievous to try to extirpate the symptom while leaving the cause unattended.

Thus, the American political mind has been engaged in a three-cornered war. It has been at war with the political realities, which do not yield to the invocation of moral principles. It has been at war with its moral principles, since it must condone implicitly what it condemns explicitly and is powerless to change. And it has been at war again with its moral principles, since it practices with a good conscience what it condemns in others. It bridges the gap between its moral principles and its political practices by juxtaposing its selfless intentions—most eloquently propounded, for instance, by Wilson in justification of the intervention in Mexico—with the evil purposes of other nations.

The war with the political realities has proved to be a quixotic futility, creating hopes sure to be disappointed and inciting actions doomed to fail. One war with moral principles opens up a gap between words and deeds, suggesting political weakness. The other war with moral principles issues in a self-confident pragmatism, which, in the best British tradition, combines moral assurance with political advantage.

A classic example of this combination is provided by the telephone conversation that was held between Secretary of War Henry Stimson and Assistant Secretary of War John McCloy in May, 1945, which Professor Kolko quotes. The issue was how to combine the exclusiveness of the American sphere of influence in the Western Hemisphere with the international organization then planned. Both officials agreed that the formation of similar spheres in Europe and Asia for the benefit of the Soviet Union would conjure up the risk of war and destroy the effectiveness of the international organization. They also agreed that the exclusive American sphere in the Americas, where the United States could act unilaterally, must be preserved. "I think," said Stimson, "that it's not asking too much to have our little region over here which never has bothered anybody." They further agreed that the Soviet Union could not object to such an arrangement, since it was building a similar sphere in Eastern Europe. Finally, they agreed that, according to McCloy, "we have a very strong interest in being able to intervene promptly in Europe . . . we ought to have our cake and eat it too; that we ought to be free to operate under this regional arrangement in South America, at the same time intervene promptly in Europe; that we oughtn't to give away either asset." Both denied that the position the United States occupies in the Western Hemisphere was analogous to the one the Soviet Union aspired to in Europe, because our intervention in the Western Hemisphere did not upset the world balance of power, while Soviet intervention in Europe would.

In other words, we could not divorce the centuries-old Russian aspirations for a sphere of influence in Eastern Europe from the world-wide aspirations of Communism, and, hence, we interpreted the Soviet Union's territorial war aims as a stepping stone toward the Communization of the world, as we later interpreted North Korea's invasion of South Korea as the opening shot in a Communist campaign to conquer the world. On the other hand, the Soviet Union, baffled by the American combination of quixotic dedication to abstract moral principles with the cold-blooded attempt of the restoration of the *status quo ante bellum*, interpreted the verbal and political opposition to the Sovet domination of Eastern Europe as still another manifestation of undying capitalist enmity. Both the United States and the Soviet Union understood, and in good measure misunderstood, their respective policies in terms of their dogmatic ideological assumptions about the unchanging nature of the other, seemingly buttressed by the experiences of the past.

This dogmatic distortion is one factor that goes into the making of foreign policy. To understand its historic manifestations and significance one does not need to search for a villain. It is enough to be aware of the frailty of human reason, carried on the waves of passion and unequal to the rich complexities of experience. In that frailty all men share: Greeks and Persians, Americans and Russians. Beholding them as brothers in blindness, we can be just to them. That is the justice of Thucydides, of which Louis Halle's *The Cold War as History* is a contemporary echo. This justice, as we have seen, is rare; for it requires a commitment to charitable understanding—"when mercy seasons justice"—which cannot help but be at odds with the commitment to particular adversary interests. It is absent from Professor Kolko's work.

Professor Kolko's justice is not charitable but compensatory. He has seen the partial and partisan justice, which amounts to injustice, of the orthodox historians and undertakes to set the record straight. Thus he pits his partisan and partial justice, which is also injustice, against theirs. From the dialectic interplay of these opposing and partial views of the truth a vision of the whole truth emerges. The one-sidedness of one impinges on the one-sidedness of the other as a qualification and a corrective. Taken together and infused with the charitable view beyond partisanship that sees weakness and error all around, they give an account of history "as it really was."

The political significance of Professor Kolko's book derives from its correspondence with the contemporary mood. That mood reacts negatively to the simple and simplistic equation, *de rigueur* during the war and postwar periods, of American interests and policies with democratic virtue and wisdom and those of their enemies with totalitarian folly and vice. As the orthodox historiography of World War II and the Cold War expressed and justified that ideological juxtaposition, so the revisionism of Professor Kolko expresses and justifies the new mood of ideological sobriety. However, given the moralism behind American political thinking regardless of its content, revisionism tends to be as moralistic in its critique of American foreign policy as orthodoxy is in defending it. While the moralistic approach remains, the moral labels have been reversed: What once was right is now wrong, and vice versa. Yet as the historical truth emerges from the dialectic of opposite extremes, qualified and tempered by transcendent charitable understanding, so sound political judgment requires both the recognition of extreme positions as inevitable and their transcendence through a morality as alien to the moralism of our political folklore as Thucydidean justice is to the compensatory justice of opposing schools.

PART II

THE MEN

9

John Foster Dulles

[1961]

A contemporary American Secretary of State must perform two basic and difficult tasks: He must defend and promote the
interests of the United States abroad, and he must establish and
defend his position at home. Whereas the former task is inherent in
the office, the latter is a result of five interconnected constitutional
and political factors inherent in the American system of government.
The position of the Secretary of State must be secured, first of all,
against competition from four quarters: the President, Congress,
other agencies of the executive branch, and other members of the
Department of State. The fifth factor is public opinion, and it, of
course, affects the Secretary's relation to the other four.

The President bears, according to the constitutional scheme, the
chief responsibility for the conduct of foreign policy. This responsibility
he is supposed to discharge with the help of the Secretary of State as
his principal adviser and administrative officer. Yet in actuality, the
distribution of responsibility between the President and the Secretary
of State has run the gamut from Presidential predominance—the
President determines foreign policy without the advice and administrative support of the Secretary of State—to the predominance of the

87

Secretary of State—the latter determines and administers foreign policy, and the President merely ratifies his decisions.

The competition between the executive branch and Congress for control of American foreign policy began in Washington's Administration and is the result of a constitutional distribution of functions that, in the words of Professor Corwin, "is an invitation to struggle for the privilege of directing American foreign policy." It is also the result of the dynamics of the American political system, which deprives the Secretary of State of most of the political weapons of rewards and reprisals with which the President and other members of the Cabinet can stave off congressional opposition and secure congressional support.

The need for the Secretary of State to maintain the prerogatives of his office against competition from other executive departments arises from the dispersal of responsibility for the conduct of American foreign policy among a multitude of executive departments. In 1949, the Hoover Commission, which investigated the organization of the executive branch, found that about forty-five executive agencies, aside from the Department of State, were dealing with one or another phase of foreign policy. The Secretary of State must maintain the over-all direction of foreign policy against the parochial interests of all these agencies.

The Secretary of State must also establish and maintain his authority within his own department. He must keep in check the members of his staff who owe their position to political influence or who otherwise enjoy political support for independent policies.

Finally, the accomplishment of these four competitive tasks depends in great measure upon the ability of the Secretary of State to marshal public opinion at large to the support of his person and his policies. Without the support of public opinion, the Secretary of State is bound to be utterly vulnerable to competition from any of the quarters mentioned, especially, however, from Congress, which in most circumstances is likely to enjoy the public support that the Secretary of State is lacking. On the other hand, with that support secured, the Secretary of State is in a strong position vis-à-vis his competitors, especially those who, like himself, draw much of their strength from public opinion.

Thus the American Secretary of State must perform a domestic political task of great complexity and delicacy as a precondition for the performance of his primary task in the field of foreign policy. Nor are these two tasks separate in execution. Quite to the contrary, each impinges upon the other. The kind of foreign policy the Secretary of

State pursues exerts an influence, favorable or unfavorable, upon his domestic position. The kind of domestic position he is able to make for himself predetermines in good measure the limits within which he is able to move on the international stage. The attempt to reconcile the demands of foreign policy and those of domestic politics, without sacrificing the indispensable substance of either, involves more complications and calls for greater finesse than any of the tasks previously mentioned. It is here that the Secretary of State faces the supreme test of his ability to do justice to the requirements of his office.

How has John Foster Dulles performed those tasks, which impose themselves with existential force upon whoever occupies the office? What conception of the office did he bring tð those tasks, and in what concrete terms did he execute them? The answers to these questions must be sought in three factors that exerted a fundamental influence on Dulles: his sense of mission, the state of mind of the Republican party, and the example of his predecessor, Dean Acheson.

Dulles's appointment to the position of Secretary of State must appear to the observer as the natural culmination of a development foreshadowed by his family background and prepared for step by step by his diplomatic career. Both his maternal grandfather, John W. Foster, after whom he had been named, and his uncle, Robert Lansing, had been Secretaries of State. Dulles had started his diplomatic career virtually at the earliest possible moment: In 1907, when he was nineteen and a junior in college, he acted as his grandfather's secretary at the Second Peace Conference at The Hague. He served in 1917 as a member of the Second Pan-American Scientific Congress and as a special agent of the Department of State in Central America. In 1918–19 he was counsel to the American Commission to Negotiate Peace, and in 1919 he became a member of the Reparation Commission and of the Supreme Economic Council. He was a member of the American delegation to the San Francisco Conference of 1945 and to the United Nations General Assembly in 1946, 1947, 1948, and 1950. He served as adviser to the Secretary of State at meetings ot the Council of Foreign Ministers in 1945, 1947, and 1949 and as consultant to the Secretary of State in 1950. In 1950–51, as special representative of the President with the rank of ambassador, he negotiated the peace treaty with Japan and the security treaties with Australia, New Zealand, the Philippines, and Japan. When Thomas E. Dewey ran for the Presidency in 1944 and 1948, Dulles was generally regarded as his choice for Secretary of State.

To Dulles himself, this record seemed to reveal a providential design, which had singled him out to be Secretary of State, had endowed him with the qualities required for that position, and would not let him fail. In a speech to the staff of the Department of State on the assumption of his office, Dulles pointed to the fact that his grandfather and his uncle had been Secretary of State, and that he was now Secretary of State. His conviction that there was something virtually inevitable and foreordained in his holding of this exalted position accounts at least in part for Dulles's confidence in his ability to shoulder alone the momentous responsibilities of his office and to face alone the dreadful uncertainties of foreign policy. The self-confidence that all statesmen need, faced as they are with these responsibilities and uncertainties, and that others have found in superstitions, such as astrology or other forms of soothsaying, exhaustive information and advice, or a simple faith in divine guidance, Dulles found in his sense of predestination, derived from his family background and his career and supported by a strong, self-reliant personality.

Dulles was destined to become Secretary of State as a member of a party whose support for an active but restrained foreign policy—moving somewhere between isolationism and imperialism—was still precarious at the beginning of the 1950's. The Republican party had entered World War II committed to isolationism and had emerged from it with a split personality. Senator Vandenberg, strongly influenced and supported by Dulles and a minority of his party, initiated bipartisanship in foreign policy. Thus one wing of the Republican party came to approve the fundamental changes by which American foreign policy was transformed in the 1940's, whereas another wing, more vociferous and more influential with public opinion at large, and represented by men like Senators William E. Jenner and Joseph R. McCarthy, remained in uncompromising opposition. Between these two groups stood a vacillating center, which hankered back to isolationism but would almost, though not quite, admit that isolationism was beyond the reach of a rational foreign policy. Senator Robert A. Taft was the most eminent spokesman of this group.

Dulles had to come to terms with the problem of gaining the support of his own party for his person and policies. Two roads were open to him. He could attempt to impress the internationalist wing and the wavering center with the rationality and even the inevitability of the foreign policy to which he was committed, letting the intransigent right wing wither on the vine, or else he could try to gain the support of the right wing by giving the appearance of being really one of them and of actually pursuing their policies. Dulles chose the latter course, primarily under the impact of what had happened to his predecessor.

The third fundamental experience that molded Dulles's conception of his office, and the policies realizing it, was the opportunity of witnessing, and contributing to, the fate that befell Dean Acheson. Here was a Secretary of State who was, intellectually at least, as well equipped for the office as any of his predecessors since John Quincy Adams; whose dedication to the common good was exemplary; and whose achievements in fashioning a new foreign policy for the United States commensurate with its interests was outstanding. In short, in terms of the requirements of foreign policy, here was one of the best Secretaries of State the United States had ever had. Yet here was also, in terms of the requirements of domestic politics, one of the least successful Secretaries of State. For large sectors of American public opinion, Acheson's State Department became synonymous with softness toward Communism—if not toleration of, or even connivance in, treason. When Acheson's loyalty was attacked and his resignation asked for in Congress, not a member dared to come to his defense. Only the President's support kept him in office.

Witnessing the terrifying spectacle of a good and able man—as great a Secretary of State in terms of foreign policy as Dulles could ever hope to be—hounded as a threat to the Republic and shunned as an outcast, Dulles resolved that what happened to Acheson would not happen to him. In consequence, to secure his domestic position became his overriding concern. To that end, he set out to achieve three objectives: to create for the American public the image of himself as a stanch and dynamic fighter against Communism and thus as a Secretary of State without any of the faults attributed to his predecessor; to prevent at all costs the development of an opposition in Congress to his person and policies; and to establish and maintain a relationship with the President that would assure his control of foreign policy.

The creation of the image of a foreign policy radically different from that for which the preceding Administration had been responsible proceeded essentially through six spectacular pronouncements: "liberation," the unleashing of Chiang Kai-shek, "agonizing reappraisal," the "new look," intervention in Indochina, and "brinkmanship."

During the election campaign of 1952 and during the first months of his tenure of office, Dulles and other spokesmen for the new Administration announced that the old policy of containment, which Dulles had called in the Republican platform of 1952 "negative, futile, and immoral," was to be replaced by a policy of liberation, which carried with it the risk of war. The Eisenhower Administration, however, shied away from the risk of war at least as much as had its predecessor. And when the East German revolt of 1953 and the Polish revolt and Hungarian revolution of 1956 put the policy of liberation to the test of actual performance, it became obvious that liberation was indistinguishable from containment.

In his State of the Union message of February 2, 1953, following Dulles's public and private advice, President Eisenhower declared: "In June, 1950, following the aggressive attack on the Republic of Korea, the United States Seventh Fleet was instructed both to prevent attack upon Formosa and also to insure that Formosa should not be used as a base of operations against the Chinese Communist mainland." In view of the Chinese intervention in the Korean conflict, the President declared that he was "issuing instructions that the Seventh Fleet no longer be employed to shield Communist China." This announcement implied a fundamental change in the Far Eastern policies of the United States from the preservation of the *status quo* to the active attempt to restore Chiang Kai-shek's rule on the Asian mainland. In actuality, no such change occurred. Quite to the contrary, the Eisenhower Administration seems to have been at least as anxious as its predecessor to limit the military activities of Chiang Kai-shek to strictly defensive measures. By making this limitation part of the agreements negotiated with Chiang Kai-shek at the end of 1954, the Eisenhower Administration went even beyond the unilateral declaration of policy contained in President Truman's instruction to the Seventh Fleet of June, 1950.

On December 14, 1953, Dulles declared at the meeting of the North Atlantic Council: "If, however, the European Defense Community should not become effective, if France and Germany remain apart, so that they would again be potential enemies, then indeed there would be grave doubt whether Continental Europe could be made a place of safety. That would compel an agonizing reappraisal of the basic United States policy." This statement implied that in certain contingencies the United States might lose its interest in the military defense of Europe and leave it to its fate. This threat called forth much comment but little anxiety in Europe and elsewhere. As an incentive for France to ratify the European Defense Community, it was ineffective. For in order to take this threat seriously, one would have had to assume that the United States had committed itself to the defense of Western Europe, not because it deemed its own security dependent upon it, but because it happened to approve of the policies of certain European nations. Few observers, and no responsible statesmen, were willing to make such an assumption.

The most far-reaching and most widely commented-upon announcement of this kind, however, was Dulles's speech of January 12, 1954, proclaiming a "new look" in American foreign policy as the result of "some basic policy decisions" which the President and the National Security Council had taken. This new policy was anchored to the concept of "massive retaliation." Lester Pearson, then Canadian Secretary of State for External Affairs, thought as late as March 15, 1954, that this speech "may turn out to be one of the most important of our times." The present writer, on March 29, 1954, published an article in the *New Republic* interpreting and evaluating this speech as if it meant what it said. Yet Walter Lippmann could say on March 18 that "the official explanations of the new look have become so voluminous that it is almost a career in itself to keep up with them." Characterizing Dulles's speech as "a case of excessive salesmanship," Lippmann concluded:

> There is no doubt that the words of the text convey the impression that something momentous and novel has been decided. But everything that has been said since then by the Chiefs of Staff, notably by Admiral Carney, and no less so by Mr. Dulles himself, make it plain that there has been no radical change in our strategic policy.

On the same day, the *Manchester Guardian* summed it all up by saying:

> The "new look" in American military strategy is mainly old merchandise in a new package. There is really nothing new in relying on "massive mobile retaliatory power" as the principal safeguard of peace—nothing new, that is, except the sales campaign by which the Administration is trying to persuade the American people that some small changes make the strategy of 1954 fundamentally sounder than the strategy of 1953.

On March 19, the Senate Committee on Foreign Relations was the scene of the following dialogue between Senator Mike Mansfield and Dulles, who for all practical purposes buried the "new look" under the cover of military secrecy:

> Senator Mansfield: Do you consider this new policy a new policy?
> Secretary Dulles: It certainly has new aspects.
> Senator Mansfield: What are they?
> Secretary Dulles: Well, I am sorry I cannot go into that here. All I can say to you, and you will have to take it on faith, is that a series of new decisions have been taken by the National Security Council and many have been involved, close, and difficult decisions, but there is today on the record a series of decisions which are largely derived from this basic philosophy which were not there a year and a half ago.

Although the "new look" was the most sweeping of these announcements, the official declarations concerning the Indochina War were politically and militarily the most serious; for they dealt not with general principles of United States policy but with a concrete situation that required action here and now. On March 25, 1954, the President declared at his news conference that the defense of Indochina was of "transcendent importance." On March 29, the Secretary of State announced:

> Under the conditions of today, the imposition on Southeast Asia of the political system of Communist Russia and its Chinese Communist ally, by whatever means, would be a grave threat to the whole free community. The United States feels that that possibility should not be passively accepted, but should be met by united action. This might have serious risks, but these risks are far less than would face us a few years from now if we dare not be resolute today.

The President and the Secretary of State referred to Indochina as the cork in the bottle of Southeast Asia and as the first in a row of dominoes whose fall would necessarily cause the downfall of the others. Yet no action of any kind reflected even faintly the conception of policy that these words seemed to convey. It was, in the words of the *Economist* of August 21, 1954, this "spectacle of vociferous inaction" that led to the "worst diplomatic disaster in recent American history."

The most sensational and also the most patently implausible of these pronouncements concerned "brinkmanship." In an article in *Life* magazine of January 16, 1956, Dulles was reported as having declared, in the course of an interview, that his policy of firmness and daring, fully supported by the President, saved the peace and protected the interests of the United States on three occasions: in Korea, Indochina, and the Formosa Straits. "Of course," Dulles was quoted as having said, "we were brought to the verge of war. The ability to get to the verge without getting into the war is the necessary art. If you cannot master it, you inevitably get into war. . . . We walked to the brink and we looked it in the face. We took strong action." The article praises this technique as "the greatest display of personal diplomacy since the great days of the Franklin-Adams-Jefferson triumvirate in the Europe of the 1780's."

Although this is obviously not the place to test these claims in detail against the available historical evidence, it must be pointed out that, in regard to Indochina, Dulles was prevented from going to war by the unwillingness of the President and of Great Britain to do so. Whether the Government of the United States had really resolved to use atomic weapons against Manchuria in June, 1953, if the Communists renewed the war in Korea, and whether the Communists were deterred by that knowledge are at present matters of speculation. It is also a moot question whether the congressional resolution of January, 1955, authorizing the President to defend the offshore islands in the Formosa Straits under certain conditions was interpreted by both the administration and the Chinese Government as a threat implying the certainty of atomic war. Yet what in actuality was either speculative or simply untrue was presented, in the *Life* article, as a set of historical facts supporting a most favorable evaluation of Dulles's policies.

Dulles's six major pronouncements served the purpose of creating the image of a new, forceful, aggressive foreign policy in order to gain the support of public opinion for both the person of the Secretary of State and the foreign policies he pursued, which were not essentially different from those of his predecessor and were certainly not different in the respects in which they were claimed to be. These endeavors culminated in the first Cabinet meeting ever televised, in which Dulles reported on the London Conference that met from September 28 to October 3, 1954. Arthur Krock recalled in *The New York Times* of May 6, 1960, that "the television show . . . was billed as a 'Cabinet meeting' . . . and turned out to be more of a sham performance than any rigged quiz program." In the *Manchester Guardian Weekly* of October 23, 1954, Alistair Cooke gave a striking account of that performance:

> The whole show had a relaxed, closed-door air, almost like a Cabinet meeting. In the lead part . . . Mr. Dulles gave a naturalistic performance of great ease and articulateness. Mr. Henry Cabot Lodge made the most of a single-sentence tribute to the President for his peaceful atomic energy proposals. Cast as the unsleeping watchdog of the people's purse, Mr. Secretary of the Treasury Humphrey expressed with moving verisi militude his concern that the Paris Agreement should not cost the American taxpayer one extra nickel. Mrs. Hobby conveyed an intelligent anxiety over the Saar.
>
> Only Secretary of Agriculture Ezra Benson, an artless man from the West, had to be prodded into his line by Mr. Dulles, who suggested after an anxious pause that some of them might now be wondering "how the Soviet Union is taking this." Mr. Benson was indeed wondering just that, and made an alert retrieve. It was the only missed cue in an otherwise flawless performance, surely an enviable record for any amateur dramatic company.

The position of the Secretary of State vis-à-vis Congress was secured by two basic tactics. Dulles disarmed the potential Congressional opposition, consisting of the right wing of the Republican party, by pursuing its policies and by allowing it to exert a governing influence, at least temporarily, over certain personnel and substantive matters, which remained but nominally under the control of the Secretary of State.

Dulles's execution of the personnel policies of the Congressional right wing was predicated on the assumption, with which the Republican party had attacked the preceding Administration, that the Department of State at the very least was not a reliable guardian of the interests of the United States vis-à-vis other nations, particularly Communist ones. In carrying out these policies, Dulles proceeded in two stages: The first was a purge and the second the application of stringent security regulations. By the end of 1953, most members of the Foreign Service who had held high positions in the Department of State had been dismissed, had voluntarily resigned, or had been transferred to politically nonsensitive positions.

Executive Order No. 10450 of April 27, 1953, as applied to the Department of State, in effect institutionalized the purge by establishing extremely stringent security regulations for employment, promotion, and surveillance. The case of John Paton Davies, Jr., a prominent member of the Foreign Service, who underwent nine security investigations before he was dismissed, is but an extreme example of what was then a fairly typical situation. His case is typical also in that it reveals clearly the political purpose of the purges, which, insofar as the Secretary of State was concerned, were undertaken primarily in order to satisfy the potential opposition in Congress. Davies, who had been stationed in China after World War II and who afterward joined the Policy Planning Staff, was a favorite target of that opposition. There can be no doubt, even though the documentary evidence to prove it is not yet available, that Davies was deliberately sacrificed, regardless of the merits of his case, and was subjected to as many security investigations as were necessary to prove him a security risk. It is revealing in this connection that, after the last investigating board had rendered the desired unfavorable verdict and Davies had been dismissed, he received a telephone call from the Secretary of State congratulating him upon his attitude before the board and authorizing him to use Dulles's name as a reference in his search for a new position.

Executive Order No. 10450, which provided the legal basis for these proceedings, was a general order, issued under the authority of the President for all executive departments. Yet since this order left wide discretion to the heads of the departments, the Secretary of State was responsible for the way it was implemented in his own Department. Not only did he establish, and suffer to be established, a rigid system of security regulations, but he also added to this system measures of his own. Deparment Circular No. 95 of April 15, 1954, for instance, imposed upon all officials of the Deparment of State the duty to be informers:

> I am aware that no agency of the government can improve, or even maintain its level of effectiveness unless it is receiving a stream of new ideas and constructive criticisms. I hope that the inspection operation will be the focal reception point of that stream. I have told Mr. McLeod that in his capacity as administrator of the inspection operation he should be available at any time to receive personally from any of our people the benefit of their thinking on improving operations and procedures or on other problems, official and personal.
>
> In brief, I regard the internal inspection operation of the Department as one of its most important concerns. Its success will depend upon the cooperation and aid received generally from employees of the Department.

Dulles's efforts to disarm the potential opposition by pursuing its policies were assured success by the ability of that opposition to place its representatives in key positions within the Department of State. The right-wing bloc thus came to dominate the Bureau of Security, whose leading officials controlled, directly or indirectly, security, consular affairs, personnel, and inspection of United States missions abroad. The bureau adopted the political philosophy and the policies of the members of Congress to whom its principal members owed both their positions and their primary loyalties. It reported to them and executed their orders. To an extent that changed with the ebbs and tides of political fortune, it was these members of Congress, and not the President or the Secretary of State, who determined the operations of the Department of State and its affiliated agencies.

The most spectacular instance of this extraconstitutional influence that has come to light is provided by the International Information Administration. The report published by Martin Merson, the chief consultant to the director of that agency, leaves no doubt that, at least from February through July, 1953, Senator McCarthy and his friends in Congress had taken over the functions which, according to the Constitution, the President and the Secretary of State are supposed to perform. These members of Congress determined, in large measure, both the substantive and the personnel policies of the International Information Administration. It was to them that the top officials of the agency reported, it was their approval they had to seek, and it was their orders they were supposed to execute. And when they finally incurred the displeasure of their congressional masters, they had to resign.

In *The New York Times* of January 17, 1954, five of the most distinguished older diplomats of the United States, four of whom have been Ambassadors and an equal number Under or Assistant Secretaries of State, summarized the "sinister results" of these policies:

The conclusion has become inescapable, for instance, that a Foreign Service officer who reports on persons and events to the very best of his ability and who makes recommendations which at the time he conscientiously believes to be in the interest of the United States may subsequently find his loyalty and integrity challenged and may even be forced out of the service and discredited forever as a private citizen. A premium therefore has been put upon reporting and upon recommendations which are ambiguously stated or so cautiously set forth as to be deceiving.

When any such tendency begins its insidious work it is not long before accuracy and initiative have been sacrificed to acceptability and conformity. The ultimate result is a threat to national security. In this connection the history of the Nazi and Fascist foreign services before the Second World War is pertinent.

The forces which are working for conformity from the outside are being reinforced by the present administrative set-up within the Department of State which subordinates normal personnel administration to considerations of security.

It is obvious, of course, that candidates for the Foreign Service should be carefully investigated before appointment and that their work should at all times be under the exacting scrutiny of their professional superiors. But when initial investigation attaches undue importance to such factors as even a temporary departure from conservative political and economic views, casual association with persons holding views not currently in fashion or subscription to a periodical labeled as "liberal"; when subsequent investigation is carried to the point of delaying a promotion list for a year and routine transfers from one post to another; when investigations of individual officers must be kept up-to-date to within ninety days; when an easy path has been opened to even the anonymous informer; and when the results of these investigations are evaluated not by persons experienced in the Foreign Service or even acquainted at first-hand with conditions abroad, but by persons of quite different experience, it is relevant to inquire whether we are not laying the foundations of a Foreign Service competent to serve a totalitarian government rather than the government of the United States as we have heretofore known it.

Fear is playing an important part in American life at the present time. As a result the self-confidence, the confidence in others, the sense of fair play and the instinct to protect the rights of the nonconformist are—

temporarily, it is to be hoped—in abeyance. But it would be tragic if this fear, expressing itself in an exaggerated emphasis on security, should lead us to cripple the Foreign Service, our first line of national defense, at the very time when its effectiveness is essential to our filling the place which history has assigned to us.

As far as personnel policy was concerned, the potential opposition was pacified simply by the dual device of pursuing its policies and handing over to it in good measure the control of those policies. With regard to substantive policies, three different devices were used to propitiate the opposition. First, the great pronouncements, which, as we have seen, were intended to impress public opinion at large with the novelty, dynamism, and aggressiveness of Dulles's foreign policy, served the same purpose for congressional opinion. Although the foreign policies that had been established by the preceding Administration and had proved their worth by their success were essentially continued, the Secretary's pronouncements created the impression of a succession of drastic innovations. Second, the department shunned actual initiative and innovation where they were called for by new conditions, for a new departure in foreign policy might antagonize the potential opposition and was bound to create the domestic political complications that Dulles was resolved to forestall. Thus the twofold need of giving the appearance of innovation and avoiding it in practice resulted in a consistent contrast between what American foreign policy was declared to be and what it actually was.

In regard to the Far East, however, Dulles did permit a certain degree of innovation. His third major conciliatory tactic was to pursue a substantive foreign policy in support of Chiang Kai-shek, to which the potential opposition was committed. He identified himself, at least to some extent, with that commitment and handed over the control of foreign policy in that area to men who were committed to pursue that policy vigorously. There can be no doubt that the majority of the leading officials who advised Eisenhower on foreign affairs during his first years in office were opposed to his policies in the Far East. That majority was composed of two groups: By far the larger of the groups wanted to advance toward a more aggressive position, even at the risk of a limited war with Communist China; the smaller group would have liked to retreat into less exposed positions. The actual policy of the United States was to maintain an intermediate position between those two extremes, which followed the line of least resistance by trying neither to advance nor to retreat but to maintain the *status quo*.

Yet a rational examination of the forces opposing each other in the Far East and their probable dynamics could only lead to the conclusion that a commitment to the *status quo* was not likely to be tenable in the long run. Both the United States and Communist China would have to go forward or backward; they were not likely to remain indefinitely where they were. Why, then, was the policy of the United States based upon an assumption that could not be supported by rational argument? The answer is to be found in the surrender to the concepts, if not the policies, of an opposition whose reasoning, contradictory in itself, could not provide the basis for a rational policy but whose voice, by default of the executive branch, was powerful enough to mold public opinion.

Public opinion with regard to Communist China was dominated by two strong contradictory desires: to make good somehow the defeat the United States had suffered through the defection of China to the Communist camp, and to do so without getting involved in a major war on the continent of Asia. The opposition presented a program designed to meet these two emotional demands. It promised the overthrow of the Communist regime of China and the restoration of Chiang Kai-shek's rule through aerial bombardment and a naval blockade, using Formosa as a springboard. Yet a careful reading of the minutes of the joint Congressional committee investigating in 1951 the dismissal of General MacArthur can leave no doubt in the mind of the unbiased reader about the military and political emptiness of this program. For the opposition could not devise any policy, short of all-out war, that would assure the destruction of the Communist regime of China. In short, the program of the opposition served as an effective instrument to achieve an illusory reconciliation of policy with popular demands, but since the two could not be reconciled in practice, it offered no basis for a rational policy.

Nevertheless, the Eisenhower Administration, frightened like its predecessor by the specter of public opinion, at least appeared to have accepted the objectives and expectations of the opposition and thus allowed its own policies to be judged by the standards of the opposition. By these standards, its policies could not help but be found wanting. For, on the one hand, the Administration was responsible enough not to embark upon military adventures; on the other, it committed itself at least to the defense of Formosa, whose indispensability for the defense of the United States was accepted as a dogma by government and opposition alike. In consequence, the executive branch found itself continuously on the defensive, apologizing, as it were, for not living up to its own standards and feeling compelled from time to

time to substitute for policy a momentous announcement or a grandiose gesture suggesting the imminence of forceful action. The executive branch had thus become the prisoner of the opposition. Too
responsible to do what the opposition wanted it to do, but prevented
by its fear of public opinion from devising and executing a positive
policy of its own, the President and Secretary of State were reduced to
having no policy at all, while trying to make it appear as though they
were following, however cautiously, in the footsteps of the opposition.

Dulles's task of making his position and policies secure with public
opinion and Congress was greatly complicated by his uncertainty
about the extent to which public opinion and Congress were willing
to endorse him as Secretary of State and to support his policies. It was
this uncertainty, amounting in Dulles's mind to extreme doubt, that
resulted not only in his opening of the gates of the State Department
to the potential opposition, allowing it to influence substantive policies, but also in his making pronouncements on foreign policy that
contrasted with the policies he actually pursued.

Dulles's task of making his position and policies secure with the
President encountered no such complications and hence necessitated
no such complex measures for its achievement. President Eisenhower
very soon trusted Dulles so completely and admired his ability as Secretary of State so unreservedly that he gave him, for all practical purposes, a free hand to conduct the foreign policy of the United States as
he saw fit. Although Dulles was continuously and deeply concerned
with the support he could expect from Congress and public opinion,
he did not need to worry about the President's support.

Echoing Thomas E. Dewey's statement that Dulles was "no ordinary
mortal" in his ability to understand and conduct foreign policy, President Eisenhower paid frequent tribute to Dulles as the greatest Secretary of State he had known. On the occasion of Dulles's fiftieth
anniversary as a diplomat, on June 15, 1957, President Eisenhower
wrote him a personal letter, saying: "Your accomplishments will establish you as one of the greatest of our Secretaries of State." And when
Dulles's tenure as Secretary of State was at an end, President Eisenhower said in his press conference of April 18, 1959: "I personally
believe he has filled his office with greater distinction than any other
man our country has known—a man of tremendous character and
courage, intelligence and wisdom." The President acted in accordance
with his estimate of Dulles's ability, for he almost always followed his
Secretary's advice in things great and small. The only important instance on record in which Dulles was overruled by Eisenhower occurred

in 1954, when the President refused to accept Dulles's advice to intervene with military force in the Indochina War.

Although Dulles did not need to exert much effort to create his extraordinary relationship with the President, he was from the very outset careful lest it be disturbed by third parties. And, as in his relations with public opinion and Congress, it was his knowledge of what had happened to other Secretaries of State in this respect that determined his attitude. According to a report by James Reston in *The New York Times* of February 2, 1958, Dulles remarked privately at the beginning of his tenure of office "that he would oppose any system of divided authority between the White House staff and the State Department for the conduct of foreign policy." He called attention to the examples of his own uncle, Robert Lansing, who had been hampered by the influence Colonel House had exerted upon Woodrow Wilson, and of Edward R. Stettinius, Jr., many of whose functions as Secretary of State had been performed by Franklin D. Roosevelt's assistant, Harry Hopkins. Dulles concluded, therefore, that "he could not take lightly any attempt to establish in the White House a competing center of foreign policy information and negotiation."

Thus Dulles opposed successfully a plan, devised by the White House staff, to reorganize the office of the President by creating three Vice Presidents, one of whom would have been in charge of foreign policy. He did not oppose in 1956 the appointment of General Walter Bedell Smith, who had served as his Under Secretary, as special adviser to the President in the field of foreign policy; this appointment fell afoul of the opposition of Herbert Hoover, Jr., then Under Secretary of State. But the men who were actually appointed to similar positions, however limited in scope—C. D. Jackson, Nelson A. Rockefeller, William Jackson, and Harold Stassen—met with Dulles's opposition and sooner or later had to yield to it by resigning. Of these conflicts, the most dramatic was the controversy with Stassen, the President's adviser for disarmament. Stassen, who had strong ideas of his own on the conduct of disarmament negotiations, challenged openly the authority of the Secretary of State, and the latter did not hesitate to take up the challenge. To this conflict over policy was added a clash of personalities. The result was a complete triumph for Dulles. In February, 1958, Stassen was forced to resign, the possibility of his further employment by the Eisenhower administration having come to an abrupt end.

The position of Dulles vis-à-vis other executive departments and the Department of State itself was made secure both by his unique relationship to the President and by his extraordinary forensic ability and force of personality. When Dulles spoke in the councils of the government, he spoke not only as the President's principal adviser on foreign affairs, as would any Secretary of State, but also and patently as the President's alter ego. When Dulles spoke, it was for all practical purposes the President of the United States who spoke. The voice of so trusted and admired a servant was not challenged lightly. This relationship between the President and his Secretary of State made it impossible from the outset for any executive department to bypass the Secretary of State by gaining the ear of the President and to pursue a foreign policy of its own in competition with that of the Secretary of State. Yet that same relationship allowed the Secretary of State to bypass other executive departments, either singly or assembled in the National Security Council, and to obtain without bureaucratic complications the President's approval for what he had decided.

The voice of the Secretary of State, however, carried an authority derived not only from his identification with the President but also from the qualities of Dulles's personality and mind. In force of personality, only the Secretary of the Treasury, George Humphrey, was his equal in the councils of government; in knowledge of foreign affairs and skill of argumentation, Dulles was clearly superior to all the President's other advisers. Thus, in the National Security Council, the Cabinet, and the informal discussions on foreign policy, Dulles generally carried the day. He was in uncontested control of American foreign policy. In its conduct he had no rival above him, that is, in the President; beside him, that is, in other executive departments; or below him, that is, in the Department of State itself.

Rivalry from within the department was precluded by two facets of Dulles's *modus operandi*. It has been frequently asserted that Dulles carried American foreign policy under his hat. Although this is an exaggeration, it contains an element of truth. It is true that Dulles used to confer with a small number of aides and that these conferences, especially during President Eisenhower's first term, were frequently characterized by a vigorous give and take. But they apparently served less to provide the Secretary with information and advice than to give him an opportunity of trying his ideas out in informal debate. The Department of State at large was not affected by these debates in its day-by-day operations and was hardly aware of them. Nor was the Secretary of State, in either his thinking or his decisions, much affected by what the Department of State knew and did. Dulles devised the foreign policies of the United States by drawing upon his own knowledge, experience, and insight, and the Department of State merely implemented these policies.

Dulles assumed personal responsibility, not only for formulating American foreign policy, but also, in good measure, for carrying it out, at least on the higher levels of execution. The public image of Dulles as a constant traveler comes indeed close to reality. During his tenure of office, he traveled 559,988 miles, of which 479,286 were outside the United States. He visited 47 nations—France, 19 times; Great Britain, 11 times; Italy, 4 times; and West Germany, 6 times. By personally performing many of the major political functions which had traditionally been performed by high-ranking diplomats, Dulles greatly reduced opportunites for the latter to take political initiative of any kind. By divorcing his operations to a considerable degree from those of the Department of State and at the same time taking over the higher political functions of the Foreign Service, Dulles for all practical purposes disarmed the Department of State as a rival in the management of foreign affairs. It must also be kept in mind that the purge of 1953 and the regime of surveillance accompanying and following it had made it inadvisable for a member of the Department of State to develop a foreign policy of his own.

Thus the *Life* article quoted above had a point when it commented:

Dulles . . . altered drastically the basic concept of the job of Secretary of State. . . .

President Truman's Secretaries of State worked essentially in the pattern of the administrative executive. They counted time away from Washington as serious neglect of the Department. Dulles took the opposite view. He regarded too much time spent in Washington as neglect of the U.S. task of free world leadership.

Reverting to an older tradition, he undertook personal direction of the country's foreign affairs, assigning himself the role of No. 1 diplomat of the U.S. The day-to-day routine of departmental administration he has delegated to his undersecretaries.

However, operational efficiency was bound to suffer from Dulles's methods of securing his position from the rivalry of subordinates and of other executive departments. The price of his success was lack of political coordination for all concerned. In some cases the Secretary made decisions without regard to political and military information available in the Department of State and other executive agencies; in other cases he neglected to prepare the Department of State and the related agencies for the policies to be adopted. For instance, the concept of massive retaliation, taken at its face value, was obsolete from the military point of view when Dulles presented it as the "new look" of American foreign policy in 1954. On the other hand, the decision to intervene in Lebanon in 1958 took many high officials of the State Department by the same surprise that it did the general public.

Comparing Dulles's conception of the office of Secretary of State with the results of his administration of the office, one cannot doubt that he was eminently successful. Everywhere he seemed to achieve his purposes. When he took office, he resolved that what had happened to Dean Acheson would not happen to him; that he would make himself master of American foreign policy, without competition from any of the quarters from which such competition had traditionally come; that he would give the appearance of being the initiator of new, dynamic, and successful foreign policies. Dulles accomplished what he had set out to do. Yet it is characteristic of the dilemma that of necessity faces a modern Secretary of State that Dulles had to pay a price for his triumph in making his position and policies secure on the domestic political scene, just as Acheson had to pay a price for shielding his foreign policies from the intrusion of domestic policies. Although what happened to Acheson did not happen to Dulles, something else did. The price Dulles had to pay for his domestic success consisted in the stagnation of American foreign policy and the diminution in prestige that both his person and his office suffered abroad.

Although Dulles consistently strove to make it appear that his foreign policies were different from, and superior to, the foreign policies of his predecessors, it is a historical fact that he essentially continued those very policies. Refusal to recognize the legitimacy of the *status quo* in Europe and defense of the *status quo* in Europe and elsewhere through containment, as well as foreign aid, were the cornerstones both of his and his predecessors' foreign policies. Dulles introduced only two major variations: He endeavored to extend the policy of military containment, originally applied to Europe, systematically to the Middle East and Asia through a network of alliances, and he postulated the inadmissibility of violence as an instrument of national policy, putting that principle into effect by opposing the 1956 invasion of Egypt by France, Great Britain, and Israel.

Regardless of the intrinsic merits of these policies, it is hardly open to doubt that they were not sufficient to meet the new issues arising from the growing military, economic, and political power of the Soviet Union, the emergence of Africa from colonial rule, the unrest in Latin America, and the endemic crisis of the Atlantic alliance. A case can of course be made in support of the thesis that Dulles, acting essentially as the resourceful advocate of his client, the United States, was constitutionally incapable of transcending his responsibility to defend the position in which he found his client, that is, the *status quo*, and of creating new situations by virtue of new policies more in tune with the interests of the United States in a new environment. However, even if Dulles had had the attributes of the creative statesman, he would have been greatly handicapped in his creative task by his overriding concern with his domestic position. To stand as still as possible while appearing to move was the safest course to take in view of this concern, and so was the limitation of any actual movement to the military sphere. A fresh political initiative, a really creative political effort, would in all likelihood have raised a domestic political issue, dividing Congress and public opinion at large into supporters and opponents, and it was such a division that Dulles was resolved to forestall.

The support Dulles enjoyed at home was not matched by a similar response from abroad. Neither his person nor his policies were popular with foreign statesmen and foreign peoples. To a degree, unpopularity is the price that powerful nations and forceful personalities pay for their power and force, and to that extent it cannot be helped. In Dulles's case, however, the negative foreign reaction was in good measure the direct result of the preoccupation with domestic support that dictated both the conception and the administration of his office. Foreign public opinion and foreign statesmen were more sharply aware than American public opinion could be of the contrast between what American foreign policy was declared to be and what it actually was. Once this contrast had developed into a consistent pattern, Dulles's public and private pronouncements were bound to be carefully scrutinized abroad for their real meaning. Since foreign statesmen could not be sure that Dulles's policies would conform to his pronouncements, they lost confidence in his person and his policies.

Dulles's *modus operandi* also contributed to the distrust he ultimately encountered abroad. By concentrating not only the direction but, to a large extent, also the implementation of foreign policy in his own hands, he escaped the handicap of involvement with the bureaucracy of the State Department but created another hazard. By taking over the functions ambassadors have traditionally performed, Dulles deprived himself of that protection with which ambassadors are intended to shield their chiefs from too frequent contacts with their opposite numbers. Such contacts breed not only familiarity but also distrust; for it is in the nature of diplomacy to try, sometimes by devious means, to use other statesmen for its own purposes. The statesman who has been so used for some length of time is likely to get tired of, and lose confidence in, the man who has so used him, and then it is time to replace that man. For that reason ambassadors frequently become expendable after a few years of service in a particular capital and are transferred elsewhere. The foreign minister who assumes the task of his ambassadors simultaneously in many capitals cannot easily be replaced when, for the same reason, his usefulness has been impaired. Thus he carries on with his prestige damaged and his trustworthiness compromised.

Dulles compounded the liability inherent in his *modus operandi* by his use of the advocate's technique. The advocate, trying to advance his client's case as far as possible, can afford to disregard the interests and reactions of other parties who have advocates of their own, both relying upon the judge to sift the truth from ex parte statements, hyperbole, and deception. What the advocate can afford, the foreign minister cannot. For the foreign minister is not only the advocate of his nation, but, in a manner of speaking, also the advocate of the other side and the judge who recognizes and respects the interests of the other side and at least tentatively decides how the two interests ought to be reconciled. The foreign minister who limits himself to being the advocate of his nation will be acclaimed at home as the stanch defender of the national interest, but he will be handicapped in his conduct of foreign policy because he will be distrusted personally and will be incapable of performing the supreme task of diplomacy: to create out of disparate and contradictory national interests a higher harmony.*

Such was the price in terms of substantive foreign policy that Dulles had to pay for his domestic triumph. Did it have to be paid? The answer to that question depends upon one's judgment of the strength of the potential domestic opposition and of the need for different foreign policies. This writer is convinced that the price was unnecessarily high by far; for Dulles, fully supported by President Eisenhower's unprecedented prestige, could have pursued whatever foreign policies he chose without fear of a domestic opposition. But, then, would different foreign policies have been desirable, and would Dulles have wanted to pursue them had he not feared that opposition? Future historians will debate these questions, and perhaps history will one day answer them.

---

* A close associate of Dulles has graphically described in private conversation one facet of Dulles's technique and its results. He compared Dulles, as he would deal with two foreign ministers, to a man who had to explain the same landscape to two associates. Knowing that foreign minister A was interested in mountains, he would tell him only about the mountains. Knowing that foreign minister B was interested in valleys, he would tell him only about the valleys. When the two foreign ministers later compared notes, they both felt that they had been deceived.

10

Charles de Gaulle: The Grand Design

[March, 1963]

Europe has a set of primary interests, which to us have none or a very remote relation. Hence she must be engaged in frequent controversies, the causes of which are essentially foreign to our concerns. Hence, therefore, it must be unwise in us to implicate ourselves, by artificial ties, in the ordinary vicissitudes of her politics, or the ordinary combinations and collisions of her friendships or enmities.

We accepted, and acted upon, this formulation of our relations with Europe, which Washington's Farewell Address gave us, for a century and a half. Our interventions in the two World Wars we considered at the time temporary exceptions to the rule of noninvolvement, justified by "extraordinary" vicissitudes, combinations, and collisions. Then, in the spring of 1947, we radically changed the conception and course of our foreign policy by identifying our interests with those of Europe in what we thought was virtual permanence through the Truman Doctrine, the Marshall Plan, and the military containment of the Soviet Union.

Since then, Europeans have from time to time expressed their fear lest we define our interests differently from theirs and go back into isolation. It was for us to reassure them. Now Europe turns Washington's formulation against us and proclaims the separateness of its interests from those of America. I have advisedly attributed this proclamation to "Europe" and not to Charles de Gaulle alone; for de Gaulle has but given trenchant and uncompromising expression to a mood and trend that are by no means limited to the French leader.

It is revealing that both de Gaulle and Harold Macmillan justify their contradictory positions with the furtherance of the emancipation of Europe from America. De Gaulle opposes British membership in the Common Market because it would lead to the formation of "a colossal Atlantic Community under American dependence and leadership" (press conference of January 14, 1963). Macmillan, on the other hand, insists on British membership because only so can Europe become "great and strong enough to build a more equal and worthy partnership" with the United States (speech at Liverpool on January 21, 1963) and anticipates the end of the alliance if the United States were given "for all time the sole authority" over the nuclear deterrent (broadcast of January 30, 1963). Macmillan, having just been expelled from Europe by de Gaulle and having to choose between a far-from-splendid isolation and utter dependence upon the United States, cannot refrain from paying tribute to the emancipation of Europe while being careful to stress the American connection. De Gaulle, on the other hand, thinks he can afford to declare the independence of Europe from America in so many words and to make it perfecty clear to us that what he wants is the exact opposite from what we want.

We have responded to that declaration with surprise and indignation. While none of us has gone so far as to suggest, as did the London *Economist* on January 26, 1963, that de Gaulle's scheme was "demented," we have certainly proved the point that the distinguished Italian paper *Giornale d'Italia* made on January 22, 1963: "It is perhaps easier to criticize de Gaulle than to understand him." De Gaulle's policy may well be wrong in that it will prove either unsuccessful or, if it should succeed, detrimental to France. It may also run counter to the interests of the United States and, if so, must be opposed by American policy. Yet, whatever one's conclusions are, they ought to derive not from emotional reactions but from a rational understanding of what de Gaulle is after. Whatever his chances for success may be, and in whatever ways his success or failure may affect the interests of France and the United States, de Gaulle's design is rational in itself and not devoid of audacity and even grandeur. That much is obvious from a dispassionate examination of de Gaulle's press conference of January 14, 1963, put in the context of his general political philosophy, and from interviews held with prominent Frenchmen, especially in the military field, during the week following that press conference.

De Gaulle's European policy derives from five basic propositions, which are not peculiar to France but are of general validity.

First, an alliance among nations unequal in power of necessity gives to the most powerful nation a decisive voice in the determination of the policies of the alliance. This fact of political life, which Machiavelli recognized in Chapter 21 of *The Prince* when he warned weak nations against making alliances with strong ones except by necessity, can be obscured, but cannot be eliminated, by talk about "interdependence" and "equal partnership." "Interdependence" means for the weak to be dependent upon the strong, and there can be no equality among those who are unequal in the qualities that count in the political scales.

Second, such dependence is tolerable for the weak only if there exists so complete an identity of interests between the weak and the strong that the policies pursued by the strong in their own interests also serve the interests of the weak. Such identity of interests is rare in peace and cannot be taken for granted even in war. It exists among the members of the Atlantic Alliance only on the most general plane: The Atlantic Alliance is united in its opposition to Communist aggression and subversion. But this interest is not a policy in itself; it must be implemented by common policies. Such policies, to which all members of the Alliance are committed, do not at present exist.

In reviewing the outstanding issues that face the Atlantic Alliance, one is struck by the fact that there is not a single one on which all members of the Alliance see eye to eye. The United States stands alone in its policies vis-à-vis China, South Vietnam, and Cuba. In the Congo, it had the support of neither Great Britain nor France. In the rest of Africa, the allies go their separate ways. With regard to Berlin, Great Britain, on the one hand, and West Germany and France, on the other, have taken contradictory positions, while the United States, after a period of vacillation, has ended up in the Franco-German camp. The same observation applies to the German question as a whole and to the over-all relations between the West and the Soviet Union: In view of irreconcilable divergences of interest and policies, abstention from initiative and a passive commitment to the *status quo* have been the order of the day. The policies of the United States and France toward the United Nations are diametrically opposed, while Great Britain takes an intermediate position. A similar cleavage separates France from the United States and Great Britain in the field of disarmament.

As concerns military strategy and the policies to implement it, the United States is at loggerheads with its major European allies on two basic issues: the role of conventional forces and the disposition of nuclear weapons.

Third, the availability of nuclear weapons to the United States and the Soviet Union has administered a death blow to the Atlantic Alliance, as it has to all alliances. It has made alliances obsolete. In the prenuclear age, a powerful nation could be expected to come to the aid of a weak ally, provided its interests were sufficiently involved, risking at worst defeat in war, the loss of an army or of territory. But no nation can be relied upon to forfeit its own existence for the sake of another. Thus, the same doubt about American intentions that deters Khrushchev disheartens de Gaulle. Khrushchev cannot be sure that the United States would not be willing to blow itself up over Berlin and, hence, is deterred. De Gaulle cannot be sure that the United States *would* be willing to blow itself up over a vital interest of France and, hence, is disheartened.

The independent national nuclear deterrent, then, becomes the substitute for obsolete alliances. Since no nation can be expected to risk destruction for the sake of another nation, all nations must protect themselves as best they can. While France could not hope to match the deterrent of a major nuclear power quantitatively, it is able to develop a minor nuclear capability. It could say to a major nuclear power: If you do this, I shall cut off your leg. And the major nuclear power could reply: If you do that, I shall kill you. But is it likely for an issue to arise between France and a major nuclear power for the sake of which the latter would be willing to risk losing a leg? And if it were to arise, the major nuclear power would in all likelihood save its leg by wiping France off the face of the earth in a preventive nuclear war.

Fourth, what has been said of alliances also applies to federations of states. Strong and weak nations can federate effectively only on a hierarchical, not on an equalitarian, basis. Here, de Gaulle's conception is not so much Napoleonic as Bismarckian. That is to say, he applies the principles through which Bismarck united Germany a century ago to the unification of Europe. Bismarck had two choices: the "greater German" solution, including Austria, or the "little German" solution, excluding it. Bismarck rejected the former solution on two major grounds: Austria would have been a rival to the predominance of Prussian power, and its imperial interests stood in the way of a full commitment to the German cause.

The unification of Germany in 1871, dominated by Prussia and excluding Austria, was preceded by two international organizations:

the German Confederation, established in 1815 under the leadership of Austria and composed of 38 sovereign German-speaking nations, and the German Customs Union, established in 1819 by Prussia. Prussia was able to thwart Austria's attempts to join the Customs Union or to break it up, and by 1853 the Customs Union comprised all German states with the exception of Austria. On the other hand, Prussia's attempt in 1849 to unite Germany politically under its own leadership, with the Austro-Hungarian monarchy occupying an associate position, was frustrated by Austria in the so-called Punctation of Olmütz. The defeat of Austria by Prussia in the War of 1866 led to the dissolution of the German Confederation and the Customs Union and its replacement in 1867 by the North German Confederation and a new Customs Union under Prussian dominance. The South German states joined the Customs Union and sent representatives to an all-German customs parliament. This process of exclusion and integration culminated in 1871 in the so-called little German solution of the German problem, the establishment of a German Reich under the dominance of Prussia and without Austria, in the aftermath of the victorious war against France, in which all German states except Austria participated.

In de Gaulle's design, the nucleus of Franco-German power takes the place of Prussia, Great Britain takes the place of Austria, and now as then economic arrangements are used as means to political ends. Faced with a similar choice, de Gaulle follows Bismarck's example and prefers a "little European" solution, excluding Great Britain, to a "greater European" one comprising it. De Gaulle sees himself as choosing between a Europe dominated by the United States and a Europe dominated by the Franco-German combination. He sees Great Britain not only as the spearhead of American power but also as a non-European influence within Europe, by virtue of its worldwide interests and commitments. Furthermore, the British presence in Europe would endanger the viability of the Franco-German combination; for the British political presence could offer Germany an alternative to the association with France and threaten France with isolation. In other words, it would be a threat to the predominance of France.

Lastly, de Gaulle realizes that Europe thus united under Franco-German auspices is but a fragment of the true Europe, the other part of which forms the western part of the Soviet empire. To unite the two parts is the task of a united Western Europe and, more particularly, of France. The accomplishment of that task is, of course, predicated upon an accommodation with the Soviet Union. The main issue of such an accommodation is the stabilization of the territorial and military *status quo* in Central Europe. The Soviet Union has tried to compel the United States to accept such a stabilization by raising the issue of Berlin. That attempt has come to nothing, in good measure because of West Germany's and France's veto. But might not France succeed where the United States failed, if it could offer the Soviet Union a Europe without the American presence and a Germany immobilized in the French embrace? Such a vista must appeal to de Gaulle, for it portends power and security for France. It might appeal to Germany, for which it holds out the prospect of unification in peace. And it cannot fail to attract the Soviet Union, threatened as it feels itself to be by the United States today and, in all probability, by China tomorrow; for here is the promise of security at the Soviet Union's sensitive frontier and of the settlement of the single issue that at present most acutely endangers the peace of the world.

We said before that de Gaulle's grand design is rational in itself. The issue it poses concerns the power to carry it through. It is at this point that the analogy between de Gaulle and Bismarck appears to break down. The power of Prussia was supreme in Germany after 1866, and the power of Germany was paramount in Europe after 1870. The power of France, such as it is and is likely to be until France possesses, if ever, a nuclear deterrent of its own, can come into play only under the umbrella of the American nuclear deterrent. As long as that umbrella protects him, de Gaulle can play the role of the Bismarck of Europe. Without that protection, he would be the Nasser of Europe, declaiming big lines in an implausible act.

It is de Gaulle's paradoxical good fortune that he can count upon the protection of the United States regardless of what he says and does. However much he may annoy American sensibilities and antagonize American interests, we cannot help but protect him, not for his sake but for ours. What was true in 1953, when John Foster Dulles threatened France with an "agonizing reappraisal," is true today. Regardless of what France does or does not do, we have a vital interest in preventing the addition of French and, through it, European power to that of the Soviet Union. In the awareness of that vital interest of the United States, which makes France secure, de Gaulle can afford to attempt the realization of his grand design, the purpose of which is to be done with the need for that American protection. Hegel would have enjoyed seeing "the ruse of the idea" thus at work.

Regardless of whether de Gaulle succeeds or fails, the relations between the United States and Europe can never again be what they were before January 14, 1963. For de Gaulle has laid bare in simple and stark outline the ills that have ailed the Atlantic Alliance for a decade and that governments on both sides of the Atlantic have been pleased to gloss over with fine phrases and manipulate with petty schemes. We may be able to continue this convenient yet self-defeating tradition for the time being; but the sooner we face the facts, however startling and unpleasant they may be, and act upon them, the better will we be capable of moulding them to our interests. Thus far we have talked and acted as though we were dealing here with the idiosyncracies of one man and not with the revelation of objective conditions that concern all of us, not only de Gaulle and France.

Thus, we have declared that we intend to go ahead with our proposals for a so-called multilateral nuclear deterrent to be put at the disposal of NATO as well as of selected allies, regardless of what de Gaulle has said and done. According to this scheme, NATO should have possession of a nuclear deterrent of its own. Yet the all-important question as to who shall determine its use has not yet been authoritatively answered; General Norstad, former Supreme Allied Commander in Europe, for instance, has suggested a committee of three. Furthermore, Great Britain and some other members of the alliance shall also possess a nuclear deterrent of their own, whose use they could determine independently "in moments of great national peril." It is this scheme that de Gaulle has almost contemptuously rejected. His reasons for doing so, it seems to me, are good, and they lose nothing of their force by being brushed aside.

The issue de Gaulle has raised and our government ought to join is an issue akin to that of sovereignty. It concerns the question as to who shall die for what and under what circumstances. As long as the United States has that power of decision through the possession of a nuclear monopoly within the Atlantic Alliance, it has the power to make Frenchmen die for causes that may not be their own (e.g., Cuba), and refuse to let Americans die for the causes of France (e.g., Suez). If Great Britain or France has that power of decision, albeit only "in moments of great national peril," while the two countries are allies of the United States, it is they who have the power to decide that Americans should die in causes that are not their own.

There are only two ways in which this issue can be resolved. Either the United States retains its power of decision, in which case the present Atlantic Alliance must be transformed into a true federation capable of bringing the political interests peculiar to its members upon a common denominator; or the power of decision must be put into the hands of the individual allies that wish to exercise it, in which case the alliance will for all practical purposes be dissolved. The former alternative requires for its achievement a series of constructive and delicate political settlements and arrangements, eliminating the present points of friction among the allies. The other alternative requires the return of the United States to isolation in a world dominated by four power centers instead of two: the United States, the Soviet Union, Europe, and China. In other words, the alliance will go either forward or backward, but it cannot stand still. Nor is there a middle ground on which the two alternatives could be reconciled.

It is such a middle ground that the Kennedy Administration has been seeking with its different schemes for a "multilateral" deterrent. Yet the control of nuclear weapons is like sovereignty: It is indivisible. It cannot be shared. It is either here or there, and it cannot be in two places at the same time. We have learned through the bitter experience of a civil war how futile and dangerous it is to gloss over and obfuscate the issue of ultimate decision for the sake of a fleeting political advantage. We ought to be able to apply that lesson to the issue at hand. There are advantages and risks in either of the alternatives from which we must choose. There are nothing but tremendous risks in a "compromise" that leaves the ultimate power of decision in the hands of the President of the United States under certain conditions and transfers it to individual nations or a committee under others, or, worse still, leaves it in abeyance.

Whether or not we find these policies to our taste or in our interest, we are indebted to de Gaulle for having posed the great issues of the day with simple and accurate clarity. De Gaulle has made clear what some of us have pointed to for a decade without anybody listening— that the political, military, and economic foundations upon which the Atlantic Alliance was constructed are in the process of erosion or have altogether ceased to exist, and, hence, the institutional superstructure of the alliance has lost its empirical supports. De Gaulle is hailed in France as the great realist who, after "demythologizing" Algeria and French parliamentarism, now performs the same beneficial operation on the Atlantic Alliance. His grand design may well come to naught. Yet great men are remembered even for their failures, and lesser men can learn from them. For even their failures shed an illuminating light upon a reality obscured by high-sounding yet inaccurate words and distorted by spurious actions. So will de Gaulle be remembered, even if he should fail.

11

Khrushchev: The Inner
Contradictions of Communism

[October, 1964]

Even if one were to assume that he was retired from supreme power for reasons of ill health—an assumption obviously rendered untenable by the humiliating circumstances of his retirement
—Khrushchev would go down in history both as the liberalizer of Communist totalitarianism and as the victim of that liberalization. That is
to say, he will go down in history as a truly tragic figure. Yet Khrushchev's personal tragedy is but a reflection of the contradictions that,
in the course of the twentieth century, have shattered one after the
other of the foundation stones of Communist philosophy. And it has
been the ex-Premier's historical mission to push that process of destruction a mighty step forward while trying to arrest it. Here, indeed,
is the element of tragedy in classic terms, as well as of Hegelian-
Marxian irony: The hero trying to master fate only hastens its consummation, the political leader seeking to arrest the historical process on
behalf of the interests of a particular class or nation only pushes the
process forward toward the destruction of those interests.

Marxism as a living political philosophy, that is, a rational guide to
political action, has been undermined by two sets of contradictions:
contradictions with historical reality and contradictions within itself.

116

The former prove Marxism to be untrue in one or the other respect; the latter prove Marxism to be absurd altogether. Marxists could take the former in their stride, even though their cumulative effect could not fail to put in question the credibility of Marxism *per se*. But Marxism as a living political philosophy could not survive the revelation of its inner contradictions, and it has been Khrushchev's historical mission to reveal two of them.

The two great contradictions that have shattered Communism since 1956, of which Khrushchev has been both the instrument and the victim, not only put into question the correctness of one or the other of the Marxist dogmas but also deny the validity of Marxism itself as a scientific system of political thought. Both contradictions stem from Khrushchev's revelation of Stalin's crimes in 1956: the polycentric replacement of Moscow's leadership of the world Communist movement and the internal challenge to Communist totalitarianism.

To appreciate fully the enormous and lasting destructive impact of Khrushchev's revelation of Stalin's crimes, one must remember that Marxism claims to be a body of scientific truths, the only science of society worthy of the name. Those who rule in the name of Marxism do so by virtue of their monopolistic possession of the Marxist truth. The Marxist rulers have risen to their position by a process of selection that has tested their understanding of Marxism against the practical tasks at hand. Lenin is venerated as the authentic disciple of Marx, who developed and applied the master's teaching, thus becoming a master himself and earning the right to supreme rule. Similarly, Stalin was praised in the Soviet Union until 1956, and still is praised to a certain extent in China, as the incomparable genius who followed in the footsteps of Lenin and, hence, had the right to rule supreme. Thus, the legitimacy of Communist rule derives from the monopolistic relationship between the ruler and the Marxist truth.

What Khrushchev did when he denounced Stalin in 1956 was not only destroy the legitimacy of Stalin's rule but also cast doubt upon Marxist legitimacy as such. If a blood-stained tyrant could rule supreme for twenty years in the guise of Marxist legitimacy, how trustworthy was the test by which the successors of Marx and Lenin were chosen? That question was raised in 1956 implicitly by the revolts in Poland and Hungary with regard to the legitimacy of their regimes and explicitly by Khrushchev with regard to Stalin, but it was bound to be raised with regard to Khrushchev as well. And so it was raised, in 1957, by a majority of the Presidium of the Central Committee, but Khrushchev managed, through the plenum of the Central Committee, to have it answered in his own favor. He was less lucky in October,

1964. The question, however, is bound to be raised again with regard to his successors, and it will be answered with less and less confidence. If Marxist selection could produce a Stalin and a Khrushchev in succession, why should it be trusted to produce a good ruler for a change, and by what standards shall we know whether or not the ruler is good?

In the realm of practical politics, two sets of consequences have ensued from the erosion of Marxist legitimacy, set in motion by Khrushchev: the polycentric disintegration of the Soviet camp, and the relaxation of totalitarian rule within the Soviet Union and elsewhere.

The monolithic character of the Communist camp under Stalin rested upon the moral foundation of the Marxist infallibility of the Soviet Union as incarnated by Stalin. Since the Soviet Union was the "Fatherland of Socialism," the most advanced Communist nation, guided by the genius of Stalin, the duty of Communists everywhere to put the interests of the Soviet Union ahead of their respective nations was clear. The testimony of the members of the Communist spy ring operating in Canada and the United States during World War II, as reported by the Canadian Royal Commission on the Gouzenko case, conveys a vivid impression of the strength with which that duty was felt. When Khrushchev stripped Stalin of his Marxist infallibility, he also deprived the Soviet Union of its moral claim to lead the Communist camp. It was only after the destruction of this claim that the divergent interests of different Communist nations and parties could assert themselves.

Polycentrism manifests itself in two different ways: as independence from the Soviet Union, pure and simple, and as rivalry with the Soviet Union for leadership of the world Communist movement. The former manifestation is typically represented by Rumania and the Italian Communist Party, and the latter, by China. China, by denying Khrushchev's claim to Marxist legitimacy, has invoked the authority of Marx, Lenin, and even Stalin. How could Khrushchev meet that Chinese challenge? Here was one of Khrushchev's dilemmas.

He could reassert Lenin's and Stalin's claim that Moscow was in the monopolistic possession of the Marxist truth. But that claim had lost its plausibility, not only because the exposure of Stalin had drastically weakened Marxist legitimacy but also for two additional reasons stemming from that weakening. The claim of Soviet infallibility and, hence, supremacy could no longer be enforced against recalcitrant Communist governments and parties. The restoration of Soviet rule in Hungary in 1956 in the face of the threat of complete disintegration could not be repeated elsewhere in the face of much more gradual and insidious threats. And it is characteristic of the ineluctable character of that process of disintegration that this process is taking place even in Hungary, where less than a decade earlier Soviet supremacy was most drastically restored.

Thus, Khrushchev was reduced to arguing with Communist governments and parties, most particularly the Chinese, which he could no longer command. Only if his arguments carried conviction and, more particularly, his conclusions coincided with the interests of other Communist governments and parties, would the Soviet position prevail. Otherwise, he had to swallow the intransigence of the Rumanians and accept in silence the challenge of Togliatti's political testament. As for the Chinese, whose interests are irretrievably at odds with those of the Soviet Union, he was reduced to vituperation.

Nevertheless, all the while Khrushchev had to maintain the claim that Moscow was the sole repository of Marxist truth. This inevitable contrast between claim and reality constituted one of the ironies of Khrushchev's position. It made him a comic figure in the tragic sense. In the process of trying to reconcile claim and reality, Khrushchev had to weaken the substance of the claim itself. He had to relax the totalitarian rule he had inherited from Stalin. This, too, was a result of the erosion of Marxist legitimacy.

The dethronement of Stalin prompted within the Soviet Union, and within the other Communist countries and parties, the same doubts and questions about the legitimacy of Marxist rule encountered in the relations between the Soviet Union and other Communist nations and parties. The dilemma with which Khrushchev had to cope here is different from that posed by the challenge of China and the assertion of independence on the part of the other Communist governments and parties. As regards that dilemma, Khrushchev really had no choice. When the Chinese challenged the supremacy of Moscow, he could rant against them as heretics; when the Rumanians went their own independent way, he could do nothing at all; for he had no effective power to restore Moscow's supremacy. Within the Soviet Union, however, he had a choice, for there he had effective power. He could make concessions to the doubters and questioners, or he could refuse to make them, or, once made, he could take them back completely or in part.

But the outer limits to the concessions Khrushchev could afford to make were prescribed by the need of his own rule to survive. This is another way of saying that these concessions were bound to be narrowly circumscribed and, as such, unsatisfactory to the doubters and questioners. For the latter had questioned, always implicitly and sometimes explicitly, the very legitimacy of Khrushchev's rule, which Khrushchev could not afford to have questioned. Thus, Khrushchev was forced by the very logic of his position to take the stand of a modified and moderate, yet uncertain, Stalinism. He could not answer the question he was asked without putting in jeopardy the very foundation of his power, and he allowed it to be raised but intermittently and surreptitiously. He had to vacillate between giving in to popular pressures with small concessions and taking them back in part or in whole when the pressure subsided or became so strong as to endanger his regime.

Thus, the destroyer of Stalinism became its victim. He could not escape the logic of the rule by which Lenin and Stalin had governed. Precluded from invoking the grace of God or the will of the people to legitimize his rule, he could only fall back upon the claim to monopolistic possession of the Marxist truth, which he himself had discredited by his attack upon Stalin. There is, then, deep historical significance and also poetic justice in Mikhail Suslov's indictment of Khrushchev (according to *The New York Times* of October 17, 1964) before the Central Committee for the same crime Khrushchev had accused Stalin of: the "cult of personality." Khrushchev was guilty of that crime. It is in the nature of Communist totalitarianism that he could not help being guilty of it.

It would be an illusion to expect that the successors of Khrushchev can escape the dilemmas to which he fell victim. The successors may patch up the conflict with China and prevent it from degenerating into an open break; they may make more or fewer concessions at home; and they may be more or less intransigent in their dealings with other nations. But they are caught in the same contradictions that were the undoing of Khrushchev. They may mitigate or aggravate them by their policies, but they cannot escape them.

The disintegration of the Communist camp will continue, and so will the oscillation between harsh and moderate rule at home and abroad. Thus, political life in the Soviet Union is likely to continue to be "solitary, poor, nasty, brutish, and short." If and when the objective conditions of Soviet politics have radically changed, or a statesman of genius has transcended and thereby transformed them—only then will the rulers of the Soviet Union be able to rule without being stifled, and in the end ruined, by the inner contradictions of Communism.

12

U Thant

[January, 1963]

The United Nations Charter envisages the Secretary-General as the "chief administrative officer of the organization." It limits his political initiative to "bring[ing] to the attention of the Security Council any matter which in his opinion may threaten the maintenance of international peace and security." In the performance of other nonadministrative functions, he shall act upon the initiative, and as the agent, of the General Assembly, the Security Council, the Economic and Social Council, and the Trusteeship Council. He and his colleagues are enjoined to "refrain from any action which might reflect on their position as international officials responsible only to the organization."

This limited and subordinate character of the functions assigned by the Charter to the Secretary-General is predicated upon the assumption that the main political agencies of the United Nations—the Security Council and the General Assembly—are able to act in accordance with the intentions of the Charter. The assumption has proved illusory, because the Cold War between the Soviet Union and the other permanent members of the Security Council has rendered that body impotent, and because the General Assembly has been made unwieldy by the increase in membership from the original 51 to the present 110. As the Security Council has been immobilized by the Russian veto, so a large and disparate membership threatens the ability of the General Assembly to marshal a two-thirds majority behind any substantive policy. The present eminence of the office of the Secretary-General, unforeseen and unintended by the Charter, is a function of this decline of the Security Council and the General Assembly as the main political organs of the United Nations. First, the weight of political decision shifted from an impotent Security Council to the General Assembly, and then it shifted from an unwieldy General Assembly to the Secretary-General.

Yet the second shift would not have been possible without the fortuitous circumstance that during the decisive period, from 1953 to 1961, the office of Secretary-General was occupied by a man endowed with unsurpassed qualities of wisdom, skill, and courage: Dag Hammarskjöld. Without him, the United Nations could never have become what it is today and might well have followed the League of Nations into oblivion as an operating political institution. Hammarskjöld became a kind of prime minister of the United Nations, assuming through his office political functions that the Security Council and the General Assembly should have performed but could not. Through their delegations of power, the Secretary-General became the initiator and executor of policies. The terms of the delegation were frequently most vague, such as the restoration of peace and order in the Congo, and thus gave broad discretion to the Secretary-General's initiative, limited only by the willingness of member states to implement it with the required financial, technical, and military means.

Mr. Hammarskjöld's initiative, however cautiously and skillfully conceived and executed, could not help being controversial. More particularly, he and his policies were violently attacked by the Soviet Union. It was inevitable that this conflict should have arisen between the great imperialistic power of the age and the chief political officer of an international organization that by its very nature is committed to the defense of a particular *status quo*, to be changed only by peaceful and lawful means. Mr. Hammarskjöld could be, and was, impartial in his attitude toward different nations; he could not be, and was not, neutral when it came to the fundamental issue of changes in the *status quo* by violent or illegal means. Thus, political opposition was added to the lack of a constitutional base and the weakness of institutional support to threaten Mr. Hammarskjöld's new conception of the Secretary-General's office. That his conception prevailed is above all a tribute to the extraordinary qualities of the man. That triumph of one man—

powerfully supported, it is true, by the universal fear of war—has served to conceal the inner weakness of the organization on behalf of which he spoke and acted. He walked on the most brittle of grounds. It was only the sureness of his step that made those grounds seem less brittle than they actually were.

These observations are prompted by the George Huntington Williams Memorial Lecture, which the new Secretary-General of the United Nations, U Thant, gave at Johns Hopkins University on December 2, 1962. The lecture was delivered two days after U Thant's election and therefore commands special attention as a programatic statement of the new Secretary-General's political philosophy. It must be said right away that this address is disquieting in view both of its general subject matter and of the specific views it contains.

U Thant does something that, to the best of my recollection, Mr. Hammarskjöld never did: He reviews the international scene, analyzes and assesses the trends of events, praises and criticizes specific policies, and offers advice to the governments of the world. He postulates compromise as a universal principle of foreign policy. He assesses Khrushchev's foreign policy, as distinct from Stalin's, and criticizes the West for not reacting properly to it. He approves of the Cuban and Laotian settlements. He seems to favor neutralism as a general principle for the nonaligned nations. He sees "one of the root causes of political tension" in the disparity in the wealth of nations.

With these statements, U Thant postulates an entirely novel conception of the Secretary-General's office. He speaks here as a kind of superego in the conduct of foreign policy. His voice has the sound of truth and reason, to be heard above the melee by the less enlightened and less pure nations. But no man, however great his wisdom and purity of motive, can perform the function the new Secretary-General of the United Nations has here assumed, and the attempt to perform it is not only doomed to failure but also fraught with mortal danger to the United Nations. It is because the United Nations is an important, if not indispensable, instrument for the preservation of peace in the contemporary world that one must point to the weakness of U Thant's position.

U Thant obviously believes that by a sheer act of will an individual, such as the Secretary-General of the United Nations, can elevate himself above the political conflicts of the times and can judge the positions and policies of different nations by completely objective standards. He is capable of doing this, so he seems to believe, because he is identified not with any particular nation or group of nations but with the organization of all nations, the United Nations. This belief is mistaken. The United Nations does not exist in separation from the interests and policies of its members. Either it represents and puts into effect the consensus of a majority of its members, expressed through the procedures of the Charter and supported by effective power, or it does not exist at all as an effective operation. When in the past the Security Council or the General Assembly delegated its powers in a specific instance to the Secretary-General, it was left to the genius of Mr. Hammarskjöld to sense the limits within which the consensus of the members and their power would support his action; and it can well be argued that in the Congo he went to those very limits, if he did not in fact overstep them.

The Secretary-General's voice and action, then, are not his own, nor do they belong to the United Nations in the abstract. Rather, the Secretary-General speaks and acts as the agent of a temporary majority, which has coalesced in support of a particular policy on the occasion of a specific issue. He can speak for the United Nations in the abstract only on one occasion: when he offers the peace-preserving and -restoring procedures of the United Nations by pointing out what the United Nations could do if the members were only to avail themselves of its facilities. This has been the burden of the argument presented by Mr. Hammarskjöld in his classic annual reports.

A Secretary-General who tries to do more than that by pretending to judge the positions and policies of individual nations by the objective standards of truth and reason is bound to end up speaking only for himself, supported by one nation and opposed by another, as the case may be. This is as it must be in a world of many nations; it has happened to John Foster Dulles and Mr. Nehru, among others. But when it happens to the Secretary-General of the United Nations, it has happened not just to another statesman whose pretenses have left the facts behind, but to the United Nations itself. The United Nations, with its collective political organs paralyzed or ineffective, has only one agent left through whom it can act: its Secretary-General. His political purity, as it were, is his most precious political asset. When the chips are down, he cannot help antagonizing that nation or group of nations that tries to change the *status quo* by illegal or violent means. Thus, he cannot help using up his political capital as the price of his effectiveness; this was the fate of U Thant's predecessors. But neither can he afford to squander that capital in futile and dubious pronouncements that have no bearing upon the concrete issues he is called upon to deal with as Secretary-General. How can he command the political and military support of the member states necessary for effective political action, if he has impaired his reputation for impartiality by pretentiously pontificating on the affairs of the world? A few such pronouncements, antagonizing a sufficient number of nations, may well end the usefulness of the Secretary-General as the agent of a majority of member states. They may also thereby bring to an end the usefulness of the United Nations as "a dynamic instrument of governments," to use Mr. Hammarskjöld's pregnant phrase.

This would be so even if the Secretary-General's pronouncements on concrete policies were pearls of wisdom, for it would not be necessarily a wisdom palatable to the nations that possess a preponderance of numbers and power. It is doubly so when the pronouncements of the Secretary-General, far from wise, are rather trivial and beside the point. I shall not concern myself here with statements in U Thant's address that are controversial in that they express a preference for one kind of policy over another, such as his approval of the Cuban and Laotian settlements and his call for a compromise on Berlin. I shall instead analyze a statement that is so deficient intellectually that it might be subject to universal criticism, regardless of national preference:

> . . . the system created and maintained by Stalin was manifestly ruthless and obsolescent even before his departure. Mr. Khrushchev, who is now in control of the reins of government, belongs to a different category of leaders, with a coherent philosophy of the world based on the thesis, not of the inevitability of war but of the imperative of competitive coexistence.
>
> We may or may not agree with his philosophy or with his aims, but we have very good reasons to believe that he does not want war. The West does not seem to appreciate the full significance of this obvious change of political climate in the Soviet Union.

I submit that this analysis is trivial, insofar as it is correct, and that it completely misses the decisive issue.

No statesman in possession of his senses wants war as an end in itself; that was as true of Stalin as it is of Khrushchev, and as it has been of most statesmen in modern times. The real issue, to which U Thant does not address himself at all, is whether certain statesmen pursue objectives that can be achieved only at the risk or through the actual employment of war. The Communization of the world by the Soviet Union and the establishment of an Asian empire by China are two such objectives. The difference between the foreign policies of Stalin and Khrushchev is a matter of method, not of objectives; Mr. Khrushchev's words and deeds testify to that. A case could even be made in support of the proposition that Stalin's objectives were limited in the tradition of Czarist imperialism, while Khrushchev's objectives restore the universalistic aims of Lenin. How would U Thant have the West react to that change? His answer is: through bargaining and the give and take of compromise. These are indeed instruments of foreign policy that, as I have tried to point out for fifteen years, have been too little used by the government of the United States. But they must be used with discrimination; they are not universal principles. There are situations for which compromise is appropriate; there are others for which it is not. After all, the Munich settlement of 1938 was also a compromise! To return to the present, how do you bargain with a nation that believes in the inevitable universal triumph of Communism and regards its mission to be that of bringing about your doom? What can you give a nation by way of compromise, if that nation is bent on taking all? How can India bargain with China, if China seeks its downfall?

U Thant does not raise these questions, and as Secretary-General of the United Nations he has no business raising them. But the questions he raises instead are the wrong questions. By raising questions he should not have raised at all, even if they had been the right ones, he has put in jeopardy the effectiveness of his office. Since without the effectiveness of that office the United Nations cannot survive as an instrument for the preservation and restoration of peace, he has done a disservice to the international organization that, under present circumstances, must stand or fall with him.

13

Barry Goldwater: The Romantic Regression

[Autumn, 1964]

The political romantic is the obverse of the political reformer. The reformer endeavors to bridge the gap between reality and a moral and rational ideal not yet achieved by transforming reality in the light of that ideal. The political romantic carries within himself the picture of a glorious past (fancied or real or both), of a golden age once achieved by ancestral virtue and despoiled by contemporary vice, of a political paradise once attained and now lost.

Political romanticism is not identical with conservatism. Romanticism is indeed a powerful disposition in American politics; conservatism is so only in terms of philosophy and method, not of purpose. The neglect of this dual distinction between romanticism and conservatism and between two different kinds of conservatism has resulted in considerable confusion of our political thinking and argumentation. Thus, Goldwater calls himself a conservative and is actually a romantic who has recently turned conservative only by force of circumstance and, in a partial sense, by having become the champion of the segregationists.

Conservatism of philosophy and method is an intrinsic element of the American political tradition. *The Federalist* is its greatest literary monument; Alexander Hamilton is its greatest theoretician; John Quincy Adams and Abraham Lincoln are in different ways its greatest practitioners. That conservatism holds that the world, imperfect as it is from the rational point of view, is the result of forces inherent in human nature. To improve the world, one must work with those forces, not against them.

This being inherently a world of opposing interests—and of conflict among them—abstract principles can never be fully realized. They must at best be approximated through the ever temporary balancing of interests and the ever precarious settlement of conflicts. Conservatism, then, sees in a system of checks and balances a universal principle for all pluralist societies. It appeals to historical precedent rather than abstract principle and aims at the realization of the lesser evil rather than of the absolute good.

What separates Goldwater from the Republican statesmen of the recent past is not his philosophy but the positive relationship he appears to be willing to establish between that philosophy and political action. His immediate predecessors, as leaders of the Republican party —romantic though they might have been—were no fools. When their romantic philosophy came up against the hard facts of political life, it was the facts that won out.

Goldwater is a different breed of man. He is an honest man, and he at least gives the impression of being a determined man. Not only does he firmly believe in what he says, but he also appears to have the resolve to put into practice what he believes, come hell or high water. He believes in the political potency of strong action inspired by good intentions. His predecessors failed because they did not believe firmly enough and did not try hard enough. If stubborn facts seem to stand in the way of successful action, too bad for the facts. Don Quixote has mounted Rosinante and is at last ready to give battle.

Here is the source both of the enthusiasm Goldwater evokes in his followers and of the dismay with which his Republican opponents behold him. His followers are unsophisticated enough to think that the modern world has come upon us, at best, by default of a succession of misguided governments or, at worst, by their conspiratorial connivance with the forces of evil. What is needed to set things right is a good and determined man, and Goldwater appears to be such a man.

Hence Goldwater's charisma, which communicates itself to the individual visitor no less than to the crowds. This charismatic quality sets Goldwater apart from his predecessors. Eisenhower's charisma was not primarily a quality of his person but a function of the memory of his historical role, real or fancied. And whatever assets Dewey and Nixon may vaunt, charisma is certainly not one of them.

That very same apparent determination to narrow the gap between a romantic philosophy and an obstreperous reality that elates Goldwater's followers sends shudders down the spines of his pragmatic Republican opponents. These opponents bow to Goldwater's verbal picture of the lost paradise to be restored, but in practical terms they are perfectly satisified with the *status quo*. It is exactly that satisfaction with things as they are that affords them the luxury of indulging in ideological daydreams about things as they have been and ought to be.

Goldwater's apparent determination to make things over in the image of his philosophy appears to them as a reckless interference with a *status quo* that they find highly satisfactory in view of their pragmatic interests. A corporation executive may inveigh against government interference, but he does so in the knowledge that his company spends annually more federal funds than, say, the federal Department of Labor; if anything, he wants to get the federal government more deeply involved in the private sector rather than have it retreat from it. He is indeed afraid of Communism and wants it defeated, but not at the risk of blowing himself up.

Both opponents and adherents listen to Goldwater's voice as to the prophet's, promising salvation. Yet, while the opponents may applaud the prophet and dismiss his message, the adherents expect the prophet to transform reality in the image of his message and look at themselves as so many apostles of salvation.

This tendency toward activism, which is the result of Goldwater's personality, is powerfully reinforced by the objective conditions under which he competes for the Presidency of the United States. The activist romanticism of Goldwater coincides with the crystallization of a genuine conservative position, exceptional in American history. That is the position of the segregationists, North and South. Here indeed is a group that has a stake in the *status quo*, that has a political, social, and economic position to defend against change—and is resolved to defend it. Goldwater has become the champion of that group.

The traditional romanticism of the Republican party is now being fused with the conservatism, old in the South, new in the North, of the segregationists. A romantic tenet, such as state rights—which in the past was nothing more than a specious incantation—now takes on concrete political significance in that it provides both Governor

Wallace and Goldwater with a weapon for the protection of the seg-regationist position. For the first time, the romanticism of the Republican party has a concrete political cause for which it can fight, not from the rostrums, as in the good old, purely romantic days, but from the barricades and from the White House. This is the novelty of our situation. Goldwater's political romanticism tending toward action has converged with a conservatism requiring action. This makes Goldwater's candidacy so portentous and ominous an event in the history of our country.

Trying to assess the chances of Goldwater's candidacy, one must sharply distinguish these two elements in his position. Romanticism has been the curse of the Republican Party since 1932—Eisenhower's victories are but accidents without consequences in the history of the Republican Party—and activist romanticism is bound to be a greater curse still. Considering Goldwater as nothing but an activist romantic, he is bound to go down to resounding defeat in November; for there are not enough voters who would take the risk of acting out their romantic daydreams. But Goldwater is also the champion of segregationist conservatism, and here one must distinguish between the old conservatism of the South and the new kind of the North. Even if one were to add the old conservatives of the South to the traditional romantics of the Republican Party and deduct the pragmatic Republicans deterred by Goldwater's activism, Goldwater could not win.

The great unknown in the equation is the conservatives of the North. To them Goldwater offers himself as the savior of America from social change. His success in November will depend upon the number of Northern Democrats and habitual nonvoters who feel strongly enough the need to be saved, and believe strongly enough that he is the man to save them, to vote for him. How large is that group? It is certainly larger than the group of Republicans who will be deterred by Goldwater's activism. But how large is it likely to be in terms of electoral votes? Nobody has the answer to that question. More particularly, the pollsters do not have it; for they cannot identify the number of nonvoters aroused enough to vote for Goldwater this time, nor can they isolate the prospective conservatives of the North from the rest of the voting population. It is upon the answer to that question that the future of Goldwater, of the Republican party, and of the nation depends.

If Goldwater should win, the stubbornness of the facts is bound to restrain his romantic activism, and so will his innate democratic decency. Yet it is exactly this unwitting decency that makes him the natural prey of people less decent than himself. There looms, then, the specter of a victorious Republican party taken over by romantic and conservative activists and pulled by its own dynamics toward an authoritarian position. For neither romantic restoration nor conservative preservation is attainable within the limits of the democratic consensus. If they are to be attained, they must be attained by violence.

14

Adlai E. Stevenson: Tragedy and Greatness

[August, 1965]

Adlai Stevenson has been praised and buried. His wit and eloquence have been duly noted; his honesty and his disappointments, commented on. Yet these qualities do not explain the impact his death has made upon the people. After all, there have been other witty, eloquent, honest, and disappointed candidates for the Presidency whom men have not mourned as they mourn Adlai Stevenson. What sets Adlai Stevenson apart from all the other seekers after high office of his time, successful or unsuccessful? What is the gift that only he has brought to American life, that made the vanquished shine more brightly than the victor? The answer is both simple and complex: It is the quality of greatness tinged with tragedy. The man in the street felt that tragic greatness without being able to define its substance. Everybody knew that here was a unique political figure, different from all others and, in an undefinable, almost mysterious sense, superior to them. Everybody also sensed that this political figure, in all his uniqueness, was more like ourselves than the common run of politicians (this is what we mean when we say that he was "more human" than they) and that his tragic failure was in some way the tragedy of all of us writ large. Adlai Stevenson

132

was, indeed, political Everyman. His promise was ours, and so was his failure, and the tears we shed for him we shed for ourselves.

Wherein did Adlai Stevenson's greatness lie? Wherein does any man's greatness lie? It lies in his ability to push the human potential for achievement in a particular respect to its outer limits, or beyond them if they are defined in terms of what can be expected in the ordinary course of events. Thus, we speak of great painters and great writers, great liars and great lovers, great statesmen and great merchants, great saints and great crooks. We call them great because they have done what others may do well, indifferently, or badly, with a measure of excellence that at least intimates perfection.

Adlai Stevenson was great in his relationship to power. He was not a great statesman, because he did not have the chance to use power for the purposes of the state. He was not a great politician, because he did not choose to be a politician. But he was a great seeker after power, and it was his very greatness in the pursuit of power that was, as we shall see, responsible for the tragedy of his failure.

In order to understand the substance of Stevenson's greatness, we must remind ourselves that there are two ways to be great in the pursuit of power. The search for power ordinarily entails, at least in a certain measure, the sacrifice of the intellectual and moral virtues. It is in the nature of the struggle for power that the competitors must deceive themselves as they deceive others. Those who have chosen power as the ultimate aim in life must use truth and virtue as means to their chosen end and discard them when they do not serve that end. The prototype of this power-seeker is endowed with what Russell Kirk, in a contemporary reference, has called a "canine appetite for personal power." He is a Borgia or a Stalin, the Machiavellian prince, who will stop at nothing to gain and hold the power he seeks. He will sacrifice all other values for the sake of power. His greatness consists in that single-minded, ruthless pursuit of power, of which lesser—and better—men are incapable. They stop at some point on the road to power, distracted and restrained by the common virtues of intellect and ethics.

Man is capable of another kind of greatness in the pursuit of power, which owes less to Machiavelli than to Plato's postulate of the philosopher-king and to the Hebrew-Christian ideal of the wise and good ruler. That greatness consists not in the single-minded pursuit of power but in the ability to subordinate the pursuit of power to transcendent intellectual and moral values. Rather than being possessed by power, those men possess it; rather than being devoured by it, they tame it. History has, indeed, known few rulers of this kind. But they all, as far as I can see, have been secure in the possession of power, generally by virtue of the automatic character of monarchical succession. Those who had to fight for the gaining and keeping of power, which is, of course, the normal situation in a democracy, have generally been precluded by this ever-present concern from attaining that greatness. The best they have been able to achieve has been an uneasy *modus vivendi*, a compromise between the demands of power and the requirements of the intellectual and moral virtues, power having an excellent chance of prevailing when the chips are down. Of those who could not take power for granted but had to fight for it, I know only one who has attained that greatness: Abraham Lincoln. And it is indeed impossible to think of the substance of Stevenson's greatness without reflecting on the greatness of Lincoln. What they have in common explains their greatness; in what they differ accounts for the triumph of the one and the failure of the other.

What Lincoln and Stevenson have in common is a high degree of freedom from illusion, to which politicians—like all men—are prey, about themselves, about their actions, and about the world. What took the place of these illusions was a lucid awareness, both intellectual and moral, of the nature of the political act, of their involvement in it, and of the consequences of that involvement for themselves and for the world. That awareness gave them the intellectual distinction and moral sensitivity that set them apart from the common run of politicians. It gave their actions the appearance of indecisiveness and the reality of moral force. It accounts for their personal qualities of eloquence, wit, and sadness.

Lincoln and Stevenson knew both the moral risks and the practical hazards inseparable from the political act. They knew that to act politically was to take a jump into the dark. Innocent people would suffer, and the outcome was uncertain. Moral absolution could not be bought with good intentions, nor could success be vouchsafed through ingenuity. The actor on the political stage takes his fate into his hands. Try as he may, he cannot escape the risks and hazards of his acts. If he is of the run of the mill, he will consult the flight of the birds, the constellation of the stars, or their modern equivalent, the public opinion polls, and receive the illusion of certainty that the facts of experience refuse him. If he is great in the manner of Lincoln and Stevenson, he cannot help but face the risks and hazards of his acts, to weigh them against the risks and hazards of alternative acts, to shudder at what he must do—and do it as though those risks and hazards did not exist. He acts in awareness of, and in spite of, these risks and hazards. Here is the measure of the heroic dimension of Lincoln's actions.

What the actor's mind knows, his action is ignorant of. It can afford to be determined and bold, because the mind has done its task of knowing, weighing, and judging. It is for that very reason that the act carries within itself the conviction of justice in the sense of being appropriate to the end to be achieved. What needs to be done will be done, but nothing more, is the message the act seems to convey. Here is the core of the moral force of Lincoln's policies.

That contrast and tension between what the actor knows and what he must do accounts for his eloquence, his wit, and his sadness. In both Lincoln and Stevenson, eloquence is more than a mere matter of rhetoric and literary skill; wit is more than a mere matter of fleetness of brain and quickness of tongue; and sadness is more than a mere matter of mood and nerves. They are the qualities of souls that have been formed by their awareness of what the political act implies and by the burden of having to act nevertheless.

Lincoln and Stevenson share the gift of eloquence and wit with other great political figures. One thinks of Bismarck, Churchill, and Adenauer. The quality of sadness is theirs alone. It is the function of an intellectual and moral sensitivity in the face of power that, so it seems, is peculiarly American. It gives immunity from that ultimate illusion to which even the intellectually aware and morally sensitive political actor is apt to succumb. His heroism makes him act; his intellect makes him explain himself; his wit makes him transcend the incongruities of his political existence, at least in thought. And so he may delude himself into believing that now he has mastered the political world. Lincoln and Stevenson were incapable of that ultimate illusion. They knew that, when all is said and done, they were still faced, without remedy or escape, with the moral ambiguities and practical pitfalls of the political act. Knowing what they knew about themselves, their actions, and the world, they could not but be sad. Their sadness denotes the resigned acceptance of the moral and intellectual imperfections of the political world and of their precarious place within it.

It is hardly necessary to point out that these qualities of greatness are more fully developed in Lincoln than they are in Stevenson. They were not clearly visible before Lincoln entered the White House; it was the pain of great decisions that brought them to the fore. Thus, they have a grave and somber aura, which Stevenson's qualities are lacking. Stevenson's greatness was not the result of an ineluctable confrontation between personality and fate: The only great decision he had to face—three times, it is true—was whether or not to seek the nomination. Rather, it was the spontaneous expression of a great personality in intellectual anticipation of the fateful decisions he might have to make. Hence the peculiar quality of playfulness, of the aimless intellectual exercise, which is alien to Lincoln.

What is the relevance of this difference between Lincoln and Stevenson for the latter's failure to gain political power after his initial success in Illinois? The answer to that question is obscured and rendered speculative by the intrinsic hopelessness of the 1952 and 1956 campaigns and by his failure to win the nomination in 1960. But why did he pursue the aspiration, foredoomed to failure, of becoming Secretary of State? And why did he silently suffer for four and a half years the humiliation of being Ambassador to the United Nations? Can these questions be explained away as accidents of history? Or do these persistent failures point to a fatal flaw, a tragic defect in Stevenson's greatness, which barred his way to power but which might not have barred him from making great use of it, had he been able to achieve it? I think, indeed, that there was such a flaw. In order to understand its nature, let us return for a moment to Lincoln.

Abraham Lincoln, we have said, revealed his greatness only after he had reached the highest office. He made his way to that office as a politician competing with other politicians, seeking power in the manner of politicians, always tough and sometimes ruthless and devious. Lincoln made no bones about wanting power, and the people gave it to him. It was only after he had reached it that he also achieved an awareness of, and detachment from, it; and it is here that we found the key to his greatness.

Stevenson showed his awareness of and detachment from power from the very outset. No doubt, he wanted power. When it eluded him in 1952, he said that he envied one man, the Governor of Illinois. When, as Ambassador to the United Nations and nominal member of the Cabinet, he had the trappings of power without its substance, he complained about the "disadvantage in being anywhere other than the seat of power." He never forgave himself for his indecision in 1960. He wanted power, but he wanted it only with intellectual and moral reservations openly revealed. He wanted power, but not with that "canine appetite," with that single-minded animal ferocity, which carried his competitors in the Democratic party to success. He wanted power, but he did not want it badly enough. His was a civilized pursuit of power in a barely civilized political world. But the people want their politicians to be wholehearted and uncomplicated in their pursuit of power. By being so, the politicians give a token that they can hold and use power when they have it. It was this distance between the core of Stevenson's person and the pursuit of power, and the interplay between the two, articulated by him and sensed by the people, that fascinated the masses and gained him their admiration but not their confidence.

It was that very same distance that saved the defeated Stevenson from the disintegration that is the common lot of frustrated seekers of great power. They hate or drink themselves to death. Stevenson in defeat could fall back upon that moral and intellectual core of his person that remained unaffected by the lust for power. He remained what he had been: eloquent, witty, and sad, but now he was so in a peculiarly purposeless way. The desire for power, too, remained; yet surviving the possibility of its satisfaction, it became patently futile and carried within itself a measure of humiliation.

Stevenson wanted to be Secretary of State, and I suggested him in 1960 to the President-elect for that position; for I thought then, as I think now, that he was far better qualified than his competitors. But it should have been obvious to him—and to me—that politically the appointment was impossible; for the victor did not owe him that much, and, more important, he could not be expected to countenance a star at Foggy Bottom that shone brighter than the sun of the White House.

Stevenson's acceptance of the Ambassadorship to the United Nations, to which I was opposed from the outset, and his unwillingness to relinquish it reveal most poignantly the desperation of his pursuit of power. The services he rendered to the country in that position could have been performed as well by lesser men, and they do not compensate for the personal diminution he suffered as a mouthpiece for policies on which he had no influence and was but rarely consulted.

Had Stevenson been a more unrestrained seeker of power, he might have disintegrated in defeat. Had he been less addicted to the pursuit of power, he might have given it up in defeat altogether and become one of the great reflective men of the nation. He did neither. What could already be discerned in 1952, 1956, and 1960 now became almost pathetically obvious: the conflict between intellectual and moral awareness and the pursuit of power, spoiling both.

There, then, is the rub. The intellectual and moral component was too dominant in Stevenson's personality for the good of his political ambitions. It made Stevenson reveal his greatness prematurely. In a democracy, ordinariness, not greatness, gains power. Once a great man, such as Lincoln, has gained power under the cover of ordinariness, he can afford to bare his greatness to the mutitude, but not before. Lincoln's greatness evolved from his ordinariness, buttressed by power. Stevenson's greatness was a gift of nature, not grown from the successful conquest of power, but anticipating it. Yet, had Stevenson possessed that quality of ordinariness necessary for the democratic conquest of power, behind which his greatness could for the time being have been hidden, he would, in all probability, still have lost in 1952 and 1956, and the world might never have known how great a man he was. Thus all may have turned out for the best. Alas, poor Adlai. Such is the irony of your life.

15

John F. Kennedy

KENNEDY AND FOREIGN POLICY

[July, 1961]

After five months in office, the Kennedy Administration cannot boast of anything that can be called a success in foreign policy. But it has registered two glaring defeats: the Cuban disaster and the Communist conquest of Laos. In consequence, everybody is disenchanted with the Kennedy Administration. The Republican opposition is naturally, one might say professionally, disenchanted and advocates "strong action" on the model of what President Eisenhower did in Lebanon and Guatemala. The Democrats are disenchanted because their expectation that everything wrong with American foreign policy would be set right after January 20 is unrealized. Most significant, the Administration is disenchanted with itself; it has come to recognize that intelligence and initiative are not enough to vouchsafe success in foreign policy. Quite a number of Hamlets must have walked the battlements of the White House in recent nights, debating with themselves the relation between thought and action.

Two strands can be distinguished in this negative attitude toward the foreign policy of the Kennedy Administration, one rooted in the psychology of the public, the other stemming from actual deficiencies of Kennedy's policy. We all share to a greater or lesser degree the ineradicable tendency to expect from a new administration all the achievements—and without delay—that we awaited in vain from its predecessor. We expect dramatic and spectacular reversals of fortune. These expectations are bound to be disappointed. However unwise and unsuccessful the preceding Administration may have been, and however wise the new one may be, the very vices and failures of the predecessor put strict limits upon the successor's freedom of action.

The policies of its foreign counterparts, friend and foe alike, limit the freedom of action of a new administration even more significantly. Regardless of the intrinsic merits of its own policies, an administration, unless it chooses to try to impose its will upon other governments by force, can go only as far as the other governments will allow. As long as Khrushchev insists upon a Soviet veto over the political decisions of international organizations, the disarmament policies of the Kennedy Administration must remain a dead letter. As long as President de Gaulle seeks an independent position for France within Europe and an independent position for Europe, under French leadership, within the Atlantic Alliance, it will remain impossible for the Kennedy Administration to do what it wants to do, e.g., to strengthen the Atlantic Alliance.

Furthermore, insofar as a new administration has and uses the freedom to start new policies, the results of those new policies are not likely to be visible at once. The Kennedy Administration, for instance, has embarked upon a new policy of foreign aid, derived from what appears to be a sound philosophy of the conditions and purposes of foreign aid. It will take some time for this new policy to filter down through the ranks of the officials in the field, if it ever does. Most of these officials have operated on certain primitive assumptions, deeply ingrained in the folklore of American politics, about the relations between foreign aid and economic development, economic development and social stability, social stability and democracy, democracy and a peaceful foreign policy. They are not likely to have been selected for their political sophistication and manipulative skills. Even after they have learned how to translate the new philosophy into effective action it may take years for the results of the new policy to show.

Our disenchantment is nourished further by the nature of the tasks it has fallen to the Kennedy Administration to solve. One of them is the liquidation of overextended commitments. That is to say, the United States, if it does not want to risk war in the defense of indefensible and, at best, nonessential positions, must retreat from these positions. It has already retreated from Laos and has been trying, thus far in vain, to obtain the cooperation of the Communist powers in covering up that retreat. It will soon be faced with a similar choice in South Vietnam and perhaps, later, in Iran. The American people are utterly unprepared for these retreats. As concerns American power vis-à-vis the power of other nations, they are living in a dream world, which antedates the atomic age, especially its bipolar period. The dream world is dominated by the power of the United States, which need only use it with determination to get what it wants. It is the misfortune of the Kennedy Administration that it assumed office at a moment when the veil that had hidden an obstreperous and dangerous world from the eyes of America had worn thin enough to show at least some of the contours of a disturbing reality. The reassuring slogans that for eight long years we have taken to describe reality (such as "massive retaliation") now start to clash openly with the facts of life. Since nobody in authority has yet told the American people what the facts of life are, the Kennedy Administration is widely suspected of weakness in the face of Communist aggression: It does not live up to the slogans it has not dared to repudiate.

The people are disenchanted with the Kennedy Administration for its failure to do what it was expected to do but was incapable of doing in the objective circumstances. What is worthy of blame here is the people's judgment, not the actions of the government. However, the Administration is also being blamed deservedly for failures of commission and omission. Its outstanding failure of commission is, of course, the invasion of Cuba. What has shocked our sensibilities is not so much that the Administration tried to intervene in Cuba by force of arms, or even the failure of the intervention, as the manner in which it failed. It is that manner, the incredible folly of the whole thing, that points to actual weaknesses in the Administration's conduct of foreign policy. The weaknesses are conceptual, organizational, and intellectual.

In Cuba, as elsewhere, the Administration has operated with an outdated concept of revolution. When it staged the invasion of Cuba, it expected the Cuban people to rise against Castro. It assumed that the Castro revolution was not a genuine popular revolution or that, if it once was, it was no longer. The people, it was reasoned, are anti-Communist by nature, as it were, and when they happen to live under a pro-Communist government, it must be under duress. Thus, the overthrow of the Communist governments of Russia and China has been predicted and expected time and time again. When such countries as Cuba go Communist, or are in danger of doing so, as are Laos and South Vietnam, it can only be through foreign intervention, not by popular consent. All that is needed, then, is military intervention to free an unwilling people from Communist domination. Since the Communists are gaining control through guerrilla warfare, we must reply in kind. The Kennedy Administration therefore places special emphasis on what it calls "paramilitary operations" or "counterinsurgency."

But the modern totalitarian regimes, fascist and Communist, have not been imposed by a tyrannical minority upon an unwilling population. Aside from the Franco regime, which came to power on the bayonets of Nazi Germany, and the satellite regimes of Eastern Europe, which came to power on the bayonets of the Red Army, the modern totalitarian regimes have come to power and maintained their rule with the support of populations willing to sacrifice individual freedom and self-government, actual or potential, for order and what they consider to be social justice. Such regimes are to be overthrown not by counterrevolutionary invasions but only by the vision of a social order superior to the *status quo* and capable of realization.

Where guerrilla warfare is an instrument of foreign invasion, as it was in Greece and Malaya, it can indeed be countered in kind. But where guerrilla warfare is the spearhead of popular revolution, as it was in Cuba and is today in South Vietnam, "counterinsurgency," operating in hostile territory without a popular base, is doomed to failure. The Kennedy Administration, by seeming to look to "counterinsurgency" as its main answer to Communist revolution, falls into the trap of assuming that what works well for the Communists must work equally well for us, if only we make the effort to imitate it.

Both the Cuban invasion and the official sanction of the prisoner-tractor deal point up another real weakness of the Administration's foreign policy: the process of policy formation. President Kennedy has made a conscious effort to avoid his predecessor's isolation from both relevant information and effective control. To that purpose, he has done away with the committee system of governing, at least at the top level, and has surrounded himself with a number of individual advisers, in different degrees brilliant, knowledgeable, and experienced. The advisers, equals in the eyes of the President, are supposed to present him individually with a variety of views and recommendations from which he can choose. This concept of Presidential government, indeed, has considerable merit when compared with the committee system it is intended to replace, but it is not likely to work in practice.

The successive presentation of views and recommendations by isolated individuals is no substitute for the dialectic confrontation of such views and recommendations in a group, which puts differing opinions to the test of empirical verification and logical analysis. Also, in a contest among equals for the President's ear those with offices in the White House are likely to be more equal than those with offices, say, in Foggy Bottom. And those who are supposed to have a monopoly of at least some of the *arcana imperii*, such as officials of the CIA and the Pentagon, are likely to have an advantage over those who can boast of nothing more than intelligence with a small i. This system also tends to separate the men of ideas from the men of facts and gives an inevitable advantage to brilliant presentation, unchecked against practical experience. Thus, the President, when he had to make a decision on Laos, was compelled by the objective requirements of government to restore the National Security Council to its original function as the President's principal adviser on issues of national security.

The equalitarian diffusion of the advisory function raises another issue: the role of the intellectual in the process of policy formation. We all smile in memory of what was once a maxim of our government: A man who knows how to run General Motors by definition knows how to run the Department of Defense, and a man who has met a payroll must also be capable of meeting the requirements of government. It is, however, no more self-evident that a man who knows how to run a university is thereby qualified to run the foreign policy of the United States, or that an intellectual who knows how to lecture and write books by definition knows how to make foreign policy. The intellectual does not need to have, and is frequently devoid of, that quality which is indispensable in the statesman: practical wisdom. It is possible to be very intelligent without being very wise or, for that matter, being wise at all; which is another way of saying that one can be very intelligent and very foolish at the same time. Woodrow Wilson was a brilliant intellectual without, to say the very least, the full measure of wisdom. Harry Truman had practical wisdom without being an intellectual.

Two qualities, essential in the statesman, are not necessarily present in the intellectual: a sense of limits—limits of knowledge, of judgment, of successful action—and a commitment to a grand design, born of a sense of purpose that neutralizes the doubts arising from the awareness of limits. The intellectual is rather sure of himself, satisfied with himself, and out for the next little triumph in his little world. In the world of the intellectual, ideas meet with ideas, and anything goes that is presented cleverly and with assurance. In the political world, ideas meet with facts, which make mincemeat of the wrong ideas and throw the pieces into the ashcan of history. To stand one's ground in this battle of ideas, which will determine the course of history, is a different matter, requiring different qualities of mind and character, from that innocuous and frequently irrelevant pastime we pretentiously call the academic dialogue.

Perhaps it is not by accident that an administration whose style to an exceptional degree is determined by intellectuals speaks a great deal about purpose but appears to lack a sense of direction, that it calls upon the people for sacrifices without being able to tell them what to do. Here, indeed, is the Administration's failure of omission. And it is first of all the President's failure. When the President finally spoke in positive terms about the national purpose, he and his advisers could think of nothing better than being first in sending a man to the moon, a patent publicity device, which an unexcited public took in its stride. It is another instance of that trap of imitating the Russians and playing the game according to their rules. And whenever the President called for sacrifices, he said hardly anything of substance, but he said it in beautiful prose.

The quandary of the Administration—knowing that it must give American foreign policy a new direction and instill it with a new purpose, but not knowing how to go about it—stems from the contrast between the nature of the tasks before it and the quality of its thinking about them. The Administration has found, to its dismay, that it has even less freedom of action than it thought it had when it assumed office. The negotiations on the cessation of atomic tests are at a dead end. Consequently, the chances for disarmament are virtually nil. The positions on Berlin appear irreconcilable. The Atlantic Alliance remains in disarray. Our positions in Asia are deteriorating.

This being so, the Administration is naturally tempted to reconcile itself to the inevitable and to put its stakes upon the unabated continuation of the nuclear armaments race, hoping for the best but knowing in the back of its collective mind the inevitability of the worst. It is the easiest policy to pursue and is bound to be popular, but it cannot fail to lead to disaster. Here the Administration is offered a great opportunity to put its brain power to work on a task of constructive statesmanship. It must try to break out of the sterile patterns of past policies and put forward proposals of a boldness commensurate with the novelty of our tasks and the urgency of the dangers that face us. The tasks of greatest urgency are Berlin, the supranational control of nuclear power, and, intertwined with these, the revitalization of the Atlantic Alliance.

If the Administration were to embark upon these and other tasks with sufficient boldness, it could no doubt expect the kind of sacrifices it must ask of the American people—sacrifices not primarily of money or of toil but of long-held, cherished convictions that have turned out to be illusions. The President must set an example for the American people by offering up popular illusions on the altar of truth. This task is politically risky in the short run, but in the long run it is the precondition for both the restoration of the vigor of our national life and the renewal of our foreign policy. Our awareness of the Administration's failure to perform that task is perhaps the deepest source of our disenchantment: We have been told, and we know, that there is something fundamentally wrong with our national life and our foreign policy. Yet the Administration seems to think, and certainly acts on the assumption, that traditional remedies will cure our ills. What gives us pause is the discrepancy between the actual foreign policies pursued, with the kind of thinking that apparently goes into them, and what we have been led to believe about our condition or know to be true. History will judge the Kennedy Administration on how well it performs the task of bringing its thought and action up to the level of that truth.

KENNEDY THE POLITICIAN

[January, 1962]

On September 30, 1961, the eminent French sociologist and columnist Raymond Aron addressed an open letter to President Kennedy in *Le Figaro*. It is both a moving and an important document. It is moving because it is written with sympathy and concern by a man who calls himself an "enthusiastic partisan" of the President. It is important because it raises one of the two great issues of government that will ruin the Kennedy Administration, and perhaps the country, if the President does not meet them successfully.

Mr. Aron addresses himself to the President's method of deciding issues of foreign policy, taking as his point of departure the invasion of Cuba. The President had to choose between two incompatible courses of action suggested by his advisers: to stage an invasion of Cuba, with American military support, if necessary, or not to intervene. In order to avoid the risks that either course of action, consistently pursued, would have entailed, the President tried to steer a middle course, intervening just a little bit but not enough to assure success. Confronted with a choice between black and white, he chose gray. "Yet in foreign policy," as Mr. Aron puts it, "the half-measure, the compromise, ordinarily combines the disadvantages of the two possible policies."

Mr. Aron was, and perhaps still is, afraid that the President might repeat this error in his approach to the Berlin crisis. For, here again, the President must choose between counsels recommending diametrically opposed courses of action: a negotiated settlement, which is bound to weaken the American position in West Berlin and West Germany, and an intransigent position, which, at the very least for the immediate future, increases the risks of war. As Mr. Aron sees it, the President has chosen, at least in theory, the "hard" line; yet in his style, method, and language he has committed himself also to "flexibility." In consequence, nobody can be sure whether Mr. Kennedy intends to play the role of Churchill or of Chamberlain. Nobody— not the American people, not our allies, nor, probably, Mr. Khrushchev himself—knows what our negotiating position is, assuming we have one.

Mr. Aron left one question unanswered: What has been the matter with Kennedy? The indecisiveness of the Cuban intervention and the apparent indecisiveness of Mr. Kennedy's approach to the Berlin crisis are but the manifestations of a deficiency deeply embedded in the President's experience and personality. To put it bluntly, the President does not know what the statesman's task is, while he knows only too well the politician's, and thus he endeavors to accomplish the task of the statesman with the tools of the politician. Yet the virtues of the politician can easily become vices when they are brought to bear upon the statesman's task.

The decision of the statesman has three distinctive qualities. It is a commitment to action. It is a commitment to a particular action that precludes all other courses of action. It is a decision taken in the face of the unknown and the unknowable.

The politician can take words for deeds, and insofar as his words seek to influence people to vote for him or for his measures, his words actually are deeds. He can make promises without keeping them, and his promises may not even be expected to be kept. He can run on a platform every two or four years and take his stand on quite different ground in between. He can equivocate between different courses of action and bridge the chasm between incompatible positions by embracing them both. He can vote one way today and another way tomorrow, and, if he can't make up his mind, he can abstain from voting. He can try to reduce to a minimum the uncertainties of the future by preparing his action with proper attention to the facts, organization, and planning.

The statesman, especially in his dealings with other nations, can hardly ever afford to do any of these things. His rhetoric is verbalized action, an explanation of deeds done or a foretaste of deeds to come. What still moves us today in the recorded oratory of a Churchill or a Roosevelt is not so much the literary quality *per se* as the organic connection between the words and the deeds. Listening to those words, we remember the deeds, and we are moved.

The statesman must commit himself to a particular course of action to the exclusion of all others. He must cross the Rubicon or refrain from crossing it, but he cannot have it both ways. If he goes forward he takes certain risks, and if he stands still he takes other risks. There is no riskless middle ground. Nor can he, recoiling before the risks of one course of action, retrace his steps and try some other tack, promising risks different and fewer. He has crossed the Rubicon and cannot undo that crossing.

The statesman must cross the Rubicon without knowing how deep and turbulent the river is, or what he will find on the other side. He must commit himself to a particular course of action in ignorance of its consequences, and he must be capable of acting decisively in spite of that ignorance. He must be capable of staking the fate of the nation upon a hunch. He must face the impenetrable darkness of the future and still not flinch from walking into it, drawing the nation behind him. Rather than seek unattainable knowledge, he must reconcile himself to ineluctable ignorance. His is the leading part in a tragedy, and he must act the part.

The extent to which the style of the Kennedy Administration resembles the politician's rather than the statesman's is revealed not only by the policies it has pursued but, more particularly, by its mode of operation. Rhetoric has been divorced from action and has tended to be taken as a substitute for it. To give only one glaring example: In July, 1961, the President committed himself in a speech to a program of fallout shelters, without having a policy. Ever since, his aides have searched for a sensible policy that would not be too much at variance with the President's words.

Yet the President cannot help making decisions, and the method by which he has reached them suffers from three defects. It is informal to the point of being haphazard. It tends to lose sight of the distinction between what is paramount and must be decided by the President and nobody else, and what is only important enough to be decided not by the President but by somebody else. It has the quality of indecisiveness, because it vainly seeks a certainty that is beyond its reach.

The President has wisely discarded the committee system through which his predecessor governed, shielding himself from direct contact with the issues in all their complexity. Yet he has unwisely replaced this system with another that threatens to overwhelm him with an unmanageable variety of issues and opinions.

The President exposes himself deliberately to advice from a great variety of sources. These sources are generally individuals who talk to him at length in his office or over the phone. This system, or lack of it, has the virtue of making the President familiar with all shades of opinion. It has the double vice of making it either too easy or too difficult for the President to make up his mind.

The President may well be swayed by a particular counsel, especially when it is presented with that subjective self-assurance which some mistake for objective certainty, and with that facility for expression and brilliance of formulation which some mistake for depth. Impressed with these qualities of form, he may commit himself to the substance of the advice without being fully aware of the meaning of that commitment. It has been reported on good authority that the President was once presented with advice concerning a policy of capital importance. He approved of that policy orally and asked the individual concerned to instruct the head of the department within whose jurisdiction the policy fell to put it into operation. This was done. When the head of the department some weeks later informed the President of the progress made in the execution of that policy, the President questioned its wisdom, obviously unaware that he had approved it and ordered its execution.

This casualness of policy formation puts two obstacles in the way of the President's making up his mind. Taking counsel on the spur of the moment with all kinds of people on all kinds of issues, the President is overwhelmed with issues to be decided and advice to be weighed. In consequence, his mind can no longer perceive clearly the vital distinction between the paramount issues he alone must settle, and the merely important ones that others may decide, with or without his guidance. The President has lost sight of the natural relationship that exists between the gravity of the issue to be decided and the level of authority that decides it. Thus, some paramount issues will remain unattended or will be ineffectually attended to by officials lacking sufficient authority, while the President will concern himself with secondary issues that could be more effectively disposed of by subordinate authorities.

Thus it has come about after many months of deliberations by a great many officials that if we have a policy with regard to Berlin, neither the American public nor the allies of the United States are aware of it. *The New York Times* could publish on October 21, 1961, a report from Washington under the headline "Allied Confusion Stalls Thompson. Envoy Unable to Get Clear Stand for Moscow Talks." The result is not only confusion but also the surrender of the determination of policy to some other nation whose interests may or may not coincide with those of the United States. Thus, again, the *Times* reported on October 26 as the official position of the United States Government that "the United States could not get nearer to war than the West Germans wish to go, and could not get nearer to peace than they were willing to go." Many months of contingency planning did not prepare the Administration for the possibility that the East Germans might effectively seal East Berlin off by erecting a wall. Hence, the Administration did not know what to do when the wall went up in August, 1961, and did nothing. The show of force through which the United States in October tried to maintain the *status quo* concerning the access of its military personnel to East Berlin ended in confused retreat.

The President must overcome the indecisiveness of his own mind. That mind seeks the predictability to which it is accustomed from domestic politics. There, meticulous ascertainment of the facts, precise planning, and elaborate organization years in advance paid off in victory in the primaries, the nominating convention, and the elections. To be sure, a margin of uncertainty remained, but it was small compared with what was known, what had been prepared and planned for.

The President searches for the same kind of certainty in his conduct of foreign policy. He tries to eliminate the darkness of ignorance and to probe the depth of uncertainty that even so astute a mind as his cannot penetrate, by drawing upon the most luminous and knowledgeable minds he can find and by making use of all the information he can lay his hands on. Yet those dark spots on the landscape of foreign policy are impervious to the most brilliant intelligence, and factual knowledge cannot prevail against them. Thus the President's mind hesitates and his will falters when he seeks the answer to the riddle in more advice and additional information.

The frantic search for advice and information performs for the President the same function the employment of astrologers and soothsayers did for the princes of old: to create the illusion of certainty where there can be no certainty. The more facile the President's advisers are with words and the more self-assured they are in their convictions, the more adept they are in encouraging the President in such futile search. They cannot give him what he needs more than anything else: the tragic sense of politics. In view of that need, he could do worse than add to the ranks of his advisers a philosopher who would remind him at regular intervals that there are more questions than answers and that the great decisions must be made in ignorance and without certitude. The President, who knows his history, will remember that the princes of old reserved a place among their advisers for a man who called their attention to the limits of their power beyond which there is the realm of Providence and fate.

This particular issue of government stems from the President's personal approach to his task. He has created it; it has never before in American history appeared in this way and is not likely to appear so again. The other issue of government with which the President must come to terms is inherent in the American system. All Presidents have had to face it and live with it one way or another. It concerns the relationship between domestic politics and foreign policy.

The issue is posed by the incompatibility between the rational requirements of sound foreign policy and the emotional preferences of a democratically controlled public opinion, to which Tocqueville referred in a famous passage.* Confronted with this dilemma between the requirements of good foreign policy and the preferences of public opinion, the President has the supreme task of reconciling the two. The dilemma is tragic because it can never be fully resolved. If the President pursues uncompromisingly the foreign policy he regards to be sound, as Woodrow Wilson did, he risks losing the support of opinion at home; if he accommodates himself to that opinion at the expense of what sound foreign policy requires, he risks jeopardizing the interests of the country. In order to be able to avoid these two extremes—the one fatal to his personal power, the other fatal to the power of the nation—the President must perform the two historic functions of his office: to be the educator of the people and the conciliator of seemingly irreconcilable positions. The President must impress upon the people the requirements of sound foreign policy by telling them the facts of political life and what they require of the nation and then must strike a compromise that leaves the essence of sound foreign policy intact while assuaging domestic opinion.

It is the measure of Mr. Kennedy's failure that he has performed neither task. Instead, substituting again the politician's concerns for the statesman's, he has tended to subordinate the requirements of sound foreign policy to the requirement of winning elections in 1962 and 1964. The President knows that our Far Eastern policy has so far failed to result in catastrophe not because it is sound but because of

* See page 43.

circumstances that are likely to change drastically to our disadvantage. The President knows that what we call our German policy has been for fifteen years a verbal commitment to the illusion of unification rather than a policy. But the great mass of the American people know nothing of this, because the President has not dared to tell them. To return to the fallout shelters: Not only did the President commit himself in words to a fallout shelter program before he had a policy, but he now has committed himself to a policy in order to be able to compete in 1962 and 1964 with Mr. Rockefeller, who has developed such a policy for the state of New York.

Yet the President, with his sense and knowledge of history, and groping as he does for his proper place in the scheme of things, cannot but feel where his true mission lies.

It is for the President to reassert his historic role as both the initiator of policy and the awakener of public opinion. It is true that only a strong, wise, and shrewd President can marshal to the support of wise policies the strength and wisdom latent in that slumbering giant—American public opinion. Yet while it is true that great men have rarely been elected President of the United States, it is upon that greatness, which is the greatness of its people personified, that the United States, from Washington to Franklin D. Roosevelt, has had to rely in the conduct of its foreign affairs. It is upon that greatness that Western Civilization must rely for its survival.

These words I addressed in 1949 to Mr. Truman and in 1956 to Mr. Eisenhower. It is the measure of the chronic weakness of Presidential leadership that the same words must be addressed to Mr. Kennedy in 1962, at the beginning of his second year in office.

THE KENNEDY LEGACY

[December, 1963]

History is likely to associate the Kennedy Administration with seven developments, four domestic and three international: the intellectual as public servant, governmental concern for culture, the responsibility of the executive branch for civil rights, permanent unemployment, the demonstrated implausibility of nuclear threats, the disintegration of the Atlantic Alliance, the crisis of foreign aid. Domestically, we have witnessed the expansion of the public sphere; internationally, attempts at reorientation without conclusive results.

The pure intellect and the arts have traditionally occupied a lowly place in the estimation of the American people. The "long-haired professor," the "egghead," the impractical fellow "who never met a payroll" might be appreciated privately as a virtuoso or enjoyed as highbrow entertainment, but certainly public affairs had to be managed by businessmen, who had already provided proof, calculable in dollars and cents, that they were practical. The candidacies of Adlai Stevenson were a first indication of a change in that popular attitude, as his defeats were perhaps an indication of its persistence.

It is the historic merit of Kennedy to have made the intellectual respectable as a manager of national affairs. Especially in its upper-middle layers, his Administration was dominated by professors and professional Ph.D's. It was indeed an extraordinary and awe-inspiring spectacle to see the Department of Defense, over which a succession of businessmen had presided in hapless ineffectiveness, transformed by a group of young intellectuals. Such people compelling generals and, more particularly, admirals to do what they did not want to do—here, certainly, was something new in military administration. I have been told that a survey shows Ph.D's to have a superior chance of becoming administrative assistants of members of Congress.

I would note in passing what I pointed out at the beginning of the Kennedy Administration * that politics has its own standards of excellence and that intellectuals, especially on the level of policy-making, are not *a priori* better qualified to manage public affairs than businessmen. But they are not less qualified either. Intellectuals have been as spectacular failures in public life as businessmen. What was wrong was the *a priori* assumption in favor of businessmen and professional politicians and against intellectuals. It is this wrong that Kennedy righted.

Kennedy made not only the intellectual respectable in the public eye, but culture in general as well. The arts have been flourishing in America through private initiative, and it is only our cultural inferiority complex vis-à-vis Europe that has made us unaware of the original and vital force of our artistic life. The public powers in the United States, in contrast to their contemporaries and predecessors throughout Western civilization, have acted by and large as though culture were no more their concern today than was economics thirty years ago. Opera and theater still flourish in the country according to consumer response and not because of their intrinsic quality, which does not necessarily coincide with the consumer's judgment and, hence, needs support from independent private or public sources. It was a historic

---

* See pages 139–45.

innovation for Kennedy not only to pay his personal respects to the arts but also to make a beginning in supporting them through the instrumentalities of the federal government.

What Kennedy did for the arts he has also done for civil rights. It is irrelevant for the purposes of this account, which does not seek to evaluate the merits of persons and policies but rather to point up the great historical changes associated with the Kennedy Administration, that this concern for civil rights was imposed upon the Kennedy Administration by a spontaneous popular initiative. The historical fact remains that under Kennedy the executive branch of the federal government transformed itself from a mildly interested bystander into an active proponent and champion of civil rights. The extension of the public power, which was at its most spectacular during the period of the New Deal, was continued by the Kennedy Administration. In the 1930's, the federal government assumed responsibility for the economic welfare of the nation. In the 1960's, it began to extend that responsibility to culture and civil rights.

In the area of economic welfare, the Kennedy Administration tried to come to terms with a new kind of unemployment, which appeared impervious even to prolonged prosperity. It proposed to attack this problem with the Keynesian methods of increasing purchasing power. Yet it is a moot question whether we are here in the presence of a temporary discrepancy between productive capacity and purchasing power, to be removed by Keynesian remedies, or whether we are not rather face to face with radical changes in the structure of the economic system, due to a technological revolution that is replacing human labor with machines permanently and on an unprecedented scale while at the same time enormously increasing productive capacity. If the latter should be the case, as I think it is, Keynesian remedies will not cure the disease.

What will be required is a radical transformation of our economic thinking, more radical than was the Keynesian departure from classical economics. The magnitude of the task that would have faced the Kennedy Administration, and will face its successor, is illuminated by the fact that the Keynesian measures it proposed (probably obsolescent), must overcome powerful and widespread opposition to their allegedly revolutionary nature. Perhaps history will see the significance of this era of economic thinking and practice as that of a dual backwardness of a public opinion that has not yet assimilated the Keynesian revolution, and the backwardness of a government that tries to apply Keynesian methods to a situation that has left the Keynesian model behind.

It is indicative of the character of the historical era in which we live that the quandary that beset the Kennedy Administration in the economic sphere was duplicated in international relations. In foreign policy, the Kennedy Administration at least made a start at coping with the fact that we have been living for a decade in a world whose objective conditions have outpaced our traditional modes of thought and action. This contradiction between tradition and reality had to be faced in three fields: nuclear war, alliances, and foreign aid.

The United States and the Soviet Union have continued to threaten each other with nuclear war, although this threat has always been implausible in view of the radical difference between nuclear and traditional violence. Thus in the successive Berlin crises and the Cuban crisis of October, 1962, the U.S. and the U.S.S.R. tried to convince each other that they were irrational enough to incur their own destruction by supporting their respective positions with nuclear violence, assuming at the same time that the other side would be rational enough not to provoke such an irrational reaction. The new nature of these nuclear threats and counterthreats, which had been analyzed before in theory, was now demonstrated in practice.

Conventional force is an instrument for breaking the will of the opponent through either successful defense or attack; it is in the effectiveness of its physical application that its primary function lies. But the primary function of nuclear force lies in making its physical application superfluous by deterring the prospective opponent from using it. While conventional force operates psychologically through the intermediary of actual physical employment, nuclear force has a psychological function pure and simple. The prospective opponents are kept constantly aware of the inevitability of their own destruction should they resort to nuclear force, and this awareness prevents them from resorting to it.

It is worth noting that in the prenuclear age the threat and the counterthreat of force could always be, and frequently were, put to the test of actual performance, and either the threat or the counterthreat was then proved to be empty. In the nuclear age, the very purpose of threat and counterthreat is to prevent the test of actual performance from taking place. The appearance of possessing both the ability and the resolution to make good threat and counterthreat becomes, then, of paramount importance as a condition for the success of mutual deterrence.

The nature of this condition, it will be observed, is political rather than military; for what is essential is the *appearance* of possessing the ability and resolution to make good threat and counterthreat, not the reality of such possession. In order to make mutual deterrence work, two nations need only to create the mutual belief that they are willing and able to destroy each other in nuclear war. As long as this belief exists, it is irrelevant whether or not the reality corresponds to it. In other words, the mechanics of mutual deterrence require an element of bluff, either real or suspected.

At this point, the mechanics of mutual deterrence raise a most serious political dilemma. No nation can afford to yield to a threat of nuclear war that is only a bluff; nor can it afford to stand up to a threat that turns out not to be a bluff. Miscalculation is bound to be fatal either to the interests of the nation concerned if it yields to the bluff, or to its existence if it stands up to a nuclear threat that is not a bluff. Yet—and here is the dilemma—a nation cannot determine with certainty when the other side is bluffing without the test of actual performance, a test that it is the very purpose of mutual deterrence to avoid. Deterrence has thus far worked only because there has remained in the minds of both sides a doubt as to whether the other side was really bluffing. Or, to put it the other way around, both sides were able to give the threat of nuclear war at least a certain measure of plausibility.

While the Kennedy Administration demonstrated the dilemma of nuclear deterrence, it was unable to devise policies capable of transcending the dilemma. It made a gesture toward arms control in the partial test-ban treaty. In the sphere of military strategy, it attempted to "conventionalize" nuclear war, that is, to overcome the irrationality of nuclear weapons by using them as though they were conventional ones. This last effort, the so-called counterforce strategy aimed at military objectives rather than industrial and population centers, is no less certainly doomed to failure than were its predecessors, such as the "clean bomb" or tactical nuclear war. For there is no way of overcoming the immensity of nuclear destruction, which is out of all proportion to the ends sought and, hence, is irrational.

The issue of counterforce strategy has fortunately remained in the realm of theoretical planning, but the nuclear dilemma has had a destructive impact upon political reality in that it has called into question the survival of the Atlantic Alliance. President de Gaulle raised that issue in his press conference of January 14, 1963. In doing so, he spoke not only for himself and for France but for the major European powers as well. The issue is a logical extension of the nuclear dilemma. On the one hand, the nations of Europe cannot be absolutely sure that the United States is willing to commit suicide on behalf of their interests. On the other hand, they are not willing to commit suicide for the interests of the United States.

An independent nuclear deterrent for France, and eventually for Europe, was de Gaulle's answer to this dilemma, an answer which conjures up the specter of the uncontrolled proliferation of nuclear weapons. Our answer has been a multilateral seaborne nuclear force, a military monstrosity and a political evasion. Here again, the Kennedy Administration was groping for a military answer to what is essentially a political problem. That problem consists in the coordination of the political interests of all concerned to such an extent that no member of the Alliance would want to use nuclear weapons for a purpose for which all the other members of the Alliance would not want to use them, too.

Finally, the Kennedy Administration developed a new conception of foreign aid, which found its most persuasive formulation in the philosophy of the Alliance for Progress. This philosophy tries to connect foreign aid with the political interests of the United States, on the one hand, and the demonstrated capacity of the recipient countries for economic development, on the other. Thus we took a decisive step away from that naïve philosophy that equated foreign aid with economic development, economic development with social stability, social stability with democracy, and democracy with a peaceful foreign policy.

But the new philosophy of foreign aid came up against intractable political conditions in the recipient countries. Many of the recipient governments were unable or unwilling, for political reasons, to create the domestic preconditions for the effective use of foreign aid. Yet under the threat of imminent collapse or communization they claimed and received foreign aid just the same. Here, therefore, was another dilemma that the Kennedy Administration brought to the fore but could not transcend.

The Kennedy Administration is, then, marked by a transitional quality both at home and abroad. At home, it staked out new areas for the public sector and had just begun to fill these areas with new accomplishments. On the international scene, it became aware of novel problems, and when it came to an end it was still groping for solutions to them.

MONUMENTS TO THE LATE PRESIDENT

[January, 1966]

When I met John F. Kennedy in 1956, at a symposium sponsored by the American Friends of Vietnam, I tried to size up the man and was baffled. What, if anything, I asked myself, is behind that bland, slick, polished façade, acting in word and gesture with almost mechanical precision? Fate has allowed history to answer that question only in part. There was indeed something of substance behind that façade. But what was it? Messrs. Schlesinger and Sorensen say it was greatness. Their books * are monuments to that greatness. However, it is a greatness assumed but not proved. I am not saying that Kennedy could not have become a great President, had fate allowed him to test his inner resources against a series of momentous challenges. I am saying only that the record is inconclusive. But it was not without promise. That promise rested on three qualities, of which these two books provide abundant evidence.

First, Kennedy had the ability to make fun of himself. To be able to look at oneself from a distance without being overly impressed is indeed, in a statesman, an attribute of greatness. It allows a man to see the world as it is, undistorted by the involvement of his ego. Of recent contemporaries, Eleanor Roosevelt and Adlai Stevenson had that gift. I remember vividly a conversation I had with Eleanor Roosevelt in which she related how her husband had once used her for his political purposes without the slightest concern for her feelings, let alone for her worth as a human being. She spoke with complete detachment, with an objectivity suggesting that it was not she who had suffered, but somebody else; she permitted herself no display of emotion, only the desire to understand.

Kennedy's detachment was closer to the mocking self-deprecation of Stevenson. Capable of beholding himself with ironic detachment, he could do justice to the situation he had to master. He lived up to Goethe's saying: *"Wer sich nicht selbst zum Besten haben kann, gehört gewiss nicht zu den Besten."* (The play on words cannot be translated; it means, "Those unable to make fun of themselves are not among the best.") When Kennedy was reminded that Schlesinger had written a memorandum opposing the Bay of Pigs invasion, Schlesinger reports, he said: " 'Arthur wrote me a memorandum that will look pretty good when he gets around to writing his book on my administration.' Then, with a characteristic flash of high sardonic humor: 'Only he better not publish that memorandum while I'm still alive. . . . And I have a title for his book—*Kennedy: The Only Years.*' " Again according to Schlesinger: "When the first volume of Eisenhower's presidential reminiscenses came out, he said drily to me, 'Apparently Ike never did anything wrong. . . . When we come to writing the memoirs of this administration, we'll do it differently.' "

* Arthur M. Schlesinger, Jr., *A Thousand Days: John F. Kennedy in the White House* (Boston: Houghton Mifflin, 1965). Theodore C. Sorensen, *Kennedy* (New York: Harper & Row, 1965).

The second quality of Kennedy's personality that carried the promise of greatness is related to the first: a keen and open intellect, an unusual intellectual voracity, energy, and restlessness, an openness to new ideas, a hospitality to experiments. His impatience with the Department of State derived from his awareness that, from top to bottom, it was lacking in those very qualities. The Cuban crisis of 1962 provided a dramatic opportunity for a fascinating interplay of minds —proposing, debating, criticizing, thinking aloud. The President made his decision in full awareness of this intellectual process. What is important, in view of the intellectual qualities of the decision, is not whether it was right or wrong (I thought then that it was wrong, because it did not go far enough, concentrating upon the tactics to be used against Khrushchev rather than the strategy against Castro), but that it was the distillation of a collective intellectual effort of a high order, the like of which must be rare in history.

The promise of greatness rests upon still another quality, which the historical record does not show clearly but of which the two books give impressive evidence. It is the ability to grow, not just to learn from experience, as we all do and as Kennedy did from the Bay of Pigs debacle, but to transform experience into a new intellectual quality, wisdom. Two incidents that Schlesinger reports make the point. Kennedy was bound to be annoyed and embarrassed by the open hostility of some of the leading generals to his policies. While he did not allow them to influence his policies substantially, he lived with them and even placated them with secondary concessions, as he did in the settlement of the Cuban crisis of 1962 and the partial test-ban treaty. He recognized their value in their proper sphere, that is, in the conduct of military operations. "It's good to have men like Curt LeMay and Arleigh Burke commanding troops once you decide to go in," he told Hugh Sidey. "But these men aren't the only ones you should listen to when you decide whether to go in or not. I like having LeMay head the Air Force. Everybody knows how he feels. That's a good thing."

When Kennedy told the Congressional leaders about the Cuban crisis of 1962 and his plan for a quarantine, Senator Russell of Georgia disagreed and recommended invasion; he was supported by Senator Fulbright, who, together with Chester Bowles, had been alone among Kennedy's top advisers in opposing the invasion in 1961. "The trouble is," Kennedy told Schlesinger later, "that when you get a group of senators together, they are always dominated by the man who takes the boldest and strongest line. That is what happened the other day. After Russell spoke, no one wanted to take issue with him. When you can talk to them individually, they are reasonable." One is reminded of the wisdom of the Roman saying: *Senatores boni viri, Senatus autem mala bestia* (The Senators are good men, but the Senate is an evil beast).

The two books cannot fully reveal, because in a sense it was not their purpose to do so, what I regard to be the three great weaknesses of Kennedy's personality. They are the vices of his intellectual virtues: a tendency to take rhetoric as the equivalent of action, the absence of a communicable political passion, and disorderly administration.

To a great extent, Kennedy's rhetoric was divorced from action. It was political literature of a high order. But it was not, as was Churchill's or Roosevelt's, verbalized action, an explanation of deeds done or a foretaste of deeds to come. There was in Kennedy's rhetoric no organic connection between the words and the deeds. The classic example is the speech of July, 1961, in which Kennedy committed himself to the construction of fallout shelters without having decided on the purpose the shelters should serve. It was only after the rhetorical event that his aides searched for a sensible policy that would not be too much at variance with the President's words.

Similarly, there was no organic connection between Kennedy's grandiose pronouncements on foreign policy, for instance, with regard to Berlin and relations with the Communist world, and the actual policies pursued. Nor could there be, since the policies proclaimed in one speech were incompatible with those announced in another. During his triumphal tour through Germany, Kennedy identified himself unreservedly with the national aspirations of Germany. He spoke as though he were a German statesman, and he was received with the enthusiasm befitting one. His declaration *"Ich bin ein Berliner"* was not only hyperbole; it epitomized his rhetorical commitment to German policies. On the other hand, in his speech at American University, Kennedy opened up the vista of improved relations with the Soviet Union. Yet the great unsettled issue from which the Cold War arose twenty years ago and on which it has fed ever since is the issue of Germany. The United States cannot simultaneously take an uncompromising stand on the German question and work for the elimination of tensions with the Soviet Union. It must choose between the two mutually exclusive policies. Germany and the Soviet Union have been aware of this, but Kennedy's rhetoric showed no sign of such awareness.

Because of this divorce between words and actions, Kennedy failed to move us as did Roosevelt and Churchill. We would admire the intellectual and literary qualities of his speeches, but we would not be moved to tears and to action. Only once, listening to the Madison Square Garden speech on Medicare, have I felt at least a suggestion of the emotion that comes naturally, even today, when I listen to the recorded speeches of Roosevelt and Churchill.

Kennedy's intellectual curiosity, energy, and restlessness were also responsible for the disorderly procedures of his administration. Both books give many examples of this weakness, naturally without dwelling on them. Kennedy exposed himself to advice from a great variety of sources, official and unofficial. He would receive information from, and give orders to, second-level officials without informing their chiefs, and it happened that when an issue was later discussed in the formal councils of government, he had forgotten that he had already given an order contrary to his current position. From Schlesinger's discussion of Kennedy's Vietnam policy emerges a melancholy tale of ignorance, miscalculations, confusion, and absent-mindedness. The initial decision to withdraw support from Ngo Dinh Diem, for instance, derived from a Presidential misunderstanding of the actual position of the different executive departments concerned.

Kennedy's stewardship, then, bears the mark of extraordinary intellectual awareness, brilliance, and activity, far outpacing its political achievements. These very intellectual qualities impeded not only the ability to act effectively but even the determination so to act. Time and again, Kennedy demonstrated that he knew the score, but either he did not act at all upon that knowledge or he acted ineffectually. Thus he was fully aware, as we have seen, of the proper role of the military in the determination of policy, and he stood his ground in the Cuban crisis of 1962, at least on the issue of airstrikes, and compromised on the test-ban treaty. Yet even after he had burned his fingers in the Bay of Pigs, he accepted the military assessment—consistently wrong—of the situation in Vietnam and acted, however half-heartedly, upon it. He was by no means convinced of the merits of the MLF (the NATO multilateral seaborne nuclear force), but he allowed that outlandish scheme to become our European policy. Kennedy was aware of the defects of the State Department, but at the end of his tenure they were at least as pronounced as they had been at the beginning. He committed himself in words to great innovations in the field of civil rights and social reform, yet it remained for his successor to get them on the statute books.

What is impressive in Kennedy's administration, then, is the gap between intellectual awareness and actual performance, and it is the high degree of that awareness that makes the breadth of that gap starkly visible. Time and again, in Schlesinger's account, we are presented with a vivid picture of a new intellectual departure. But when we ask what happened in the real world as a consequence of that departure, we are left with nothing but a change in the intellectual climate. Kennedy, as it were, told us what the promised land would be like, but he hardly began to make that promise a reality.

It was not to be expected that the two books would dwell on these and similar weaknesses. Monuments present their subjects as heroes, simplified in their grandeur; but they must also make convincingly visible the positive qualities of their object. Judged by this standard, Schlesinger's book is far superior to Sorensen's. Schlesinger's is a surprisingly good book; for Schlesinger, a close personal friend of Kennedy's and a member of his court, could have been forgiven had he written a panegyric to his friend and chief. As it is, he has written a history of the Kennedy Administration that is first rate by even the most exacting standards. His narrative is informed by high intelligence, great knowledge, and excellent political judgment. His character sketches of Rusk, Harriman, and Bowles—to mention only three whose accuracy I can test against my personal knowledge—are brilliant, penetrating, and just. It is but occasionally marred by petty malice, as when the author refers to a brilliant Harvard sociologist who happens to look at the political scene from a different point of view as "a sociologist named Barrington Moore, Jr."

Schlesinger's book is not only first-rate history but also an impressive human document: Its prose is graceful and its human sympathy with its subject pervasive. It is sustained and carried forward by an underlying emotion, which bestows upon the work a melancholy nobility and envelops the reader.

Mr. Schlesinger writes from a distinct point of view. This is as it should be: All historians who are more than chroniclers or antiquarians must write so. It is the fatal flaw of Mr. Sorensen's book that he tries to write as if he did not have a point of view. He tries to let the facts speak for themselves. Yet the facts are mute if they are not filtered through a perceptive intelligence that distinguishes what is important from what is not, and establishes a hierarchical order, derived from its point of view, among the amorphous multitude of facts. His book is shapeless and has a pedantic quality. The index, for instance, contains references to Kennedy "and drinking," "as driver," "and gambling," "and prejudice," "as smoker," "and touch-football," "and coat-of-arms." All this and more appears in the book as undigested raw material, and the reader's curiosity about the significance of such items goes unsatisfied. Mr. Sorensen conceives of himself as a chronicler, not a historian. In consequence, over all-too-long stretches Mr. Sorensen's book is so boring as to be a sure cure for all but the hardiest cases of insomnia.

Yet Mr. Sorensen, too, cannot help having a point of view, and sometimes he lets himself go and says something profoundly revealing. Of Kennedy's decision not to send combat troops to Vietnam, Sorensen has this to say:

> Formally, Kennedy never made a final negative decision on troops. In typical Kennedy fashion, he made it difficult for any of the prointervention advocates to charge him privately with weakness. He ordered the departments to be prepared for the induction of combat troops, should they prove to be necessary. He steadily expanded the size of the military assistance mission (2,000 at the end of 1961, 15,500 at the end of 1963).

Such asides occasionally illuminate not only the past but also the present.

16

Lyndon B. Johnson

THE SUMMIT OF POWER

[March, 1966]

As Lord Bryce wrote in *The American Commonwealth,*

Someone has said that the American Government and Constitution are based on the theology of Calvin and the philosophy of Hobbes. This at least is true, that there is a hearty Puritanism in the view of human nature which pervades the instrument of 1787. It is the work of men who believed in original sin, and were resolved to leave open for transgressors no door which they could possibly shut. Compare this spirit with the enthusiastic optimism of the Frenchmen of 1789.

And compare it with the spirit and the political practices of the Americans of 1966!

The American system of government reposes upon two premises, which are in strict logic mutually exclusive: first, that the government must be strong enough to govern, and second, that it must not be so strong as to be able to abuse its powers. Thus on the one hand, the Constitution, supported by the dynamics of American politics, confers upon the President powers that, as the Founding Fathers recognized with awe, are the equal of those of any king. On the other hand, it confines those powers within a strait jacket of checks and balances, which interposes seemingly insuperable obstacles to their effective exercise. The dynamic interplay between these two contradictory principles has called forth a dialectic in which the Supreme Court and Congress have tried to shackle the President's powers while the President has tried to free himself of the shackles. In the short run, Congress and, more sporadically, the Supreme Court have been able to hamstring a succession of Presidents, to delay, water down, and divert their policies. In the long run, however, strong Presidents have known how to mobilize their constituency, that is, the nation as a whole, in support of their policies, and Congress and the Supreme Court have not been able to resist that combined pressure of President and people for long. Yet after each new departure, Congress and the Supreme Court have known how to reassert their limiting functions, calling forth a new Presidential initiative.

Thus the American political system has fulfilled the intentions of its founders: It continuously oscillates between the ascendancy of the President and that of Congress and the judiciary. It is indeed a system of checks and balances. In consequence, whenever the Presidential scales are heavy, one must wish for an increase in the weight of the congressional and judicial ones, and vice versa.

Today the President's power sweeps all before it. The Supreme Court has become his ally, and Congress stirs but half-heartedly and ineffectually in its bondage. The mass media of communications, with very few, and again half-hearted, exceptions, are at his service. The individual citizen, opposing the President's power and policies, fulfills the mission of keeping the voice of conscience alive, but as concerns his political effectiveness, he might as well talk to himself. When Theodore Roosevelt said that he had only one wish—to be for twenty-four hours President, Congress and the Supreme Court at the same time— he was daydreaming. Lyndon B. Johnson has achieved what Theodore Roosevelt was dreaming about, and for more than twenty-four hours.

What is so ominous in our present situation is not that the President has reasserted his powers but that in the process he has reduced all countervailing powers, political and social, to virtual impotence. What the Founding Fathers feared has indeed come to pass: The President of the United States has become an uncrowned king. Lyndon B. Johnson has become the Julius Caesar of the American Republic.

> Why, man, he doth bestride the narrow world
> Like a Colossus, and we petty men
> Walk under his huge legs and peep about
> To find ourselves dishonorable graves.

Men at some time are masters of their fates.
The fault, dear Brutus, is not in our stars,
But in ourselves, that we are underlings.

What makes opposition to such a concentration of power particularly burdensome is its exercise on behalf of aspirations that are the common possession of the great majority of the American people. If Lyndon B. Johnson were a selfish tyrant, protecting, say, "the interests" against the popular aspirations, the people, Congress, and the Court would cut down his powers, for they would find distasteful the ends on behalf of which those powers are being used. If a contemporary Mark Antony were to tell us what Caesar has done and will do for the people, who then would care that Caesar is "ambitious," that is, that he has, and seeks, too much power? *

But the benevolence of inordinate power must not blind us to the dangers inherent in such power, regardless of the intentions and purposes of its holder. For no man, however good and wise, is good enough and wise enough to be trusted with unlimited power. This is the perennial truth, which the Founding Fathers wrote into the structure of American government. "Th'abuse of greatness is, when it disjoins remorse from power." That is what Brutus feared in Caesar; that is what we must fear in Lyndon Johnson.

This astounding imbalance in the distribution of governmental powers has become obvious in Lyndon Johnson's Administration, but it has not been created by it. Comparing the powers of Napoleon III and the President of the United States, the London *Economist* remarked on January 27, 1866:

> The key-note of the American Constitution is the existence of an Executive which during its term of office is responsible to the people, which acts by its own volition, which can pursue if necessary a policy diametrically opposed to the wishes of those who elected it. That also is the key-note of the system established by the Second Empire. The President does as he pleases in all matters within his province just as the Emperor does, and like him is irresponsible to the Legislature—need not, indeed, explain to the representatives of the people his own official acts.

Almost a decade ago, a French writer, Amaury de Riencourt, referred to the President's "powers of truly Caesarian magnitude." The objective conditions for the ascendancy of Presidential powers have been long in the making; they only awaited a President willing and able to

---

* The people forced Lyndon Johnson out of political life when they became convinced that his power no longer served their interests.

make full use of them. First of all, the President has a natural advantage over the other branches of the government because he can take the initiative, he can act, while the others can only prevent and delay. This natural advantage of the executive has since the beginning of the Republic been particularly marked in the conduct of foreign policy.

Second, and most important, our age has witnessed a drastic shift in power from the people at large to the government, within the government from the legislative to the executive branch, and within the executive branch from the democratically responsible officials to certain technological elites. These shifts of power are the result of the revolutions in the technologies of transportation, communication, and warfare. The revolutions have transformed the business of government into an esoteric undertaking, unintelligible to the uninitiated and far removed from the life experiences of the man in the street. In consequence, political participation has given way to apathy, and "consensus" has taken the place of political controversy. It is the signal contribution Lyndon B. Johnson has made to American political life that he has taken advantage of these objective conditions with extraordinary skill and with an extraordinary taste for power. He has well-nigh exhausted the power potential of the modern Presidency, dwarfing the other branches of the government and reducing the people at large to the role of a helplessly approving bystander.

James MacGregor Burns has addressed himself in a previous book, *The Deadlock of Democracy*, to one force in the dialectic of American politics: the decline of Congress and the four parties operating within it. In this new book,* he deals with the other force, the President. But it must be said right away that he does not really come to grips with the central problem of imbalance created by the ascendancy of the President and the decline of Congress. This book does not have a single focus or thesis, but is rather in the nature of a collection of essays, approaching the modern Presidency from different angles. In one chapter, Professor Burns gives us a typology of the Presidency in terms of the Hamiltonian, Madisonian, and Jeffersonian models. In another chapter, he surveys the attitudes of the historians and political scientists toward the Presidency. Elsewhere again, he analyzes the different forces that are brought to bear upon the making of the President's decisions. In a last part, he assesses the modern Presidency in terms of its relation to the national purpose, individual liberty, representative government, and national leadership.

* James MacGregor Burns, *Presidential Government: The Crucible of Leadership* (Boston: Houghton Mifflin, 1966).

Professor Burns is fully aware of the enormous concentration of power in the hands of the modern President. "Thus the Presidency has absorbed the Cabinet, the executive departments, the Vice-Presidency. It has taken over the national party apparatus. Through consistently liberal appointments over the years it has a powerful influence on the doctrine of the Supreme Court. It has transformed the federal system." And Congress is tied to the President by the consensus on freedom and equality. Yet Professor Burns is not concerned with the perils of imbalance and the restoration of the system of checks and balances. Rather, he wants "to set to rest some of the fears of people that worry about the perils of the presidency":

> The old and accepted fears of presidential power . . . do not seem justified on the basis of actual experience. Increased authority and scope have not made the Presidency a tyrannical institution; on the contrary, the office has become the main governmental bastion for the protection of individual liberty and the expansion of civil rights. The office "represents" the electorate at least as effectively and democratically as does Congress, though in a different way. The office has attracted neither power-mad politicians nor bland incompetents but the ablest political leaders in the land, and these leaders in turn have brought the highest talent to the White House . . . as a general proposition, the stronger we make the Presidency, the more we strengthen democratic procedures and can hope to realize modern liberal democratic goals.

Professor Burns fears not an excess of power in the President but a lack of it.

> The real danger, it seems to me, is just the reverse—whether we have created such an institutionalized Presidency that the President will be smothered by the machinery, whether he will lose the vitality, independence and inventiveness necessary for creative leadership. . . .
> The danger . . . lies not in the failure to achieve our essential contemporary goals of freedom and equality but in their substantial realization and in the incapacity of presidential government to turn to new human purposes.

Professor Burns's mood thus seems to be utterly at variance with the distrust of power that has inspired the American Constitution and the American political system. Since Presidential power thus far has been in benevolent hands, Professor Burns argues, let us have more of it, and let us not worry about its possible abuse. But Professor Burns is not a son of the Enlightenment. He shares the failing of many academics who, for themselves, must be satisfied with the appearances of power: He is dazzled by real power. But interestingly enough, he is not blinded by it. In the same breath, he extols Presidential power and calls for opposition to it.

> The greatest need of the Presidency . . . will be an opposition that challenges presidential values, presidential methods, presidential institutions, that is eager to take power and to present its own definition of the national purpose. . . . The impotence of the opposition becomes more serious as presidential government becomes more powerful. No matter how benign a government may be, it will be tempted to manipulate public opinion, to try to dominate the flow of opinion, to cover up mistakes, and to cast doubt on the patriotism or at least the honesty of outside critics. The more that government represents a consensus, or claims to, the more tempted it may be to succumb to some of these tendencies.

Professor Burns here clearly recognizes the complementary relationship that exists between an overpowering Presidency and an impotent opposition. Thus he cannot have it both ways: He cannot, on the one hand, look complacently at unchallengeable Presidential power and even advocate its increase and, on the other, call for a strong opposition. He cannot at the same time yield to his fascination with Presidential power and satisfy his concern with democratic restraints. If he wants an all-powerful Presidency, he cannot want a strong opposition, and vice versa. Here is indeed the dilemma that the institution of the Presidency has posed from the very beginning for the theory and practice of American democracy.

An impotent opposition is a mere function of an all-powerful Presidency. To affirm the latter and to call for a strong opposition to check it is a contradiction in terms. It is the very existence of an all-powerful President that reduces the opposition to impotence. The opposition can criticize the President's conduct of the Vietnam war. But it can do nothing but talk, and it is the President who acts. By virtue both of the constitutional arrangements and the dynamics of American politics, the congressional opposition cannot prevail against the President as a parliamentary opposition can. The remedies are both broader and narrower than that.

On the one hand, the congressional opposition can mobilize the people at large, who will render their verdict in the next congressional and Presidential elections. On the other hand, Congress can refuse to grant the President the financial means with which to implement his policies. Both the general remedy of bringing about a change in policies by changing the policy-makers and the specific one of forcing the President to give up certain policies by withholding financial support from them must be nurtured by a spirit of political realism and of democratic independence, which recognizes both the need for Presidential powers and the necessity to restrain them. At this point we return to the wisdom and dilemma of the Founders: a system of checks and balances that will promote the effective use, and prevent the abuse, of Presidential power.

THE INNER WEAKNESS

[August, 1966]

This is by far the best book * written on the Presidency of Lyndon B. Johnson. It excels by the same psychological acumen, quality of political analysis, and wealth of detailed and in good measure new information as do the best books written on John F. Kennedy's stewardship. It is eloquent testimony to the ability of an adroit and discriminating journalist to penetrate the secrets of state, obvious classified documents not excluded. The author pays tribute to his sources of information, who "are men living or working somewhere within Lyndon Johnson's ken. . . . In any case, it is in the nature of things, above all in Lyndon Johnson's Washington, that anonymity is the price of a reasonable degree of candor about an incumbent President."

However, the book is not just a character study of Lyndon B. Johnson as the molder of American foreign policy. It is also a study of American foreign policy as conducted during the Presidency of Lyndon B. Johnson. What the book is really about is the impact of Lyndon B. Johnson's personality upon the conduct of American foreign policy. That impact has been dramatic and profound. The results have been gratifying in certain secondary matters; they have been disquieting in the great affairs of state. For better or for worse, the foreign policy of the United States is the foreign policy of Lyndon B. Johnson and bears the mark of his mind and character. What mind and character does the foreign policy of Lyndon B. Johnson reveal? It reveals a mind narrow in the substance of its knowledge and understanding, but superbly suited for the tasks of the tactician. It reveals a character of extraordinary complexity, beset by contrasts that render extremely hazardous the prediction of future courses of action.

* Philip L. Geyelin, *Lyndon B. Johnson and the World* (New York: Praeger, 1966).

The President's thinking on foreign policy has been molded by his domestic experience. As far as his modes of thought are concerned, he is incapable of making a distinction between foreign policy and domestic politics.

> He had heard the fashionable concepts, be they containment or disen-
> gagement or neutralism or parallelism. But he didn't speak that language
> because he did not think in it; he thought in analogies to the New Deal
> or Munich, to "another Korea" or "another Cuba"; the Mekong Basin
> was to be "another TVA."

Thus, as the author cleverly remarks, the President does not practice "foreign policy" so much as "foreign *politics*."

Yet, as James Byrnes found out as Secretary of State twenty years earlier, when, according to his own recollection, in the negotiations with the Soviet Union he used every trick he had learned in the Senate, but to no avail, the issues of foreign policy do not necessarily yield to the techniques that have proved successful in American politics. It is this experience that brought to the fore an innate trait of Lyndon B. Johnson's character: his deviousness and impetuosity. On the one hand, in the words of "a close but reasonably dispassionate associate," "This President wants the world to work to his clock." On the other hand, he came to realize that, in his own words, the trouble with foreigners "is that they're not like folks you were reared with."

One reaction to the gap between intent and reality was the attempt to obliterate the gap by misrepresenting reality. It brought out what Geyelin calls "the Munchausen in the man. His public and extemporaneous description of the carnage in Santo Domingo, during the April, 1965, uprising, went so far beyond the demonstrable facts that U.S. officials on the spot could only throw up their hands when badgered by newsmen for some supporting evidence." He could tell "one of the Senate's more serious students of foreign affairs that 'if we don't stop the Reds in South Vietnam, tomorrow they will be in Hawaii, and next week they will be in San Francisco.' " In the summer of 1965, he assured Senator Gruening that "the U.S. troops would be beginning to come home from Vietnam by the early part of 1966." Mr. Geyelin adds, "At that time, mid-1965, no responsible American official thought American troops could be withdrawing from Vietnam anything like that soon; the President didn't think so; and it is even doubtful if Senator Gruening really thought so." This "credibility gap" has become a persistent aspect of Johnson's conduct of American foreign policy.

In the field of action, Johnson has tried to fill the gap between intent and reality by forcing the American intent upon a recalcitrant world. When, on the occasion of John F. Kennedy's funeral, the Foreign Minister of Pakistan rose to depart after having delivered a message of condolence from his government, "Mr. Johnson ordered him to sit down and delivered an impromptu discourse on Pakistan's increasing antipathy to Western causes and growing preference for those of Peking . . . even U.S. officials present were taken aback." When anti-American riots broke out in Panama, "he startled his advisers by grabbing for the phone and calling the Panamanian President direct." Johnson's massive military reaction to the Dominican revolution is a matter of historical record.

Yet the experienced inadequacy of the policy of frontal assault brought out another trait of Johnson's character: a caution sometimes blending into inaction where action is called for. After more than a year in office, he complained about being "new here" and said that he was "in the position of a jackrabbit in a hailstorm, hunkered up and taking it." The MLF (the multilateral seaborne nuclear force) and Vietnam in different ways illustrate the point. The MLF had been sold to the reluctant policy-makers by a group of zealots in the State Department with the argument that it was necessary to satisfy our main European allies. When Johnson realized by way of firsthand contacts that these European desires were by and large a figment of the inflamed imagination of our men in the State Department, an explosion occurred in the White House, of whose magnitude Mr. Geyelin gives no more than an inkling, and the MLF was shelved for good. Since then, the President has been most careful not to be swayed by the anti-Gaullist emotionalism that before had been common in the highest councils of the White House and State Department, and to leave the initiative for change to de Gaulle while trying to preserve as much as possible of the *status quo*.

In Vietnam, the President has been trying to wage a limited war for the limited objective of a negotiated settlement. He has shied away from both liquidation and drastic escalation. While he has probably committed as many American troops as could be supported logistically at any particular time, he has been very slow—much too slow for the preferences of the Joint Chiefs of Staff—in expanding the war against the North. He has gone to extraordinary lengths to keep control over both the selection of targets and the kind and frequency of attacks.

While the conduct of the war in Vietnam provides an example of Johnson's caution, it also demonstrates the outstanding and most successful gift Johnson has brought to the conduct of American foreign policy: his unsurpassed mastery of the tactics of political manipulation. Domestically, he maneuvered himself into a position where he appeared to resist in equal measure the "escalators" and the "de-escalators," threading carefully and cautiously a middle course. In truth, he never ceased to escalate the war. But he did it almost imperceptibly, in unspectacular little steps. He never sided openly with the "escalators." Quite to the contrary, he made it appear that there was really no great difference between his position and that of his senatorial and academic critics. Did he not do everything to achieve peace with honor, and what alternative had his critics to suggest? When he had to take a major step on the road to escalation, he covered it up with a "peace offensive," aiming at, and in good measure succeeding in, taking the wind out of the sails of the opposition.

The conduct of foreign policy through the methods of domestic political manipulation was but temporarily successful with regard to Vietnam, because sooner or later that policy was bound to come up against the facts of international life, which do not yield to this kind of manipulation. A "peace offensive" may temporarily disarm the domestic opposition; internationally, if it is divorced from the facts of interests and power, it will be no more than a propagandistic flash in the pan. However, where the international component is insignificant or susceptible to manipulation, that method has proved stunningly successful.

Mr. Geyelin shows in impressive detail how the Johnson approach has succeeded in reforming our policy of foreign aid and marshaling our support for the Asian Development Bank. Here Johnson the magic tactician carried the day. More importantly, his tactical virtuosity was here at the service of objectives of whose soundness his domestic political experience had convinced him. Here he was on sure ground. Thus he could not fail to see that much of foreign aid neither served the interests of the United States nor met the needs of the recipient countries. Emotionally dedicated to the projection of the Great Society onto the international scene, especially as an alternative to military intervention, he was more keenly interested than were his subordinates in the economic potentialities and political advantages of an Asian Development Bank.

It is at this point that we approach the crux of the matter. What is the President's general conception of foreign policy? Through what kind of philosophic presuppositions does he try to understand the world and master it? What is the strategy his tactics are to serve? This book makes abundantly clear that it is impossible to give a coherent answer to these questions. For the most disparate elements coexist in the President's mind without any awareness on his part of their disparity. On the one hand, the President approaches foreign aid with the hard-headed calculations of the politician; on the other hand, he accepts a book as intellectually shallow and politically preposterous as Barbara Ward's *The Rich Nations and the Poor Nations* as the ultimate revelation of political wisdom. On the one hand, he is resolved not to repeat the error he thinks the United States committed in the 1930's: to encourage its enemies by failing to make its resolution clear from the outset. On the other hand, he can quote a passage from the Bible praising faith, virtue, knowledge, temperance, patience, Godliness, brotherly kindness, and love, and add: "That's what the Peace Corps is to me. That is what my religion is—that is what the Great Society is . . . and that is the foreign policy of the United States."

One has to read the book in order to experience the shattering impact of the variety of these contradictions, which operate upon the President's mind simultaneously or alternately without any coherence, let alone hierarchical order. This being the state of the President's mind, it is impossible to define the President's approach and predict the action he will take on the world scene. As an expert of the Johnson record put it: "You will search without success for any evidence of deep commitment or firm philosophy." "I have known him for fifteen years and I don't think I could predict what he will do in any given circumstance," is the judgment of "one of the White House men from Texas."

What restrains a President intellectually so constituted is the gnawing doubt about his own adequacy and the correctness of his policies. Thus he searches for reassurance outside himself in a consensus, as revealed by the public opinion polls. These polls perform for the President the same psychological function the flight of the birds or the configurations of the stars did for the statesmen of old. They put his doubts to temporary rest and enable him to act with assurance. They prove his policies right, because they approve of him.

Thus comes into play the other motive force of the President's nature: the urge to prove himself, to be a great President. Yet that urge toward greatness bespeaks his unacknowledged inner weakness. Greatness is a quality inherent in men, not something to be acquired like power and riches. It is not to be conquered, like a woman, by conscious effort; rather it is a gift of heaven that is given to those who deserve it (because in a sense they already have it), not to those who seek it. Those who seek greatness with frenzied effort reveal through their very frenzy that they are lacking what it takes to be great.

17

J. William Fulbright

[May, 1964]

Senator J. William Fulbright of Arkansas is one of the ablest and most responsible members of the Senate. He is one of an impressively large group of eminent Senators whose individual excellence has been overshadowed by the dismal spectacle that, because of antiquated procedures and domination by an antidemocratic minority, the Senate as a collective deliberating body frequently presents to the world. It was an ironic demonstration of this contrast between individual excellence and collective failure that Senator Fulbright delivered his important address on American foreign policy entitled "Old Myths and New Realities" on March 25, 1964, before a virtually empty Senate chamber.

Having hoped and urged since the 1950's that the Senate Foreign Relations Committee under the leadership of Senator Fulbright develop an American foreign policy of its own as a counterfoil to the official one, I ought to have welcomed Senator Fulbright's speech with unqualified enthusiasm. Instead, my reaction is mixed. I welcome the fact that Senator Fulbright has spoken out at all in criticism of our foreign policy. I admire the high intellectual qualities of the speech and I agree with much of what the Senator had to say, especially

174

on the nature of the Communist threat, Latin America, and the mythological nature of much of American thinking on foreign policy. But I must disagree with his central assumption, and I regret that he has not applied his analysis to certain acute and fundamental issues, more important than, say, the issue of Panama, on which he dwelt so extensively.

Senator Fulbright assumes that a "radical change" has occurred "in relations between and within the Communist and the free world" and that in consequence "the character of the cold war has, for the present, at least, been profoundly altered." It has been so altered "by the drawing back of the Soviet Union from extremely aggressive policies; by the implicit repudiation by both sides of a policy of 'total victory'; and by the establishment of an American strategic superiority which the Soviet Union appears to have tacitly accepted because it has been accompanied by assurances that it will be exercised by the United States with responsibility and restraint." Senator Fulbright's assessment of Cuba as a mere "nuisance" and not as "a grave threat to the United States" is predicated upon this assumption of a radical change in the foreign policies of the Soviet Union.

However, the correctness of that assumption, at the very least, has not been proved. It is of course true that there has been no direct military confrontation between the United States and the Soviet Union since the Cuban missile crisis of October, 1962. But can it be said that this is due to the Soviet Union's drawing back "from extremely aggressive policies"? Or could it not be said that our unwillingness to face up to Soviet challenges made a direct military confrontation unnecessary for the Soviet Union? Cuba and Cyprus are cases in point.

It cannot be too often repeated, since there is such a deep-seated unwillingness to face this simple and central fact, that the Soviet Union has achieved what it set out to achieve in the summer of 1962 and what we declared to be intolerable: the transformation of Cuba into a political and military base for the Communization of Latin America under the auspices of the Soviet Union. Official talk about Russian "technicians" and about "offensive" missiles, as distinct from other types, has obscured this fact, but it has not affected its existence.

Cyprus has been delivered into the hands of Makarios as a result of his brilliant and ruthless diplomacy, the deft maneuvering of the Soviet Union, the unwitting support of the United Nations, and the short-sightedness of American foreign policy. This is not the place to analyze in detail the fascinating power game that has been played for the control of Cyprus and that has ended in victory for Makarios and the Soviet Union. To support our argument, it is necessary only to point to the different aims and patterns of action with which the Soviet Union and the United States have been identified.

The Soviet Union has pursued two aims: to gain a foothold in the eastern Mediterranean and to weaken the relations between the NATO powers and Turkey, after Germany the most potent military force at the Western frontiers of the Soviet Union. The United States had one aim: to prevent an open military conflict between Greece and Turkey. Both sides have, paradoxically enough, succeeded. But the United States has succeeded only in terms of the pacifist goal it set itself, not in terms of its true interests, that is, to prevent the weakening of Western ties with Turkey and the transformation of Cyprus into a Mediterranean Cuba. We are here in the presence of a mode of action very similar to that which determined our Cuban policy in October, 1962. In other words, we are in the presence of a pattern that threatens to frustrate our foreign policies wherever it is applied.

In Cuba and Cyprus, both we and the Soviet Union were compelled to come to terms with the dilemma of being armed with nuclear weapons and having to avoid their use while protecting and promoting our respective interests with the threat of violence. Neither we nor the Soviet Union can afford to go to the brink of nuclear war; we must pull back before we get there. It is the risky art of foreign policy in the nuclear age to stop neither too early nor too late. A nation that stops too late destroys itself. A nation that stops too early sacrifices its interests to an exaggerated fear of war, and its policies end up by seeking peace at almost any price.

Concerning Hungary and Suez in 1956, Cuba in 1962, and Cyprus in 1964, American and Soviet foreign policies have consistently shown two different patterns: The Soviet Union has been willing to take greater risks than the United States, and consequently the Soviet Union has been more successful in protecting and promoting its interests. Why should the Soviet Union, then, not draw back from "extremely aggressive policies," since it is able to achieve its goals without them? Why should it, to give still another example, continue its pressure on the Western presence in Berlin, when the Berlin Wall has closed the gap in the Iron Curtain that the Western presence in Berlin had provided?

Since the days of Lenin, Soviet foreign policy has combined consistency in the pursuit of objectives with extreme flexibility in the choice of means. While the pursuit of objectives has been determined by national interest and political philosophy, means have changed in response to changes in the international environment. Thus Lenin's policy of world revolution was transformed by Stalin into the policy of "socialism in one country," and Stalin's policy of limited expansion into territories adjacent to the Soviet Union was transformed by Khrushchev into world-wide economic and ideological competition and support for "wars of national liberation." The foreign policy of the Soviet Union has indeed changed in recent years, and it is likely to change again, to become either more or less aggressive, as the case may be. If one wishes, one can say that in consequence "the character of the cold war has, for the present, at least, been profoundly altered." But it has not been ended, as Senator Fulbright himself points out, nor has its conduct by the Soviet Union become less dangerous to the West for having undergone yet another transformation.

In view of these arguments, little needs to be said about the other two points Senator Fulbright makes in this connection: implicit refutation of a policy of "total victory" and Soviet acceptance of American strategic superiority. The United States repudiated the policy of "total victory" even when it had a monopoly of nuclear weapons, and when that monopoly was replaced by the nuclear stalemate, such a policy became utterly irrational for both sides. The very term "stalemate," accepted by both sides, negates the idea of victory. It is similarly a misnomer to speak of "American strategic superiority" with regard to nuclear weapons. What we have is superiority in quantity and variety of nuclear weapons. It gives us at best a tactical advantage, but it cannot affect the strategic balance of terror. Nothing in Soviet military doctrine and dispositions supports the statement that the Soviet Union has "accepted" this superiority in reliance upon our assurances to use it "with responsibility and restraint." Quite to the contrary, the Soviet Union has tried to counteract it with a small number of multimegaton weapons and an elaborate system of anti-aircraft and anti-missile defenses. Least of all does the Soviet Union rely upon our "responsibility and restraint" in the use of nuclear weapons, a phrase I take to be a reference to counterforce strategy. For the Soviet Union, in both its military doctrine and its dispositions, has emphatically denied the possibility of limiting the use of nuclear weapons to military targets.

While the radical change in the relations between the United States and the Soviet Union that Senator Fulbright postulates turns out to be a myth rather than a reality, the inability of our foreign policy to anticipate new conditions, or at least to adapt to them when they have occurred, is indeed an established fact. Our alliance policies provide a prime example of that inability. We were unable to rebuild the structure of an originally sound alliance, such as NATO, when its foundations crumbled, and we were equally unable to divest ourselves of the burden of an originally unsound alliance, such as that with Pakistan, when it became an obvious hindrance to the protection and promotion of our interests.

Outside observers have been calling attention since the second half of the 1950's to the impending crisis of NATO, caused by the economic and political recovery of the nations of Western Europe and, more particularly, by the ability of the Soviet Union to counter the American nuclear threat with a threat of its own. Yet when that crisis became acute in the aftermath of de Gaulle's press conference of January 14, 1963, we responded with shocked surprise and righteous indignation, not with constructive proposals taking cognizance of the objective character of the crisis, which de Gaulle brought into the open but did not create. And so it has remained to this date. The only positive contribution we have made to the restoration of the Atlantic Alliance has been the multilateral seaborne nuclear force, and the character of that device is itself eloquent commentary upon our technical ingenuity and the sterility of our political thinking. For this device attempts not so much to restore the Atlantic Alliance but to give our European allies the illusion of participating in nuclear decisions while at the same time isolating France. It is, in truth, a subterfuge, one that uses a costly, useless, and dangerous military device to bypass a political problem of vital importance to the Western world.

The alliance with Pakistan has been from the outset a useless and counterproductive instrument of American foreign policy; it could truly be called a diplomatic act against nature. For the military forces of Pakistan, built up with our massive support, have as their primary target not the Soviet Union or China, but India. Yet we have an obvious vital interest in the political and economic success of India, an interest far transcending any other we have in Asia. Our military support of Pakistan has forced India to divert a proportionate fraction of its scarce resources to military purposes, and we, anxious to prevent India's collapse, have been compelled to replace at least a part of those diverted resources with foreign aid.

It was possible to dismiss this armaments race with ourselves as a costly absurdity until China invaded India and, in the aftermath of that invasion, Pakistan reached a political and, it is generally believed, a military understanding with China. Everything points to the likelihood that China will repeat the invasion on a larger scale as soon as it has solved its logistic problems. It is also obvious that, when India is fighting for its life, Pakistan will bring the weapons supplied by us into the camp of its enemies while we support India—by improvising a crash program after the invasion has started.

All this has been known for almost a decade, first by conjecture and then by empirical observation. Why is it that, aware of the facts and of what action they require, we cling with desperate tenacity to policies that, if they ever served our purposes, have now lost their usefulness? So it has been with NATO, and so it has been with India and Pakistan. Our Latin American policies provide another example. During the election campaign of 1952, John Foster Dulles dedicated a whole speech to Latin America, chiding the Truman Administration for its neglect and pointing to the dangers our traditional interests were facing in that part of the world. His concern was then shared by at least some of the professionals in the Department of State. But it took nine years to translate that concern into action.

We are here in the presence of another pattern of our foreign policy: the inability to act decisively in anticipation of a crisis rather than in response to it. What accounts for this pattern, which Senator Fulbright calls "a malady of chronic and excessive caution"? The Senator mentions the fear of public opinion, and he says wisely that "an effective foreign policy is one which concerns itself more with innovation abroad than with conciliation at home." Yet the foreign-service officer must of necessity take his cue from the Secretary of State and the President. If the President subordinates foreign policy to domestic policies, and if the Secretary of State would rather administer established policies than create new ones, there remains nothing for the Department of State to do but implement the defective policies. Thus the responsibility for a foreign policy that has become the slave of a leaderless public opinion lies with the President and, to a lesser extent, with the Secretary of State.

Another factor, however, deserves consideration: the size and organization of the Department of State. The Department of State is absurdly overstaffed, as are its rivals for the determination of American foreign policy, the Department of Defense and the Central Intelligence Agency. The elimination of half of its employees could by itself not fail to improve its operations. Overstaffing means that, say, ten people—able, mediocre, and incompetent—spend twenty man-hours preparing a paper on which one able or even mediocre man would spend two. As it is, say, three members of the group of ten will prepare different versions of the paper, which will be shuffled back and forth over ten different desks to be revised, amended, and commented upon. These versions will then be discussed in meetings of the whole group until finally the whole collective effort will produce a paper more likely than not inferior to what could have emerged from the desk of one able or mediocre official. The same process may be repeated a couple of times on different levels of the bureaucratic hierarchy, both within the Department of State and between it and other agencies of the executive branch.

This inflated collective method of policy-making has three results, all detrimental to the new departures Senator Fulbright wants our foreign policy to take. First of all, it makes sustained thinking impossible. It may seem like belaboring the obvious to say that great political decisions require sustained and solitary thought. Field Marshal Montgomery, in a series of television broadcasts about his campaigns of World War II, stated as the first condition for the success of a commander the preservation of his ability to think, for which purpose he must keep his staff small and keep visitors away from his headquarters. Yet I dare say that in the conduct of our foreign policies nobody, from the President to the lowliest desk officer, meets that requirement. I have watched high officials of our government receiving visitors and paying visits, convening and going to committee meetings, placing and receiving telephone calls, reading, dictating, and signing papers from morning to night, day after day, six or seven days a week. I am told that an official was allowed five minutes to brief the President on an important issue of foreign policy. If anyone were to suggest that the President, the Secretary of State, the under secretaries, and the assistant secretaries ought to have time to reflect for hours on the great issues that require decision, Washington would probably consider him a practical joker. But great decisions cannot be made without such thought. As Napoleon put it: "I meditate a great deal. If I seem always equal to the occasion, ready to face what comes, it is because I have thought the matter over a long time before undertaking it. I have anticipated whatever might happen. It is no genius which suddenly reveals to me what I ought to do or say in any unlooked-for circumstances, but my own reflection, my own meditation."

Second, the collective method of policy-making is hostile to new departures because it tends toward the establishment of consensus at the lowest common denominator. The official who has the insight and courage to propose a break with an outworn policy will find himself hemmed in by colleagues who are less endowed with those qualities, who prefer inconspicuous continuation of the *status quo* to risky experiments. Both intellectually and politically, continuation of the *status quo* is more convenient than innovation, so the prospective innovator is likely to lose out to colleagues who are fearful of innovation.

Third and last, the collective method diffuses responsibility. Since nobody is responsible for anything in particular, nobody can be blamed for failure or praised for success. I have often wondered, sometimes aloud, what happens to a foreign-service officer whose judgments prove consistently wrong, and I have been told time and again that he is transferred to another bureau or another diplomatic post. The collectivity, as it were, absorbs him and makes his incompetence in a sense innocuous. But the same happens to the innovating deviationist whose judgment is prematurely right. The collectivity pulls the incompetent up—and the innovator down—to its own level of unoffending mediocrity. After all, innovation is typically the achievement of one man who takes the risks and seeks the rewards, not of a faceless collectivity.

Thus when one reflects with Senator Fulbright on the need for American foreign policy to adapt itself to new realities, one becomes aware, first of all, of how hard it is to distinguish between old myths and new realities. One man's new reality is likely to be another man's myth, old or new. But even agreement on that vital distinction is but the first inconclusive step in the reform of American foreign policy. For, as the examples we have cited show, intellectual awareness is by no means tantamount to action. Action will continue to follow its established grooves, if the Department of State remains an elephantine colossus, if the Secretary of State prefers administering established policies to creating new ones, and if the President does not educate the people in the realities of a new age.

18

Robert F. Kennedy

[August, 1968]

The emotions have had their day. We have witnessed a funeral that for most of us must have been the most moving we ever saw, quite different in its monumental privacy from the somber pomp and circumstance of John F. Kennedy's state funeral. The grief of a family was made visible to millions. We went with the widow to St. Patrick's at five o'clock in the morning, watched her at solitary prayer, and followed her to the coffin, averting our gaze when she embraced that part of it where the shattered head of her husband lay.

Yet even in those moments of private grief, which the nation shared, it was impossible not to think of politics. The President of the United States paid his respects three times to the dead man—at St. Patrick's, at the Washington railroad station, and at the graveside—but he had hated that man as that man had hated him. Robert Kennedy regarded Lyndon Johnson as a usurper. He had become Vice President by a fluke, by accepting an offer that he was not expected to accept and that was seriously intended for Stuart Symington. He had been elevated to the Presidency through an assassin's bullet. It was by virtue of both accidents that Lyndon Johnson held supreme power. Thus Robert Kennedy contemplated not attending the first Cabinet meeting of

President Johnson and then made it a point to be late; the symbolic significance of that late entry was not lost upon the President. And in the early morning of the day of President Johnson's inauguration, Robert Kennedy went to his brother's graveside, and he went there again in the afternoon for the benefit of photographers. He held a grudge against his brother-in-law Sargent Shriver for continuing to work for Lyndon Johnson.

What Robert Kennedy expected and worked for, Johnson feared and tried to prevent; that his tenure of office would be an interregnum between the Presidencies of two Kennedys. Thus Johnson said in 1963 that he would never have a Kennedy on his ticket, and in 1967, in a face-to-face confrontation, he threatened Robert Kennedy with political extinction within six months. To prevent Robert Kennedy from becoming President of the United States had become one of his major political goals, and now, for the second time, not his efforts but an assassin's bullet had settled the issue. How galling must it be for a proud man to contemplate that he owes his elevation to supreme power and the elimination of a hated rival to the accident of two assassinations!

Robert Kennedy, like Lyndon Johnson, was a beneficiary of his brother's assassination. The most precious inheritance John F. Kennedy left him was the myth of his unfinished stewardship. Nobody can say what President Kennedy would have accomplished had he lived. But it is certainly fair to say, as I did at the time, that while he lived as President he achieved little of substance. His domestic program was hopelessly stymied in Congress. In foreign policy, he was responsible for the fiasco of the Bay of Pigs; the Alliance for Progress never got off the ground; he achieved a tactical success and suffered a strategic defeat in the Cuban missile crisis; he started our serious involvement in Vietnam by increasing the number of military advisers from 400 to 16,000; he endeavored to counter the disintegration of the Atlantic Alliance with the stillborn multilateral seaborne nuclear force. Only the limited test-ban treaty and the development of mobile conventional military forces can be counted real successes. The rest was rhetoric—well-chosen, knowing, forward-looking words, political literature of a high order, from which no action followed.

Nevertheless, those words raised the great issues of the day, of which the preceding Administration was not even aware, and proposed action to meet them. They engendered the expectation of great deeds and were for the time being taken as a substitute for them. Thus when John F. Kennedy died without having performed these deeds, it was easy to hold the accident of premature death rather than intrinsic disability responsible for that deficiency. And it was likewise easy to expect from the living brother the achievement of the deeds that the dead President's rhetoric had promised. The public mind, as well as his own, identified Robert Kennedy with his dead brother: what John Kennedy would have done had he lived, Robert Kennedy was called upon to do in his stead. This was his mission, ordained by fate. For him to aspire to the Presidency, then, was not a matter of choice but an ineluctable duty, dictated not so much by personal ambition and love of kin as by the natural order of things. As a king's oldest son becomes king on his father's death, so Robert had to succeed John as a matter of course. So he saw himself, and so he was seen by untold millions at home and throughout the world.

This identification of the living with the dead brother was in an unintended and ironic sense to the point. For while Robert was lacking in the literary and rhetorical gifts and the intellectual sophistication in which John Kennedy had excelled, both had in common the inability to mold political forces, which they could not control, in support of their aims. In other words, both were lacking in the quality that distinguishes the statesman from the politician. For this reason, both were adept at organizing election campaigns where they were in control of their workers as a general is in control of his army. And for the same reason, both were indifferent members of the Senate—and Robert was a bored and unhappy one to boot—because neither knew how to deal with senators, who are not to be ordered about but must be induced by peculiar senatorial diplomacy to support a measure advocated by one of them. They must be approached, very much like sovereign rulers, on the basis of equality. They must be flattered, argued with, threatened, promised and given advantages. And all this has to be done on a strictly pragmatic basis. Senators, like nations, to paraphrase Palmerston, have no permanent friends and no permanent enemies, but only permanent interests.

This approach to politics was alien to both John and Robert Kennedy. They were imperial characters who found it difficult to relate themselves to others on the basis of equality. They wanted victory for themselves and defeat for the enemy, but not compromise which by definition is less than victory. They could give orders, rewarding those who obeyed and punishing those who did not. They had permanent friends and permanent enemies, and they never forgot who was who. The courtiers of John F. Kennedy were accepted by Robert as a matter of course. He never repudiated Joe McCarthy, and he never forgave Eugene McCarthy for nominating Adlai Stevenson in Los Angeles in 1960.

Thus Robert Kennedy was an efficient campaign manager, campaigner, and Attorney General; for in all those capacities he was in control. Yet when he had to deal with the uncontrollable warring factions of the Democratic Party in New York State he was helpless; his intervention in the gubernatorial campaign of 1966 was a fiasco. And he made a mess of things when he tried to come to terms with William Manchester, author of *The Death of a President*, who could not be controlled either.

This disability, common to both brothers, was aggravated in the case of Robert by his moralistic approach to life in general and politics in particular. His moral revulsion against evil, manifesting itself in the persecution of wrongdoers and sympathy for the victims of wrongdoing, was one of the two genuine determinants of his being. Thus he persecuted Hoffa, the head of the Teamsters, with single-minded ferocity, and he opened his heart to the poor at home and abroad. These simple and clear-cut positions, emotionally attractive in themselves, require in the actor an absolute certainty of what is right and what is wrong. Nobody who has deeply reflected upon the issues of morality can have such certainty. But, then, Robert Kennedy was not reflective but emotional. He saw wrong-doing and suffering and was revolted by them. He had to do something about it. But since he was unaware of the ambiguity of moral judgments, he was also unaware of the moral and pragmatic ambiguity of the political act performed in emotional response to a moral judgment. His approach was morally fundamentalist and politically simplistic: Put Hoffa behind bars, and stamp out poverty throughout the world. Yet it never occurred to him that such remedial action would call forth new problems and new evils, which a statesman must take into account before embarking upon it.

The other genuine determinant of Robert Kennedy's being was dedication to personal success. He was not a crusader for a cause nor the protagonist of a political philosophy. He wanted to win the election he contested. He might, in the process of that contest, pick up a cause that could be used for increasing his electoral chances, then drop it as soon as it had done its work. But he would not allow a cause, or even an emotion, to stand in the way of his personal success. Thus in 1964 his hatred of Johnson did not prevent him from actively seeking the Vice-Presidential nomination and, after being rebuffed, the ambassadorship to Vietnam. He would be cautious, calculating, and ambiguous rather than indignant if such a posture appeared to enhance his chances for personal success. His attitude toward the Vietnam war and his entry into the Presidential primaries are cases in point.

Some Senators, such as Church, Fulbright, Gruening, and Morse, opposed our military involvement in the Vietnam War from the outset. Kennedy was not among them. When the first wave of protest struck the country in 1965 in the form of teach-ins, Kennedy did not join it. He did not go on record as opposed to the war itself but only voiced doubts about its tactics. One of his most prestigious advisers, Arthur Schlesinger, took the side of the Johnson Administration. Another of his principal advisers, Richard Goodwin, in 1966 published a book advocating continuation of the war in South Vietnam. When, in 1966, sixteen Senators addressed a letter to the President asking for the continuation of the bombing pause, Kennedy's name was not among them. He spoke out clearly against Administration policies for the first time in February, 1966. He dismissed military victory and withdrawal and advocated a negotiated settlement that would allow the Viet Cong "participation" in the government and would exclude "domination or internal conquest." For more than a year following this speech, Kennedy kept silent on Vietnam. When he spoke again, in March, 1967, he reiterated his previous proposal, amplified by the suspension of the bombing of North Vietnam and the commitment of both sides not to escalate the war. We are not concerned here with the intrinsic merits of those proposals but only with their relation to the position of the Administration. They appear as modifications of that position rather than clear-cut alternatives to it. Their motivation has been formulated by William V. Shannon in these terms:

> His cold shrewdness and his passion enabled Kennedy to abandon his previous commitment to the Vietnam War. Like his father, he has a speculator's ability to size up a proposition and decide whether it looks like a winner. No emotion, no ideological fixation, no wishful romanticism clouds or confuses this analytic process. Self-interest is the controlling criterion. . . . Passion, too, played its part. Robert Kennedy's dislike of Lyndon Johnson, bordering upon hatred, made it easier for him to change his mind about Vietnam the more he thought of it as Mr. Johnson's war. . . . Actions in Vietnam that Robert Kennedy would have stoutly defended if JFK had ordered them became suspect in his eyes since their author was LBJ.*

A clear example of cautious calculation—and miscalculation—is provided by the manner in which Robert Kennedy entered the Presidential primaries. It is of course axiomatic that in normal times it is a

---

* William V. Shannon, *The Heir Apparent: Robert Kennedy and the Struggle for Power* (New York: Macmillan, 1967).

hopeless, if not suicidal, undertaking to contest the renomination of an incumbent President. Kennedy complied with this axiom and probably went beyond it by repeatedly endorsing the re-election of the incumbent President. The axiom required abstention from active competition; it did not require a declaration on television to the effect that "I have great admiration for President Johnson." Yet when McCarthy's victory in the New Hampshire primary showed that the times were not normal, Kennedy recalculated his chances and decided to compete for the Presidential nomination.

It is this conjunction of moral certainty about right and wrong with calculating opportunism that accounts for Kennedy's reputation for ruthlessness. The issue, however, is more complex than that. If Kennedy had gone after Hoffa the way he did for purely selfish reasons, he would indeed deserve the epithet. However, if one sees oneself as the champion of justice against a monstrous evil, does not the nobility of the end and the magnitude of its denial justify the extraordinary character of the means used? Furthermore, if unconsciously the defense of right against wrong merges with the promotion of one's own political success, so that personal success and the triumph of right come close to being interchangeable, is one not entitled to be as "ruthless" in, say, misrepresenting the record of Senator Keating in the campaign of 1964 as one was in disregarding procedural niceties in the prosecution of Hoffa? Such argumentation naturally does not concern itself with the fundamental question as to whether the democratic ethic permits anyone to be so certain in distinguishing right from wrong in the pursuit of personal success. Among the many quotations Robert Kennedy used, you are not likely to find what Cromwell said to the representatives of the Church of Scotland.*

The same conjunction of an emotionally founded moral certainty with opportunistic calculation accounts for Kennedy's lack of intellectual perception. The vital force of his being was in his emotions, not in his mind. When, in November, 1965, he went down into the coal mines of Lota in Chile and saw the misery of the miners, all Communists, he reacted in these words, "If I worked in this mine I'd be a Communist too." That is to say, he implicitly affirmed the moral right and political necessity of revolution. He even affirmed it explicitly by telling his student audience in Lima, Peru, that "the responsibility of our times is nothing less than a revolution. . . . We can affect its character; we cannot alter its inevitability." Yet while he was in the government he was the main promoter of counterinsurgency, intended to counter Communist revolution. That technique has proved to be utterly useless in Vietnam. Its failure derives from a profound misun-

* See page 40.

derstanding of the nature of contemporary revolutions. For it is absurd to expect that these revolutions, nourished by the vital national and social aspirations of great masses of people, can be successfully opposed by a military technique developed by academic theorists and applied by military tacticians.

When Robert Kennedy, after his trip to Latin America, presented his philosophy and program for Latin America in May, 1966, to the Senate in a long and thoroughly researched address—so long as to have to be delivered in two parts—he again missed completely the fundamental problem of revolution. Robert Kennedy had a personal stake in the Alliance for Progress as one of his late brother's great innovations in foreign policy. Yet he failed to see—and he was, of course, not alone in this failure—the fatal ailment that had paralyzed the Alliance for Progress from the very outset. That ailment was the attempt to bring about radical social, political, and economic change through the instrumentality of oligarchies whose political power derives from the *status quo* and who have therefore a vital interest in preventing such radical change. Thus his emotional moral reaction to the evils he saw in Latin America and elsewhere in the underdeveloped world was translated into conventional political proposals that had proved to miss the basic political point in the past and, hence, could not succeed in the future, even if they were supported with greater efforts and more refined techniques.

However, and most importantly, that selfsame emotional moral reaction, which proved to be a dubious asset for Robert Kennedy as a politician, became the source of his final triumph as a charismatic leader. He entered the Presidential primaries as a calculating politician who was quick to see a miscalculation and set it right, and he was still one in the Indiana campaign, when he played down to the prejudices of the electorate. Yet when he made his last speech in Los Angeles, he had become the adored leader of millions of disillusioned people and the incarnation of the hopes of the disinherited of America. His capacity for moral indignation had found its cause, the voice of moral protest had found its audience, the malaise that ailed America appeared to have found its cure. In this last respect, Robert Kennedy came to perform the same function in 1968 his brother had performed in 1960. That is, he faced the problems of the day with the rhetoric appropriate to them rather than with that of yesterday or the day before. This was the great advantage he had over Humphrey and Nixon.

It is, of course, idle to speculate as to what Robert Kennedy would have made of this great asset had he lived. There is no doubt that he was ill at ease bearing the mantle of the charismatic leader. His hair was turning gray, his face became deeply lined, his hands were trembling, and there was frequently a stridency in his voice and a tenseness beneath his composure that one does not expect to find in a man destined to be a charismatic leader. Was he the driver on a road he had freely chosen, or was he driven by a fate he could not escape?

But even if Robert Kennedy had not fulfilled the promise that millions of people saw in him, he would have performed a vital function for America. He noticed three months before his death that the mood of the country and, more particularly, of large groups within the Democratic party does not conform to the traditional pattern of the two-party system. Large masses of the people are aware of the bankruptcy of the philosophies, the programs, and the policies abroad and at home by which we have been governed. They are aware of the unbridgeable gap that exists between the reality of the issues with which we must come to terms and the modes of thought and action by which we are being governed. They think that it is time for a change, not just in the personnel of the government—replacing Mr. Johnson with either Mr. Humphrey or Mr. Nixon—but in the modes of thought and action themselves. Kennedy gave a voice to these aspirations.

That this voice has been forever stilled is the great loss the country has sustained. Even if Robert Kennedy had lived, in all likelihood he would not have been nominated in 1968. Yet this passionate voice, contemporary and addressing the future, would have reminded us that there exists an alternative to Humphrey's liberalism of thirty years ago and to the timeless opportunism of Nixon. It would have been proof to those of us who were ready to opt out of the American political system altogether at the beginning of this year, not only that there are alternatives to the obsolete philosophies and policies of the powers-that-be, but also that there are men who are willing to search for those alternatives and put them into effect.

Only Eugene McCarthy today fulfills that function. That so relatively ineffectual a campaigner can have such a success is a measure of the extent and the depth of the dissatisfaction in the ranks of the Democratic party. It is also the measure of the success Robert Kennedy might have achieved had he lived—and indeed, what might still happen if a sufficient number of disenchanted voters demonstrate to the managers of the Democratic convention that Humphrey cannot win.

Conversely, McCarthy's success points to the danger the Republic now faces. If these masses, deprived of a charismatic leader, should find McCarthy's candidacy faltering, they would have no place in the American political system as now constituted. The unrepresentative character of American democracy might well become so extreme as to be intolerable to them. In consequence, they may either sink into political apathy or attack the system from without. In either case, the political force most likely to benefit from the disintegration of the Kennedy camp would be the defenders of the *status quo*, which, in view of the widespread disaffection from it, can be defended only by fascist means. It goes without saying that such a defense would be undertaken in the name of law and order and democracy.

Thus the myth of Robert Kennedy is likely to be very similar to that of his late brother: the leader who showed us the promised land and would have led us into it had he lived. On the strength of the historical record, one can say only that they knew there was a promised land, and knew also that it wasn't the one we were living in. It will forever remain a moot question as to whether they would have been able to lead us into it had they lived. But that intellectual and emotional awareness of the distance between the actual conditions of American life and what they ought to be set them apart from Nixon and Humphrey. For Nixon is convinced that the *status quo* is all we need to have, promoted by private enterprise and protected by fiscal responsibility and the police. Humphrey, on the other hand, enthusiastically believes that there is nothing wrong with America that could not be remedied by liberal reform. His call for a domestic Marshall Plan shows clearly the limits of his political imagination. For, as I pointed out in 1956,

> while the Marshall Plan has regenerated the productive capacity of Western Europe, it has left its economic, social, and political structure by and large intact. The dangers to the stability and strength of Western Europe which have grown in the past from the defects of that structure have continued to grow because those defects were not repaired. The Marshall Plan almost completely lost sight of those roots of instability and unrest, which antedated the emergency and were bound to operate after it was over.

(This statement, by the way, has been used by the White House, with Mr. McGeorge Bundy as the spokesman, to show that I am "opposed" to the Marshall Plan.) What was true of the original Marshall Plan would also be true of Humphrey's domestic version.

Their breadth of vision set the two dead Kennedys apart from their contemporary rivals. For that alone, they have earned the gratitude of their countrymen, and no myths are needed to evoke or deepen it.

19

Eugene McCarthy

[August, 1968]

Talking to Eugene McCarthy again after an interval of a couple of years, one is first of all impressed with the absence of any effect of the momentous events of 1968 upon his personality and behavior. Most public men—and, for that matter, most private men as well—play roles that either they or others or events have assigned to them. Their dreams, their ambitions, or the functions they are called upon to perform compel them to make it appear that they are different from what they actually are. Look at Humphrey, Nixon, Reagan, Rockefeller, Wallace (the order is strictly alphabetical): They all play, in different admixtures, the role of the leader, the savior, the man of action. I know a public figure of great eminence, famous for his humility, whom another public figure of similar eminence has called the proudest humble man in America!

What has always struck me in Eugene McCarthy's personality, and what struck me again the other day with renewed force, is the complete absence of any visible contrast between the public role he plays and the man he is. There is no pretense, not even the intimation of an attempt to impress, and there is in consequence the impact of an extraordinary measure of poise, serenity, and inner strength. For only

191

the man who either is not sure of himself or seeks rewards beyond his merits is compelled to conceal his true self and deck it out in borrowed robes. More particularly, those who have dedicated their lives to the pursuit of power and who compete for the highest political prize must make it appear that they are seeking power not for its own sake but only as an instrument for the attainment of different and higher goals.

What the other candidates for the Presidential nomination are compelled to pretend is an obvious fact in McCarthy's case. It would certainly be false to say that McCarthy has no sense of power. He would have liked to get the Vice-Presidential nomination in 1964, and he would like to get the Presidential nomination in 1968. But he wants the nomination this year not because he has dedicated his life to the pursuit of supreme power but because the events of this year have shown him that he can perform three functions for America no other candidate appears to be able to perform. He can restore a philosophy of government and of the American purpose that is in tune with the genius of the American people. By doing so, he can move large masses of the American people and, more particularly, of the younger generation back into active participation in the democratic processes. Finally, he presents clear-cut alternatives to the policies of the present Administration as well as of his competitors, especially in the field of foreign policy.

Once he has achieved these goals he would be willing, as he made clear to me, to relinquish supreme power, that is, he might not seek re-election after one term. Immediately after the New Hampshire primary and before Robert Kennedy declared his candidacy, McCarthy tried to persuade Kennedy to stand aside by arguing that he wanted the Presidency only for one term and that Kennedy would have his chance four years later. This instrumental and restrictive conception of supreme power, an organic outgrowth of McCarthy's ethos, was met with startled disbelief by his rival, whose conception of supreme power was quite different.

It is in accord with these personal qualities that what McCarthy has to say about foreign policy is far from startling. It is common sense restored to its rightful place. The unspectacular character of McCarthy's foreign policy is, moreover, accentuated by the combination of neglect and misguided activity characteristic of the foreign policies of the Johnson Administration, which resulted from the lack of a sense of national priorities. A bloody anti-Communist crusade in Asia is obviously more spectacular than its liquidation, as an insane act is more spectacular than a sane one. To advocate the latter is not a mark of originality.

Rather it is a mark of that very sanity which ordinarily we tend to take for granted and which we miss and long for only when it is conspicuously absent.

The general tone of McCarthy's foreign policy is indicated in the title of his book *The Limits of Power* and in its first sentence: "If this book has a principal theme, it is that our foreign policy should be more restrained and, insofar as prudent judgment can determine, more closely in keeping with the movement of history." McCarthy does not believe in the philosophy of American paramountcy, as propounded by Professor Brzezinski, until recently an enthusiastic supporter of the Vietnam War and the principal foreign-policy adviser of Vice President Humphrey. This philosophy has whittled down Henry Luce's "American Century" of twenty years ago to an "American Decade," during which the United States is supposed to have a preponderance of power sufficient to provide stability and order to the world. McCarthy does not see the United States as standing outside history, the chosen nation enabled by a unique combination of virtue and power to reform the world. Rather, the United States is the creation of history, as are the other nations, and therefore must try to change the world from within the historical process.

In this view, the solution of our domestic problems is in the long run more important for our ability to change the world than the power we are able to bring to bear directly upon other nations. Thus we serve our goal of promoting racial justice throughout the world better by setting an example in the ordering of our race relations at home than by exerting pressure on South Africa. The American mission is not to dominate but to lead. Leadership for McCarthy does not mean to impose one's will upon unwilling citizens and nations but to educate and direct, thereby releasing the energies of peoples and institutions.

This conception of the American mission abroad harks back to the concept that originally informed American foreign policy: America as a model for other nations to emulate. This conception of the American mission at home postulates a philosophy of the Presidency radically at variance with that practiced by the Johnson Administration. This Administration has indeed tried to dominate, both abroad and at home, and failed. It has been unable to impose its will upon Vietnam, which it made the test of American power, and in the process it squandered that most precious and uniquely American asset, the moral attractiveness of America. Domestically, President Johnson has tried to dominate both the government and the people by the same methods of manipulation that stood him in good stead when he was Majority Leader of the Senate. In consequence, he lost control of the two most important congressional committees, Ways and Means and Foreign Relations, and he lost popular support to such an extent as to make an attempt at renomination and re-election too hazardous for him to undertake.

The McCarthy philosophy of the Presidency does not make for a weak President, nor does McCarthy's philosophy of foreign policy argue for a return to isolationism. Both objections have been advanced, but they are without foundation. What McCarthy seeks is a different type of President from the type to which we have been accustomed, a President who is strong in exactly those qualities in which President Johnson was deficient. We know from experience that a hyperactive President, concerned with the details of the execution of policy, is not necessarily an effective one. McCarthy stresses the historical functions great Presidents have performed: framing and supervising long-range policies, educating the people, embodying their aspirations, and stimulating the creative forces latent in society.

As for American foreign policy, McCarthy is convinced that the great innovations that radically transformed American policy in the spring of 1947—the policy of containment, the Truman Doctrine, the Marshall Plan—are irreversible. But he also believes that these policies suffer from two major deficiencies. They have not been adapted to drastically changed circumstances, and they have been corrupted by a disproportionate emphasis upon military measures. This is particularly true of NATO. McCarthy, however, advocates our continuing military presence in Europe for political reasons, that is, in order to support the Western orientation of Germany and to prevent its isolation.

In Asia, McCarthy favors the normalization of our relations with China, of which diplomatic recognition is, of course, an indispensable precondition. Yet in contrast to those who advocate the containment but not the isolation of China, McCarthy realizes that our relations with China must remain abnormal, carrying within themselves the seeds of war, as long as the issue of Taiwan remains unsettled. In other words, McCarthy has not fallen for the illusion that one can shove the issue of Taiwan under the rug and proceed with the normalization of our relations with China as though that issue did not exist. More than a hundred conversations between Chinese diplomatic representatives and our own in Geneva and Warsaw have made it perfectly clear that the issue of peace or war between the United States and China hinges upon the disposition of Taiwan. McCarthy realizes that no quick or easy formula will resolve this crucial issue.

Its outcome will depend upon the internal situation on Taiwan, once Chiang has left the stage, and particularly on the nature of the over-all settlement between the United States and China.

This analysis of our relations with China reveals a persistent quality of McCarthy's thinking. Debates on American foreign policy are permeated with deceptive appearances, distinctions without differences, intellectual shadow-boxing, political make-believe, and phony solutions. It is intellectually easy and politically convenient to allow oneself to be deceived and to partake in the deception of others. The debate on our China policy is a case in point. Official policy seeks both to isolate and to contain China. The "critics" appear to take a different position: They propose to end the isolation of China by establishing private and diplomatic contacts, encouraging trade, and so forth, while maintaining the policy of containment that ignores the issue of Taiwan. The real issue between the United States and China, however, is not isolation but containment. And since the "critics" are as unwilling as the Administration to face the issue of containment, their policy amounts to nothing more than a more attractive-looking variant of official policy. McCarthy has not been deceived by the apparent differences between the supporters of essentially identical positions, and he has faced the reality of the crucial issue, however intellectually taxing and politically inconvenient it is to do so.

Another case in point is foreign aid and our relations with the developing nations in general. The history of these relations has been the story of hopes disappointed, of human and material resources wasted, of an unjust and frequently unviable *status quo* supported by American resources and power. McCarthy clearly sees the inner contradiction in the attempt at stimulating radical reform through the instrumentality of oligarchic governments that have a vital interest in maintaining the *status quo*. This contradiction has spelled the doom of the Alliance for Progress. McCarthy agrees with the recent declaration of Latin American bishops, which proclaims the inevitability of revolution. The choice before the United States, then, is not between revolution and the *status quo* but between different kinds of revolutions. What remains to be decided is the auspices under which the revolution will take place.

McCarthy appears to think little of foreign aid as a political weapon because it can be used as blackmail by the receiving as well as the giving nation. He favors Senator Fulbright's proposal to maximize the economic effects of foreign aid by channeling it through international agencies.

The most spectacular case in point is, of course, Vietnam. It has become *de rigueur* among politicians who feel they must speak out about the settlement of the Vietnam war to sound "reasonable," to support "a political instead of a military solution," to advocate an "honorable compromise." It has also become a political requirement for the political and academic supporters of the war to make it appear that either they never supported it or at least they haven't done so since March 31, 1968. Since the Vietnam ship is obviously sinking, the once enthusiastic and cooperative crewmen are jumping overboard, and one can readily visualize Captain Johnson and First Mate Rusk (or will it be only the latter?) standing in not-so-splendid isolation on the bridge when the ship finally goes down. The most eminent defector is Vice President Humphrey. Yet, as I know from personal observation, the war could have had no more genuinely committed supporter than the Vice President. It is only now, in an election year, that the Vice President feels compelled to make this appear to be Mr. Johnson's war, but not necessarily Mr. Humphrey's. Considering the mood of the electorate, he must advocate an end to the war. We remember that in 1964 Mr. Johnson ran as the peace candidate against Mr. Goldwater.

The most elaborate attempt to date on the part of supporters of the war to cover their tracks is Nelson Rockefeller's four-stage peace plan of July 13, which is reported to be the brainchild of Professor Kissinger. The fatal weakness of this plan lies in its basic assumptions, identical with those that moved its authors until recently to support the war. The plan assumes that the Saigon Government is the legitimate Government of South Vietnam, threatened by foreign aggression and internal subversion. It invites the aggressors to leave and the subversives to disarm politically and militarily, in return for which act of abnegation the latter are "guaranteed a role in South Vietnamese politics." It also proposes to de-Americanize the war by letting the South Vietnamese army bear its main burden.

But is it not obvious that if the South Vietnamese army were willing and able to bear that burden and the Saigon Government could rely on its support, it would never have been necessary for more than half a million American troops to keep that government in power? Can the Viet Cong really be expected to lay down their arms and to deliver themselves to the tender mercies of the Saigon Government, armed to the teeth and of proven determination to use its arms against its political opponents? And is it likely that Ho Chi Minh, who has been sold down the river twice before—in Paris in 1945 and in Geneva in 1954—will put his trust in "free elections" and in an "international peace-keeping force," meaningless terms in the Vietnamese context? Why should the Viet Cong and the Government of Hanoi surrender what they have gained by force of arms in exchange for unenforceable paper promises, especially since they have not been defeated in the field?

Here, indeed, is the rub. The negotiating position implicit in the Rockefeller-Kissinger plan assumes, as does the negotiating position of the Administration, that we have won the war. This assumption is of course fictitious, and Governor Rockefeller has made that point himself. But President Johnson and Governor Rockefeller see eye to eye in that both try to gain at the conference table what the United States has been unable to achieve on the battlefield: the surrender of the enemy. No wonder peace overtures so unrealistically conceived have been stillborn.

In contrast to Rockefeller's deceptive and unworkable plan, McCarthy's approach to the Vietnam problem is characterized by intellectual honesty and political courage. Intellectual honesty requires the admission that, as Professor Reischauer has put it, we have lost the war in terms of our original objectives. For in spite of the presence of more than half a million American troops and an annual expenditure of approximately thirty billion dollars, there is still no government in Saigon that can keep itself in power without massive foreign support, and the Viet Cong are still providing the only military, political, and administrative organization that is both viable and indigenous. From this admission McCarthy draws two conclusions, both requiring political courage: A broadly based civilian government must be established in Saigon, and that government must negotiate the liquidation of the war with the Viet Cong. The upshot of such negotiations is bound to be a coalition government. The final outcome of such an experiment, depending primarily upon the distribution of power within the coalition, is of no concern to the United States. For the United States has fulfilled its commitment to protect the right of the South Vietnamese people to self-determination. How they use that right is their affair.

The refusal to deceive himself and to deceive others sets McCarthy apart from his peers. It connotes honesty in judgment and courage in action. When I suggested to him a certain course of action, he replied firmly and without a moment's reflection: "If I do that I am on my way to becoming a demagogue." For the same reason, he has not seen fit to lure the Kennedy people to his side or to make blatant appeals to the blacks. Such unshakeable honesty honors McCarthy as a man and as a public figure. More important, in view of the American political character and its potentialities, is the strong possibility that this man, a world apart from what the conventional wisdom has taught us a politician must be like, could, according to some polls, be nominated the Presidential candidate of the Democratic party and elected President of the United States, if our political institutions and practices truly reflected the popular will.

That so many Americans are willing to put their trust in a man of such qualities, who has come to them without money, without organization, and without prestigious sponsorship, honors them perhaps more than it honors him. Win or lose in August and November, Eugene McCarthy will have one historic achievement to his credit: to have made qualities of goodness and sanity latent in the American people active and visible, to have revealed a face of America that was concealed beneath the distorting mask of its political practices, and to have given us an intimation of what the American people could be like if they had a leader worthy of them.

20

Nixon vs. Humphrey: The Choice

[November, 1968]

Perfect democracy gives the voter a choice of alternative policies by giving him a choice of alternative candidates, each identified with a different policy. We probably had such a choice in 1952 and 1956, when we could choose between Eisenhower and Stevenson, and we thought we had it in 1964 when most of us preferred Johnson to Goldwater. What occurred in 1964 is typical of the way imperfect democracy operates, which is another way of saying the way contemporary democracy operates. The voters deceive themselves into thinking that they are choosing a policy by choosing a man. In truth, they express their preference for one man against another on the basis of criteria that may or may not be relevant to the formation and execution of policy.

It is characteristic of the situation with which the election of 1968 confronts us that it contains elements of perfect and imperfect democracy, but in such a fashion as to put into question the very survival of American democracy. That survival is threatened from two different quarters. It is threatened by the Wallace movement, which in its appeal to a perplexed and frightened primitivism is the American version of fascism, and it is threatened by the irrelevance, as far as the substance of policy is concerned, of choosing between Humphrey and Nixon.

The choice between Wallace, on the one hand, and Humphrey and Nixon, on the other, is a choice not only between men but between policies as well. But the policies Wallace has espoused—carefully couched for the time being in democratic language in order to avoid alienating prospective voters—are incompatible with the principles and practices of liberal democracy. A victorious Wallace would try to establish a totalitarian democracy in which a self-perpetuating majority, unconcerned with individual and minority rights, would have a monopoly of political power.

The next President, whoever he may be, will be faced with the task of restoring the unity of the nation, now impaired by large-scale disaffection at the bottom and the top of the social pyramid. Two methods are at his disposal: radical reforms, which will satisfy the elemental aspirations of the disaffected and thereby make an end to their disaffection, and the imposition of the government's will by force, which will make an end to the outward manifestations of the disaffection. While these two methods can be separated for the purpose of intellectual analysis, they coexist in the practice of governments. What distinguishes a liberal from a tyrannical regime is the relative weight assigned to the free interplay of social forces and the organized violence of the state. There can be no doubt that Wallace would minimize the integrative role of freely given consent induced by social reforms and rely in the main upon the power of the majority to be used for the purpose of imposing by force upon recalcitrant minorities a pattern of conduct submissive to the will of the majority.

The choice before the voter is, then, of extraordinary significance. Before he is called upon to choose between two candidates operating within the traditional context of liberal democracy, he must choose between that context and the totalitarianism the Wallace candidacy portends. For the readers of this journal, the choice must be easy in the abstract: Obviously, Wallace must be contained and liberal democracy given another chance. But the choice is hard to come by and painful to live with when one has to face the concrete issue: Who, Humphrey or Nixon, is more likely to restore the vitality of our political institutions, reunite the nation, and govern well? Let it be said right away that for different reasons, to be discussed shortly, both candidates appear to be singularly unqualified for these tasks. If the choice were simply between Humphrey and Nixon within the traditional context of the two-party system, I would have said that the choice is a matter of political taste but not of political judgment, since there is really nothing to choose between their qualifications. There is no lesser evil to be preferred, since both candidates portend evils different in kind but not in degree. It is the Wallace threat to the ethos and the institutions of America that forces a choice upon us not between the candidates' intrinsic merits but between their respective abilities to contain Wallace.

To dispose of some irrelevant arguments first: There can be no doubt, of course, that Humphrey is a more attractive human being than Nixon. If I had to choose a companion for a desert island, I would not hesitate to choose Humphrey: While Humphrey's tongue would be likely to tire before my mind gave way, Nixon would be capable of having me for dinner and making me thank him for the privilege. However, the human qualities we value in a friend are not necessarily assets for a politician. "It sometimes happens," wrote Henry Taylor in *The Statesman*, "that he who would not hurt a fly will hurt a nation." Men of good will and even of great intellectual awareness have frequently been bested in the business of politics by the smart politician who knew what he wanted for himself and how to get it. Politics has its own standards of excellence, which are different from those of other spheres of action.

It is also obvious that Humphrey has a better intellectual grasp than his opponent of some of the substantive problems with which the next President must come to terms. Humphrey is aware of the acute threats that the decay of the cities and the aggravation of racial conflict constitute for American society, and he knows that these threats must be countered by reforms rather than repression. But the reforms he has suggested by and large have been bypassed by history. They might have been adequate twenty or thirty years ago but they are only palliatives today. While Humphrey has shared the liberal illusion that disarmament is possible without at least concomitant settlement of the political issues from which the armaments race arose, he has clearly seen the enormous risks of nuclear proliferation as well as the risks and irrationality of the nuclear arms race.

On the other hand, while Nixon has not shown his hand with regard to Vietnam, Humphrey has shown his, and it is Johnson's. The best that can be said of Humphrey's speech of September 30, 1968, is that it reiterates Johnson's position. The worst that can be said about it is that it goes beyond Johnson's position in asking Hanoi not only for some kind of reciprocity—explicit or implicit—in exchange for a complete cessation of the bombing of North Vietnam, but specifically for "communist willingness to restore the demilitarized zone between North and South Vietnam."

The role Humphrey has played in the conduct of the Vietnam war has been deliberately obscured and falsified. It has been said that the Vice President could not help defending the President's policy in public while trying to change it in private, that he would emerge with a different policy once he could be "his own man." The trouble with this argument is that there never have been two Humphreys—any more than there have been two Nixons—one willy-nilly supporting the war, the other opposing it. There has only been one Humphrey, wholeheartedly and passionately supporting the war in private as well as in public. One need only read his speech of September 30 to see how completely and sincerely he is committed to Johnson's philosophy and strategy. As the new Nixon is but the old Nixon, packaged for public consumption, so Humphrey as "his own man" is just the Humphrey he always was—and that is his insuperable handicap. He has always been warm-hearted, decent, idealistic, enthusiastic, uncritical, easily swayed by emotion, intoxicated by his own rhetoric, lacking in political judgment, failing in political organization and management, and without the authority of a political leader.

The New York Times, in its editorial of October 6 endorsing Humphrey, has embellished the myth of the dovish Humphrey struggling at long last to emerge from under the wing of Johnson. *The New York Times* finds it "significant that the former members of the Johnson administration who are rallying to Mr. Humphrey's support include its best-known doves." Whom does the *Times* have in mind? George Ball, who had doubts about some of the tactics of the war but, as his recent book clearly shows, has seen eye to eye with Johnson on philosophy and strategy? Or those former members of the Johnson Administration who, far from being opposed to the war, wanted to improve its operations? Or those who enthusiastically supported the war as long as the polls supported it, and followed the polls into half-hearted opposition? In truth, it was impossible to be a member of the Johnson Administration and a dove at the same time, and Humphrey has been very careful to follow in Johnson's footsteps by maintaining the ostracism of all those who had been opposed to the very idea of the war from the outset and without reservations.

Nixon's assets and liabilities are the reverse of Humphrey's. He has shown no intellectual understanding of the momentous issues with which the next President will have to deal. Most disturbing is his apparent conviction—I stress here and elsewhere "apparent," for in Nixon's case trying to distinguish between appearance and reality is extraordinarily hazardous—that the more nuclear weapons a nation has the better off it is militarily. His remedy for the disintegration of American society appears to be private enterprise and the police. However, Nixon has one quality, indispensable but not sufficient in a political leader in which Humphrey is lacking: the gift of political organization and manipulation. He transformed the Republican party, virtually moribund four years ago, into an instrument of his power and victory. He has done this by organizing the party from the grass roots up, by giving his competitors enough rope to hang themselves, by straddling some issues, such as Vietnam, and by glossing over others with unexceptionable generalities, such as the cities and race.

These political gifts are at the service not of a great political vision, nor even of a limited political program, but of a drive for personal power. Nixon thus far has shown all the qualities of a politician of the second rank, but none of those of a political leader or statesman. The mistakes Humphrey would have made enthusiastically, unthinkingly, well-meaningly, Nixon is likely to make by limiting his calculations to the effect his actions might have upon his personal political fortunes. Thus, as Johnson, in spite of his different intentions, was reduced to executing in Vietnam approximately Goldwater's policies, so Humphrey, his intentions and insights notwithstanding, would in all likelihood be forced to put Nixon's policies into practice on the domestic scene because he would have failed in the tasks of political leadership, organization, and manipulation. While Nixon would embark upon an unlimited nuclear arms race deliberately and with conviction, Humphrey, lacking the political savvy to make his convictions prevail against strong hostile pressures, would do so hesitatingly and regretfully but would be liable to acquire Nixon's convictions in the process. However different the two contenders are in personality, ability, and style, they offer us the prospect of the same calamities.

That grim picture has only one redeeming feature, favoring Nixon. Nixon is more likely than Humphrey to make an end to the Vietnam War; for in contrast to Humphrey, he is not emotionally committed to it, nor does he bear any responsibility for it. He can afford to allow political calculations to determine his actions, and these calculations point unmistakably in the direction of speedy liquidation of the losing enterprise. If the cost of liquidation should be painfully high, the Democrats are available for the blame.

Weighing the over-all prospects the two candidates present to the people and trying to choose between them, one must suspend political judgment, which is supposed to guide us to the choice of the lesser evil. For while they present different kinds of evil, by what objective criteria is one to decide which is the lesser of the two? Political judgment tells us only that neither candidate is qualified to be President of the United States from 1969 to 1973 and that it is impossible to foresee on the basis of the record whose administration is likely to be less calamitous for the nation. This being the case, it is perfectly rational not to vote at all, since there is no basis for a rational choice. The decision to vote nevertheless becomes then a matter of subjective preference, of political taste.

The matter could rest here if the issue before us were nothing more than a traditional contest between the two major parties. In truth, the crucial issue—crucial for the future of American democracy —is not between Humphrey and Nixon, but between Humphrey and Nixon, on the one hand, and Wallace, on the other. The rational voter is called upon to answer not only the question—unanswerable on rational grounds, as we have seen—as to who, Humphrey or Nixon, would make the better President, but also, and above all, as to who is better qualified to defend American democracy against the onslaught of the Wallace movement. That latter question is indeed susceptible of a rational answer.

The Democratic party is likely to suffer a debacle similar to the one that befell the Republicans in 1964. The debacle of 1968 may turn out not to be worse than that of 1964 in terms of popular and electoral votes—although even this is quite possible—but it is bound to be worse in its political consequences. The Republicans after 1964 only needed to reformulate their philosophy, to retune their political machinery, to unite behind a leader, and to watch the Democrats ruin the country—and they look like unchallengeable winners four years later. The Democrats cannot do after 1968 what the Republicans did after 1964; for the popular base of their political power has crumbled under the impact of the Vietnam war and the racial crisis. The disaffection of the intellectuals and students, as well as large sectors of the lower middle class in the North and of virutally the whole party apparatus in the South, has left the Democratic Party with a drastically diminished population base.

To recover what it has lost, the Democratic party has two policies to choose from. Either it can compete not only with the Republican Party but, primarily, with the Wallace movement for its share of the conservative and fascist vote, or it can reconstitute itself as the progressive party of the left by creating a new combination of popular forces united by common or parallel interests. However, these are long-range prospects. In the short run, the Democratic party, tainted by failure at home and abroad and paralyzed by the irrelevance of its leaders, cannot perform the traditional task of the opposition party, to present itself as an alternative to the party in power four years hence. The opposition party is the Wallace movement, and the fate of the Republic will be decided not by the number of votes Humphrey can garner in defeat as compared with Nixon's, but by the strength Nixon can muster against Wallace. Nixon's strength is Wallace's weakness. Thus the defense of liberal democracy requires a massive popular mandate for Nixon to pursue a conservative policy in the spirit and within the institutional framework of the liberal-democratic tradition.

There are two pitfalls, which could nullify the prospects for Nixon's defending liberal democracy; there is also an opportunity that could enhance them. Nixon may feel compelled to compete with Wallace for the support of the potential fascist vote, as Eisenhower, Nixon, and Dulles competed in the fifties with Joseph McCarthy. The choice of Agnew may be a harbinger of a massive appeasement of the radical right. Such appeasement may or may not take the fascist wind out of Wallace's sails, but it will make the Republican party fascist. If Nixon should fail in providing by whatever policies he may choose an alternative to Wallace acceptable to the broad masses of the American people—and here is the other pitfall—it is possible that liberal democracy in America has played its last card and lost the game. Many of the millions who in 1968 either remained faithful to the Democratic party out of liberal conviction and traditional loyalty or voted for Nixon as the lesser evil and as an acceptable conservative choice may then find Wallace proved right in his rejection of the two traditional parties and may turn to him as the only available savior.

Yet regardless of whether Nixon succeeds or fails, they might also turn to a savior from the left, provided one is available. It is characteristic of the volatility of large sectors of the American electorate, not only in party affiliation but also in their general position in the political spectrum, that many of the people who voted for Wallace in 1964 and are likely to vote for him in 1968 voted for Robert Kennedy and Eugene McCarthy only a few months ago. They want a charismatic leader, the repository of their troubles and the incarnation of their hopes and aspirations, and they will still want such a leader in 1972. If Nixon should by then have failed, Wallace would have the field all to himself, provided the Democrats cannot counter his charismatic leadership with someone of their own.

It is for this reason that American democracy seems to be best served not only by Nixon's victory in 1968 but also by a defeat of the Democratic party so drastic as to amount to the disavowal of its present leadership, philosophy, and policies and to render inevitable the radical transformation of its philosophy and structure. For without such a defeat and the transformation following it, the Democratic party may do consistently and on a large scale what it did in Chicago only by dint of Mayor Daley's unchallengeable sway: to act out what Wallace preaches. That would be the road not of competition but of imitation and ultimate absorption. If the Democratic party is to save itself and American democracy, it must be made to pay for its political sins by being defeated in 1968. That defeat will be the defeat of Johnson, his heir, and their supporters. Only when they have been discredited and eliminated by electoral defeat will the men who could have saved it in 1968—the Kennedys, the McCarthys, the McGoverns, and their heirs—have a chance to save it in 1972.

This analysis, if there is any merit in it, presents a dismal picture indeed: pathetically dismal with Humphrey, riskily dismal with Nixon, disastrously dismal with Wallace. In a European country, stratified in its social structure and set in its political ways, the situation might well be called hopeless. It is not so in America. Many Americans do not occupy a fixed position in the philosophic and political spectrum. They move from one political position to another, as they do from house to house, city to city. In America, nothing is determined once and for all, and anything is possible, the worst and the best. Wallace may rise to become the American Hitler, or he may fade away as the American Poujade. The way we vote, or don't vote, will be a factor, however small in itself, in the determination of what will happen and what can be avoided.

PART III

THE ISSUES

21

The Coming Test of American Democracy

[January, 1964]

What is disquieting in our present condition is the contrast between the gravity of the two great domestic problems that require solutions—race relations and unemployment—and the complacency permeating the thoughts and actions of government and public alike.

After dictating that sentence, I was informed of President Kennedy's assassination. Returning after a week of horror and sorrow, pity and shame, to the task, I find the timely gravity of these issues accentuated, if anything, by the tragedy of dual violence through which we have passed. These two issues, interrelated as they are, threaten our democracy with the dissolution of the American consensus, and once it is dissolved, violence must replace it. Violence from below, actual or threatened, will call forth violence from above, or vice versa, and American democracy will transform itself, in all probability imperceptibly and gradually rather than in one glaring breakdown of constitutional processes, into a police state. This alternative to government by the consent of the governed is inescapable, for government must rest on one of two foundations: consent or violence.

The unequal condition of the black American has been an endemic denial of the purpose for the sake of which the United States of

America was created and which, in aspiration and partial fulfillment, has remained the distinctive characteristic of American society: equality in freedom. That unequal condition has been, in Jefferson's words, "a moral reproach," a "condition of moral and political reprobation." The first step toward eliminating this evil and complying with the American purpose was taken a hundred years ago with the emancipation of the slaves. We have tended, in view of the present unequal condition of the black man, to underrate the practical importance of that emancipation and to look at it as a mere change in legal status that affected the actual conditions of life but little.

But we should remind ourselves that a slave was a piece of property, like a chicken or a chair, without any attributes of legal personality. He could not marry and had no right to his children. He had no rights in court and was devoid of all other legal protection; he was, like a dog, subject to the master's punishment. In most slave states it was a criminal offense to teach slaves how to read and write. In order to assess correctly the present status of the black man in America it is necessary to compare that status not only with the ideal of equality in freedom but also with the status of slavery of a century ago. Emancipation transformed the black from a thing into a man, a precondition not only for what he has achieved and can hope to achieve in the future but also for his awareness of himself, of what he is and can become.

The problem American society faced a century ago in the form of slavery posed itself in terms quite different and much simpler than does the issue of segregation today. On the legal plane, solution of the problem of slavery required one single act: The Emancipation Proclamation changed the legal status of the Negro from thing to man. On the plane of actual enforcement, the task was first to contain slavery within a circumscribed territory and then to eliminate it altogether through a victorious war.

The problem that we face today in the form of segregation cannot be solved by legal enactment, even though legal enactment is a precondition for its solution. The Supreme Court decision of 1954 declaring segregation in public schools unconstitutional by itself made hardly a dent in actual segregation. After a protracted period of perfunctory compliance and widespread defiance and evasion, it was the spontaneous initiative of the people themselves, black and white alike, supported by the full powers of the federal government, that started to compel compliance with the decision of the Supreme Court as well as with the principle of integration in other fields of social interaction.

Furthermore, and most importantly, the problem of integration is not geographically localized, as was the problem of slavery, even though it is posed in certain Southern states in different terms from elsewhere. In consequence, segregation cannot be contained and sealed off as was slavery. Slavery was a localized cancer that could be cut out; segregation is a metastasized cancer to be treated by more complex and uncertain means. There are no segregationist and integrationist states as there were slave and abolitionist states. All states of the Union are segregationist in different degrees, with regard to different activities and by virtue, or in spite, of different legal arrangements. Even where the law requires integration in all fields of social interaction, segregation is still a social fact.

That social fact is all-pervasive and resistant to change; by no means does it apply to blacks alone. Less than thirty years ago I had to deal with American consuls who considered it their patriotic duty to violate the law in order to prevent the immigration of Jews; once I was here, I could not find a place to sleep in the White Mountains of New Hampshire until I registered under my wife's maiden name. Less than twenty years ago I could not get service at the Dartmouth Inn in Hanover, New Hampshire. And even today Jews and blacks cannot own property in one of the best residential districts in Washington, D. C. Thus segregation is a general social phenomena, nourished by social myths, fear of what is different, actual social differences, and incompatible interests, real or fancied. These factors on which segregation thrives are as such impervious to legislation, although legislation can provide levers with which to contain and weaken them through the application of irresistible pressure.

In the face of the foreseeable persistence of segregation as a social fact, the blacks of America have at their disposal four courses of action: passive acceptance of a slightly improved *status quo*; peaceful agitation and pressure; alienation; and violence. In view of the high hopes being placed in the practical consequences of legislative enactments, especially on the economic plane, militant alienation and violence—and alienation ultimately means violence, too—are bound to attract large masses of militant blacks. Violence, since it cannot organize itself against a rational political objective, is bound to appear as anarchy, a large-scale and unmanageable breakdown of law and order. No less real for being deemed an unfit subject to print, that anarchic violence already terrorizes many of our streets and schools. I have been told that in one Chicago school in one week of November, 1963, more than twenty students were attacked by fellow students with deadly weapons, one teacher was knocked unconscious by a student with a bottle, and one teacher was raped. The student who had hit the teacher was merely suspended for three days by a terrorized school administration, whereupon her father went to the school to complain about the treatment his daughter had received!

This violence, spreading unchecked, is bound to call forth counter-violence by those who feel themselves threatened. While the progress the blacks are likely to make in their actual conditions of life will be too small to integrate them into the main body of American society and, hence, meet their aspirations, it will be large enough to threaten, or at least appear to threaten, the social position of large masses of white members of the lower middle class. This problem is being aggravated by the large-scale migration of Southern blacks to the North. The black population of Mississippi, for instance, has decreased from 51% of the total in 1950 to 42% in 1960 and 36% in 1963. Here will be an additional inducement to the violence traditionally employed by a low stratum of American society that feels itself threatened by a still lower but rising one. We have had a foretaste of things to come in the protracted violence, inadequately reported or not reported at all, that has accompanied or prevented the attempts of blacks to move into white neighborhoods. Thus we are facing the prospect of a three-cornered relation of violence: the black man against the government, the lower white middle class against the black man, and the government against both.

This prospect will be gravely accentuated by the persistence and the likely spread of unemployment. The permanent unemployment we have been unable thus far to cope with is different in nature from the mass unemployment of the 1930's. The latter was the result of a temporary maladjustment, a consequence of the natural fluctuations of the business cycle, to be remedied by the techniques of Keynesian economics. The unemployment of our day is the result of structural defects due to technological innovations, to be cured only by radical structural changes.

Both economic theory and economic practice have been helpless in the face of the permanent gap that technology is opening up between a productive majority and a permanently unemployable new proletariat, which may well become a majority tomorrow. What is needed to close that gap is not the half-hearted application of Keynesian remedies, devised for quite different circumstances, but a revolution in our economic thinking and practice, commensurate in its magnitude with the changes modern technology has wrought in our economic circumstances. Such a revolution will have to recognize two fundamental facts, one economic, the other moral.

Economically, we are in the process of acquiring a productive capacity to transform our economy from one of scarcity into one of abundance. Morally, we have accepted the obligation to provide all citizens with a modicum of economic well-being and security as a precondition for having an equal opportunity to realize their human potentialities in freedom. It is only outmoded economic theory and practice that stands in the way of our using our productive power for this moral end. Once we have overcome this cultural lack by bringing our economic thinking up to date, we will have to transform radically our economic system and social organization.

The two great issues with which American democracy must come to terms—equality in freedom for the black American and the restoration of a meaningful economic and social order—are thus interconnected. The former cannot be fully achieved, and might even be ultimately jeopardized, without the latter. For even if the black American were to come into full possession of legal and social equality, he would still be exposed to the disabilities of a contracting labor market. As an unskilled laborer, regardless of discrimination, he is likely to be permanently unemployed. But as a skilled worker, even if he were to compete without discrimination for ever scarcer jobs, he would still be threatened with unemployment. The resentment of the blacks, whose new equality reveals itself as meaningless in economic terms, would be a source of alienation from America and an incentive to violence against it. The resentment of the ever swelling mass of white unemployed would be a source of alienation from the political and social *status quo* and an incentive to violence against both the Negro and the government. One resentment would be pitted against the other, fanning anew the enmity of races and jeopardizing the ability of the government to govern without the continuous use of violence.

The government, thus deprived on a large scale of the consent of the governed, will have to resort to violence in order to be able to govern. It is at this point that the political order of the states of the Deep South acquires a crucial relevance for the future of American democracy. The governments of these states are already deprived of the consent of the governed. For their legitimacy reposes upon the myth of the natural inequality of the races, a myth unacceptable to the politically conscious blacks and the white moderates alike. Thus these states can govern only by violence, and it makes a difference only for the modalities of application, not for the substance of the case, whether that violence is exerted through the instrumentality of a lynch mob, an unpunished murderer, arbitrary brutality by the police, or an equally arbitrary administration of justice, which destroys life and liberty as arbitrarily as, but more effectively than, a mob.

Worse still for the future of American democracy, this government by violence is not limited to the Deep South but rules the nation as a whole through Southern domination of Congress. The Southern leaders of Congress cannot afford to support the integration of the black man into American society, since their political power derives from the denial of the black's natural equality. Allied as they are with the most feudalistic sector of the American economy, from which they derive the economic sustenance of their power, they cannot even contemplate the radical structural changes in our economic system technology has made necessary; for them the obsolescent Keynes is a symbol of unacceptable radicalism.

Thus we are in the presence of a dual paradox. On the one hand, a minority that governs its territory through violence rather than the democratic consent of the governed is able to thwart the will of the majority of the nation, which seeks to enable American society to cope with the problems of race and permanent unemployment. On the other hand, if it succeeds, that minority will make inevitable the extension of its own methods of government by violence to the whole nation. A century ago, slavery was contained and extirpated through civil war. Today, we face the danger that government by violence may engulf the whole nation through the manipulation of the levers of political power by those who once defended slavery and now can govern their own states only through violence.

Who really won the Civil War? The Union has been preserved, but on whose terms? The house that was divided against itself a hundred years ago is still so divided. It still stands, but it has begun to wobble. If ever the explosive mixture of racial discontent and economic deprivation becomes firmly lodged in its foundations, it can then be held precariously together only through the cement of violence.

22

Modern Science and Political Power

[December, 1964]

We seemed to be moving into a new high pressure area. Mishandled, any of these crises may result in wars, little or big; at worst, they could provide an atomic convulsion capable (literally) of tearing the planet to pieces. A terrifying fact is that the men who grapple with these crises are dealing with forces of which most other people are unaware. Often they must seek solutions for which the prevailing politics and public opinion of the United States are unprepared; and the only way politics and public opinion will ever be prepared is when enough people have general awareness of the underlying considerations and facts.
—ADOLF A. BERLE

Upon the domestic political scene, the modern scientific age has had three major effects. Power has shifted from the people to the government. Within the government, power has shifted from democratically responsible officials to certain technological elites, military and scientific, which are not democratically responsible. In consequence, popular participation in and control over the affairs of government have drastically decreased.

The ultimate safeguard of popular rights has been, in modern democracy as in all other systems of government, the ability of the people to overthrow the government by force—to make a revolution. This ability provided a double safeguard. On the one hand, the fear of revolution imposed effective restraints upon the government. The popular rights in defense of which the people were willing to take up arms were safe as long as the government calculated the mood of the people correctly. On the other hand, the actual threat or fact of revolution was capable of protecting or restoring the rights of the people if the government should calculate wrongly.

The protection with which the possibility of revolution surrounded the rights of the people is predicated upon an approximately equal distribution of the means of physical violence between the government and the people. This approximately equal distribution of military power between government and people has in our age been transformed into the unchallengeable superiority of the government. Popular revolution has ceased to be a practical proposition in technologically advanced societies. It is but another illustration of the obsolescence of our modes of thought and action that our statutes still threaten with criminal penalties people who conspire to overthrow the government "by force or violence."

Thus it is not by accident that for technologically advanced nations this is the age not of popular revolution but of the *coup d'état*. That is to say, what a modern government must primarily guard against is not the disaffection of the people but the disloyalty of the armed forces. Such a government can rule over a thoroughly disaffected people as long as the armed forces support it; but it cannot rule, albeit supported by a loyal people, against the disaffected armed forces. A modern government may be overthrown by the armed forces acting alone, but it can no longer be overthrown by the people acting alone.

A people, in order to make a successful revolution, must gain the support of the armed forces and may do so in the measure that the armed forces partake of the popular mood. The success of the Hungarian revolution of 1956, however temporary, and of the Korean and Turkish revolutions of 1960 was assured when the armed forces made common cause with the people. Thus, in the last analysis, the ultimate contest is no longer between the government and the people but between the government and the armed forces.

The extent to which the fate of modern democracy is in the hands of the armed forces is clearly shown by the fate of the democracies of Germany, Italy, and France. In the rise of Nazism to power in 1933, the support of the armed forces was decisive; Nazism survived the military revolt of 1944 only because the armed forces were split and the segment that supported the revolt was half-hearted and vacillating. It was the distribution of power within the armed forces that was decisive. Both in the assumption of power by Italian fascism in 1922 and in its dislodgement in 1943, the Italian Army played the determining role. And it was only through the impetus of defeat in war and invasion, and not through a spontaneous upheaval from within, that both regimes collapsed.

Nowhere, however, has the ascendancy of the armed forces at the expense of the people been more clearly revealed than in the history of France since 1958. Once the army had resolved to make an end to the Fourth Republic, the doom of the regime was sealed. Regardless of the support it enjoyed in Parliament and in the population at large, the last government of the Fourth Republic could only choose between the voluntary or the compelled surrender of power at the behest of the army. Government with the consent of the governed had become government with the consent of the army; once the Fifth Republic had assumed power with this consent, government with the consent of the army became government by the will of the army.

In no other Western democracy has the shift of power from the people to the armed forces been revealed with such stark simplicity. Only in the Fifth Republic of France have the political consequences been drawn from this shift with such radical consistency. Yet the shift has occurred everywhere by virtue of the irresistible superiority of the means of violence that modern technology has put in the hands of the armed forces. The political consequences of that shift have differed from country to country by virtue of different political and social conditions.

To a greater or lesser extent the armed forces partake of the aspirations of the people and, hence, reflect them in their political attitudes. Thus, where the military are in the political ascendancy, it is through their intermediary that popular aspirations are brought to bear upon the government. In terms of the actual distribution of political power between government and people in the United States, it is not so much the armed forces specifically as the executive branch as a whole that has benefited from the shift. Three factors account for this.

With respect to the issues that concern the armed forces most—military strategy, assignment of missions, and appropriations—the armed forces appear on the political stage not as a unit but divided into competing branches. The armed forces are indeed a new center of power, because of new international and technological conditions, competing with other centers of power, old and new, for the determination of the policies relevant to their tasks. But, far from being a single-minded colossus, they reflect within themselves the same variety of philosophies and policy commitments that characterize American opinion in general. The determination of policy within the Pentagon is a result of the same kind of pluralistic competition and conflict that we find in the Department of State, Congress, and American society at large. The mechanics of checks and balances, characteristic of the American government as a whole, reappear within the military establishment and exert their limiting and restraining influence. And the arbiter of these contests is not a military man but the Secretary of Defense and, ultimately, the President of the United States.

Furthermore, the principle of civilian control of the armed forces is firmly established not only in the Constitution but also and more particularly in the political mores and practices of America. Heeding the wisdom of the *Federalist* (No. 8, Hamilton), America has been consistently mindful of the potential threat that a standing army constitutes to the democratic order. America has never brought itself to accept a truly unified command for fear of the man on horseback. It has compounded the military inefficiency of the committee system (the Pentagon houses more than seven hundred committees) by superimposing upon it a plethora of civilian secretaries, under secretaries, and assistant secretaries (twenty-five all told) intended to harness the armed forces to the civilian will.

Finally, the armed forces have consistently and eagerly accepted that subordinate role. Even when the civilian direction of the military establishment temporarily lapsed, as it did in Europe in the last months of World War II, leaving a vacuum waiting to be filled, the military leaders refused to fill it. In April, 1945, during the "deadly hiatus" in American political leadership to which Sir Winston Churchill referred,* when the British Government suggested in vain to the American Government that our army go as far east in Germany and Czechoslovakia as possible and in particular occupy Berlin and Prague, Generals Marshall and Eisenhower refused to take an action both militarily feasible and politically advantageous "unless," in the words of Eisenhower, "I receive specific orders from the Combined Chiefs of Staff." † The different course of action General MacArthur took under somewhat similar circumstances during the Korean War was an exception to the rule.

The subordination of the armed forces to civilian control and, more

---

* Winston L. S. Churchill, *Triumph and Tragedy* (Boston: Houghton Mifflin, 1963), pp. 455–56.

† Forrest C. Pogue, "Why Eisenhower's Forces Stopped at the Elbe," *World Politics*, Winter, 1952, pp. 356 and 366.

particularly, their own commitment to that subordination make the executive branch as a whole, rather than the armed forces specifically, the beneficiary of the shift of power away from the people. The results of that shift are in normal times intangible and potential; they become obvious and acute only when the country approaches a revolutionary crisis. The country may be said to be approaching such a crisis in view of the resistance of Southern states to the federal government's attempts to enforce the application of constitutional guarantees to the blacks. Yet while a century ago such a conflict would have raised the specter of revolution and civil war, as it actually did with regard to a different but related issue, today the unchallengeable military superiority of the federal government precludes the possibility of armed conflict. It is the absence of this possibility, of which both the government and the people are vaguely aware, that removes a restraint from the power of the government and a weapon from the armory of the people.

This shift of power from the people to the government not only results in a quantitative increase in the powers of the government but also creates the possibility for a qualitative transformation of government: It makes totalitarianism possible. Totalitarianism is a new form of government. It is not identical with traditional despotism, as some of its critics claim; nor is it identical with democracy, as its apologists claim. While different from both, it combines qualities of both. Totalitarianism, like democracy, governs with the consent of the people. But unlike democracy, it creates that consent through the monopolistic use of the mass media of communications and the instruments of terror.

It is not by accident that the rise of totalitarianism coincides with the development of the modern technologies of communication, transportation, and warfare. For these technologies have given modern governments the tools with which to penetrate and overwhelm the sphere that tradition has reserved for the individual and his freedom—to condition his thoughts and control his actions without limitation from outside. Before the advent of the modern technological age, no government, no matter what its inclination, could have become totalitarian, because of its limited technological resources; thus the freedom of the individual was protected by the inability of the government to utterly destroy it. Our age has given modern governments the ability to make themselves total masters of the individual. The freedom of the individual in our age rests upon moral and legal restraints, imposed from within or without the government, but not upon the inability of the government to destroy it.

Thus the very quality of individual freedom has changed by virtue of changes that have occurred in the nature of modern government. Whether individual freedom is more or less secure than it used to be is a matter that awaits empirical analysis. What is important to note are the different foundations upon which contemporary individual freedom rests. In the pre-modern age, government could not utterly destroy individual freedom and it was upon this physical inability that individual freedom ultimately rested. Today, if it wishes, government is physically able to destroy individual freedom; thus individual freedom now depends ultimately upon the unwillingness of the government to do what it is able to do.

The same considerations apply to the possibility of world conquest by a totalitarian government. In the age from Alexander to Napoleon, attempts at world conquest foundered on the lack of resources necessary to conquer the world and keep it conquered. A would-be world conqueror might go very far toward achieving global dominion but would quickly discover the technological impossibility of controlling from one central point his world empire. In order to do this, he needed three prerequisites: enforced social integration through centralized control over the minds of the subjects of the empire, superior organized force at any point of possible disintegration within the empire, and permanency and ubiquity of these means of control and enforcement throughout the empire. These three military and political prerequisites were not available to the would-be world conquerors of the past. But they are within his reach in our time.

Today, no technological obstacle stands in the way of a world-wide empire if the ruling nation is able to maintain superiority in the technological means of domination. A nation that has a monopoly of nuclear weapons and control of the principal means of transportation and communications can conquer the world and keep it conquered, provided it is capable of keeping that monopoly and control unimpaired. First of all, it will be able to mold the minds of the citizens of its world empire into a uniformity of submissiveness, of which the totalitarian societies of the recent past and present have given us fair samples. Under the assumption of a reasonably effective government, the will to revolt will at best be scattered and, in any case, will lack political and military significance. Second, any attempt at revolt will meet with the speedy reaction of superior power and is thus doomed to failure from the outset. Finally, modern technology makes it possible to extend the control of mind and action to every corner of the globe regardless of geography and season. What prevents the consummation of world conquest on the part of a technologically advanced nation is, then, not its lack of resources, as it was in the past, but rather the existence of another nation or nations endowed with similar resources. Thus the freedom of nations, as of individuals, rests no longer upon a government's inability to subvert it totally and permanently but on restraints upon the government's will to do what it is physically able to do.

The modern age has not only greatly strengthened the power of the government vis-à-vis the people and, more particularly, the power of the military within the government. It has also brought to the fore an altogether new kind of ruler, the scientific elite. The ascendancy of such elites is the inevitable result of the central positions science and technology occupy in the affairs of modern government, and of the inaccessibility of these branches of knowledge to the layman, that is, their esoteric nature.

Before World War II, governments were typically the beneficiaries of scientific and technological innovations achieved accidentally by private enterprise. Governments surveyed, as it were, the scientific and technological market and appropriated and developed what appeared to be useful. Gunpowder, the steamship, the railroads, the airplane, the machine gun, are cases in point.

James B. Conant reports two stories that illustrate the casual relationship that then existed between government and science:

> In World War I, President Wilson appointed a consulting board to assist the Navy. Thomas Edison was the chairman; his appointment was widely acclaimed by the press—the best brains would now be available for the application of science to naval problems. The solitary physicist on the board owed his appointment to the fact that Edison in choosing his fellow board members had said to the President, "We might have one mathematical fellow in case we have to calculate something out."
>
> Another story illustrating the popular attitude towards science and invention in 1916 concerns chemists, not mathematicians or physicists. At the time of our entry into World War I, a representative of the American Chemical Society called on the Secretary of War, Newton Baker, and offered the service of the chemists in the conflict. He was thanked and asked to come back the next day. On so doing, he was told by the Secretary of War that while he appreciated the offer of the chemists, he found that it was unnecessary as he had looked into the matter and found the War Department already had *a* chemist.*

The development of radar and the atomic bomb at the instigation and

* James B. Conant, *Modern Science and Modern Man* (New York: Columbia University Press, 1952), pp. 8–9.

under the management of the government at the beginning of World War II initiated a new relationship between scientific and technological innovation and the government. Today, both intellectually and economically the government dominates the development of science and technology. If the government does not support a supersonic or nuclear-powered airplane, it will not be built. The National Aeronautics and Space Administration determines the objectives and methods for the exploration of outer space, satellite communications, and in good measure, astronomy.

More indirectly and more persuasively, the commitment of unmatchable resources for certain scientific and technological projects chosen by the government exerts a well-nigh irresistible attraction upon scientific and industrial research. Thus the direction of scientific exploration and technological innovation is no longer left to the free interplay of intellectual curiosity and technical ingenuity but is predetermined by the interests and the power of the government. The priorities of scientific investigation and technological innovation are no longer primarily the result of the dynamic interplay of free minds and of economic competition and inchoate social needs, but are imposed by the overwhelming interests and power of the state. The actual impact of that power is indicated, but not fully reflected, by the figures.

> The Federal Government provided approximately two-thirds of total national funds for research and development in the year 1961–1962. Of the estimated $14.7 billion spent for research and development in the Nation during that year, Federal agencies financed $9.6 billion. . . . In that year the Federal Government financed about 60 percent of the money spent by industry for research and development; and Federal grants and contracts provided funds for 70 percent of expenditures by colleges and universities and other nonprofit institutions for these purposes. . . . Close to 60 percent of total funds for basic research in 1961–62 came from Federal sources. Of the estimated $1.5 billion spent that year for basic research, Federal agencies contributed over $0.8 billion.*

The federal government supports about three-fifths of the scientists and engineers engaged in research and development. Government appropriations for a number of private corporations engaged in scientific research and technological development are individually larger than those for each of the smaller executive departments represented in the Cabinet.

* U.S., National Science Foundation, *Federal Funds for Research, Development, and Other Scientific Activities* (Washington, D.C.: Government Printing Office, 1964), p. 5.

The interest of the government in science and technology is utilitarian. It was aroused by the exigencies of World War II and is being maintained by those of the Cold War. The extent of this interest is determined by the mechanization of transportation, communications, and warfare that has occurred since World War I, as well as by a succession of technological revolutions, both past and anticipated, that have transformed, and promise to transform again, the technologies of these three fields. Military power is no longer primarily measured by the possession of territory, the number of men under arms, and the number of weapons available, but by scientific breakthroughs and technological innovations; national prestige derives in good measure from scientific and technological achievements. Nations, by continuing their historical engagement in armaments races and competition for prestige, must perforce embark upon scientific and technological competition. Thus the value of science and technology has enormously increased in the calculus of national power.

In the past, the influence of science and technology on national power remained static over long stretches of history. For instance, the predominance of Europe throughout the world remained for centuries firmly based upon its technological superiority. Today, the distribution of national power derived from science and technology has become, at least potentially, dynamic to an unprecedented degree. This is the result of a number of scientific revolutions, past and anticipated, following each other in ever more rapid succession. The acquisition of the atomic bomb by the United States in 1945 changed overnight the distribution of military power in the world, and so did the acquisition of the bomb by the Soviet Union in 1949. In the late 1950's, we feared that the unilateral acquisition of powerful rockets by the Soviet Union presaged another change in the distribution of military power, this time in favor of the Soviet Union.

Such unilateral advances spell more than a shift in the relative distribution of power; in view of the destructiveness of modern weapons, they may well mean the difference between victory and defeat, survival and utter destruction. Thus not only the superpowers but also nations of the second or third rank, such as China, France, Israel, and Egypt, are engaged in frantic competition for scientific and technological advantage, and success in that competition depends upon the quality of the scientific elites. The German scientists who were working for the Egyptian Government were at that time the most important single factor bearing upon the distribution of military power in the Middle East.

This utilitarian orientation of science and technology toward the interests of the state constitutes a radical break with tradition. The great scientific discoveries of the modern age, upon which modern technology rests, have in the main been the result of idle curiosity and theoretical speculation, not of the search for the solution to practical problems imposed from the outside. The theoretical experiments of Faraday brought forth the discovery of electricity. Maxwell's mathematical speculations and Hertz's research into electromagnetic waves led to the invention of the radio by Marconi. Nobel's chemical experiments resulted by accident in the production of dynamite. The dependence of modern science and technology upon abstruse mathematical speculation is particularly striking. Gauss's "non-Euclidian geometry" was indispensable for Einstein's theory of relativity and all the scientific and technological consequences following from it, as the "group" theory of mathematics was for the quantum theory of spectroscopy. Einstein's mathematical theory of the "ideal gas" had, decades after its publication in 1925, far-reaching consequences for the chemistry of gases, and Einstein's formula $E = mc^2$, defining the relation between mass and energy, became the foundation of nuclear physics in all its theoretical and practical aspects.

It is an open question, fiercely debated by scientists, whether or not scientific creativity can flourish if the scientific mind is tied to a practical purpose extraneous to itself, and is thereby deprived of that uncommitted speculative curiosity from which the great scientific discoveries of the past have sprung. Abraham Flexner, who provided the examples of the "usefulness of useless knowledge" cited above, was emphatic in his advocacy of uncommitted scientific curiosity:

Curiosity, which may or may not eventuate in something useful, is probably the outstanding characteristic of modern thinking. It is not new. It goes back to Galileo, Bacon, and Sir Isaac Newton, and it must be absolutely unhampered. Institutions of learning should be devoted to the cultivation of curiosity and the less they are deflected by considerations of immediacy of application, the more likely they are to contribute not only to human welfare but to the equally important satisfaction of intellectual interest which may indeed be said to have become the ruling passion of intellectual life in modern times. . . . What Rutherford and others like Bohr and Millikan have done out of sheer curiosity in the effort to understand the construction of the atom has released forces which may transform human life; but this ultimate and unforeseen and unpredictable practical result is not offered as a justification for Rutherford or Einstein or Millikan or Bohr or any of their peers. Let them alone. No educational administrator can possibly direct the channels in which these or other men shall work. The waste, I admit again, looks prodigious. It is not really so. All the waste that could be summed up in developing the science of bacteriology is as nothing compared to the advantages which have accrued from the discoveries of Pasteur, Koch, Ehrlich, Theobald Smith, and scores of others—advantages that could never have accrued if the idea of possible use had permeated their minds. These great artists—for such are scientists and bacteriologists—disseminated the spirit which prevailed in laboratories in which they were simply following the line of their own natural curiosity.*

If Flexner is right, the rise of science to power in the modern state will have been paid for, at the very least, with a drastic impairment of its creativity. Its creative imagination will have been stifled by its commitment to the purposes of the state. Even if this pessimistic assessment is wrong and if the very search for, and experimentation with, solutions for practical problems should provide new impulses for scientific imagination, the utilitarian orientation of contemporary science is bound to affect its nature. The utilitarian selectivity of government commitments to scientific exploration and technological experimentation, massively supported by money, manpower, and machinery, will open certain avenues and close others. Scientific curiosity cannot help being attracted by the avenues opened by the government, regardless of the intrinsic worth of the scientific goal toward which they seem to lead. Scientific fashions, created by the conformity of scientists, are bound to call forth vested interests, defined in terms of economic rewards, research facilities, and prestige. Thus, when the avenue the government has opened turns out to be a blind alley, it cannot be easy for the scientists and administrators who have committed large human and material resources and their scientific reputations to this road, perhaps in the face of opposition, to admit in time that they were wrong and that all these resources have been wasted. The dynamics of such large-scale collective and public commitments, of which those of NASA provide prime examples, may well make for persistence in error, rationalized and justified by the expectation that all that is needed for success is just another major effort. Therefore major effort may well follow major effort in futility, reminiscent of the trench warfare of World War I, until catastrophe takes the place of timely retreat.

It is probably idle to speculate whether this kind of wastefulness is socially more burdensome than the wastefulness of independent scientific enterprise, which Abraham Flexner found redeemed by what that enterprise achieved. But it is clear that it is much easier for the in-

* Abraham Flexner, "The Usefulness of Useless Knowledge," *Harper's Magazine*, October, 1939.

dependent scientist who has found himself in error to retrace his steps than it is for the government-sponsored scientific collectivities. The new utilitarian scientists, then, face the danger of becoming the members of a scientific orthodoxy committed to one set of problems, methods, and solutions to the exclusion of all others, and science faces the risk of sterility and ossification. At best, the new utilitarian science is likely to weaken and slow down the dynamics of change that the objective test of success and failure has traditionally provided. At worst, the new utilitarian science will degenerate into an official doctrine, propounded by an "establishment," whose interests must make it hostile to change.

Two factors make this probable trend toward rigidity particularly dangerous: the ever increasing rapidity in the succession of scientific discoveries and technological innovations since the middle of the nineteenth century, and the resistance to change that, strange as it may seem in view of their reputation for open-mindedness and objectivity, is traditional with scientists. The history of science in this respect is no different from the history of any other cultural endeavor, be it religion, philosophy, literature, or art. The very novelty of a departure from tradition evokes resistance from those who are intellectually, if not personally, socially, and economically, identified with that tradition. To have to change one's habits of thought in view of a scientific discovery is in itself a burden. It is a greater burden still to have to admit that what one and one's contemporaries had believed to be the truth was actually error. These traditional intellectual positions frequently create vested social and economic interests, which may be endangered by a new discovery. Resistance will be particularly strong when these intellectual and social positions have been erected upon certain philosophic and religious foundations which might not survive the acceptance of the discovery.

The history of science is replete with instances of great discoveries having been passed over in silence or having been shoved aside by specious refutation and of technological developments having thus been retarded. The very development of science in the Western world was probably held back for a thousand years by the triumph of neo-Platonic philosophy over the fledgling science of ancient Greece. The history of modern science, from Copernicus to Einstein, is the story of a continuous struggle between the new and the old, between reason and tradition, of new discoveries missed or neglected, of misdirected energies and retarded technological progress. It is the paradox of our present situation that, on the one hand, scientific and technological revolutions follow each other with unprecedented speed and, hence, require of the scientific community a corresponding openness to scientific novelty and technological adaptability, while, on the other hand, the bureaucratization of science and its utilitarian orientation tend to impair these very qualities. In other words, the conservative trend that is an element of the scientific tradition is in need of being weakened in view of the development of modern science, while in actuality it is likely to be strengthened by the new relations existing between science and government. Thus science and technology must guard against a dual threat of stagnation and ossification: its modern utilitarian orientation superimposed upon its traditional conservative disposition.

That threat is enhanced by the artificial barriers of secrecy; new scientific knowledge and technological innovations, developed under government auspices, are kept not only from independent scientists and the public at large but also from other scientific elites within the official scientific establishment. When in 1957 the Army and Air Force competed in the development of ballistic missiles, each service withheld information from the other. In the hearings before a Subcommittee of the House Committee on Government Operations, the Army charged that when it requested information on the requirements of the Air Force Jupiter, the Air Force provided inadequate data. In retaliation, the Army refused to allow civilian contractors of the Air Force to assess the work the Army did on the Thor. When Air Force General Schriever visited the Army installations, he was not allowed to be accompanied by the head of the Air Force program. As Army General Medaris put it: "I could not buy the idea of having our system evaluated by a man who invented a different one." *

This problem shall be discussed later in greater detail in another context. Here it is sufficient to indicate the radical departure these several walls of secrecy constitute from the traditional freedom of communications within the scientific community, both on the national and international levels. This freedom has been one of the mainstays of scientific progress, for it has provided stimulation for the creativeness of individual scientists as well as a corrective to the eccentricities of that creative imagination. Scientific innovations frequently develop simultaneously in different places on identical or parallel lines; for scientists start with the same accumulated capital of

---

* U.S., Congress, House Subcommittee of Committee on Government Organizations, *Hearings on Organization and Management*, 86th Cong., 1st Sess., 1959, pp. 280–81.

knowledge, and their minds, guided by the same rational faculties, however independent of each other, pose to themselves the same problems, apply the same methods, and seek the same goals. The universal knowledge, at least within certain limits, of what everybody else is doing and has discovered calls into being a kind of implicit cooperative enterprise whose members learn from each other what to avoid, what needs no longer to be done, what promises success, and what requires further exploration. "Secrecy and science are fundamentally antithetic propositions." *

The fragmentation of such an ideal worldwide community of scientists into a number of national and subnational societies, separated from each other by artificial walls of secrecy, is intended to protect a monopoly of knowledge on the part of each society and to perpetuate ignorance on the part of the other societies. Yet such a monopoly is likely to be illusory or at best short-lived. Even in the short run, secrecy is bound to create ignorance on the part of all concerned, regardless of the temporary shielding of a certain advance from general knowledge. The result is bound to be duplication of effort and the repetition of errors or the discovery of blind alleys already revealed as such elsewhere. In the long run, moreover, secrecy benefits nobody; for universally accessible knowledge developed by minds of equal capacity will quickly equalize whatever secret advantage a particular society might have achieved. In the end, since ignorance is inevitably the complement to secrecy, retardation and distortion of scientific progress, equally disadvantageous to all competing societies, will invariably result. Paradoxically, secret science is truly counterproductive in that it furthers that very ignorance it is the mission of science to reduce. Here is, then, another impediment to that openness and adaptability that modern science and technology require.

The ascendancy of the scientific elites in the modern state derives not only from the importance of the subject matter with which they deal but also from the monopolistic and esoteric character of their knowledge. By virtue of their training, the scientists have a monopoly of the relevant knowledge, and that knowledge is inaccessible to the layman. In sharp contrast to the types of scientific knowledge that preceded it until the beginning of this century, modern scientific knowledge is esoteric. The layman does not have the competence to retrace in his own mind the arguments that underlie the

* Conant, *op. cit.*, p. 16n.

scientist's conclusions and to check them against his own knowledge; he must take the scientist's word for it. When President Roosevelt had to decide in 1939 whether or not to commit large human and material resources for the development of an atomic bomb, he had to take on faith Einstein's famous letter assuring him that the scientific knowledge necessary for the development of an atomic bomb was available to both American and German scientists. The decision of 1949 to proceed with the development of the H-bomb hinged upon the scientific estimate of its feasibility. So does the decision, pending at the moment of this writing, to develop an anti-missile missile system. Similarly, the decision of 1963 to conclude a partial test-ban treaty was based upon the scientific evaluation that the development of nuclear weapons would not be dependent upon above-ground tests.

While, as we shall see, technical feasibility is not the only factor determining the direction of any particular decision, it is an indispensable prerequisite. If the scientific advice is unanimous, political authorities, having no scientific argument with which to refute that advice, are most likely to accept it as authoritative. In that case the scientific advice tends to become identical with the decision itself, and a particular scientist or scientific elite tends to rule within the limits of its scientific competence. This is the position that C. P. Snow assigns to Professor Lindemann as scientific adviser to Winston Churchill during World War II,* that Professor Edward Teller is supposed to have occupied from 1952–1955,† and that NASA appears to occupy in the exploration of space.

This tendency of scientific advice to become identical with the decision itself accentuates and generalizes the relationship that has traditionally existed between military advice and the political decision. Political authorities are naturally reluctant to supersede the advice of the military expert; for the military expert, too, is supposed to be in the monopolistic possession of esoteric knowledge, the application of which affects the vital interests of the state. However, this dependence of the political authorities upon the advice of the military expert has in past practice been mitigated by the awareness on the part of the political authorities that military expertise provides no assurance against wrong advice—"war is much too serious a thing to be left to military men." Many have concluded that military expertise

---

* C. P. Snow, *Science and Government* (Cambridge, Mass.: Harvard University Press, 1961) pp. 63–66 and appendix (1962), pp. 33–35.

† Robert Gilpin, *American Scientists and Nuclear Weapons Policy* (Princeton, N.J.: Princeton University Press, 1962), p. 13.

is nothing more than the application of common sense to situations having particular technical characteristics. Since political authorities are supposed to be endowed with common sense, and since experience has in the past shown that the technical peculiarities of military issues are not beyond their comprehension, the political authorities have managed to resist, with different degrees of success, the monopolistic tendencies of military expertise.

Yet the relative simplicity of this traditional relationship between military advice and political decision is a thing of the past. For today, military advice derives from scientific knowledge and technological prognosis, which the political authorities may accept or reject but which they are in no position to scrutinize on the basis of their own scientific knowledge and judgment.

In the context of this discussion it is significant to note that this scientific and technological ascendancy into the realm of military advice and decision also radically affects the command structure of the military services. Traditionally, the commander has had complete authority to order a subordinate to perform specified functions, and the subordinate, in turn, was required to perform those functions with complete obedience. That relationship resulted from the complete knowledge, if not experience, the commander had of the functions he would order the subordinate to perform. Thus commander and subordinate were interchangeable insofar as the capabilities of the subordinate were concerned. The commander could command with complete authority and expect complete obedience; for he knew the technical nature of the function to be performed and could, if need be, perform it himself.

In the technologically advanced military units of today, this traditional relationship between commander and subordinate no longer exists. The subordinates have become technological specialists, sometimes of a very high order, and between the command they receive and its execution there must intervene their own expert judgment as to the feasibility of the command and the modes of its execution. The commander may be competent to check this judgment on the basis of his own knowledge and experience in one or the other respect; but he is not likely to be able, if he commands for instance a nuclear submarine or an aircraft carrier, to check, in every respect, the judgments of all his subordinates. In consequence, his hierarchic authority as commander will be curtailed by the functional authority of his subordinates, derived from the monopolistic possession of technological expertise. The subordinate, then, transforms himself, to a certain degree, into an expert adviser, thus setting limits to the discretion of the commanding officer.*

Political resistance to the monopolistic tendencies of the modern scientific and technological elites has been more difficult and less successful than to the military elites. The reasons lie in the very nature of scientific advice. As a rule, the scientific advice the political authorities receive is not unanimous but contradictory. This happened in the instances mentioned above. In consequence, the political authorities must choose. Lacking the esoteric knowledge, their choice cannot be based upon strictly scientific considerations. What, then, is it based on? The answer to that question poses the political problem of the scientific elites.

The scientific elites, by giving expert advice that must have far-reaching political and military consequences, transform themselves of necessity into political actors of the first importance. Convinced of the truth of their scientific prognosis and its beneficial political and military results, they are compelled by the logic of their position within the dynamics of government to oppose passionately contrary scientific advice with which they connect adverse political and military consequences. The examples mentioned above bear that statement out. In the process of such controversies, the scientific arguments subtly change their character. They become political and depend for their success as much upon the political skills and outside political support of their proponents as upon their scientific soundness. The political authorities, incapable of judging the scientific issue on its merits, will tend to yield to the more persuasive and potent political pressure.

Conversely, competing interest groups within the executive branch will use scientific arguments to bolster their positions. This is typical of groups within the military establishment, competing for larger shares in missions, weapons systems, and appropriations. It is also true of the arguments between the Department of Defense and the Arms Control and Disarmament Agency and between the Atomic Energy Commission and competing agencies of the government. Thus scientific arguments have become indispensable weapons in the struggle for power within the executive branch, and the scientific elites

---

* I remember vividly my amazement when a few years ago I was invited by the commander to visit a submarine chaser and witnessed for the first time the comradely if not deferential relationship between him and his technically expert subordinates. When I commented on this new experience, the commanding officer replied: "I need them more than they need me."

have become the providers of these weapons. Starting out as the disinterested purveyors of esoteric knowledge, the scientific elites end up by rationalizing and justifying political interests by dint of their possession of esoteric knowledge.

Thus the scientific elites, by being drawn into the vortex of the political struggle, change their nature. Since their monopolistic possession of esoteric knowledge is a crucial element in political and military decisions, they become themselves protagonists of political and military policies that are in accord with their scientific judgment. While for purposes of theoretical analysis one can distinguish their roles as independent protagonists and ideological supporters, in practice those two roles tend to merge. For their political decision, independently derived from scientific judgment, is likely to coincide with a political interest, or else will give rise to one, and therefore the two roles will imperceptibly blend into each other. The scientific expert, through his dynamic involvement in the political · process, will become both the proponent and ideologue of political and military policies.

This combination of esoteric knowledge and political power alters the function and character of the scientific elites. They no longer merely advise on the basis of expert knowledge; they are also the champions of policies promoted with unrivaled authority and frequently determined by virtue of it. In the eyes both of the political authorities and the public at large, the scientific elites appear as the guardians of the *arcana imperii*, the secret remedies for public ills.

As the nature and importance of scientific knowledge transform the nature and functions of the scientific elites, democratic control becomes extinguished. Scientific knowledge is by its very nature esoteric knowledge; since it is inaccessible to the public at large, it is bound to be secret. The public finds itself in the same position vis-à-vis scientific advice as do the political authorities: Unable to retrace the arguments underlying the scientific advice, it must take that advice on faith. This would be so even if it were aware of alternative arguments supporting different decisions. In general, however, the political authorities announce their decision, supported by selected arguments, and whatever public debate there might be can only be in the nature of a *post mortem*.

This is true, in differing degrees, of most of the great decisions that mold the future of the nation, and the more vital the decision is likely to be, the more removed it is, as a rule, from popular participation and attention. Thus the determination of foreign and military policies has become virtually free from democratic controls. It is of course in the nature of things that the determination of such policies is within certain limits an executive prerogative, which can be subject to democratic scrutiny only after the event. What is new and of extraordinary significance, however, is the extension of executive discretion by virtue of the ubiquity of the technological component of the decision and the apathy of the agents of democratic control. Thus small elites within the executive branch can commit us to informal alliances and undeclared wars; they can choose military strategies and weapons systems—and whatever public debate exists is like the chorus of a Greek tragedy, praising or bewailing what has already been done.

When the government of the United States had to decide in the winter of 1962 whether or not to resume nuclear tests in the atmosphere, the American people were for the first time advised in a cogent form of the arguments pro and con in a television address in which the President announced his decision. Our policies in South Vietnam and in Southeast Asia in general are subject to perfunctory discussion in Congress and by the public, but there is no crystallization of opinion that could limit the discretion of the executive branch. Our commitment to a multilateral seaborne nuclear force (MLF), which by implication raises the fundamental issues of the future of the Atlantic Alliance, our relations with Germany and the Soviet Union, and disarmament and the proliferation of nuclear weapons, has resulted from an exercise of executive discretion followed by a perfunctory discussion by experts that the public can hardly have noticed.

This naturally secretive character of scientific knowledge, removing it from both executive understanding and democratic control, is accentuated by the artificial barriers of secrecy with which politically and militarily relevant scientific knowledge has been surrounded. Since scientific knowledge is esoteric and gives those who possess it a monopoly of power, the perpetuation of its esoteric nature, through prohibition of its dissemination, so it is argued, will perpetuate the monopoly of power. Thus as soon as we found ourselves in the possession of the nuclear bomb, we took elaborate precautions to protect its "secret." The Atomic Energy Commission, as keeper of that "secret," has become a state within the state, surrounded by a special wall of secrecy. Even government officials who have top secret clearance, giving them access to our political and military secrets, need a special clearance to penetrate the secrets of the Atomic Energy Commission. Even then, most of them will not be able to learn all there is to be known. A high official of our government, charged with making important political decisions, once told me that he could not learn how many nuclear weapons we had; and as though to confirm this statement, a high official of the Atomic Energy Commission once told me that there was certain information nobody should have access to except the President and the Director of the Central Intelligence Agency.

The secretiveness of the Atomic Energy Commission is but the most prominent example of a general tendency, prevalent in our government, to withhold state secrets not only from prospective enemies but also from other government agencies. Inside the general wall of secrecy within which the executive branch of the government dwells, there are smaller walls protecting special secrets against onlookers from within. The function of that intragovernmental secrecy, whatever the intentions of its initiators and administrators might be, cannot be the prevention of unauthorized disclosure of state secrets; for if it were, it would cast doubt upon the reliability of the great mass of government officials who, while having been cleared for top secret information in general, are precluded from access to special "secrets." Rather, the function of this special secrecy is political. By protecting esoteric knowledge, it protects and enhances power. As we have seen, the possession of esoteric knowledge is a potent weapon in the struggle for political power.

The public has responded to this inaccessibility of the reasoning behind the government decision with the political apathy that has become a common characteristic of Western democracies. It is political apathy of a peculiar kind. Not only has the public been unable to participate in any way in the great decisions affecting its very survival, but it has also been unwilling to make even an attempt at participation. It has even lost the inquisitiveness and active search for the truth, however frustrated, that have in the past been the great motive forces of democratic participation and control. The public appears to regard as normal its exclusion from knowledge, debate, and decision. The government and scientific elites, in turn, must find this absence of public interest, at the very least, convenient; for it allows them to perform their duties on the "merits of the case" and without regard for what must appear to them to be extraneous considerations. As the esoteric character of scientific knowledge calls forth the apathy of the democratic public, the peculiar character of that apathy strengthens the exemption of the scientific elites from democratic control.

As seen from the vantage point of the public, this political apathy has two interrelated sources: the remoteness of the issues from the life experiences of the man on the street, and the unintelligibility of the arguments by which the decisions of these issues are supported.

The great contemporary issues that have a scientific component are in quality different from those that commanded popular participation in the past. The great issues of the past, such as slavery, free trade, and social and economic legislation, had a direct relationship to the life experiences of the individual citizen. Their solution one way or the other had a direct, intelligible bearing upon the moral values and social interests of the individual citizen. The institution of slavery and its abolition meant something to him in very simple and personal terms, and so did the outlawry of combinations of workers as criminal conspiracies and their legal recognition as bargaining representatives; free trade and the imposition of tariffs upon the merchandise he bought; and freedom of contract and social limitations upon that freedom.

It was the immediacy of that relationship between the issues and his experiences that made it possible for the citizen to identify himself passionately with those issues, and it was the intelligibility of the arguments supporting alternative positions that made it possible for him to take an active part in the political contest culminating in the decision. Slavery a century ago was a moral issue with which all citizens could come to terms one way or another. At the turn of the century, each citizen could understand the arguments for and against legislation limiting working hours for women and outlawing child labor. The same was true, at least with regard to the basic arguments, of the New Deal legislation of the 1930's.

In these two respects—experience and understanding—the situation of the citizen with regard to the great contemporary issues is radically different from that of past generations. Issues such as the peaceful use of atomic energy, the cessation of nuclear tests, civil defense, space exploration, and nuclear war itself are far removed from his life experiences. He is able to understand the import of these issues only through a process of ratiocination, whose logical conclusions he may accept as abstract probability but has not experienced as forces affecting his life. This is true even of nuclear war. It is worthy of note that the only issue peculiar to the nuclear age that has evoked something close to widespread popular concern is that of fallout—by no means the most important issue of this kind but one that through the measurable contamination of food and air and the consequent potential hazard to health enters directly into the life experiences of the man in the street.

The remoteness of these issues as experiences is matched by what the citizen considers their unintelligibility. In this respect, the man in the street is, of course, much worse off than the government official who must make a decision. The latter can be made aware by the process of successive briefings of the core of the scientific issue and its political and military consequences, while for the citizen the whole argument is completely inaccessible. This is particularly so when he is presented with contradictory advice, which presumably is derived from incontrovertible scientific evidence. How can he, under the circumstances, take a rational stand on a treaty banning nuclear tests or make a rational choice among different kinds of such treaties? How can he, in particular, make up his mind about the kind and amount of inspection needed to insure compliance with such a treaty?

What holds true of this relatively simple issue applies with much greater and well-nigh irresistible force to more complicated issues, such as the feasibility and desirability of an antimissile missile system. One need only compare the nature of these and similar contemporary military issues with those with which the politically conscious public concerned itself, say, half a century ago, such as conscription or naval policy, in order to realize the extent to which contemporary issues have become mysteries for the public mind.

This dual remoteness of the great contemporary issues has called forth the intellectual defeatism and political apathy of the politically conscious public. Since the issues do not impinge upon the life experiences of the man in the street and since the merits of alternative solutions are inaccessible to his reason, he leaves it to the experts to take care of them. The vital link between the intellectual awareness of unresolved issues and the resolution not to leave them unresolved is missing. The common man is no longer convinced that public issues will, or even ought to, yield to concerted public action. They have become remote, unintelligible, and intractable.

A few years ago, I participated in the deliberations of a political action group whose members were far above the average in intelligence, knowledge, and political consciousness. The topic was civil defense, particularly fallout shelters. A motion not to take a stand on the issue because the group was not competent to do so was narrowly defeated. What this attitude really defeats is democratic participation and control. The ascendancy of the scientific elites, then, is a function not only of their monopoly of esoteric knowledge, but also of the abdication, in the face of it, of the politically responsible authorities and of the politically conscious public.

Is this abdication justified by the actual relationship between esoteric knowledge and political decision? The relationship that exists today between these scientific elites, on the one hand, and the political authorities and the public at large, on the other, derives from a misconception of the nature of scientific expertise. We tend to consider scientific expertise as a body of objective knowledge that is accessible only to experts and from which certain conclusions follow as a matter of logical necessity. Thus the popular mind has erected a wall between the worlds of the experts and the laymen and has endowed the former with qualities of knowledge and objectivity that set them apart from the common run of men.

However, this juxtaposition of the knowledgeable and objective scientist and the ignorant and subjective layman greatly oversimplifies and distorts reality. In truth, the scientist is by no means as knowledgeable and objective as he appears to the public, nor is the layman as ignorant and subjective as he appears to himself. Concerning the relationship between scientific advice and the political-military decision, the distinction must be drawn not between scientist and layman but between, on the one hand, the scientist as the constructor and operator of existing technology and, on the other, the scientist and the layman both trying to anticipate the technological future in a political-military context.

The reasoning behind the creation and operation of technological devices is accessible only to the scientist. Here his monopoly of esoteric knowledge holds sway. How to reduce the relationship between the weight and destructive yield of a nuclear weapon or how to shield a nuclear power plant only the scientist can say, and the layman must accept that judgment. Even if the experts differ, the layman can contribute nothing of his own judgment, and his decision will be the result of those rational arguments and political pressures that have previously been discussed.

The mental processes that go into the making of a decision about the construction and political-military effects of a new technological device are of an entirely different nature. The difference is similar to that in jurisprudence between reasoning *de lege lata*, the application of existing law, and *de lege ferenda*, the formulation and consequences of new law. This is true of both the expert advice and the decision based upon it. The two operate in the realm of conjecture, the judgment of both is derived from common sense, and the decision recommended by the expert and rendered by the authorities is political in nature. The advantage that the expert has over the layman here is restricted to the delineation of the limits of rational choice, the selection of one rational alternative over another, and the technological arguments supporting a position. Otherwise, the expert shares with the layman the same uncertainties about the future, and the political interests that enter into the decision.

The expert does not know more about the likely political and military effects of the great technological decisions of our age than the man in the street or the politically responsible official would know were they endowed with technologically informed common sense. If it comes to the need for on-site inspections to police a test-ban treaty, or the feasibility of the H-bomb or of an antimissile missile system, the scientist, like everyone else, must rely on his hunches. Indeed, it is illuminating to learn that on these issues the scientific community divides along the same lines as political officials and the public at large. For while those hunches are based upon scientific information, they are themselves in the nature of a political projection of that information into the future. The impulse behind them is political, and their choice is determined by political preferences.

Reference has already been made, on the one hand, to the non-scientific influences upon which the development of science and technology depends, and, on the other, to the nonutilitarian, "idle" curiosity that fathers many scientific discoveries. The factor we are dealing with here is utilitarian in the extreme in that the scientific advice, however sound in its own terms, is tendered as an argument in support of the political position of the expert. The expert's hunches as to the feasibility and political-military effects of a new technological device are inextricably tied to the kind of future political-military world he prefers. His selection of certain facts and the emphasis given to them, his theoretical judgment, and his projection into the future are part and parcel of his total political world view. The scientist, in common with the rest of us, looks at the political world from the vantage point of his personal perspective and preferences, and what he sees and anticipates is determined by both.

The depth of the political involvement of the scientist and the consequent political determination of his expert advice are vividly illustrated by the three great scientific controversies of the postwar period: the crash program for the H-bomb, the ban on nuclear tests, and the development of an antimissile missile system. On each of these issues, the scientific community was deeply split; each camp defended its position with specific scientific arguments. Thus one group was confident that an H-bomb could quickly be built while its opponents only gave it "a better than even chance" to be produced and thought it "wrong at the present moment to commit ourselves to an all-out effort towards its development." * On another issue, one group opposed a ban on nuclear tests, partial or total, because it was afraid that such a ban would jeopardize the continuance of the nuclear superiority of the United States. It opposed in particular a total test-ban because reliable policing could not be had without on-site inspections. On still another issue, one group advocated the development of an anti-missile missile system because it expected such a system, even in an imperfect state, to increase the relative military strength of the United States and did not rule out the possibility of its perfection. Opponents did not believe that such a system, either in its imperfect or in its hypothetical perfected states, would improve the military position of the United States.

Probing into the philosophic assumptions and political preferences that these groups have brought to their divergent positions, one realizes that the scientific arguments and conclusions are simply applications of these assumptions and preferences to concrete, specific cases of scientific policy. The different groups share in the same scientific knowledge, and, to a surprisingly large extent, even in the assessment of future scientific and technological developments. Their differences concern the future state of the world, as it will, and ought to, be determined by scientific and technological developments. Their conjectures about the future differ because their philosophic and political assessments of scientific and technological developments differ. Striking a balance between scientific and technological chances and political-military probabilities, they assign different weights to the latter and, hence, arrive at different conclusions.

The proponents of a crash program for the H-bomb and of an antimissile missile system and the opponents to a ban on nuclear tests are united in what one might call the "traditional" or "complacent" view of political and military policy in the nuclear age. They assume that the rules of the game that have come down to us from the prenuclear age apply without fundamental modification to the present day. They assume in particular that there continues to exist, after the model of conventional arms, a linear relationship between the quantity and quality of nuclear weapons and the distribution of military power. Hence, when the explosion of a nuclear device by the Soviet Union in September 1949 signaled the end of the brief American nuclear monopoly, it became imperative for them to replace this fading American advantage with another one, offered in the form of the H-bomb. Once the Soviet Union had the

* U.S. Atomic Energy Commission, *Report of the General Advisory Committee,* quoted in Gilpin, *op. cit.,* p. 89*n*.

H-bomb too, the search for another advantage had to go on, and atomic testing is considered indispensable for that purpose. The development of an antimissile missile system also offers such an advantage, which the United States cannot afford to pass up. In this view, then, we are engaged in an unending scientific and technological competition, whose dynamics compel us to try to keep continuously ahead of the other side. The competition will be won by the side that is able to gain a decisive and lasting advantage. Since the other side might gain such an advantage, it is incumbent upon us to make a continuous effort at least to keep pace in that competition.

The other group of scientists is terrified by the "cataclysmic" prospects of an unending nuclear arms race and assumes that the availability of nuclear weapons requires a drastic change in the traditional rules of foreign and military policy. It considers the continuing competition for the quantitative and qualitative development of nuclear armaments both unnecessary, since an increment of destructive power above the capability of total destruction is wasteful, and dangerous, since the intensification of the nuclear arms race increases the risks of nuclear war. Therefore, it seeks the stabilization of the existing balance of nuclear weapons and opposes futile and dangerous attempts at our gaining a competitive advantage. It opposed the crash program for the H-bomb because that program promised the intensification of the nuclear arms race on a higher level of destructiveness without promising a lasting military advantage. For the same reason it has been opposed to the development of an antimissile missile system, which would force the enemy to increase drastically its power of attack in order to saturate the defense. Finally, it has favored a ban of nuclear tests as an instrument for the stabilization of the existing distribution of nuclear power.

The politically aware scientist, then, has no advantage over the scientifically informed layman; and if the former is not politically aware he is even inferior to the latter. They both try to anticipate the future by guessing, and, as history has shown, it cannot be presumed that the guesses of one are necessarily superior to those of the other. The scientist's monopoly of the answers to the questions of the future is a myth. And with this *arcanum* it is as it was with those of old: It has to be guarded, as "essential points of the Mystery—which nevertheless everyone could come to know who desired to."*

* *Encyclopædia Britannica*, 1960 ed., s.v. "Baptism."

23

International Relations

COMMON SENSE AND THEORIES

[1967]

Aristotle found the beginning of philosophic thought in the "méga thaumázein," the "great wonderment" at an unexplained fact that requires explanation. Following the contemporary attempts at developing theories of international relations, I am continuously struck by two such facts: the contrast between the novelty of these attempts and the oldness of international relations, and the contrast between the persistence of these attempts and the consistent experience of failure.

International relations are as old as autonomous political organizations, and the ancient Chinese, Indians, and Greeks have reflected upon them. Yet with the exception of the Indian Kautilya, who developed intricate mathematical models of the balance of power, and of Machiavelli, whose *Prince* is really a theoretical treatise clothed in the traditional garb of advice to the prince on how to acquire and retain power, their reflections were philosophic and moral, not theoretical. Rather than seeking to understand in a theoretical manner what international relations are all about, they tried to learn from philosophy or history, or from a combination of both, the principles of morally right and, to a lesser degree, of successful political action.

This orientation toward practicality, moral or empirical, has been a distinctive characteristic of all reflections on foreign policy until very recently. In the *Mirror of Princes*, Machiavelli's *Prince*, the political testaments and memoirs of kings and statesmen from Louis XIV to Bismarck, the systematic treatises on diplomacy from Calliéres and Mably to Cambon and Nicolson, the concern with formulating principles that are to govern the conduct of foreign policy was predominant. What distinguishes the reflections on international relations since Machiavelli from those that preceded them is not their concern for practicality but the intellectual mode with which they endeavored to satisfy that concern. The Greek and medieval mode was predominantly ethical and deductive; that of Machiavelli and those who followed him was empirical and inductive.

This concern for practical results dominated, in the most explicit fashion and to the detriment of theoretical understanding, reflections on international relations from the end of the Napoleonic Wars to World War II. For international relations, this was the age of reform. The dominant interest was less in understanding international relations as they are than in changing them. The purpose of change was to make international peace more secure. Great intellectual energies and ingenuity were spent on developing theories of international law that, if they could be put into practice, would limit the discretion of national governments. During the nineteenth century, disarmament and international arbitration were promoted as the main devices for putting international peace on a more stable foundation; in our century, collective security, peaceful change, and international organization have been added to these devices.

In the aftermath of World War II, reflections on international relations entered an entirely new phase. This phase is marked by a number of academic schools of thought—behaviorism, systems analysis, game theory, simulation, and methodology in general—that have one aim in common: the pervasive rationalization of international relations by means of a comprehensive theory. The ultimate purpose is still practical: to increase the reliability of prediction and thereby remove uncertainty from political action. Yet this practicality is different from the traditional kind. The latter endeavored to maximize rationality and success through the rational manipulation of the objective factors of international relations; the former attempts to eradicate obstacles to pervasive rationalization that are inherent in the objective character of international relations by overwhelming them with theoretical devices. The new theories, insofar as they are new in more than terminology, are in truth not so much theories as dogmas. They do not so much try to reflect reality as it actually is as to superimpose upon a recalcitrant reality a theoretical scheme that satisfies the desire for thorough rationalization. Their practicality is specious, since it substitutes what is desirable for what is possible. The new theories are in truth utopias, differing from the utopias of old only in that they replace the simple and obvious deductions from ethical postulates with a highly complex and sophisticated methodological and terminological apparatus, creating the illusion of empirical demonstration.

This illusion is made plausible by two interconnected devices: a reductionism that deprives international relations of their political content, and quantification. Reductionism has been a necessary, and hence persistent, element of all international utopias from the Middle Ages to the present. For it is only by abstracting from that quality of politics, domestic and international, that resists pervasive rationalization and is responsible for the moral dilemmas, political risks, and intellectual uncertainties inherent in politics, that it is possible to construct a morally and intellectually satisfying theoretical scheme. That distinctive quality of politics is the struggle for power. It is at the root of all that is morally repellent, politically risky, and intellectually unsatisfactory in international relations. It is morally repellent because it violates the basic precept of Judeo-Christian morality: to treat a man as an end and not as a means. For it is of the very essence of the *animus dominandi* to impose the actor's will upon another man and to make him an instrument of that will. It is politically risky because out of the conflict of opposing desires for power there arises the propensity to violence whose consummation is the physical destruction of the opponent, who resists that consummation with violence of his own. It is theoretically unsatisfactory because power, like love, is a complex psychological relationship that cannot be completely dissolved into a rational theoretical scheme. The theoretician of international relations who approaches his subject matter with respect for its intrinsic nature will find himself frustrated morally, politically, and intellectually; for his aspiration for a pervasively rational theory is hemmed in by the insuperable resistance of the subject matter.

The new theories of international relations have yielded to the temptation to overcome this resistance of the subject matter by disregarding its intrinsic nature. Thus some of these theories have assumed that since power is a difficult concept to deal with, power is not the central concept giving unity to international relations. Others have assumed that power is not the complex and elusive psychological phenomenon it actually is by equating it with military power. Still others—and they have dominated the scene during the last decade—have assumed that politics does not need to be explained in its own terms, that is, in terms of power, but can be reduced to the manifestation of something else more susceptible to pervasive rationalization. That "something else" was found, either explicitly or implicitly, in economics.

The stage for this contemporary reductionism was set by nineteenth-century Marxism and liberalism. Marxism saw in politics an element of the superstructure whose character and development was determined by the underlying economic forces. For liberalism, politics, especially among nations, was a kind of atavism, the "pastime of the aristocracy," about to be replaced by commercial relations beneficial to all. These two intellectual movements arose from, and provided the philosophic underpinning for, the climate of opinion, prevalent in the Western and more particularly the Anglo-Saxon world, that finds the existing international scene morally distasteful, and in the twentieth century also physically dangerous, and tries to escape from it either by reforming it or by making it appear as something different from what it actually is. Woodrow Wilson, trying to abolish the balance of power rather than to understand and manipulate it, is the most eloquent spokesman for that mood.

What characterizes contemporary theories of international relations is the attempt to use the tools of modern economic analysis in a modified form in order to understand international relations. Their mainstay is quantification. The use of terms such as "systems analysis," "feedback," "input," and "output" (to mention only a few common and easily accessible ones) is revealing, for these concepts were first developed by economic theory. Even more revealing is the mode of thought that dominates many of the contemporary theories of international relations. Whether they deal with the strategy of conflict or diplomatic bargaining or nuclear escalation, they visualize international conflict as a special case of social conflict in general (which is correct if one does not neglect the paramount distinctive factor that the parties to international conflict are sovereign nations with a monopoly of organized force), whose paradigm is economic conflict (which, as we shall see, is incorrect). In such a theoretical scheme, nations confront each other not as living historic entities with all their complexities but as rational abstractions, after the model of "economic man," playing games of military and diplomatic chess according to a rational calculus that exists nowhere but in the theoretician's mind.

It is widely recognized by economists that this rationalistic, quantitative approach is of limited applicability even to economics; for even here it neglects psychological forces that interfere with the smooth operation of the rational calculus. Its applicability is established by the nature of the central concept of economics: wealth. Conversely, its inapplicability to politics is established by the nature of the central concept of politics: power. Wealth is a measurable quantity that an individual aspires to, competes or fights for, controls, possesses, or loses. Power is a quality of interpersonal relations that can be experienced, evaluated, guessed at, but that is not susceptible to quantification. What can be quantified are certain elements that go into the making of power, individual or collective, and it is a common error to equate such a quantifiable element of power with power as such. It is certainly possible and necessary to determine how many votes a politician controls, how many divisions or nuclear warheads a government disposes of; but if I want to know how much power this politician or that government has, I must leave the adding machine and the computer for historical and necessarily qualitative judgment.

Modern theorists of international relations are repelled by history; for history is the realm of the accidental, the contingent, the unpredictable. They are instead fascinated by the rational model of the natural sciences, which appear to be free of these blemishes that stand in the way of the thorough rationalization of international relations. I tried to show more than twenty years ago* that this model of the natural sciences harks back to a Newtonian universe that the contemporary natural sciences have left far behind. This rational model is a utopia that reflects the desires of theoreticians but not the real physical world, dominated as that world is by the principle of indeterminacy, and predictable as it is, at least as microcosmos, only by way of statistical probability.

I have also tried to show that politics, domestic and international, is susceptible to a radically different kind of understanding from that which is appropriate to the world of nature. When we try to understand international relations, we are dealing, it is true, with men in the aggregate, but with men per se, that is, as spiritual and moral beings, whose actions and reactions can be rationalized and quantitatively understood only on the lowest level of their existence. Thus what the contemporary theories of international relations endeavor to exorcise as deficiencies in view of an ideal, per-

---

* *Scientific Man vs. Power Politics* (Chicago: University of Chicago Press, 1946; Phoenix Books, 1965).

vasively rational theory is in truth but the ineradicable qualities of the subject matter itself. A theory that does not take them into account transforms itself into a dogma, a kind of metaphysics, regardless in what empirical or mathematical garb it is clothed.

This transformation of theory has also transformed the function that theoretical reflection has traditionally performed for the practice of international politics. It has done so in two different ways. The main practical function that a theory of international relations must perform in our period of history is to confront what governments do, and what governments and peoples think, about international relations with independent prudential judgment and with the truth, however dimly perceived and tenuously approximated. International relations today is one of the major spheres in which prudence and truth are bent to the purposes of power, and in which superstition takes the place of rational knowledge. As William Graham Sumner put it at the beginning of the century: "The amount of superstition is not much changed, but it now attaches to politics, not to religion."

As it was once the task of rational demonstration to show that natural phenomena were not caused by devils, demons, and witches and that one could not master these phenomena by ritualistically exorcising their alleged causes or destroying them in their imagined human form, so a contemporary theory of international relations must put current notions about international relations, such as beliefs in world-wide conspiracies, naturally evil nations, and revolutions at the service of such conspiracies and nations, to the test of empirical verification. The contemporary theories of international relations are irrelevant to that task. They laboriously evade it.

For these beliefs, which serve the psychological needs of the believers rather than the quest for truth, a theory of international relations worthy of the name must substitute the empirical examination of the historical data that may prove or disprove, as the case may be, the assumptions upon which governments act and the unexamined beliefs by which the man in the street forms his judgments. Thus the dogmatism of the contemporary theories of international relations reveals itself as what has been correctly called a "new scholasticism,"* that is, an intellectual exercise, frequently executed with a high degree of acumen and sophistication, that tells us nothing we need to know about the real world.

However, this failure to meet the practical intellectual needs

* Barrington Moore, Jr., "The New Scholasticism and the Study of Politics," *World Politics*, VI (1953), 122–38.

that theoretical reflection on international relations ought to meet and has always met throughout history does not imply that these theories do not perform a practical function. They operate within a social context in which truth, superstition, and different conceptions of ends and means struggle for influence upon thought and action, and they contribute to the outcome of that struggle. It is not by accident that they are lavishly supported by foundations, highly prized by academic institutions, and influential at least at the margins of governmental action. For they perform two important ideological functions, one for themselves, the other for the official doctrines of international relations.

The contemporary theories of international relations provide a respectable protective shield behind which members of the academic community may engage in noncontroversial theoretical pursuits. International relations in our period of history are by their very nature controversial. They require decisions concerning the purposes of the nation and affecting its chances for physical survival. By dealing with the subject matter but not with the issues underlying these decisions, a theory can appear to contribute to the rationality of the decisions without actually doing so. This appearance is enhanced if the theory is couched in language and underpinned with charts and equations that are accessible only to a small group of initiated academics. Here is another similarity between certain branches of modern social science and religion: the suggestion of profundity and mysterious knowledge implicit in unintelligibility. It must also be said in passing that esoteric language and method allow the trivial to appear important and sloppy reasoning to take on the appearance of precise demonstration.*

Although contemporary theories of international relations are by and large neutral with regard to the great controversies over truth and superstition and different national ends and means, they inevitably tend to support the *status quo*, that is, the official doctrine. In the never-ending conflict between the official doctrine, on the one hand, and truth and dissident prudential judgment, on the other, dissent from the official doctrine is of necessity the "aggressor." It examines critically what is officially held to be true and exposes falsehood where it finds it. Theories that are by their very existence committed to the avoidance of that task probe and expose nothing

---

* Sometimes one is reminded of Lucky Jim's comment on his work "The Economic Influence of the Developments in Shipbuilding Techniques, 1450 to 1485": ". . . its niggling mindlessness, its funeral parade of yawn-enforcing fact, the pseudo-light it threw upon non-problems."

relevant and thus give by implication the sanction of truth and prudence to the official doctrine. Thus contemporary theories of international relations provide a respectable protective shield not only for their practitioners but also for the official doctrine. By saying nothing against it, they imply that there is nothing to be said against it.

THE INTELLECTUAL AND POLITICAL FUNCTIONS OF THEORY

[1964]

In the April, 1960, issue of *International Relations*, Professor Martin Wight, then of the London School of Economics and Political Science, published a paper that bore the title "Why Is There No International Theory?" While I cannot, of course, subscribe to the unqualified negativism of the title for both personal and professional reasons, I find the paper a most illuminating and penetrating discussion of the problem. Its fourteen pages contain more insights into the intellectual issues posed by theoretical concern with international relations than a whole shelf of books and articles that, following the fashion of the day, spin out theories about theories of international relations and embark upon esoteric methodological studies on how to approach such theory-making.

Professor Wight finds elements of an international theory in writings of international lawyers, such as Grotius and Pufendorf; the so-called "irenists," seekers after a peaceful international order, such as Erasmus, Sully, Campanella, Crucé, Penn, the Abbé de St. Pierre; the Machiavellians rediscovered by Meinecke; the *parerga* of political philosophers, philosophers, and historians, such as Hume's "The Balance of Power," Rousseau's *Projet de Paix Perpétuelle*, Mably's *Principes des Négociations*; and finally the speeches, dispatches, memoirs, and essays of statesmen and diplomatists, such as Gentz's *Fragments on the Balance of Power** or Bismarck's memoirs. Professor Wight concludes that "international theory is marked, not only by paucity but also by intellectual and moral poverty. For this we must look to internal reasons. The most obvious are the intellectual prejudice imposed by the sovereign State, and the belief in progress."

According to Professor Wight, the sovereign state has been the focus of Western political thought and experience since the Reforma-

* Classified by Wight in the preceding category.

tion. Almost all intellectual energies devoted to political studies have been absorbed by it. He writes: "It has been natural to think of international politics as the untidy fringe of domestic politics . . . and to see international theory in the manner of the political theory textbooks, as an additional chapter which can be omitted by all save the interested student." Political theory, centered upon the state and its survival within the existing state system, has prevailed over international theory, wherein the state system itself is studied as a phenomenon that owes its existence to the historical process and is destined to be superseded by it. This is what Wight calls "a small-scale field of political theory." International theorists "have not been attracted by the possibility of maximising the field of political theory through establishing a world State. Nor is it unfair to see the League and the United Nations as the expression of a belief that it may be possible to secure the benefits of a world State without the inconveniences of instituting and maintaining it." Wight finds it significant that none of the three most powerful influences on the development of the modern state system—the Reformation and Counter Reformation, the French Revolution, and the totalitarian revolutions of the twentieth century—has brought forth a coherent body of international theory.

The other impediment to the development of an international theory Professor Wight finds in the fact that

the character of international politics is incompatible with progressivist theory. Thus international theory that remains true to diplomatic experience will be at a discount in an age when the belief in progress is prevalent. If Sir Thomas More or Henry IV, let us say, were to return to England and France in 1960, it is not beyond plausibility that they would admit that their countries had moved domestically toward goals and along paths which they could approve. But if they contemplated the international scene, it is more likely that they would be struck by resemblances to what they remembered. International politics is the realm of recurrence and repetition; it is the field in which political action is most regularly necessitous.

Yet when the modern mind comes face to face with this immutable character of international politics, it revolts and takes refuge in the progressivist conviction that what was true in the past cannot be true in the future; for if it were, mankind would be in desperate straits. This is what Wight calls "the argument from desperation." Thus "whereas political theory generally is in unison with political activity, international theory (at least in its chief embodiment as international law) sings a kind of descant over against the movement of diplomacy. . . . International law seems to follow an inverse movement to that of international politics." This tension between international theory and international reality is already obvious in the identification of international politics with a precontractual state of nature assumed by the classical international lawyers. Yet while the state of nature among individuals leads to the social contract, establishing authority over, and peace and order among, them, international theory sees no need for a similar development among states.

Wight finds it odd that,

> while the acknowledged classics of political study are the political philosophers, the only counterpart in the study of international relations is Thucydides, a work of history. And that the quality of international politics, the preoccupations of diplomacy, are embodied and communicated less in works of political or international theory than in historical writings. There are out of date books like Seeley's *Growth of British Policy*, which were second-rate at best, that might be thought to convey the nature of foreign policy and the working of the State-system better than much recent literature concerned with the games theory, decision-making, politicometrics and psychological concepts.

Wight summarizes his position by pointing to

> a kind of recalcitrance of international politics to being theorised about. The reason is that the theorising has to be done in the language of political theory and law. But this is the language appropriate to man's control of his social life. Political theory and law are maps of experience or systems of action within the realm of normal relationships and calculable results. They are the theory of the good life. International theory is the theory of survival. What for political theory is the extreme case (as revolution or civil war) is for international theory the regular case.

Thus in the end, international theory "involves the ultimate experience of life and death, national existence and national extinction." What we call international theory, then, amounts to a kind of philosophy of history.

It hardly needs pointing out that my position coincides in large measure with that of Professor Wight.* I take, indeed, a more sanguine view of the possibility of international theory than he does,

---

* I am referring, of course, primarily to *Politics Among Nations*, 4th ed. (New York: Knopf, 1967), more particularly to Chapters 11–14, 17, 19, and 29, dealing with the balance of power, the nation-state, and world government, respectively.

finding that possibility in the very fact that "international politics is the realm of recurrence and repetition." It is this repetitive character of international politics, that is, the configurations of the balance of power, that lends itself to theoretical systematization. I would also hesitate to equate international theory with philosophy of history. Theory is implicit in all great historiography. In historians with a philosophic bent, such as Thucydides and Ranke, the history of foreign policy appears as a mere demonstration of certain theoretical assumptions which are always present beneath the surface of historical events to provide the standards for their selection and to give them meaning. In such historians of international politics, theory is like the skeleton, which, invisible to the naked eye, gives form and function to the body. What distinguishes such a history of international politics from a theory is not so much its substance as its form. The historian presents his theory in the form of a historical recital, using the chronological sequence of events as a demonstration of his theory. The theoretician, dispensing with the historical recital, makes the theory explicit and uses historic facts in bits and pieces to demonstrate his theory.

Yet both Wight's and my orientation are historical, and it is this historical orientation that sets us apart from the present fashionable theorizing about international relations. This theorizing is abstract in the extreme and totally unhistoric. It endeavors to reduce international relations to a system of abstract propositions with a predictive function. Such a system transforms nations into stereotyped "actors" engaging in equally stereotyped symmetric or asymmetric relations. What Professor Wight has noted of international law applies with particular force to these theories: the contrast between their abstract rationalism and the actual configurations of world politics.* We are here in the presence of still another type of progressivist theory. Its aim is not the legalization and organization of international relations in the interest of international order and peace but the rational manipulation of international relations and, more particularly, of military strategy in the interest of predictable and controlled results. The ideal toward which these theories try to progress is ultimately international peace and order to be achieved through scientific precision and predictability in understanding and manipulating international affairs.

* See, for instance, the special issue on "The International System," *World Politics*, Vol. XVI, No. 1 (October, 1961), and the critique of this type of thinking in Irving Louis Horowitz, "Arms, Policies and Games," *The American Scholar*, Vol. 31, No. 1 (Winter, 1961–62), 94 ff.

In view of their consistent neglect of the contingencies of history and of the concreteness of historical situations that all these theories have in common, they are destined to share the fate of their progressivist predecessors: They must fail both as guides for theoretical understanding and as precepts for action. However, the practical consequences of their theoretical deficiencies are likely to be more serious than those of their predecessors.

The straits in which the Western democracies found themselves at the beginning of World War II were, in good measure, the result of the reliance upon the inner force of legal pronouncements, such as the Stimson Doctrine, which refused to recognize territorial changes brought about by violence; of legal agreements, such as the Kellogg-Briand Pact and nonaggression treaties; and of international organizations, such as the League of Nations, which were incapable of collective action. The scientist theories of our day pretend to be capable of manipulating with scientific precision a society of sovereign nations that use weapons of total destruction as instruments of their respective foreign policies. With that pretense, these theories create the illusion that a society of sovereign nations thus armed can continue the business of foreign policy and military strategy in the traditional manner without risking its destruction. They create the illusion of the viability of the nation-state in the nuclear age. If statesmen should take these theories at their pseudoscientific word and act upon them, they would fail, as the statesmen of the interwar period failed when they acted upon the progressivist theories of their day.

It is significant that, until very recently, no explicit theory of international relations has existed; nobody even considered the possibility of writing a theory of international relations. This is a very significant fact, which ought to give us pause. For certainly theoretically inclined, reflective people have been aware, since the beginning of history, of the existence of international relations, the facts of foreign policy, the fateful results of good and bad foreign policies, the significance of success or failure in foreign policy. And certainly we have not grown so much wiser in recent years or so much more acute in self-awareness that we have all of a sudden started to think in theoretical terms of one of the crucial facts of human existence, recognized as such by prophets, statesmen, historians, and political philosophers for thousands of years. There must be a profound reason why, until very recently, nobody has thought of writing an explicit theory of international relations. Certainly, it could not have been the backwardness of Plato and Aristotle or

Hobbes and Locke which prevented them from developing such a theory.

The first reason why there has been no theory, but only history, of international relations is to be found in the philosophic outlook that prevailed until the end of the Napoleonic Wars. Until then, the relations among nations were regarded as a fact of nature that was beyond the power of man to change. The relations among nations were considered a datum of history and a state of nature, resulting from the nature of man; nothing could be said in terms of a specific theory of international relations about their characteristics and about their manipulation. Given this outlook, the best theory could do was what political philosophy actually did, that is, to describe the state of nature and the rudimentary legal order existing, or assumed to exist, among nations.

As long as man believed that the relations among nations were beyond human control, beyond reform by the human will, there was no place in the intellectual scheme of things for a theory of international relations. In this respect, international theory found itself in the same position as social theory in general. As long as people believed that poverty, for instance, was a natural state, which man had to accept without being able to change it, social philosophy could do no more than affirm this natural condition. As long as this state of mind persisted, there was no possibility for the development of a social theory, a social theory of change at least. What the *Times* said in mid-nineteenth century of the misery of the unemployed— "There is no one to blame for this; it is the result of Nature's simplest laws!"—people said of international relations. Thus the intellectual possibility of a theory of international relations depended upon the recognition that the relations among nations are not something which is given to man, which he has to accept as given, and which he must cope with as best he can; rather, it is that the relations among nations have been created by the will of man and therefore can be manipulated and changed and reformed by the will of man.

The second reason why theoretical concern with international relations was so late in emerging lies in the reformist orientation that characterized theoretical thinking on foreign policy in the nineteenth and the first decades of the twentieth century. The main theoretical concern during that period was not with understanding the nature of international relations but with developing legal institutions and organizational devices that would supersede the type of international relations then existing. "Power politics" itself as a synonym for foreign policy was then a term of opprobrium, referring to something evil, not to be understood but to be abolished. Woodrow Wilson during and after World War I provides a classic and most impressive example of that position: He was interested not in understanding the operation of the balance of power but in getting rid of it, in reforming international relations in such a way that one did not need to resort any more to the balance of power. Franklin D. Roosevelt and Cordell Hull shared that position.* As long as such a negative orientation toward the nature of international relations and foreign policy persisted, it was both intellectually and morally impossible to deal in a theoretical, that is, an objective, systematic manner, with problems of international relations.

The third and permanent factor, which does not make a theory of international relations altogether impossible but strictly limits its development and usefulness, is to be found in the very nature of politics, domestic and international. There is a rational element in political action that makes politics susceptible to theoretical analysis, but there is also a contingent element in politics that obviates the possibility of theoretical understanding.

The material with which the theoretician of politics must deal is ambiguous. The events he must try to understand are, on the one hand, unique occurrences: They happened in this way only once and never before or since. On the other hand, they are similar; for they are manifestations of social forces. Social forces are the product of human nature in action. Therefore, under similar conditions, they will manifest themselves in a similar manner. But where is the line to be drawn between the similar and the unique? The political world appears to the theoretical mind as a highly complicated combination of numerous systems of multiple choices, which, in turn, are strictly limited in number. The element of irrationality, insecurity, and chance lies in the necessity of choice among several possibilities multiplied by the great number of systems of multiple choice. The element of rationality, order, and regularity lies in the limited number of possible choices within each system of multiple choice. Viewed with the guidance of a rationalistic, blueprinted map, the social world is, indeed, a chaos of contingencies. Yet it is not devoid of a measure of rationality if approached with the modest expectations of a circumspect theory.

To take, as an example, three current situations, we may say that the situations in Laos, Cuba, and Berlin provide American foreign policy with a limited number of rational choices. For some strange reason, these choices generally number three. What a theory of inter-

* See quotations on pages 76–77.

national relations can state is the likely consequences of choosing one alternative as opposed to another and the conditions under which one alternative is more likely to occur and be successful than the other. Theory can also say that under certain conditions one alternative is to be preferred to another. But all these theoretical analyses are contingent upon factors that either occur without our knowing or have consequences beyond our foresight.

For instance, there is the crucial problem of nuclear war. It is possible to develop a theory of nuclear war, as Herman Kahn has done in his book *On Thermonuclear War*, which assumes nuclear war to be just another kind of violence, greater in magnitude but no different in kind from the types of violence with which history has acquainted us. It follows from this assumption that nuclear war is going to be much more terrible than conventional war, but not necessarily intolerable, provided we take the measures which will enable us to survive it. In other words, once you start with this theoretical assumption of the nature and the consequences of a nuclear war, you can logically arrive at Mr. Kahn's conclusion that the foreign policy of the United States does not need to limit itself to trying to avoid nuclear war, but that the United States must also prepare to survive it. And then it becomes perfectly legitimate to raise the question, provided 100 million Americans were to be killed in a nuclear war and nine-tenths of the economic capacity of the United States were to be destroyed, "How do we enable the survivors to rebuild the United States with the remaining one-tenth of economic capacity?"

The contingent element in this theory of nuclear war is its utter uncertainty, and this uncertainty is typical of all levels of theoretical analysis and prediction in the field of politics, domestic and international. Even if one were to accept all its estimates of deaths and material destruction and of the rate of material recovery, this theory would have to be uncertain about the human reaction to the kind of human and material devastation which nuclear war is likely to bring about. Obviously, if a highly complex human society could be visualized to operate like a primitive ant society, its recuperative ability could be taken for granted. If one-third of the ants of one anthill have been destroyed together with nine-tenths of the material of the anthill, it is safe to conclude that the remaining ants will start all over again, building up the anthill and reproducing until the next catastrophe will force them to start once more.

But it is a moot question whether a human society has this type of mechanical recuperative ability. Societies have a breaking point as do individuals, and there may be a point beyond which human

endurance does not carry human initiative in the face of such unprecedented massive devastation. Perhaps, under the impact of such
devastation, civilization itself will collapse.

It is at this point that theoretical understanding of international relations reaches its limits. It can develop different alternatives and clarify their necessary preconditions and likely consequences.
It can point to the conditions that render one alternative more
likely to materialize than the other. But it cannot say, with any
degree of certainty, which of the alternatives is the correct one and
will actually occur.

This is but an extreme example of the utter uncertainty of theorizing about foreign policy beyond the clarification of alternative policies and of their possibilities and possible consequences. The Munich
settlement of 1938 is another case in point. In retrospect, of course, we
all know from practical experience that it was a failure, and from
that experience we have developed the theoretical categories that
demonstrate that it was bound to be such a failure. But I remember
very well the near unanimity with which the Munich settlement was
approved by theoreticians and practitioners of foreign policy and by
the man in the street as well. The Munich settlement was generally
regarded at the time of its conclusion as a great act of statesmanship,
a concession made to a would-be conqueror for the sake of peace.
E. H. Carr so regarded it then, and A. J. P. Taylor so regards it now.
The flaw in that reasoning, which few people were, and perhaps could
be, aware of at the time, was again the neglect of the contingencies
inherent in political prediction. That which reveals itself as a simple
truth in retrospect was either completely unknown in prospect or
else could not be determined by anything but an uncertain hunch.

Apply the reasoning with which I have just analyzed the Munich
settlement of 1938 to a hypothetical Berlin settlement of 1962. One
of the alternatives for American foreign policy, which theoretical
analysis can isolate, is to make certain concessions to the Soviet Union
that change the modalities of the West's presence in Berlin but leave
that presence itself intact. Another alternative, also revealed by theoretical analysis, is to stand on the Western right to be in Berlin and
refuse to make any concessions, because whatever concessions we
make will of necessity be followed by other concessions; step by step,
then, our presence in West Berlin will be whittled down until it becomes untenable.

A third alternative assumes that our presence in Berlin is a priori
untenable. It holds that the symbolic value of our presence in Berlin
with regard to the unification of Germany has really been bypassed by

history because the division of Germany has become definitive. Sooner or later, we must recognize this fact and adapt our policies to it. Especially in view of the risks involved and the odds against success, there is no point in maintaining a symbol that has no longer any active function to perform.

A theoretical argument can be made for any of those three alternatives, and nobody can say in advance with any degree of certainty which of the courses of action indicated by the alternatives is correct in theory, is sound in practice, or is likely to be a choice for actual policy. Only in retrospect, judging from the nature and the results of the action chosen, can we answer these questions. This limitation of theoretical analysis is inherent in the very subject matter of international relations, and this subject matter places insuperable limits on the development of a rational theory of international relations. It is only within those limits that theoretical thinking on international relations is theoretically and practically fruitful. Within these limits, a theory of international relations performs the functions any theory performs, that is, to bring order and meaning into a mass of unconnected material and to increase knowledge through the logical development of certain propositions empirically established.

While this theoretical function of a theory of international relations is no different from the function any social theory performs, its practical function is peculiar to itself. The practical function of a theory of international relations has this in common with all political theory: It depends very much upon the political environment within which the theory operates. In other words, political thinking is, as German sociology puts it, *standortgebunden,* that is to say, it is tied to a particular social situation. And we find that all great and fruitful political thought, which we still remember because of its greatness and fruitfulness, has started from a concrete political situation with which the political thinkers had to come to terms for both intellectual and practical reasons. Edmund Burke is a typical example of how great and fruitful political theory develops from concrete practical concerns. It is not being created by a professor sitting in his ivory tower and, with his publisher, looking over a contract that stipulates the delivery of a manuscript on the "Theory of International Relations" by a specified date. It is developed out of the concern of a politically alive and committed mind with the concrete political problems of the day. Thus, all great political theory, from Plato and Aristotle and the Biblical prophets to our day, has been practical political theory, political theory that intervenes actively in a concrete political situation with the purpose of change through action.

A theory of international relations can perform four different practical functions by approaching political reality in four different ways. I shall try to exemplify these four different ways with my own experience as a theoretician of international relations, attempting to come to terms with the issues of international relations and of American foreign policy, in particular, since the end of World War II.

I had my first experience as a theoretician of international relations under the Truman-Acheson administration of America's foreign policy. Theory then provided a theoretical justification for what the policy-makers were doing, one may say, instinctively—what they were doing pragmatically on a mere day-by-day basis.

By 1947, the new pattern of American foreign policy was set. It manifested itself in four political innovations: the Truman Doctrine, containment, the Marshall Plan, and the American alliance system. These policies have in common the permanent assumption, by the United States, of responsibilities beyond the limits of the Western Hemisphere. The heart of that new policy was the policy of containment. Yet the policy of containment was never officially formulated. It grew as an almost instinctive reaction to the threat of Russian imperialism. It called a halt to the territorial expansion of Russian power beyond the line of military demarcation drawn, at the end of World War II, between the Soviet orbit and the Western world.

There was no theory in support of these new policies. It was only as an afterthought that theoreticians developed a doctrine in the form of a theoretical framework that gave rational justification to the new policies. The policy-makers "played it by ear"; they did what they thought they needed to do under the circumstances. They embarked upon courses of action that at the time appeared to them almost inevitable in view of their knowledge of the threat and of their objectives. It was only as a kind of intellectual reassurance that a theory of American foreign policy was developed that put the stamp of rational approval upon policies already established.

The function of the theoretician of international relations under the two Eisenhower Administrations, dominated by the foreign policy of John Foster Dulles, was of an entirely different nature. It was a function that had many precedents in the history of political thought. One can even go so far as to say that it is one that political theories have traditionally performed. Theory here developed a coherent system of thought, which was supposed to embody the sound principles of foreign policy. The actual conduct of American foreign policy was judged by the standards of that theory and frequently found wanting. Criticism directed at that theory was similarly judged and justified or found wanting, as the case might have been, by the standards of the theory. I remember very vividly that whenever I published an article critical of the foreign policy of Mr. Dulles, I found nowhere more enthusiastic approval of that criticism than in the Department of State. Theory here provided a rational framework for a nonorthodox, critical political position either within the government or outside it. Theory gave a rational justification to that position.

The situation in which the theoretician of international relations has found himself since the Kennedy Administration took office on January 20, 1961, is, of course, quite extraordinary. What is the function of the outside theoretician when the government itself is staffed in the command posts of foreign policy by theoreticians? It stands to reason that he has become in good measure technologically obsolete. I have, since January 20, 1961, reflected with a great deal of embarrassment upon this change of position. Hardly anybody asks my advice now, because the people in government know at least as much as I do, and probably some are convinced that they know much more—and perhaps they actually do.

What, then, is the function of the academic theoretician of international relations in a society in which foreign policy itself is determined by theoretically conscious policy-makers? There is still a function to be performed. For it is in the very nature of the conduct of foreign policy in a democracy that what theoreticians regard to be the sound principles of foreign policy must be adapted to the preferences of public opinion and to the pressures of domestic politics, and thereby corrupted and distorted. I remember the statement I once heard a former Secretary of State make to the effect that he had always regarded it as his function to give the President advice on the basis of what he thought the principles of a sound American foreign policy required, leaving it to the President to decide how much of those sound principles could be safely put into practice in view of the state of domestic public opinion and the pressures of domestic politics.

Thus, the actual foreign policies pursued by a government staffed even by theoreticians are bound to fall short, from time to time, of the requirements of a pure theoretical understanding of what American foreign policy ought to be. It is here that the theoretician of foreign policy must perform the function of an intellectual conscience which reminds the policy makers as well as the public at large of what the sound principles of foreign policy are and in what respects and to what extent actual policies have fallen short of those principles.

There is a final task—and perhaps it is the most noble of all—that a theory of international relations can and must perform, particularly in an age in which the very structure of international relations has radically changed. It is to prepare the ground for a new international order radically different from that which preceded it. Theoretical analysis can show that the principle of political organization that has dominated the modern world from the French Revolution of 1789 to this day is no longer valid. The sovereign nation-state is in the process of becoming obsolete. That is to say, the fact of nuclear power, together with the modern technologies of transportation and communications, which transcends the ability of any nation-state to control and harness it and render it both innocuous and beneficial, requires a principle of political organization transcending the nation-state and commensurate with the potentialities for good or evil of nuclear power itself. Theoretical analysis can show that the availability of nuclear power as an instrument of foreign policy is the only real revolution that has occurred in the structure of international relations since the beginning of history, because it has radically changed the relationship between violence as a means of foreign policy and the ends of foreign policy.

Until the end of World War II, there existed a rational relationship between violence as a means of foreign policy and the ends of foreign policy; that is to say, the policy-maker could rationally ask himself whether he should pursue the aims of his country by peaceful means or whether he ought to go to war. If he chose the latter alternative and if he lost the war, his nation lost in general only a bearable fraction of its human and material resources. If he won, then the risks taken were justified by the victory gained. This rational relationship between violence as a means and the ends of foreign policy has been obliterated by the availability of nuclear power. Nuclear power provides governments with a destructive force transcending all possible rational objectives of foreign policy. For all-out nuclear war is likely to obliterate the very distinction between victor and vanquished and will certainly destroy the very objective for which such a war would be fought. It is here that a theory of international relations has a creative and vital task to perform, a task that has been performed throughout history by the political theories of domestic politics. It is at this point that the realistic and utopian approaches to politics in general, and to international relations in particular, merge.

It is a legitimate and vital task for a theory of politics to anticipate drastic changes in the structure of politics and in the institutions which must meet a new need. The great political utopians have based their theoretical anticipation of a new political order upon the realistic analysis of the empirical *status quo* in which they lived. Today, political theory and, more particularly, a theory of international relations, starting from the understanding of politics and international relations as they are, must attempt to illuminate the impact nuclear power is likely to exert upon the structure of international relations and upon the functions domestic government performs. Further, it must anticipate in a rational way the intellectual, political, and institutional changes that this unprecedented revolutionary force is likely to require.

There is another function of international theory, which is not so much intellectual as psychological in nature and is of interest primarily to the sociology of knowledge. It is to provide a respectable shield that protects the academic community from contact with the living political world. That function is performed by much of the methodological activities carried on in academic circles, with sometimes fanatical devotion to esoteric terminology and mathematical formulas, equations, and charts, in order to elucidate or obscure the obvious. These activities can be explained psychologically by the fear of many academics to come into too close a contact with the political world, to become controversial in consequence, and to be contaminated in their objective scholarship by contact with political reality. By engaging in activities that can have no relevance for the political problems of the day, such as theorizing about theories, one can maintain one's reputation as a scholar without running any political risks. This kind of international theory, then, is consummated in theorizing for theorizing's sake, an innocuous intellectual pastime engaged in by academics for the benefit of other academics, without effect upon political reality and unaffected by it.

In conclusion, it may be said that the nature of a theory of international relations and the intellectual and political functions a theory of international relations performs and ought to perform are not, in essence, different from the nature of general political theory and the functions such theories have performed since the beginning of history. The fact that we have only in recent years turned toward explicit theoretical reflection about international relations is, in good measure, due to our recognition that international relations is not something to be taken for granted but something to be understood and to be changed and, more particularly, to be changed beyond the present limits of its political structure and organization. Here lies, indeed, the ultimate theoretical and practical justification of our interest in a theory of international relations. Threatened by the unsolved political problems of the day, we have come to think more and more in terms of a supranational community and a world government, a political organization and structure that transcend the nation-state. Reflecting on a theory of international relations, the politically conscious theoretician cannot help reflecting upon the political problems whose solution requires such novel structures and types of organization.

24

Government and Private Enterprise

[January, 1964]

Private enterprise is threatened from two quarters: from within the economic sphere itself through the accumulation of uncontrolled power in the hands of economic organizations, such as giant corporations and labor unions, and from the intervention of the state in the economic sphere. Thus the economic sphere, at least on the corporate level, has lost much of the autonomy it has had in the past: It is subject to political control as it, in turn, tries to control political decisions. We are in the presence of the revival of a truly political economy, and the major economic problems are political in nature.

This interconnectedness of the political and economic spheres is not peculiar to our age. Even in the heyday of nineteenth-century liberalism, the strict separation of the two spheres was in the nature of a political ideal rather than the reflection of observable reality. The monetary, tax, and tariff policies of the government had then, as they have now, a direct bearing upon the economic life—and so had the outlawry of the associations of working men as criminal conspiracies. Yet the ideal of strict separation served the political purpose of protecting the economic forces from political control without impeding their influence in the political sphere.

What is peculiar to our age is not the interconnectedness of politics and economics but its positive philosophic justification and its all-pervasiveness. The state is no longer looked upon solely as the umpire who sees to it that the rules of the game are observed and who intervenes actively only if, as in the case of the railroads, the rules of the game favor one player to excess and thereby threaten to disrupt the game itself. In our age, aside from still being the umpire, the state has also become the most powerful player, who, in order to make sure of the outcome, in good measure rewrites the rules of the game as he goes along. No longer does the government or society at large rely exclusively upon the mechanism of the market to insure that the game keeps going. Both deem it the continuing duty of the government to see to it that it does.

In the United States, the state pursues three main purposes in the economic sphere: observance of the rules of the game, maintenance of economic stability, and national defense.

The rules of the game are oriented toward the pluralistic objectives of American society. Thus they seek to prevent any sector of the economy from gaining absolute power vis-à-vis other sectors of the economy, competitors, or the individuals as such, by controlling and limiting its power. Regulatory commissions, legislation controlling and limiting the strong and supporting the weak, and tariff and monetary policies serve this purpose.

While the state started to assume responsibility for the rules of the game in the last decades of the nineteenth century, it made itself responsible for economic stability in the 1930's. Economic stability, in this context, signifies the mitigation, if not the elimination in certain sectors, of the business cycle. Its main positive characteristics, as conceived by the Government of the United States, are stability of employment, stability of the value of the dollar, and stability of agricultural prices. A plethora of legislative and administrative devices serves this purpose.

Since the end of World War II, technological research and industrial production have become to an ever increasing extent the backbone of military defense. The regular annual expenditure by the government of close to 50 billion dollars on national defense, its decrease or increase from year to year, and its shift from one sector of the economy to another all exert a sometimes drastic influence upon the economic life of the nation. They have made the government the most important single customer for the products of the national economy. In addition, many tax and monetary policies and price and wage policies are determined by considerations of national defense.

With the government thus exerting an enormous controlling, limiting, and stimulating influence upon the economic life, the ability to influence the economic decisions of the government becomes an indispensable element in the competition for economic advantage. Economic competition manifests itself inevitably in competition for political influence. This political influence is exerted through two channels: control of, and pressure upon, government personnel.

The most effective political influence is exerted by the direct control of government personnel. The economic organization that has its representatives elected to the legislature or appointed to the relevant administrative and executive positions exerts its political influence as far as the political influence of its representatives reaches. In so far as the representatives of these economic organizations cannot decide the issue by themselves, the competition for political influence and, through it, economic advantage will be fought out within the collective bodies of the government by the representatives of different economic interests. While this relationship of direct control is typical in Europe, it is by no means unknown in the United States. State legislatures have been controlled by mining companies, public utilities, and railroads, and many individual members of Congress represent specific economic interests. Independent administrative agencies have come under the sway of the economic forces they were intended to control. The large-scale interchange of top personnel between business and the executive branch of the government cannot help but influence, however subtly and intangibly, decisions of the government relevant to the economic sphere.

However, in the United States the most important political influence is exerted through the influence of pressure groups. The decision of the government agent—legislator, independent administrator, member of the executive branch—is here not a foregone conclusion by virtue of the economic control to which he is subject. His decision is in doubt, for he is still open to divergent economic pressures. The competition for determining the decisions of the government takes place not among the government agents themselves but between the government agent, on the one hand, and several economic pressure groups, on the other. Only after this competition among several pressure groups has been settled one way or another will the government agents compete with each other, provided the issue is still in doubt.

This interconnectedness between government and economy is likely to be strengthened by drastic changes that are occurring in the structure of our economic system. While our economic system is dedicated to ever increasing productivity, it finds itself hampered by its inability to sell at a profit what it is able to produce. This inability is not the result of a temporary maladjustment in consequence of the natural fluctuations of the business cycle, to be remedied by the techniques of Keynesian economics. Quite to the contrary, our economic system suffers from structural defects that are the result of technological innovations and can be cured only by radical structural changes.

Technological innovations have affected the structure of our economic system in three different respects. Automation is replacing human labor with machines. Machines are making unskilled labor permanently unemployable and are assigning to skilled labor an ever more limited scope. Machines are increasing productivity far beyond the ability of a market economy to consume. In consequence, an enormous and ever expanding productive apparatus and the ever shrinking segment of the population profiting from it finds itself face to face with an ever increasing segment of the population permanently severed from the productive processes.

Thus technology is opening up a gap between a productive majority and a permanently unemployable new proletariat, which may well become a majority in the future. This development is likely to have three consequences: increased intervention of the state in the economic processes, decline of the labor unions, and a radical transformation of our society.

The government is committed to the maintenance of full employment. That is to say, the government will have to take measures to protect an ever increasing segment of the population from the consequences of technological change. To that end, the government has a choice among three different types of measures. It can artificially maintain the disadvantaged segment of the population through the dispensation of benefits, public works, and subsidies. Our agricultural policies exemplify this type of measure. It can try to narrow the gap through the Keynesian methods of deficit financing. Or it can assume planned control of an economy that is one of abundance rather than of scarcity, and one can well imagine that it will then provide free of charge food, clothing, power, transportation, medical care, and other services, as it does already water, roads, police, and fire protection.

Whatever course or combination of courses the government will take, the power of the labor unions is likely to decline. The issue to which labor unions owe their existence has been the division of the social product between management and labor. The issue of the future will be who shall have the opportunity to work. As concerns that issue, the unions can do no more than try to protect the vested interests of their members against what is likely to be irresistible technological change. The decrease in the labor force and the inability of the unions to stave off the threat of technological unemployment will lead to a decrease in union membership and morale. In other words, the unions as presently constituted can only fight a rear-guard action in the face of certain defeat.

Visualizing an economy of abundance in full bloom, one must also visualize an entirely new society. In such a society, the meaning of work will radically change. People will work less and for different purposes. They will work not in order to earn a subsistence but in order to avail themselves of benefits of a higher order. Leisure will become more extensive and widespread and will pose with renewed urgency the question of the purpose of man's life. People will cease competing for sheer survival; but on the basis of an economically assured survival, they will fight for the realization of what they regard as their respective purposes in life.

The future of American democracy will depend in good measure upon the solution of the economic problem outlined above. At present, American democracy is weakened, but it is not threatened by a political movement seeking to do away with it. Domestic Communism is negligible as a threat to democratic institutions. Certain Communist nations threaten the United States from without, not from within. But if the ranks of the permanently unemployed were to be swelled continuously until they comprised large masses, especially among the young, there can be little doubt that a political movement of whatever coloration would take advantage of the grievances of those permanently deprived of the economic benefits of American society. In view of the failure of democracy to solve this problem, such a movement would be bound to be antidemocratic. Its antecedents in the 1930's point in the same anti-democratic direction.

Since we have assumed, however, that American democracy will be able to solve this impending economic problem, we must be concerned here with the two main weaknesses of democracy that are visible today and are likely to be aggravated in the future. These weaknesses present themselves as two paradoxes. On the one hand, the people have lost much of their power to control the government in spite of an ever more pronounced deference to the will of the majority as the ultimate standard for political action. On the other hand, the government, in spite of an unprecedented accumulation of power in its hands, has likewise lost much of its ability to influence events. Thus we are in the presence of a thwarted majority and a thwarted government, an over-all loss of the ability to govern effectively.

The decline in the power of the government is the result of two factors: the feudalism of semi-autonomous executive departments and the feudalism of the concentrations of private power.

When we refer to the executive branch of the government, we are really making use of a figure of speech in order to designate a multiplicity of varied and more or less autonomous agencies that have but one quality in common: their authority has been delegated to them either by the President or by Congress. But neither the President nor Congress is able to control them. The reason must be sought in the inadequacy of the Presidency and of Congress for the control of the executive branch as it has developed in our time.

The executive branch of the American government has become an enormous apparatus of the highest quantitative and qualitative complexity. The functions of the executive branch have been divided and subdivided and parceled out to a plethora of agencies. Most of the functions these agencies perform overlap or are at the very least interconnected to such an extent that an agency needs the support of other agencies in order to perform its functions. There can be but few policies of any importance that an agency is able to pursue without regard for the position of other agencies. In the absence of hierarchical direction and control, one agency can act only with the consent of another agency, and how to secure that consent—through cooperation or competition—becomes a vital issue upon which the usefulness of the agency depends.

The quantitative proliferation of the executive function is accompanied by its qualitative atomization, which is due to the technological complexity of many of the most important executive functions. This complexity gives the agency that masters it an advantage in policy formation which may well amount in some of the most important areas to a virtual monopoly. Such specialized knowledge, which is a unique source of power, is typically guarded by a wall of secrecy, and excluded from it are not only the general public and Congress but also other—especially rival—agencies.

Upon this sprawling and unwieldy agglomeration of executive agencies, which legally speaking are but an arm of the executive and the legislature, the President and Congress try in vain to impose their will. The President as chief executive and Commander in Chief has of course the constitutional power to impose his conception of policy upon the executive departments, with the exception of the independent regulatory commissions, which are supposed to operate according to the statutory standards laid down by Congress. However, reality diverges sharply from the constitutional scheme. Even so strong and astute a President as Franklin D. Roosevelt was incapable of assuming full control even over the State Department, the constitutional executor of his foreign policy. His successors have had to an ever increasing degree to limit themselves to laying down general principles of policy in the hope that they would not suffer too much in the far-flung process of execution. On the other hand, the main weapon at the disposal of Congress, the investigating power, is clumsy; it can at best deal effectively with abuse and violation of the law, but it is hardly able to correct an executive policy that is at variance with its own. For the statutory standards by which Congress must judge the executive performance are generally so vague as to leave to the executive branch and, more particularly, the regulatory commissions a vast area of discretion.

Thus the constitutional intent to translate the Presidential and congressional will into purposeful action, as the movements of the arm reflect the impulses emanating from the brain, has produced instead the anarchy of a war of all against all, fought among as well as within the executive departments. The objective of the war is the determination—either directly or by influencing the decisions of higher authority—of at least that segment of policy which falls within the jurisdiction of the agency. The proliferation of agencies with overlapping functions and the equal status of many of them make the interagency phase of the war almost inevitable. The absence of clear lines of authority and of an organization appropriate to the functions to be performed invites intra-agency war and in certain departments, such as State and Defense, makes it inevitable. To win these wars, the belligerents enter into alliances with other belligerents, with factions in Congress and in the White House, with business enterprises, and with the mass media of communications. The deliberate leak to a journalist or a member of Congress becomes a standard weapon with which one agency tries to embarrass another, to force the hand of higher authority, or to establish an accomplished fact.

This process of policy formation and execution resembles the feudal system of government in that the public authority is parceled out among a considerable number of agencies which, while legally subordinated to a higher authority, are in fact autonomous to a greater or lesser degree. The executive agency, competing for the determination of a policy with other agencies, more and more resembles a feudal fief that owes its existence to the delegation of powers by higher authority but becomes in active operation an autonomous center of power, defending itself against other centers of power and trying to increase its power at the expense of others. This system of government resembles the feudal system also in that the fragmentation of public power carries within itself a diminution of the sum total of public power. Fragmented power is weak power, and the sum total of the fragments, each following its own impulse, is of necessity inferior to what the public power would have been had it remained in one piece, harnessed to a single purpose. The government, instead of speaking with one strong and purposeful voice, speaks in many voices, each trying to outshout the others, but all really weak as well as contradictory.

It is worthy of note that this fragmentation and consequent diminution of the public power, which characterizes the executive branch of the government, was erected by the Constitution into a fundamental principle of the American system of government in the form of the separation of powers. The separation of the public power into three separate departments, in good measure independent of one another, seeks to prevent one branch from imposing its will upon the whole and thereby becoming too strong for the liberty of the citizens. It seeks to weaken the government by dividing it. What the Constitution sought to achieve for the whole government by intent, the executive branch has achieved for itself through haphazard, fissiparous growth.

The debilitating effect which the separation of powers was intended to exert upon the government was innocuous as long as the functions which the government had to perform were limited and exercised in normal circumstances. However, when a crisis required strong action by the government and, more particularly, by the executive, which alone is capable of direct action in the true sense of the word, it was the President who, through the authority of his office, the strength of his will, and the persuasiveness of his vision, gave the government that unity of purposeful action commensurate with the task to be performed. And the Constitution designed the Presidency to be equal to such a crisis situation by investing the President with the powers of an "uncrowned king."

What the philosophy of the Constitution could conceive only as the extreme and exceptional conditions of crisis have become the normal conditions of American existence. The revolutions of the Civil War, the Square Deal, the New Deal, and the Cold War have established in permanence the dominant role of the government in the affairs of the nation. The quantitative proliferation of executive agencies implements that role. Yet the organization of the Presidency is adequate only to lead and control the weak and but sporadically active federal government of bygone times, not a Federal government that has become in permanence the determining factor in the vital concerns of the nation. No President can perform at the same time the functions of head of state, chief executive, Commander in Chief, and head of his party. He cannot even plan, formulate, coordinate, and supervise the execution of policy at the same time. The President has the constitutional authority to do all these things, but he has not necessarily the extraordinary combination of knowledge, judgment, and character required for such a task; most certainly, he does not have the time. In the absence of an effective Cabinet system, the President is separated from the day-by-day operations of the executive branch by a gap that he can but occasionally bridge. Normally, he presides over the executive branch, but he does not govern it.

Congress, on the other hand, is kept from effective control of the executive branch by the constitutional separation of powers, especially as interpreted by the executive branch itself. This impotence, bred in good measure by ignorance of what the executive branch is doing, has engendered in Congress an endemic mood of frustration and irritation which seeks relief in the harassment and persecution of persons rather than in the formulation, supervision, and enforcement of policies. Lack of party discipline and archaic rules of procedure make it difficult for Congress to discover a will of its own and impose it upon the executive branch.

The disintegration of the executive branch and the debilitation of the public power resulting from it must be cured by infusing the executive branch, on the one hand, with a purpose transcending the feudal interests and loyalties that rend it asunder and, on the other, by superimposing upon it a power capable of neutralizing, subduing, and fusing the fragments of feudal power, which tend to be a law unto themselves. Both purpose and power can come only from the President's office. For only here do we find the visible authority and the fullness of implied powers necessary to make the national purpose prevail over the parochialism of feudal fiefdoms. As in sixteenth- and seventeenth-century Europe the monarchical authority and power had to be called into being in order to create a nation out of the fragments of a territorial feudalism, so in our age must the Presidential power and authority come forward to save the unity of the national purpose from functional fragmentation.

The debility of the executive power, caused by its inner fragmentation, invites attack from the concentrations of private power, especially in the economic sphere. Throughout history, factions within the state have frequently made common cause with a foreign enemy in order to improve their position in the domestic struggle for power and have thereby delivered the state itself into the hands of its enemies. So the feudal lords within the executive branch ally themselves with the princes of private power, each ally pursuing his particular goal. The former seek to expand their fiefdoms within the executive branch and thereby increase their share in the power of the government. The latter seek to turn the instruments of government control to their own advantage and expand their own power without regard for, and at the expense of, the public power. Thus the public power is diminished through concerted action from within and without.

The recovery of the power of the government will depend upon three factors: strengthening of presidential power, radical retrenchment in the personnel of the federal government, whose enfeeblement is in good measure the result of extreme overstaffing, and the decline of the concentrations of private power.

Presidential power is primarily a function of the President's personality and, hence, must be left to the accidents of history. The present concentrations of private power are likely to decline, as was pointed out above, as the result of radical technological changes, in all probability to be replaced by others. Retrenchment in the federal personnel would require an act of will to reverse a trend of long standing. This trend is likely to be strengthened by the increase in the number of the permanent technologically unemployed, who will look to the federal government for employment. Thus while the retrenchment of the federal bureaucracy is rationally required, it is doubtful whether it will be accomplished.

Modern technology, which has given the government a decisive potential advantage over the people in the over-all distribution of power,* has also actually strengthened the hand of the government in its day-by-day operations. The great issues of state in the fields of foreign policy, military organization and strategy, economics, and finance can no longer be understood, as they formerly were, by any knowledgeable man of average intelligence. Their understanding requires a large degree of expert knowledge, which is much more readily available to the government than to the individual citizen and part of which, because of its classified nature, is available only to the government. Thus the government can speak in these matters with an authority unmatched by that of any individual or group outside it.

Not only can the government speak with superior authority, but it can also act with finality. The natural advantage of the executive branch in being able to confront the people and their elected repre-

---

* See above, pages 215–16.

sentatives with an accomplished fact is increased by its control over the technological initiation and implementation of policy. Once the executive branch has started building, say, one kind of missile or radar warning system, it becomes impractical for Congress or for the people at large to insist upon a different program; for the complicated technology, costliness, and lead-time of such programs preclude the possibility of changing them in view of—perhaps but temporary— Congressional or popular pressure. The disavowal of the government's policies in elections, provided their import could be clearly ascertained, could influence policy at best only in the long run and only if there were a reasonable assurance, which of course there is not, that later elections would not reverse the position again. In consequence, the democratic corrective of elections has become at best a tenuous instrument of the popular will.

The preferences of the people and their representatives, insofar as they can be articulated at all, have in these matters hardly any relevance for the substance of the policies of the executive branch. They may, however, influence greatly the manner in which these policies are presented to the public and the amount of information the executive branch is willing to make public to begin with. Thus in these matters of the highest importance, while the executive branch acts, setting the course of policy perhaps for years to come, the people and Congress can but deliberate, investigate, and resolve; they can approve within the limits of the information accessible to them, or if they have no knowledge to go on, forego judgment altogether, on the assumption that the executive branch knows best since it knows more. This advantage of the executive over the legislative branch and the people at large derives of course from the nature of the executive function itself and, hence, is inherent in a system of government that makes the executive independent of the legislative branch. What is unprecedented is the qualitative shift—paralleling the shift in the control of the means of violence—of the power of decision from the people to the government in matters of life and death. It has made the government the master of the national fate.

This dual decline of democratic government—the decline of the government's ability to govern and of the people's ability to control the government—is not limited to the United States. It is a general phenomenon noticeable in differing degrees in the old democracies of Europe. It is in good measure the result of objective conditions which are beyond purposeful control. There is no reason to expect that these conditions will disappear in the foreseeable future. Quite to the contrary, insofar as democratic control is concerned, the complexity of the issues to be decided and their remoteness from the life experiences of the man in the street is likely to increase.

Considering the decline of democratic government in the old democracies due to world-wide objective conditions, it can hardly be expected that democracy will flourish in the rest of the world, especially in the new nations. More particularly, two prerequisites, without which democracy cannot exist, are largely absent in the rest of the world. One is a consensus on the fundamentals of the social and economic order, which all participants in the political process must be willing to accept. The other is the willingness of a temporary majority to give a temporary minority a chance to become a majority tomorrow, which in turn will give the new minority a chance to become a majority the day after. It is of course possible that such a consensus and such a willingness on the part of a majority to give up power in compliance with the operation of the democratic processes will emerge somewhere outside the Western world. But it must be recognized that at present there is no empirical evidence that such a development might take place.

What stability exists in the world today derives, on the one hand, from the bipolar distribution of nuclear power and the concomitant mutual deterrence and, on the other hand, from the extreme weakness of most of the non-nuclear nations, especially the new ones. Both elements of stability are likely to decline in the future.

No nation-state is capable of protecting its citizens and its civilization against an all-out nuclear attack. Its safety rests solely in preventing such an attack from taking place. While in the prenuclear age a nation-state could count upon its physical ability to defend itself, in the nuclear age it must rely upon its psychological ability to deter those who are physically able to destroy it. The prospective enemy must be induced to refrain from attacking; once he attacks, the victim is doomed.

This psychological mechanism of deterrence operates only on the condition that the prospective nuclear aggressor is clearly identified beforehand, that is, that no more than two nations are capable of waging all-out nuclear war; for it is only on this condition that deterrence operates with automatic certainty. Today, the Soviet Union knows that if it should attack the United States with nuclear weapons, the United States would destroy it, and vice versa; that certainty deters both. Yet the time is close at hand when other nations will have the weapons with which to wage all-out nuclear war. When that time has come, nations will have lost even the preventive capacity of psychological deterrence, which they still possess today. For the United States, if then attacked with nuclear weapons, will no longer be able to identify the aggressor with certainty and, hence, deter the prospective aggressor with the certainty of retaliation. When this historical moment comes—as it surely must if the present trend is not reversed—the nation-state will connote not life and civilization but anarchy and universal destruction.

The age that has seen the nation-state become obsolete witnesses the emergence of a multitude of new states fashioned from the fragments of the colonial empires. The number of sovereign states has more than doubled since World War I. Many of these new states would not have been viable political, military, and economic entities even in the heyday of the nation-state, deficient as they are in the essential prerequisites of nationhood. They could not have fed, administered, and defended themselves then, nor can they now. The disorder and threats to peace that the dissolution, first of the Turkish and then of the Austro-Hungarian and the western part of the Russian empire brought in its wake is being spread, in the name of nationalism, to ever wider areas of Africa and Asia. Is it then reasonable to expect that these new nations, some of them so artificial as to be even lacking the ethnic and historical foundations of nationhood, will be able to create a viable order among themselves and with their more powerful neighbors?

Three alternatives appear to be in store for them, perhaps one following the other: Balkanization and anarchy, a new colonialism, and regionalism. It is possible that the present trend toward fragmentation and impotence continues with the result that the new nations will either have to be supported from the outside or else sink back into the anarchy and barbarism of precolonial days. It is more likely, however, that the present lack of viability of most new nations will call forth the formation of larger, more viable political units. The rivalries that have beset the successor states to the European empires have already appeared among them. Some of the former colonies would like to have colonies of their own. The natural resources of some continue to make them attractive as colonies for stronger nations that need these resources. Their weakness, necessitating continuous support from stronger nations, predestines them as pawns in the power struggles of the latter. Their attractiveness, coupled with weakness, is thus a standing invitation to conquest, conquest by one or the other of them or else from the outside. In any event, the disorder taking the place of the old order of empire is likely to call forth, as it did before in Europe, a new order, which will be again an order of empire of one sort or the other.

Regionalism is likely to be a variant of the order of empire rather than the voluntary fusion of a number of autonomous political units on the basis of equality. The effective fusion of a number of autonomous political units requires as a rule a politically and militarily predominant unit that is able to prevent recalcitrant members from destroying the union. Thus historically most regional unions have been the result of conquest from within or from without. Austria-Hungary, Italy, and Germany are cases in point.

Nationalism would not necessarily be mitigated, but might well be aggravated, by a successful regionalism. The nations of Western Europe, for instance, are too weak to make themselves singly the effective spearheads of nationalism. The time has passed when the French or the Germans could dream of making the world over in their own image. But if the nations of Western Europe were able to unite and form a new political and military unit of very considerable potentialities, they would then have acquired the power bases for a new nationalism, common to all of Western Europe, to compete effectively with the nationalism of the present two superpowers. That the traditional nation-state is obsolescent in view of the technological and military conditions of the contemporary world is obvious. Yet its replacement by larger regional units, better attuned to these conditions, may well call forth a more effective vehicle for nationalistic competition.

The cessation of the conventional armaments race through disarmament depends upon the settlement of the outstanding political issues, such as Germany, China, and others, from which the armaments race arose. The chances for such settlements in the foreseeable future are remote. In consequence, the chances for a cessation of the conventional armaments race through disarmament are correspondingly remote.

The abatement of the nuclear armaments race through arms control has a better chance to be realized either through a formal agreement or unilateral measures. The two major nuclear powers, if they pursue a rational policy, are likely to adapt their policies to the realization that it is futile to try to gain or maintain nuclear "superiority" over the prospective enemy once one has attained a multiple capacity of utterly destroying him. The multiplication of nuclear devices and delivery systems is, then, likely to slow down and ultimately cease altogether in the foreseeable future. Production might then be limited to replacement and the technical refinement of existing facilities.

This probable trend may, however, be counteracted by technological innovations, opening up new possibilities for offense or defense. While most scientists believe such a development to be unlikely, prognosis cannot rule such a possibility out altogether.

It is hazardous enough to make political predictions, and anybody who must make them from time to time in the course of his professional work is lucky if he can say with Winston Churchill that he has not always been wrong. It is also hazardous to make business predictions. General Motors, to give only one example among many, predicted in 1939 that 38 million cars would be on the road by 1960, a prediction that was off the mark by 100 per cent. The separate hazards of political and business forecasts are compounded when it comes to predicting the influence of one sphere of action upon the other. Within the two distinct spheres, it is of course possible to project certain present trends into the future, especially for the short run; otherwise, rational action would be impossible altogether. Political and economic experience, built into abstract propositions which we call laws, enables us to make such short-range predictions. Yet the more long range the predictions are, the more uncertain they become, because experience can tell us less and less the farther we advance into the future. And experience can teach us very little indeed when we try to predict the mutual relations between the political and economic spheres in some distant future. Thus our equation contains three unknowns: the political future, the economic future, and their mutual relations. It is with this caveat that one must approach the predictions we are going to make.

If there is anything one can say about the future with any degree of confidence, it is that the present fusion of the political and economic spheres will continue; for the technological, social, and political factors that are responsible for it in the present are likely to continue in the future. In other words, a return to the relative separation that existed in the nineteenth century appears to be virtually impossible. This fusion appears to be a universal phenomenon that manifests itself in different ways throughout the world. What is uncertain is the terms on which that fusion will take place.

The actual relationship between government and business, especially in terms of the distribution of power between them, will depend primarily upon the degree of economic rationality and independent political strength, with which the government of a particular country is endowed. Weak governments, regardless of their economic rationality, will fall prey to domination by politically conscious economic forces. Politically strong governments, without economic rationality, will impose their will upon the economic forces regardless of the economic consequences. Examples for both extremes can be found in Latin America.

However, the type of relationship that is likely to prevail in North America and Europe, the Soviet Union included, will be marked by two characteristics: the politically strong government setting economic goals for political and social purposes and planning the economic measures to achieve them, and a managerial group operating the economy in a rational fashion within the framework set by the government. All developed industrial economies, regardless of their starting point, tend toward this type of political-economic system. This is true of Spain, Italy, France, Poland, the Soviet Union, Great Britain, and the United States.

The predictions made thus far assume that the political unit whose actions must be predicted is the traditional nation-state. However, two tendencies in the contemporary world run counter to the continuing importance and even existence of the nation-state: regionalism and technological potentialities.

Regionalism is in good measure a fact in Europe and an aspiration in Africa, Southeast Asia, and Latin America. It is a moot question as to whether a united Europe, for instance, would simply be a politically, militarily, and economically more efficient unit than were the nation-states composing it, or whether it would pursue toward the outside world a less nationalistic policy. The question is, in other words, whether the nationalism of the nation-state would simply be replaced by the nationalism of a larger regional unit. I am inclined to accept the latter alternative, since regional units will have to protect and promote their interests vis-à-vis other regional units and surviving nation-states in quite the same manner as do nation-states now.

As concerns the relations between a united Europe and the United States in the economic sphere, all will depend upon their political and military relations. If a united Europe should be a close ally of the United States, their economic relations are likely to reflect their political and military unity and American corporations in Europe will profit from it. If, on the other hand, a united Europe should be a truly third force, loosely or not at all connected with the United States in the political and military fields, that disunity would be reflected in the unfavorable treatment American companies would receive in Europe. Thus the key to economic prediction in this field lies in the political and military spheres.

The technological conditions in which the world finds itself today require the replacement of the nation-state not with regional but world-wide organizations. The international corporation, producing and merchandizing throughout the world regardless of national or regional boundaries, reflects this requirement. Will we be able to create a political organization commensurate with the technological and economic potentialities of the age? Nobody can answer that question. But in view of the continuing strength of nationalism one can say with a great deal of confidence that if such a development should occur it will be slow and gradual rather than dramatic.

25

Understanding Military Strategy

[June, 1965]

Until about fifteen years ago, military strategy was beyond the pale of scholarly investigation. The threat or use of force in support of foreign policy was regarded as an abnormality to be resorted to only *in extremis,* and then with maximum effect in order to get the emergency over with as quickly, as thoroughly, and as cheaply as possible. During the last decade, we have gone to the opposite extreme. Academic studies in military strategy have become the fashion, and a great number of learned and sophisticated volumes have probed into all aspects of military strategy, from nuclear war to counterinsurgency. This radical change is the result of the conjunction of our permanent involvement in the affairs of the world with the emergence of new types of warfare for which the traditional use of force with maximum economy would obviously be inappropriate. Thus nuclear war, the relation between nuclear war and conventional war, and the emergence of types of undeclared war in the form of insurgencies and guerrilla actions have challenged our ingenuity, and the academic community has risen with alacrity to that challenge.

Yet that ingenuity, in accord with our national genius, has tended toward looking at military problems as self-sufficient technical ones to be dealt with on their own terms without regard for the political context. Herman Kahn's *On Thermonuclear War* is a classic example of this trend. On the basis of a quantitative analysis of the likely consequences of nuclear war, it concludes that, given the necessary measures of active and passive defense, nuclear war does not need to be an unmitigated catastrophe and that therefore nuclear war can serve as an instrument of national policies in the traditional manner. Herman Kahn could arrive at this conclusion only by disregarding the psychological effects upon the survivors of the massive human and material losses, which he too assumes to be the inevitable result of nuclear war.

In the present book,* Mr. Kahn has progressed beyond the lack of political sophistication of *On Thermonuclear War*. The topic of the book already indicates that; for escalation is a general phenomenon of foreign policy through which hostile nations try competitively to exert pressure upon each other. Literature on the balance of power contains indeed many incidental references to this competitive threat or use of force at the service of foreign policy. Its elucidation is particularly necessary in the nuclear age, when nations threaten each other with nuclear weapons and are anxious to avoid their actual use. And it is particularly necessary in the American context, which has traditionally known only the two extremes: the abnegation of force and its unlimited use. Mr. Kahn puts it very well when he says:

> The "crusade," and even an initial pacifism as well, comes more naturally to Americans than the kind of cool, restrained, and moderate willingness to threaten or use force that will be suggested in this book. . . .
>
> There are thus two traditional American biases: an unwillingness to initiate the use of moderate levels of force for limited objectives, and a too-great willingness, once committed, to use extravagant and uncontrolled force. Both biases are potentially dangerous and should be guarded against. They could have most serious consequences unless we deliberately and consciously think about ways in which violence may occur and still be kept relatively limited.

It is on this problem that Mr. Kahn reflects in this book, and he does so with his customary acuity and ingenuity. His ability to see distinctions where ordinary minds see none is indeed astounding, and so is his gift for developing a variety of imaginary situations derived from these distinctions. These qualities were already prominent in

*Herman Kahn, *On Escalation: Metaphors and Scenarios* (New York: Praeger, 1965.)

Mr. Kahn's previous books; they established his reputation as a uniquely original thinker. What was not prominent in the previous books, if it existed at all, was the demonstration of the relevance of theoretical concepts to concrete politico-military situations. What Mr. Kahn has to say, for instance, about escalation in World War II and during the Cuban crisis of 1962 is new and very illuminating. He provides the first persuasive theoretical analysis of the nature of the Cuban confrontation, which is quite different from that popularly accepted. Similarly, he sheds new light upon the crisis of the Atlantic Alliance created by de Gaulle's insistence upon an independent national deterrent.

Yet once one has paid one's tributes to the very considerable merits of this book, one must call attention to its basic defect. That defect is not so much the property of this book as of the school of thought of which it is an outstanding representative. That school tries to transform foreign and military policy into something approaching an exact science, endowed with exactly defined concepts, rigorous analysis, and quantitatively distinguishable models. This is a praiseworthy aim but incapable of attainment; for the very nature of foreign and military policy with all its ambiguities, its contingencies, and the hunches derived from them militates against it. This incongruity between the empirical raw material and the intellectual enterprise results in conceptualizations and theoretical constructions much too refined and elaborate to do justice to the data of experience. The result is what has been aptly called a "new scholasticism," an intellectual exercise of astounding sophistication but of very limited cognitive value and practical use.

Mr. Kahn himself refers to "the seeming artificiality and abstractness of this book," and he admits that he will "tend toward discussion of possibilities *as* possibilities, without giving full attention to their credibility or likelihood." The result is "an escalation ladder" consisting of seven general phases called "subcrisis maneuvering, traditional crises, intense crises, bizarre crises, exemplary central attacks, military central wars, civilian central wars." These phases are broken down into forty-four "rungs," starting with "ostensible crisis, political, economic and diplomatic gestures, solemn and formal declarations" and ending with "slow-motion countercity war, countervalue salvo, augmented disarming attack, civilian devastation attack, some other kinds of controlled general war, spasm or insensate war." This scheme is supplemented by another one which, I must admit, I am unable to understand. It is called "varying degrees of skill on different rungs," subdivided into "current situation, feared situation, more likely, possible." Each subdivision consists of a series of numbers from one to eleven of different sizes and expansions. Looking at this scheme, I feel as I do when I look at modern art: I admire the ingenuity, wonder what it is all about, and ask myself, Is this really necessary? As concerns foreign and military policy, I am emphatic in asserting that it is not.

26

Pacem in Terris and the World Community

[Summer, 1963,
and Autumn, 1965]

The encyclical *Pacem in Terris* is a historic document of the first rank. It does for the political order—and, more particularly, for the international order—what Leo XIII's *De Rerum Novarum* did for the economic and social orders seventy years ago: It brings the eternal verities of the Church to bear upon the modern world as it is and as it ought to be. Both speak indeed *de rerum novarum*. We find here and there a total confrontation and a creative relationship between what is ancient and immutable and what is so modern that it has hardly entered the consciousness of the contemporaries and has in any event not yet been fully accepted by them, let alone been able to mold their thoughts and actions.

Yet it is exactly this modernity, this contrast between a teaching which belongs to an age that has passed and a new and unexpected teaching, both stemming from the same unalterable source, that engenders both enthusiasm and doubt. Enthusiasm results from the clarification of issues whose urgency had been felt and whose nature

283

had not been understood. Doubt arises from a human tendency to identify the eternal verities with their application to a particular historical situation and the consequent hesitation to disentangle these verities from that situation and give them a new content appropriate to new conditions. Thus forty years after *De Rerum Novarum* Pius XI could write in *Quadragesimo Anno* that "certain doubts have arisen concerning either the correct meaning of the same parts of Leo's encyclical or conclusions to be deduced therefrom, which doubts in turn have even among Catholics given rise to controversies that are not always peaceful." And Pius XI set himself the task of putting the doubts to rest and clarifying the conclusions. John XXIII's *Pacem in Terris* awaits a similar fate, and that fate has already begun to take shape.

Officially there has been nothing but praise for *Pacem in Terris*. On the very day I am writing these words I have listened at the Geneva Disarmament Conference to the eulogies of the late Pope by a Canadian Chairman and the American, Bulgarian, and Soviet delegates, all praising the encyclical. Yet Soviet spokesmen have praised it in the name of general and complete disarmament and peaceful coexistence. Others have found it worthy of support because it is supposed to contain nothing new and, more particularly, no change from the teachings of Pius XII. It has been criticized by a prominent German Catholic writer for "political incompetence," and an outstanding American Catholic theologian has endeavored to prove that a key passage, to which we shall return, does not refer to contemporary Communism but to eighteenth- and nineteenth-century liberalism and socialism. Yet another prominent American Catholic theologian has interpreted the same passage as "the widening of the 'opening to the left.'"

Considering the encyclical not in view of one's own political preferences nor even of its august origin and consequent import but rather as a self-contained analysis of the world situation and as a prescription for action with regard to it, one is struck by the papal recognition of the novelty of the age in which we live. One dominant aspect of that novelty is the result of modern science and technology. Modern science and technology reveal a rational order, which unites man and nature, and testify to the greatness of man who can understand and master that order.

This mastery enables man to satisfy wants and aspirations that formerly were at least in part beyond his ken. Thus the encyclical presents a catalogue of the rights of man, all serving "the dignity of the human person" and unprecedented in their scope: life, bodily integrity, food, clothing, shelter, rest, medical care, social services, security in case of sickness, inability to work, widowhood, old age, unemployment, "or in any other case in which he is deprived of the means of subsistence through no fault of his own." Man has also "the right to share in the benefits of culture, and therefore the right to a basic education and to technical and professional training" and to higher education.

The reason why the encyclical could plausibly present such a comprehensive catalogue, far surpassing what any of its predecessors had claimed, is to be found in the potential abundance modern science has put at the disposal of society. For it would be idle for a document oriented toward the practice of government to stipulate individual rights that are beyond the resources of contemporary governments to grant. It is in this context worthy of note that the encyclical takes a very positive position toward the democratic welfare state. It recognizes the duty of the state "to bring about a situation in which individual citizens can easily exercise their rights and fulfill their duties as well." The state must "take suitable action with regard to economic, political, and cultural matters" in order to correct inequalities among the citizens. It must "give whole-hearted and careful attention to the social as well as the economic progress of citizens." It must take care of "the building of roads, transportation, communications, water supply, housing, public health, education, facilitation of the practice of religion, and recreational facilities."

It is responsible for insurance systems, which guarantee the citizens "the necessary means to maintain a decent standard of living." It is also responsible for employment opportunities, a just wage, the place and functions of workers in the industrial organization. The encyclical declares itself to be "fully consonant with any truly democratic regime." It declares the separation of powers to be "in keeping with the innate demands of human nature."

Similarly, the achievements of modern science and technology have created new types of international relations and call for radical new approaches. The encyclical points to two fundamental empirical transformations in the structure of international relations: the obsolescence of war and of the nation-state. It deems it "hardly possible to imagine that in the atomic era war could be used as an instrument of justice." In consequence, it opposes the armaments race, especially in the nuclear field, and the continuation of nuclear tests. It advocates the equal and simultaneous reduction of nuclear stockpiles, the banning of nuclear weapons, a general agreement about "progressive disarmament and an effective method of control." As substitutes for war, it advocates foreign aid and negotiations.

This is, however, not enough. For

> the public authorities of the individual political communities—placed as they are on a footing of equality one with the other— . . . are no longer capable of facing the task of finding an adequate solution to the problems mentioned above. And this is not due to a lack of good will or of a spirit of enterprise, but because of a structural defect which hinders them. It can be said, therefore, that at this historical moment the present system of organization and the way its principle of authority operates on a world basis no longer correspond to the objective requirements of the universal common good.

What the world needs are "public authorities which are in a position to operate in an effective manner on a world-wide basis," that is, world government. The encyclical regards the United Nations as an important step in this direction.

The encyclical mentions three further novelties characteristic of the age: the total emancipation of the working class, the total emancipation of women, the emancipation of all races. It is this last emancipation that is having the most far-reaching political consequences. It signifies the end of colonialism and of the division of the world into master and subject nations. It also signifies—as do the other emancipations—a radical political and social egalitarianism. As applied to race relationships, it excludes discrimination "at least doctrinally and in theory." Thus it apparently leaves the door open for discriminatory practices, at least for the time being and domestically, while in the relations among nations, the encyclical calls "for the elimination of every trace of racism."

These are the novelties in the actual world to which the encyclical points and by which it is moved to call for innovations commensurate with them. The encyclical contains other innovations of a philosophic nature, which appear to have no direct connection with the new facts of contemporary life but which, if they are taken to heart, are bound to exert a profound influence upon the political life of the world. Two such novel philosophic postulates have a direct bearing upon politics: "the duty of men to claim their lawful rights," and the distinction, both for theory and practice, between false doctrines, on the one hand, and the persons holding such doctrines and their actions, on the other.

The natural-law doctrine of the Church has in the past undergone one great transformation: from the formulation, in classical natural law, of objective laws imposing obligations to the modern doctrine of natural rights. It was an enormous step, pregnant with political consequences of which we are all aware, from the mere conception of an objective order, compliance with which was to be enforced by conscience and Church, to the postulation of a quasi-contractual relationship between individual claimant and the individual obligé. The present encyclical takes another enormous step, similarly pregnant with political consequences, by postulating the duty of the person endowed with natural rights to claim them. There is obviously a world of difference between a person having the right, say, to a just wage that another person may withhold from him at the risk of divine punishment, and a person who has also the right to claim a just wage from the person who refuses him that wage.

There is another world of difference between a person who possesses these two rights, and the person who has a duty to make them prevail. While in the classical doctrine the obligé had the duty to comply with the natural order by giving what is the other person's right to receive, while in the modern doctrine it was left to the discretion of that other person to claim what he was entitled to, the doctrine of the present encyclical imposes a positive duty upon that other person to comply with the natural order by claiming his rights. For a person to submit passively to a violation of his rights, then, is a violation of duty on his part.

Yet this duty must be fulfilled not through revolution but through gradual reform, "by working from within." Thus the active promotion of social, economic, and political reform in the pursuit of one's rights is not only a right but also a duty. Certainly nothing of the kind, at least posited as a general principle binding upon all men, has ever been heard before in Christendom.

The other doctrinal innovation of the encyclical, the distinction between false doctrines, on the one hand, and the persons who hold them and their actions, on the other, is startling not so much for its philosophic novelty as for its implications for moral judgment and political action. The encyclical postulates that "the person who errs is always and above all a human being and retains in every case his dignity as a human person." It follows from this imperishable quality, common to all men, that the person who errs "must always be regarded and treated with that lofty dignity." "Meetings and agreements in the various sectors of daily life" with such a person are not only permitted but can be advantageous by leading to the discovery of truth.

What is true of the persons holds true also for their actions. Judgment regarding them must be separated from the judgment of the false doctrines from which these actions sprang. As a person who holds false doctrines remains entitled to our respect, so "historical movements that have economic, social, cultural or political ends" do not lose their claim upon our support because they stem from false doctrines and are inspired by them. Here the encyclical draws a crucial and novel distinction—not surprising, perhaps, since it is suggested by the history of the Church—between the doctrines, which "remain always the same", and the movements, which, "working in historical situations in constant evolution, cannot but be influenced by this latter and cannot avoid, therefore, being subject to changes, even of a profound nature." This being so, it is possible to approve of such movements, which deserve approval, and to cooperate with them "for the attainment of some practical end" while continuing to condemn the erroneous doctrines that inspire them. Thus while the negative attitude toward erroneous doctrines is a matter of principle to be decided by the ecclesiastical authorities, the attitude—positive or negative as the case may be—toward the movements inspired by the doctrines is a matter of prudence to be decided by the competent secular authorities in accordance with the teachings and guidance of the Church.

It is obvious that this fundamental distinction between doctrines and the movements inspired by them applies to all non-Catholic doctrines and the movements inspired by them. It applies with particular force to Communism, which claims for its doctrine both immutability in essence and a monopoly of truth, and which derives from this doctrine rational and moral justification. But this distinction does not necessarily connote an "opening to the left." Rather, it does not *a priori* preclude such an opening. The encyclical draws a lesson from general historical experience, for which the relations between the doctrine and the policies of the Church throughout the ages provide a classic illustration, and, more particularly, from the specific contemporary experience of the changes in Communist movements in both time and space. Khrushchev's Communism is different from Stalin's, Mao's is different from Khrushchev's, and Togliatti's is different from both, while they all claim inspiration from the same doctrine. Prudence requires that one's practical attitude toward these different movements be determined not by one's condemnation of the erroneous doctrine, which condemnation is as immutable as the doctrine itself, but by the nature of the movements as judged in the light of the principles of right action.

What the encyclical envisages throughout is change, unprecedented and unforeseeable. In its recognition of the changes that have occurred and in its own doctrinal innovations, it is itself a testimony to that change. One can best summarize its spirit in its own words:

In fact, all human beings ought rather to reckon that what has been accomplished is but little in comparison with what remains to be done. This is so because organs of production, trade unions, associations, professional organizations, insurance systems, political regimes, and institutions for cultural, health, recreational or sporting purposes must all be adjusted to the era of the atom and of the conquest of space, an era which the human family has already entered, wherein it has commenced its new advance towards limitless horizons.

The effects of *Pacem in Terris* in the realm of practice are commensurate with its doctrinal importance. The revival of the worker-priest experiment in France would have been impossible without it. And so would have been the dialogues between Catholics and Communists, both in person and in books and magazines, that are taking place in France and Italy and even between West German Christians and East German atheists. Can anyone imagine Italian Catholics and Communists meeting face to face in order to debate the relative merits of their positions in the reign of Pius XII? John XXIII made it possible with *Pacem in Terris*. He also made possible Paul VI's visit and address to the United Nations in 1965.

The fact that Paul's message emanated from the head of a powerful world-wide religious organization established its importance. No other religious leader could have spoken with the same authority. His authority derives from the circumstance, peculiar to the Catholic Church, that the Pope's expressed opinion on a secular matter has a direct influence, to a greater or lesser degree, upon the moods and attitudes, if not the opinions and actions, of close to 600 million Catholics dispersed throughout the world. In some nations, Catholics are politically dominant, in others they form a politically potent minority. For all of them, the Pope's pronouncement on an issue such as international peace sets the tone to which their attitudes, opinions, and actions will more or less conform. Had the Pope chosen to speak as the champion of Western religion against godless Communism or of Western civilization against the "yellow peril," the response his message would have evoked throughout the Catholic world in terms of attitudes, opinions, and actions would have been one of militant defense and attack against the enemies identified by the Pope. Since his message was one of universal peace, regardless of religious and ideological differences, the Catholic response is likely to be one of toleration, conciliation, and coexistence.

Nor is the influence of the Pope's message likely to be limited to the Catholic world. This is already obvious from what has been said about the dialogue between Catholics and Communists. On a larger

scale, we must remember, there exists in all conflict situations—ideological and political, international and domestic—a reciprocity of
attitudes. The attitude of one side is bound to have an effect upon the
attitude of the other. The active hostility of one side may
evoke a similarly active hostility of the other side, or it may result in
the other side's retreat. When Soviet and Western Communists were
in their active, conquering period, conciliatory attitudes on the part
of their intended victims would have stimulated rather than abated
these aggressive attitudes. In a period of history that witnesses the
polycentric disintegration of the Communist bloc into its national
components, it is a counsel of political prudence to replace indiscriminate hostility on ideological grounds with a discriminating political
posture, which is conciliatory when the national interests involved do
not require hostility, and which is hostile when national interests
require militant attack or defense. The Pope's message to the United
Nations at the very least keeps the possibility of such discriminating
policies open, if it does not actually encourage them.

On the plane of concrete political issues, the Pope's message carries
three distinct implications. First of all, the Pope proclaims peace as
the paramount interest of the Church and of mankind. Peace, in the
eyes of the Pope, is no longer preferable to war on moral grounds, as
it has been in the tradition of the Church and of Western civilization
at large. Nor does the Pope distinguish, as his predecessors did, between just and unjust wars. War now has become an evil *per se,* and
in consequence all wars have become equally unjust. Both reason and
morality require the preservation of peace. The Church Militant has
become the Church Pacificant.

Second, the Pope's message gives moral support to the United Nations. The United Nations has certainly declined from the heyday of
the political influence it achieved in the 1950's under the stewardship
of Dag Hammarskjöld. Its political influence is threatened by the
reassertion of the principle of national sovereignty by some of the permanent members of the Security Council. National sovereignty and
an effective international organization cannot coexist. One must yield
to the other. There was a time when the ascendancy of the United
Nations, especially in the person of its Secretary General, seemed to
herald the weakening, if not the end, of national sovereignty. Today,
national sovereignty is clearly in the ascendancy, and the political
effectiveness of the United Nations has correspondingly declined. The
Pope, by honoring the United Nations with his presence, by identifying his aspirations for peace with those of the United Nations, and by
identifying the United Nations as the main instrument for the pres-

ervation of peace, has put the moral weight of his position and of his Church behind the peace-keeping endeavors of the United Nations and, by implication, against the attempts to preserve national sovereignty at the expense of the United Nations' political effectiveness.

By doing so, the Pope has also removed his moral sanction from the Catholic detractors and enemies of the United Nations throughout the world. Here we are in the presence of a typical example of the Pope's influence upon the attitudes of Catholics. Had the Pope kept silent or glorified the state at the expense of international organization, he would have given moral support to the detractors and enemies of the United Nations. As it is, he has put those Catholic groups in the same position in which he put Catholic racists. They are without the moral support of their Church and, hence, are handicapped in pushing their positions and proselytizing in the name of Catholicism.

Finally, by emphasizing the universality of the United Nations, the Pope has by implication condemned the exclusion of nations from representation within the United Nations. It would be naïve to assume, considering the political sophistication of the Vatican, that this emphasis was not intended to be understood as advocacy of the seating of the Communist Government of China as the representative of China in the United Nations. It is beside the point that the real problem is not whether or not to seat the Communist Government of China but under what conditions the Communist Government of China would accept the representation of China in the United Nations. What is important in the context of our discussion is the fact that this emphasis upon the universality of the United Nations carries the implicit disapproval of the exclusion of Communist China.

It must be obvious from what has been said that the impact of the Pope's visit falls into the realm of the imponderable. It is in the nature of things impossible to put one's finger on any specific, concrete achievement. To dismiss the visit as irrelevant because of the lack of such achievement would be to fall into Stalin's error, when he asked how many divisions the Pope has. The Pope indeed has no divisions, that is, no tangible power, but he has a moral authority that is susceptible of being translated into political attitudes, opinions, and actions. The Pope, through his visit and message to the United Nations, has used that moral authority on behalf of peace, the United Nations, and its universality. Important consequences are bound to flow from that papal intervention, and they will not be less important for not being clearly visible and definable at present.

27

The Police in Their Political Setting

[1963]

A police force, domestic or international, must meet three requirements: It must be reliable, effective, and impartial. While obviously it cannot be effective if it is not reliable, it can be reliable without being effective, and it is for this reason that the two prerequisites must be distinguished. A police force, in order to be reliable, must be loyal to the political authorities and share their conceptions of law and justice. A police force, in order to be effective, must stand in a certain relation of power to that fraction of the population likely to call forth police action by breaking the law.

The police within the state are the instrument of a central authority, which is supposed to be endowed with a will culminating in decisions, and it is these decisions that the police are called upon to put into practice. In legal terms, the police have the function of enforcing the laws; in political terms, they have the function of upholding the authority of the government; in social terms, they have the function of protecting a *status quo* as defined by the laws and expressed in the government's policies. In a well-ordered society the police are but rarely called upon to enforce a change in the *status quo;* the enforcement of new race relations against groups committed to an outlawed *status quo* is a case in point in our society. In revolutionary societies, on the other hand, the police force is the main weapon with which a revolutionary minority imposes its will upon a recalcitrant population.

It follows that the police force will be reliable in the performance of its functions only if either it has been forged into so disciplined an instrument of the government's will that it will execute whatever orders it is given regardless of content, or else its convictions and interests are at the very least not openly at odds with those of the government. Thus the police force, knowingly or without knowing it, is bound to be deeply involved in the political controversies of the society in which it operates.

Lenin maintained correctly against his opponents within the Marxist camp that the dictatorship of the proletariat could not afford to take over the enforcement agencies of its bourgeois predecessor and use them for its own purposes; forged for the purpose of maintaining the rule of an exploiting minority over the exploited majority, they could not be so used. Instead the proletariat had to create its own police, open and secret, appropriate to the special tasks of a new society. During certain periods of violent labor struggles in our society, the police force, regardless of the legal merits of the case, tended to transform itself into a protective guard for the employers, reinforced at times by the latter's private police. The police have at times refused to enforce the law for the protection of members of racial minorities. In certain regions of the United States they have habitually used their power to deprive such members of their rights through positive action. During the crisis at the University of Mississippi in 1962, state and federal police tried to enforce incompatible legal rules and conceptions of justice. Wherever a society is rent by deeply felt controversies, even though they do not lead to open violence, the political preferences of the police are likely to color the performance of its function.

On a lower level of motivation, the police, frequently individually and sometimes collectively, have yielded to the temptation of private gain and neglected to enforce the law against certain types of violations, of which traffic, gambling, vice, and housing code violations are outstanding. If this corruption occurs on a massive scale, the police may transfer their loyalty altogether from the legal government to another, private one in the form of a crime syndicate. The police will remain a reliable instrument of law enforcement only as long as no more than an insignificant number of them will be opposed to the legal order they are called upon to enforce.

The reliable performance of its functions by the police force within the state is thus not a simple technical matter to be expected with mechanical precision. Quite the contrary, it depends upon political, social, and moral conditions that may or may not be present in individual members of the police or the police force as a whole. These conditions must be created and maintained through a continuous effort of the political authorities. In other words, the functioning of a police force depends not only upon its internal technical qualities but also upon the political, social, and moral climate within which it operates. If the latter is not favorable, the former will avail little.

The effectiveness of a police force is determined, aside from its reliability, by the power relation that exists between itself and the recalcitrant fraction of the population. For the police to be effective, that power relation must meet three prerequisites.

Of all the citizens of a particular society only a very small fraction must be engaged at any one time in breaking the law. If large numbers of citizens simultaneously break the law, as they did with regard to prohibition and rationing and as they are still doing with regard to gambling, the police force, although it meets the standards of reliability, ceases to be an effective agency of law enforcement. Second, however great the differences in power are within a given society, the combined power of law-abiding citizens must be distinctly superior to any combination of even the most powerful lawbreakers. If it is otherwise, as in the case of the medieval feudal lord and his modern counterpart in the form of private concentrations of economic power, the police are bound to be almost as impotent as the citizenry at large. Finally, the police force must be manifestly capable of coping effectively with all foreseeable threats to the legal order. This obvious capability serves to deter attacks upon the legal order that go beyond the piecemeal violations of individual legal rules. In other words, its visible readiness for effective action makes its actual employment in good measure unnecessary.

This quality of unchallengeable superiority, aside from being the result of the reputation for reliability, is a function of the two other prerequisites. In consequence, the government is able to rely upon a numerically small and lightly armed police force to maintain law and order. In the absence of these prerequisites, the state would need a numerous and heavily armed police force in order to meet frontal attacks upon the legal order itself. That is to say, the state would need an army rather than a police force, and the relations between government and people would be tantamount either to civil war or a military dictatorship.

The inquiry into the impartiality of the police issues in four propositions.

First, the police perform two different functions for the maintenance of peace and order: a law-enforcing function in the strict sense,
concerned with piecemeal violations of the legal order, the survival of
which is not in question; and a political function, dealing with all-out
challenges to the legal order and the political, social, and economic
status quo itself.

Second, the issue of the impartiality of the police arises only with
regard to the former function, while the latter presupposes partiality
of the police in favor of the legal order and the *status quo*.

Third, there exists a complementary relationship between the political functions and the popular consensus supporting the legal order
and the *status quo*. The more there is of the latter, the less there
need be of the former, and vice versa.

Fourth, the quantitative relationship between police and consensus
depends upon the quality and the policies of the government. The
government can afford to dispense with the use of police in the measure that it has the voluntary support of the people and trusts the
people in giving that support.

In order to understand the functions an international police force
would have to perform in a disarmed world and, more particularly, to
assess the conditions for an impartial performance of its functions, it
is necessary to beware of too close an analogy with the police as we
know them from our national experience. That police appeared relatively late in the history of the modern states. Their appearance coincides with the development of the *Rechtsstaat*, the state whose
relations with its citizens are regulated by objective legal rules of general application. Thus the modern police appear on the European
continent in the eighteenth century and were established in England
through Peel's Metropolitan Police Act of 1829.

The police perform for the modern state,* under normal circumstances, specialized functions. Considered in the over-all context of
the functions the modern state fulfills, especially for the maintenance of peace and order, these functions are marginal. The police
cooperate in the enforcement of certain regulatory laws, concerned,
for instance, with motor traffic, licenses, and closing hours. They try
to prevent the violation of criminal laws and concern themselves with
the apprehension of criminals. They aid in the administration of justice through the collection of evidence.

Yet it is not upon the performance of these functions that the
maintenance of peace and order within the modern state primarily
depends. The police can protect peace and order from individual in-

---

* We are using this term here as synonymous with *Rechtsstaat*.

fractions and keep those that occur within tolerable bounds because of the deterrent effect the likelihood of their effective intervention has upon the prospective criminal. Yet when a national society is rent by deep dissensions over vital issues, threatening disintegration, revolution, or civil war, it is not to the police but to the sum total of the human and material resources of society, especially in the form of its government and of the armed forces, that the state must appeal.

The modern state is enabled to assign the police this specialized and marginal place in the overall scheme of things because it can draw for the maintenance of its peace and order upon the psychological resources of unorganized society. The peace and order of the modern state rests primarily upon the psychological predispositions of the great majority of its citizens, supporting that peace and order. Modern society has created a network of interests, of social and economic dependencies, of power relations, and of political loyalties, which converge in creating and continuously re-creating a consensus in favor of peace and order. The great majority of the citizens of the modern state are committed to the perpetuation of the political, social, and economic *status quo*, at least in its essentials, and insofar as they are not, their interest in the maintenance of peace and order outweigh their desire for change.

In the creation and preservation of this consensus, the quality of government plays a decisive role. This consensus is in good measure a reflection of four qualitites of government. The government allows for peaceful change. It is the focus of popular loyalties overriding parochial ones. It creates in the people the expectation that its policies will result at least in an approximation to justice. And it appears to have the power, in the form of the means of organized violence, to make its will prevail. Yet this last quality stands in a subsidiary and complementary relation to the other three. For it remains normally in the background as a general deterrent to be used only *in extremis*, and it tends to enter the picture as an active force in the measure that the other three qualities are not sufficient to maintain a voluntary consensus.

The impartiality of the police has two different meanings within the context of the modern state. As concerns the legal order and the political, social, and economic *status quo*, the police cannot be impartial; for it is their purpose to defend that legal order and maintain that *status quo*. If they perform their duty, they cannot help but be partial to them; if they violate their duty, as they do when they do not enforce certain laws, such as those against gambling or racial discrimination, they are partial against the legal order. But in the nature

of things, an institution whose purpose is the defense of the legal order cannot be impartial with regard to it. It must be either for or
against it.

The appearance of impartiality is here a mere optical illusion. It
stems from the near-general acceptance of the legal order, which thus
appears as the objective framework within which society functions
and in whose objectivity the police partake. The reputation for impartiality the police enjoy, however unfounded in fact, is important
because it fulfills an ideological function. By making it appear as
though the police were not an institution of organized violence on
behalf of a particular legal order and *status quo* but somehow the
impartial manifestation of the objective order of things, that reputation necessarily strengthens obedience to the law and submission to
the police. It becomes an active factor in the maintenance of peace
and order. In this respect, the reputation of the police for impartiality
performs a social and political function similar to that performed by
the reputation of the courts for being the impartial "mouthpiece" of
the law, arriving at their decisions by a rational process of logical
deduction.

The other meaning of impartiality, as applied to the police, is identical with equality before the law. The police are in this sense impartial if they mete out equal treatment to persons and situations that
the law requires to be so treated. They lack in impartiality if they
discriminate among persons and situations in a manner unsupported
by the law or, to use the formulation of American jurisprudence, if
they deliberately deny a person the enjoyment of a right that is commonly afforded others in like circumstances.

It, then, obscures the issue to say with Charles Reith that the
democratic police force "gives service wholly to law, and not to policy."* It would be more correct to say that the modern police are of
course the instrument of policy, that is, of that set of policies which
are supported by the consensus of the great majority of citizens, and
that the issue of impartiality normally comes to the fore only when
policy has to be applied to individual persons and circumstances.
Were it not for this consensus, codified in objective laws of general
applicability, the issue of the impartiality of the police could not
arise at all. Without that consensus, the police would simply be an
organization of violence through which the state imposes its will
upon a recalcitrant or, at best, indifferent population. The police
would then be not the instrument of a national consensus but a

* Charles Reith. *The Blind Eye of History* (London: Faber & Faber, 1952),
p. 253.

substitute for it. Both qualitatively and quantitatively their functions would be utterly different from those they perform normally in the modern state. This was indeed generally the case before the beginning of the nineteenth century, and it is still the case today in numerous countries.

The functions the police perform for the maintenance of peace and order in the state that is not a *Rechtsstaat* are entirely different from those discussed thus far, and, in consequence, the problem of its impartiality is posed here in entirely different terms. This observation is true both for the autocratic state, historically preceding the modern state, and for the autocratic and totalitarian states simultaneous with it. The functions of the police are here neither specialized nor marginal but general and central. They are so central to the state's existence and so pervasive throughout its activities, they are to such an extent the distinctive characteristic of the state, that we call such a state a "police state." For the same reason, in the usage of the sixteenth, seventeenth and eighteenth centuries the term "police," derived from the Greek word for state, covers the sum total of state activities concerned with internal peace, order, and welfare. According to Doctor Johnson, it connotes "the regulation and government of a city or county, so far as regards the inhabitants," * and the *Oxford English Dictionary* defines the term as "a body of men officially instituted, or employed, to keep order, enforce regulations, or maintain a political or ecclesiastical system." † One of the most influential nineteenth-century writers on the subject defines police as the sum total of the domestic policies of a state.‡ An eighteenth-century writer defines police as "the ordering of a state with regard to its internal security, beauty, convenience, population, morality, and standard of living." § Definitions of this type abound in the literature of the period. Or, as a contemporary writer put it: "*Police* anciently meant policy, social organization, civilization; the art or technic of so organizing a community that a civilized society would be the result."** Yet even in contemporary American jurisprudence police

* Samuel Johnson, A *Dictionary of the English Language* (London: W. Strahan, 1755), Vol. I.
† Sir James A. H. Murray, (ed.), A *New English Dictionary on Historical Principles* (Oxford: Clarendon Press, 1909), VII, 1069.
‡ Robert von Mohl, *Die Polizei-Wissenschaft nach den Grundsätzen des Rechtsstaates*, 3d. edition (Tübingen: H. Laupp. 1866), I, 6 ff.
§ Carl Gottlob-Rössig, *Lehrbuch der Polizeiwissenschaft* (Jena: Academische Buchhandlung, 1786), p. 2.
** Asher Brynes, *Government Against the People* (New York: Dodd, Mead, 1946), p. 20.

power is defined as the power "to promote the health, safety, morals and general welfare,"* or in the words of chief Justice Taney as "nothing more or less than the powers of government inherent in every sovereignty to the extent of its dominions."

Another aspect of this comprehensive concept of the police, important for our discussion, is its association with the army and with the exercise of arbitrary, oppressive power. This association exists both in verbal usage and in substance. A modern constable is the diminished successor of the commander of an army and the keeper of a royal castle or fortified town of medieval times. Gendarmes are etymologically "men-in-arms." In Pakistan and certain parts of Northern India the officer in charge of a police station is called "Faujdar," that is, military officer, and the central police station of a large city is called "Kotwali", that is, the fort.† As concerns the association of arbitrariness and oppression with the police, a bipartisan committee reported in 1818 on the establishment of a professional police force in Great Britain in these terms:

> Though your committee could imagine a system of police that might arrive at the object sought for; yet, in a free country, or even in one where any unrestrained intercourse of society is admitted, such a system would of necessity be odious and repulsive, and one which no country could carry into execution. In despotic countries it has never yet succeeded to the extent aimed at by those theorists; and among free people the very proposal would be rejected with abhorrence; it would be a plan which would make every servant of every house a spy on the actions of his master, and all classes of society spies on each other.

And another committee reported thus in 1822 on Peel's proposal for the establishment of a professional police:

> It is difficult to reconcile an effective system of police with that perfect freedom of action and exemption from interference which are the great privileges and blessings of society in this country; and your committee think that the forfeiture or curtailment of such advantages would be too great a sacrifice for improvement in police or facilities in detection of crime.‡

The facts have borne out this picture which the language and ex-

---

* Edward S. Corwin, *The Constitution and What It Means Today* (Princeton, N.J.: Princeton University Press, 1954), p. 51.
† Cf. John Coatman, *Police* (London: Oxford University Press, 1959) pp. 1, 14.
‡ Quoted in Charles Reith, *op. cit.*, pp. 144, 147, 148.

pectations of men have painted of the police. Aside from the primitive decentralized system of what has been called "kin police"* in which a chief or other ruler delegates the authority to preserve peace and order on the local level to the community as a whole, and aside from self-help, widespread throughout history, this power was exercised until the eighteenth century by organized armed forces, which either were identical with the regular armed forces or were, except for organizational or functional peculiarities, indistinguishable from them. This was true of the *cohortes vigilum*, which Augustus established as protection against fires, thieves, and robbers,† as it was true of similar institutions in later periods of history. These military and paramilitary forces were typically oblivious of those piecemeal disturbances of peace and order that are the routine concerns of the police today, but they were put into action whenever there was a major threat to peace and order. The Peterloo Massacre of 1818, for instance, resulted from an attempt by the army to perform what we would regard today as a typical police function, that is, the dispersal of a crowd. The same was true of many of the riots that preceded that massacre for almost a century. The same was true even of the American War of Independence.

It was exactly this disproportionate and indiscriminate use of force, the only kind an army is capable of, that revealed to an "enlightened" age the inappropriateness of the army as a routine instrument of police power. For either the army would not act at all, leaving the protection of individual rights to self-help, or its intervention would be so devastating as to make the cure worse than the disease. The search for a modern police force was the result of this dilemma, foreshadowing the dilemma with which the availability of nuclear weapons confronts modern nations in their relations with each other.

Thus professional police forces were established to replace the army, as was done in Great Britain by virtue of the Act of 1829. Or a segment of the army was transformed into a professional police force; the Texas Rangers and the Canadian Mounted Police are cases in point. Yet it is worthy of note that even the nations that established professional police forces for the purpose of coping with piecemeal disturbances of peace and order have retained armed forces, one of whose major purposes is to meet a major challenge to the legal order and *status quo*. We look to our armed forces primarily as a protection

---

* *Ibid.*, p. 20.

† Joachim Marquardt, *Römische Staatsverwaltung*, 2d ed. (Leipzig: S. Hirzel, 1884), II, 484 ff.; Theodor Mommsen, *Römisches Staatsrecht*, 4th ed. (Tübingen: Wissenschaftliche Buchgemeinschaft, 1952), II, 1055 ff.

against foreign enemies, and it is exactly the all-pervasive consensus, making outright challenges to the domestic legal order and *status quo* at present unlikely, that allows us to look to them that way. Yet even in our society the state militias, the National Guard, and the federal army are the foundation stones upon which public peace and order ultimately rest. This becomes obvious in the rare crisis situations, such as Little Rock and the University of Mississippi, in which the police are not able to maintain peace and order, not only because of the magnitude of the challenge but also and most importantly because they prefer a different kind of order from that to be enforced.

While in the United States the armed forces constitute a kind of reserve power the federal and state governments can fall back upon in case of emergency, in other countries specialized armed forces, backing up the regular police in cases of outright challenge against peace and order, are institutionalized into paramilitary organizations. Thus in France the *gendarmerie nationale* is under the authority of the Ministry of National Defense. So is the *garde republicaine,* which fought as a unit in the two world wars and in Indochina. The *garde mobile* created in 1921 to deal with the revolutionary strikes and disturbances of that period, was transformed in 1948 into the Republican Security Companies. The Italian *carabinieri* and Spanish Civil Guards are paramilitary organizations that symbolize and enforce the authority of the state *per se* rather than perform regular police duties.

In other words, the functions of such paramilitary organizations are primarily political in the sense that they are a visible and effective demonstration of the power of the state for the benefit of the citizenry and, more particularly, of its actually and potentially recalcitrant members. These organizations are generally, as they are intended to be, reliable instruments in the hands of the government. But they can also become a state within the state, pursuing policies of their own. Thus the police prefect of Paris has at times been able to pursue his own policies in defiance of the French Government, for he commands all the police forces of the Department of the Seine and is for all practial purposes the head of the municipal government of Paris.

It is revealing that the political purpose of these paramilitary organizations is perfectly understood by the population at large. Those groups of the population, in particular, who are opposed to the government or the legal order and the *status quo,* or else are alienated from society altogether, hate this type of police as an odious instrument of oppression. It has for long been the favored target of collective violence.

Paramilitary political police, which in the *Rechtsstaat* gives symbolic or emergency support to the government, are in modern totalitarian societies developed into a full-fledged institutional system of oppression, administration of justice, punishment, and terror. In Nazi Germany and in the Soviet Union, especially under Stalin, the police established a second state, duplicating and at times superseding the administrative, judicial, and military institutions of the regular one. They were so powerful that not only the population at large but also the officials of the regular government held them in awe. Both Himmler and Beria commanded large, well-equipped elite forces that in quality were at least the equal of the regular army. These potent police organizations owed their existence to the lack of confidence—probably unfounded—of Hitler and Stalin in a voluntary consensus that could support their rule. Distrustful of the regular officials and the people at large, they created special organizations of violence fanatically loyal to themselves, a special state, as it were, with a reliable consensus of its own. That special state imposed upon the regular state and the population at large peace and order with the methods of the totalitarian police state.

Before applying these propositions to a police force in an international setting, it is interesting and relevant to take a look at history. The armed action of the Holy Roman Empire against Frederick II of Prussia during the Seven Years War vividly illustrates the dependence of an international police force upon the political purposes it is intended to support. In fact, it is surprising that to the best of my knowledge nobody has analyzed the Holy Roman Empire, as it existed from the Peace of Westphalia of 1648 to its dissolution in 1806, as the prototype of an international organization that shows revealing similarities with its twentieth-century successors—the League of Nations and the United Nations.

The medieval Emperor of the Holy Roman Empire was supposed to perform the peace-preserving and law-enforcing functions for the sake of which modern international organization has also been established. In the words of James Bryce:

> He was therefore above all things, claiming indeed to be upon earth the representative of the Prince of Peace, bound to listen to complaints, and to redress the injuries inflicted by sovereigns or peoples upon each other; to punish offenders against the public order of Christendom; to maintain through the world, looking down as from a serene height upon the schemes and quarrels of meaner potentates, that supreme good without which neither arts nor letters, nor the gentler virtues of life can rise and

flourish. The mediaeval Empire was in its essence what its modern imitators have sometimes professed themselves: the Empire was Peace: the oldest and noblest title of its head was "Imperator pacificus." And that he might be the peacemaker, he must be the expounder of justice and the author of its concrete embodiment, positive law.*

Originally the Emperor was supposed to perform these functions as the head of a universal empire, that is, as the highest secular authority within the Empire's territory. The Treaty of Westphalia reduced these functions to international ones by recognizing the territorial sovereignty of the princes and cities subject to the Emperor. The Emperor was in consequence precluded from interfering directly with the administration of any territory belonging to the Empire. All major political decisions concerning the Empire, such as the making of war and peace, levying contributions, raising troops, building fortresses, passing or interpreting laws, were the exclusive competence of the imperial Diet. Yet the Diet, in the words of James Bryce,

> originally an assembly of the whole people, and thereafter of the feudal tenants-in-chief, meeting from time to time like our early English Parliaments, became in A.D. 1654 a permanent body, at which the electors, princes, and cities were represented by their envoys. In other words, it was not so much a national Parliament as an international congress of diplomatists.†

The Diet had the authority to protect the legal order and the political *status quo* of 1618 by summoning the members of the Empire to collective military action. In addition France and Sweden, which were not members of the Empire, had in 1648 been made guarantors of the order of 1648 and hence had received the right to intervene in the affairs of the Empire on behalf of that order. But the Diet, similar to the United Nations, could only request member states to put money and armed contingents at the disposal of the Empire, taking what the member states were willing to give; it could no longer, as it once did, enforce the "matricula" specifying the quota of contingents each state was obligated to furnish to the imperial army. Thus the Holy Roman Empire developed in a way that is the reverse of the development many expect the United Nations to take: Starting as a supranational organization, it ended as a federation of sovereign states.

* James Bryce, *The Holy Roman Empire* (New York: Macmillan, 1923), p. 259.
† *Ibid.*, p. 396.

After Frederick II of Prussia invaded Saxony in August, 1756, the Elector of Saxony appealed against this breach of the peace to the Emperor and the imperial Diet. After the Emperor had exhausted the peace-preserving and law-enforcing measures with which the imperial constitution empowered him (the so-called *Dehortatoria*, addressed to the King of Prussia; the *Avocatoria*, ordering the Prussian armed forces to leave the seditious service of their king; and the *Monitoria*, the *Excitatoria*, and the *Inhibitoria*, addressed to the imperial territories in order to prevent Prussian enlistments), the Council of Princes of the Diet decided on January 17, 1757, by a vote of 60 to 26 to declare in the name of the Empire war against Prussia and to employ the military resources of the Empire for the purpose of restoring the Elector of Saxony to his throne. Pursuant to this resolution a special tax was levied on all the states of the Empire, and an imperial army was raised.* The composition of that army, the factors determining its composition, and its fate shed a significant light upon the problems facing an international police force.

The states of the Empire split according to their religious and political preferences. All the Catholic states took the side of Austria; the majority of the Protestant ones, that of Prussia. The Protestant princes of Hanover, Brunswick, Lippe, Waldeck, Hesse, and Gotha protested against the resolution of the Diet; they were allied with Great Britain, which in turn supported Prussia. On the other hand, the King of France as guarantor of the Treaty of Westphalia—which guaranty had originally been aimed at Austria—declared his support for Austria in its struggle with Prussia, and it was especially due to his efforts that the imperial army was assembled. In other words, it was not so much the resolution of the Diet but special political relations between France and individual German states which induced the latter to provide contingents for the imperial army. Thus the King of France requested the Electors of Cologne and the Palatinate to provide the number of troops promised him in previous treaties. He concluded new treaties with the Elector of Bavaria and the Duke of Wurtemberg in which he promised them subsidies as compensation for a number of regiments to be provided. He made similar agreements with a great number of minor German princes. As a result of these efforts an imperial army numbering 32,000 men was assembled. They marched into Thuringia in September, 1757, to join a French army numbering 24,000 men.

* F. C. Schlosser, *Geschichte des Achtzehnten Iahrhunderts* (Heidelberg: J. C. B. Mohr, 1837), II, 319; Reinhold Koser, *König Friedrich der Grosse* (Stuttgart and Berlin: J. G. Cotta, 1903), II, 47 ff.

When 9,500 of this "Combined Army," as it was officially called, encountered 1,900 Prussians on a reconnoitering expedition, they were put to flight. As the *Cambridge Modern History* put it:

> Here the extraordinary deficiencies from which the combined army suffered for the first time made themselves evident. . . . The army of the Empire was composed in motley fashion of contingents supplied by numerous small dynasts. This had not hindered Marlborough and Eugene from winning partly by means of the army of the Empire the Battle of Höchstädt; but in their day English and Dutch subsidies had helped to establish that army on a satisfactory footing. At present, in consequence of lack of money, such intolerable conditions prevailed among the Imperial troops that Hildburghausen [the commanding general] despaired of being able to keep his forces together for long, and therefore impatiently sought a decision by battle.*

On November 5, 1757, the day of the Battle of Rossbach, the imperial army had shrunk to 11,000 men. Of these, 7,000 were disbanded at the beginning of the battle. Those who remained were put to flight. The Bavarian and Franconian infantry threw their rifles away while the Prussians were still in the distance. The precipitous and disorderly retreat of the runaway army at the beginning of the battle became in the eighteenth century a by-word for cowardice and disorganization.

The Battle of Rossbach signified the end of the imperial army. According to Ranke, the very name disappeared.† The reasons for this catastrophe must be sought in the unreliability of the imperial army, which was the result of both religious and political factors. The appearance of France in Germany as the ally of Austria against Prussia could not fail to be considered a Catholic alliance against the foremost Protestant power in Germany. Thus the Protestant elements of the imperial army quite openly sympathized with Frederick II. The disintegrating effects of the religious preference were reinforced by divergent political sympathies. This became obvious at the Battle of Leuthen, following the Battle of Rossbach by a month. The Austrian commanders could not trust ten Bavarian battalions because of the political conflicts that then existed between Bavaria and Austria; the same was true of fourteen battalions of Wurtembergers who hated their tyrannical ruler and admired the victor of Rossbach as the champion

---

* *Cambridge Modern History*, Vol. VI: *The Eighteenth Century* (New York: Macmillan, 1909), pp. 265, 267.

† Leopold von Ranke, *Sämmtliche Werke*, Vol. XXX: *Zur Geschichte von Österreich und Preussen zwischen den Friedensschlüssen zu Aachen und Hubertusburg* (Leipzig: Duncker Humbolt, 1875), p. 312.

of German Protestantism. The Austrian commander placed those contingents on the left wing, where he did not expect the Prussian attack. Frederick attacked exactly at this point, with the result that eleven out of the fourteen battalions of Wurtembergers fled immediately, leaving behind only a few killed and wounded.*

What are the general lessons to be learned from these historical considerations? First of all, an international police force by definition cannot be at the service of a single government to which it gives allegiance and whose orders it executes unquestioningly because of that allegiance. An international police force can only be the instrument of an international organization, such as the United Nations. It is this relationship that makes its reliability a continuous problem. In a society of nation-states it is possible for some outstanding individuals to transfer their loyalty from their respective nation-state to an international organization either on a particular issue or even in general. But it is too much to expect that large masses of individual members of different nations could so transfer their loyalties that they would execute reliably and without question whatever orders the international organization might give them. The reliability of an international police force cannot be taken for granted on the assumption that it has the morale and discipline we have come to expect from the domestic police.

The reliability of an international police force is a function of the legal order and the political *status quo* it is called upon to uphold. Yet the enforcement of an international legal order and the protection of an international *status quo* present a police force with problems quite different from those the national police have to solve. Great international conflicts that lead to the violation of international law and conjure up the danger of war and therefore call for the intervention of an international police force are typically the ones in which the survival of the existing legal order and of the political *status quo* is at stake. The task the international police force must here perform is the defense of the legal order and. of the political *status quo* not against piecemeal violations but against an all-out attack. What is at stake here is not the enforcement of a particular legal rule but the survival of the legal order itself.

One nation or group of nations will be committed to the legal order as it is and to the existing political *status quo*; another nation or group of nations will be opposed to them; a third will be indifferent. The

* Schlosser, *op. cit.*, p. 335; *Cambridge Modern History, op. cit.*, p. 275.

members of the international police force belong to all three types of nations, and their sympathies concerning the issues at stake are bound to vary with the preferences of their respective nations. The members of an international police force will be a reliable instrument of an international organization only in the measure that their legal preferences and political sympathies happen to coincide with the policies of the international organization they are called upon to support.

In consequence, the international organization commanding a police force will have to cope with three different contingencies with which national political authorities do not have to deal under normal circumstances. If the challenge to the legal order and the political *status quo* emanates from, or is supported by, a great power, the police action reverts to the traditional pattern of a coalition war. That is to say, an army composed of contingents of the nations supporting the legal order and the political *status quo* will be opposed by contingents of the nation or nations opposed to the legal and political *status quo*, with the contingents of neutral nations tending to one or the other side. This was the pattern of the Korean War. That this war was called a police action by the supporters of the *status quo* did not affect the nature of the operation. At best, it made it easier for certain nations, which otherwise might have been inclined toward neutrality or a half-hearted effort, to join the defense of the *status quo* or to commit themselves more fully to it.

If the *status quo* is challenged by a nation of the second or third rank that has a vital stake in changing it, the sympathies and interests of many other nations are likely to be actively engaged on one or the other side. This contingency will confront an international police force with choices that are bound to be detrimental to its reliability or efficiency or both. If the international police force is composed of national contingents assembled in advance of, and without regard for, the particular conflict, those of its national contingents that are out of sympathy with the *status quo* may not be relied upon to defend it. If the international police force is being assembled *ad hoc* in view of this particular conflict and, hence, is being composed only of reliable national contingents, it faces the risk of being too small to provide an effective defense of the *status quo* against the forces opposing it.

Even if an international police force appears at the beginning of a conflict to be a reliable and effective instrument of an international organization, it is still faced with an ever present threat to its reliability and effectiveness. An international police force may be politically cohesive at the beginning of a conflict on the basis of a community of sympathy and interests on the part of the nations to which its individual members belong. Yet it is a moot question whether and to what extent such a community of sympathy and interests can survive the initial stages of the conflict. New interests may replace or modify the initial ones; new opportunities may present themselves for the pursuit of old ones. As the interests of the nations concerned change, so will the reliability of the respective contingents of the international police force to defend a *status quo* that may run counter to those interests. A multinational military force, be it called an international police force or an army, is thus always threatened with partial or total disintegration. Its survival as a reliable and effective force depends upon the persistence of the national interests on which it rests.

What distinguishes an international police force from a national one is, then, the lack of an automatic commitment to a particular legal order and political *status quo*. Such a commitment can be taken for granted, at least normally and except for piecemeal or marginal deviations, in a national police force. It cannot be taken for granted in an international one but must there be created and re-created and maintained for each issue. The task an international organization faces in fashioning a police force for a particular issue parallels that of a group of nations seeking political and military support for a particular *status quo*. The international police forces that have been organized by the United Nations have reflected both the composition and the political and military character of the two-thirds majorities of the General Assembly to which they have owed their existence. That is to say, no nation that did not support the police action by its vote in the Security Council or General Assembly supplied contingents for the police force, and of those that so supported it only a small minority supplied contingents. The contributions of these nations were a manifestation of their political interests and military capabilities.

Thus, of the then sixty members of the United Nations only sixteen provided armed forces of any kind in 1950 against North Korea, and of those only the United States, Canada, Great Britain, and Turkey can be said to have contributed more than token forces. South Korea and the United States provided about 90 percent of the armed forces that fought in Korea on the side of the United Nations. For the United Nations Emergency Force stationed along the Egypt-Israel armistice demarcation line, the international frontier south of the Gaza Strip, and at the Gulf of Aqaba, the following nations provided troops: Brazil, Canada, Colombia, Denmark, Finland, India, Indonesia, Norway, Sweden, and Yugoslavia. The United Nations force in the Congo was originally composed of contingents from Ethiopia, Ghana, Guinea, Morocco, Tunisia, Sweden, and Ireland. The composition of that force subsequently changed according to changes in the policies of some of the participating nations. However, what remained as the distinctive feature of the United Nations force in the Congo was the numerical predominance of contingents from African nations, which had a special interest in the pacification of the Congo without the intervention of non-African nations. What this United Nations force had in common with that of the Middle East was the absence of great-power contingents, pointing to the policy of the United Nations to use its armed forces for the purpose of isolating the territorial issues from great-power intervention.

The tenuous character of an international police force reflects the tenuous character of the commitment of a number of sovereign nations to a particular legal order and political *status quo*. The deficiencies of an international police force are the deficiencies of the international order revealed in the perspective of a particular task. In a world of sovereign nations the idea of a reliable and effective international police force, after the model of the national police, is a contradiction in terms. An international police force, by dint of being international rather than national or supranational, cannot be more reliable and efficient than the political interests and military capabilities of the nations supporting it allow it to be.

This situation would not be materially affected by arms control or limited disarmament. At best the control and limitation of national armaments might increase the effectiveness of an international police force in conflicts among major powers, provided that the stabilization and decrease of national armed forces were to go hand in hand with a corresponding increase in the strength of the international police force. Without the latter proviso, arms control and disarmament might well have an adverse effect upon the effectiveness of an international police force; for they might adversely affect the ability and willingness of national governments to put armed forces at the disposal of an international organization. The best that can be expected from arms control and limited disarmament is a change in the distribution of armed strength between national forces and the international police force in favor of the latter. But the basic political issue bearing upon the reliability of an international police force will continue to make itself felt even in a partially disarmed world; for such a world would still be a world of sovereign nations.

The situation would be radically different in a totally disarmed world. Total disarmament can no more be envisaged in isolation from the over-all structure of international relations than can an international police force. Total disarmament requires as its corollary the existence of a supranational authority capable of committing organized force to the defense of the legal order and the political *status quo*. In other words, total disarmament and world government go hand in hand; they complement each other. In a totally disarmed world the problem of an international police force ceases to exist and re-appears in the form—new in its dimensions and old in its substance —of the police of a world government.

Applying this analysis and the propositions deduced from it to an international police force in a disarmed world, one must make two assumptions, which are likely to prevail regardless of other, unforesee-able aspects of a disarmed world.

First, the world could be disarmed only in the sense that no nation will be able to wage a major war after the model of the two world wars. It is generally admitted that nations will retain police forces for the purpose of law enforcement. But it ought to be obvious as well that nations will also retain the paramilitary and military forces necessary for the protection of the legal order and the domestic *status quo* itself. The extent of these armed forces will be propor-tionate to the precariousness of the legal order and the *status quo*. The more a nation is lacking in stability spontaneously provided by society, the more will it be in need of armed forces to enforce stability. The two types of police will continue to perform for the individual na-tions the same functions they are performing now.

Second, the day-by-day enforcement of legal rules in the relations among nations will not be appreciably affected by general and com-plete disarmament. The multitude of unspectacular technical rules of international law that regulate the relations among nations with re-gard to matters such as diplomatic immunity, territorial limits of sovereignty, postal service and telecommunications, and so forth, are being enforced primarily by the reciprocal self-interest of the na-tions concerned and, under exceptional circumstances, through re-prisal, retaliation, and judicial determination. This virtually automatic enforcement of legal rules, which makes the intervention of a spe-cial police force unnecessary, is not likely to be affected by general and complete disarmament.

This being so, there is in a disarmed world but one law-enforcing function, in the strict sense, left for an international police force to perform: the enforcement of disarmament itself. This function can require of the international police the performance of four different tasks: control of production and transportation of weapons and of military installations, the ascertainment of facts concerning alleged violations, the restoration of the legal status of disarmament after violations, and the punishment of the culprit either individually or collectively—that is, the nation that has allowed or ordered the violation.

The issue of the impartiality of the international police in the performance of these tasks can arise only on the condition that the binding force of the disarmament provisions as such is not in question, that these provisions are generally accepted as legitimate and valid, and what is at issue are only piecemeal violations of individual rules by either negligence or intent. In other words, the situation is assumed to be similar to that facing the national police in the day-by-day performance of their law-enforcing functions. In consequence, the issue of impartiality, too, poses itself in similar terms.

If impartiality is the equal treatment of persons and situations that the law requires to be treated without discrimination, then the impartiality of the police rests on two foundations, one objective, the other subjective: efficiency and fairness. A police force that is slipshod in supervision and control, in the collection of evidence, and in the apprehension of suspects cannot be trusted to meet the requirements of equal treatment of equal persons and situations, however impartial it intends to be. Its partiality is a function of its inefficiency. It does not know how to be impartial, since it does not have the technical competence to identify the persons and situations deserving equal treatment. The remedy lies obviously in the maximization of technical competence and the establishment of strict inside and outside controls assuring a continuous high level of performance.

The risk of unfairness is inherent in the multinational composition of the international police. It is likely to manifest itself in two different ways. On the one hand, national loyalties and divergent national interests are likely to survive in a disarmed world, however mitigated and neutralized by more comprehensive loyalties and interests. Thus an international police force must guard against distortion of the impartial performance of its tasks resulting from the national preferences of some of its members.

The other risk of unfairness stems from the very desire of the international police, composed primarily of members of uncommitted nations, to be fair. There has been a tendency among uncommitted nations, such as India, to regard themselves almost by definition as fair with respect to the disputes of other nations and to take an intermediate position in any conflict that does not concern themselves. It has been said that if nation A takes the position that two and two make four and nation B takes the position that two and two make six, then the neutralist nation, in order to be fair, will commit itself to the proposition that two and two make five. In other words, such a nation equates impartiality with compromise. Yet when it comes to the enforcement of unambiguous legal rules, as those concerning complete and general disarmament are supposed to be, compromise between the legal and the illegal position, far from complying with the requirement of impartiality, actually meets the illegal position halfway. The temptation to confound impartiality with compromise is likely to be particularly strong when the correct assessment of legal responsibility might conjure up a major conflict among great powers.

The remedy for partiality as the result of national bias lies in a judicious national composition of the international police. Two contradictory patterns have been developed by the United Nations, one through the operations in the Congo, the other through those at the southern frontiers of Israel. The rationale underlying both patterns is the exclusion from the police force of those nationals that can a priori be presumed to be biased by virtue of their national allegiance. Both patterns exclude nationals of the great powers, opposing each in conflict and competition throughout the world, which can be presumed to be interested in a particular settlement, favorable to them, of any local issue. Yet as concerns the actual composition of the police force, the application of the same rationale has led to diametrically opposed standards of selection. The Middle Eastern operation has excluded members of Middle Eastern nations, since the latter are all committed to partisan views of the local issue. The Congo operation, on the other hand, has preferred contingents from Africa and Asia, whose sympathetic disinterest and support for United Nations policies are assumed, while white contingents, especially from former colonial powers, are regarded as less trustworthy, regardless of whether or not they actually are.

If follows that an international police force needs to be impartial not only in fact but also in appearance. If the nation or nations concerned do not trust its impartiality, its actual impartiality will be of little avail, for its measures will be received, and it will be treated, as though it were actually lacking in impartiality. Suspicion, however unfounded, will destroy what the requirement of impartiality aims to create and preserve: the voluntary acceptance, on the part of the subjects of the law, of the measures of the police, of the police as an institution, and of the legal order on behalf of which the police act.

The application of these considerations might require a flexible composition of the international police force in view of both its actual impartiality and its reputation for it. One can imagine as many patterns for its composition as there are situations requiring special attention to the impartiality of the police. For instance, in order to insure impartiality, the international police force might on occasion have to be composed of contingents of the great powers concerned, operating on the basis of equality, after the model of the quadripartite police operating in Vienna during the Allied occupation. Aside from the interests at stake, the composition of the international police force will depend upon the nature of the issue as presented by the kind of disarmament provisions to be enforced.

We have thus far tried to answer the question "Who shall perform the functions of the international police?" in such a way as to guard against one of the two possible types of unfairness. We are now raising the question, What freedom of action should the international police have, in order to dispose of both possible types of unfairness? It is obvious that the opportunities for partiality are proportionate to the freedom of action the actor possesses. The more discretion an actor has, the greater are his chances to substitute his own standards of action for those required by the law. Insofar as the law prescribes the equal treatment of persons and situations under certain circumstances defined by itself, the requirements of legality and impartiality coincide. Exclusively concerned in the context of this paper with maximizing the impartiality of the international police, we must emphasize the paramount importance of strict legal standards reducing the discretion of the police to that minimum compatible with the effective performance of their tasks. Two devices serve that purpose: the rule of law and judicial review.

Strict legal rules that clearly define what the police must do, can do, and cannot do under clearly defined circumstances not only maximize the ability of the police to act with impartiality but also increase its reputation for doing so. The parties affected by the action of the police are in large measure capable of determining for themselves whether or not the police have acted with impartiality. I can tell without the benefit of legal counsel that the police who have singled out my home for a search without a warrant have acted not only illegally but also with partiality.

Judicial review of the actions of the police serves the same dual purpose of maximizing impartiality and increasing the reputation for it. The availability of judicial review will in itself have a restraining influence upon the police. The actual intervention of judicial review will have a corrective effect upon police actions violating the standards of impartiality. Review procedures could be set up within the police organization in a quasi-judicial fashion, or independent courts could determine the legality of police actions, or the two procedures could be combined. Whatever the procedures chosen, the subjection of the police to clearly defined and enforceable legal standards will assimilate the international police as a law-enforcing agency both in their actual operations and in public esteem to the police in a *Rechtsstaat*. That is to say, the international police would attain the highest degree of impartiality with which we are acquainted in the history of the police.

Even in a disarmed world conflicts among nations will continue to occur. This will be so even if the conflicts that at present divide the major powers are peacefully settled as a precondition for general and complete disarmament. For even then, the distribution of political, social, and economic power will change within and among nations, and the groups benefiting from the *status quo* and protected by the legal order will be challenged by groups demanding changes in both. Insofar as these conflicts will take place among nations, the international powers-that-be will require a political international police force strong enough to deter potential challengers and keep actual ones in check. In other words, the political tasks assigned to an "international" police force require a world government with a supranational police force at its disposal.

As I have pointed out before,* the issue here is not the impartiality of the police but its effectiveness and reliability and, first of all, the quality of government and of society. In other words, the issue here is political and military; it concerns the viability and nature of world government. The choice will be between a world-wide police state with unprecedented powers of oppression and an ordering of international society in such a way that it will create and maintain a world-wide consensus in support of the legal order and the *status quo*. In the latter alternative, the world order will repose, as does the domestic order of the *Rechtsstaat*, upon the twin pillars of a political police, to be used only as the *ultima ratio* of the world government, and of a political, social, and economic order which allows for peaceful change, commands the loyalties of the great majority of mankind, and holds out to them at least the expectation of an approximation to justice.*

* Morgenthau, *Politics Among Nations*, 4th ed. (New York: Alfred A. Knopf, 1967), p. 484 ff.

28

The Principles of Propaganda

[May, 1960]

Even the most optimistic observer of the international scene or the staunchest defender of present policies cannot deny that the prestige of the United States has sunk in recent years to what is probably an unprecedented low. A Gallup Poll published in February, 1960, showed that eight out of nine nations friendly to the United States—the exception being Greece—believed, most of them by wide margins, that by 1970 the Soviet Union would be ahead of the United States in science and military power. A Gallup Poll taken in New Delhi in 1958 elicited the following answers to the question, "Which is doing more to help peace in the world, Russia or the West?": Russia, 55 per cent, the West, 18 per cent, don't know, 28 per cent. A wave of anti-Americanism sweeps over the world, by no means all of it inspired by the Communists, even though all of it is being exploited by them. It has been reported that in Latin America politicians, in order to compete with a chance for success, must at least pay lip service to anti-American slogans. And the Castro regime of Cuba provides an example of the lengths to which anti-Americanism can be carried in practice with the enthusiastic support of the people.

Thus large masses throughout the world look at the United States

315

with resentment, envy, contempt, and even hatred. They oppose America for what it is, for its wealth and power. But they also oppose it for what it is not, for its asserted lack of culture, its supposed indifference to freedom, and its alleged warlike intentions. Yet the very same people who have thus been alienated from America in their day-by-day reactions have shown an entirely different attitude on exceptional occasions. When the Vice President of the United States visited Poland in the spring of 1959 and when the President in the fall of that year visited India, the major uncommitted nation, they were greeted with popular enthusiasm, which was meant not for their persons but for the nation they represented. They were greeted, as Woodrow Wilson and Franklin Delano Roosevelt had been before them, as living symbols of what the nation was thought to stand for, and the enthusiasm the nation evoked in the person of its representatives was due, it is safe to assume, not to its wealth and power but to its achievements and promise as the champion of freedom.

How is this contrast between the images of two different Americas and between the hostility and affection these images evoke to be explained? The contrasting images and reactions are the result of the contradiction between what America has stood for throughout its history and what it has appeared to stand for in recent years. It has stood throughout its history for freedom at home and abroad, but in recent years it has appeared to the outside world to be indifferent to the cause of freedom. Ironically enough, the outside world seemed to understand America better than did America itself, and the outside world had to recall the American message to an America that is incapable of making clear to the world what it is about.

What accounts for that faltering voice of America, a voice that not only is inarticulate in telling the world what America is all about but also has a bent toward telling people things they don't want to hear? Three factors are in the main responsible for this failure of America to tell its story to the world: the kind of foreign policies the United States pursues and, more particularly, the way it pursues them; the over-all quality of national life to which America appears to have been committed in recent years; and the very conception of an information policy as a self-sufficient technical enterprise, divorced both from the substantive policies of the nation and from the mainstream of national life at home and abroad.

Information policy, political warfare, propaganda—synonyms for the attempt to influence the minds of whole nations over the heads of their governments—are but the reflection, in the realm of ideas, of the political and military policies they seek to support. They can be worse than these policies and they can also be better, but they cannot be a substitute for them. They can improve these policies by interpreting them, emphasizing their strong points, and glossing over their weak ones. But we, living in an open society in contrast to totalitarian countries, cannot use propaganda as a substitute for policy; we cannot use words without relation to deeds. Whenever the present Administration has tried to do this, it has been found out. For us, the call for victory in the struggle for the minds of men, to be effective, must therefore be first of all a call for political and military policies that have the makings of victory. Here, too, deeds speak louder than words.

The United States comes out second best in the struggle for the minds of men because its deeds contradict, or give the appearance of contradicting, its words. What America can offer to the world is what, throughout its history, it has tried to achieve for itself and what it has actually achieved for a substantial majority of the people: equality in freedom, a happy life for all under a government governing with the consent of the governed. Yet this achievement and promise of America have been overshadowed in the eyes of other nations by two outstanding qualities of recent American foreign policy: the quest for military alliances and the support of the political *status quo* throughout the world. In consequence, the traditional image of the United States as the last best hope of freedom has been widely replaced by the picture of a powerful, wealthy, and conservative nation, seeking to increase its power and wealth with the help and at the expense of other nations and to that end supporting the powers-that-be throughout the world.

The foreign and military policies of the United States have needlessly contributed to this revision of the traditional American image. That the United States needs allies and that, more particularly, the Atlantic Alliance is an essential prerequisite for American security goes without saying. But it is quite a different matter for the United States, as it did in the heyday of Mr. Dulles, to make the willingness of foreign nations to conclude an alliance with the United States the touchstone of our mutual relations. During that period, the United States conceived of its relations with the outside world primarily in military terms. It saw itself surrounded by allies, by uncommitted nations which thus far had refused to become allies, and by satellites that Russian power had thus far prevented from becoming allies. The Baghdad Pact, SEATO, and the Eisenhower Doctrine were open-ended—and largely unsuccessful—invitations to the uncommitted nations of Asia and the Middle East to become allies of the United States, or at least to accept military assistance from it. Thus it was little wonder that the world looked at the United States as the United States looked at the world:

primarily in military terms. The United States presented itself to the world primarily as a military power seeking military goals, and the world accepted the estimate that America appeared to give of itself, and found it wanting in view of what America had stood for during most of its history.

In its search for, and support of, allies, the United States has had to weigh its military needs against the political liabilities it might incur by associating itself with a government unpopular at home and abroad. Political preferences must obviously yield to military necessity, and in such a situation the United States has had to act on the principle that Winston Churchill stated in 1941 after the German attack on the Soviet Union when he said that if "Hitler invaded Hell I would make at least a favorable reference to the Devil in the House of Commons." Yet there is a difference between dealing with the "Devil" at arm's length out of necessity and embracing him as a friend, "our boy," the champion of freedom, the embodiment of all the virtues. Instead of dealing with the "Devil" as one businessman with another, in a matter-of-fact way, we have fraternized with him and convinced ourselves that the "Devil," since he is on our side, must really be an angel.

Our attitudes throughout the world have been consistently oblivious of this subtle but crucial distinction. We have proved ourselves incapable of having certain dealings, required by our interests, with foreign governments without identifying ourselves with them politically. Since it so happens that most of these governments are unpopular with their own peoples, we have paid for military benefits, such as they are, with a drastic decline in our prestige and influence among those peoples. In many of these nations, America is looked upon, with differing degrees of intensity, not as the last best hope of freedom but as the ally and main support of unpopular regimes. In certain countries, such as Spain, the United States is even blamed, quite unjustly, for the survival of a regime that, it is widely believed, could not keep itself in power without American support. And many of those who thus vent their opposition to, and hatred of, their own government upon the United States find the only alternative to the *status quo* in Communism and its fountainhead, the Soviet Union. Thus the policies of the United States, committed throughout the world to the containment of Communism and of the influence of the Soviet Union exercised through international Communism, unwittingly serves Communist expansion and, hence, the purposes of the Soviet Union.

The United States seems to have turned its back on its historical mission of providing the mainspring of equality and freedom for all nations desiring it, not only because it has fashioned its policies without regard to this mission, but also, and more particularly, because the quality of its national life appears to have fallen short of what the world had learned to expect of America as the champion of freedom. Throughout its history America has exerted its influence on other nations not so much through what it did abroad as through what it did at home. The men to whom the United States owes its existence intended to create a new kind of society and of government for the benefit not only of Americans but of all mankind. They wanted to demonstrate to all the world that it was possible to establish a viable government and society deriving their strength not from inherited privilege or class distinctions but from the equality and freedom of all citizens. They offered America as a model for other nations to emulate. America, to quote Thomas Paine, "made a stand not for herself only, but for the world, and looked beyond the advantages which *she* could receive."

Throughout the better part of its history, America has endeavored to live up to this mandate. Mass immigration, a civil war fought over the issue of equality and freedom, a succession of drastic social reforms, and above all a quality of national life, manifesting itself most spectacularly in a succession of great statesmen, humanitarians, and social and technological innovators, demonstrated to the world America's dedication to this mandate.

That image of the United States has faded in recent years. Restrictions on immigration reducing it to a trickle, humiliating requirements for admission even of visitors, and the outrages of McCarthyism made it appear that America had gone back on its commitment to equality in freedom. The great innovations of the New and Fair Deals, of the Truman Doctrine and the Marshall Plan were replaced by the uninspired and timid defense of the *status quo*. And that *status quo* was primarily conceived not in terms of the traditional aspirations and achievements, which had indeed made America a model to be emulated by other nations, but rather in terms of a hedonism of production and consumption, which has made America an object of envy rather than of emulation.

The very office of the President, in former times the active symbol, proponent, and support of American aspirations and achievements, has been in a fair way of being reduced to a ceremonial platform for the utterance of homilies to which nobody can take exception and to which nobody at home or abroad feels a need to rally, because they have no relevance to the concerns of living men. The President and influential spokesmen for his Administration have declared themselves to be unperturbed by the Russian triumphs in the space and missile fields and have refused to see a connection between these triumphs, on the one hand, and the soaring of Russian and the decline of American prestige, on the other. Nothing has been done to dramatize the real achievements of America in the space field, which for being less dramatic are no less important than the Russian ones. Russian visitors asked to be shown the place on the campus of the University of Chicago where the first atomic chain reaction was achieved in 1941, but there was nothing to show them, for not even a plaque commemorated then this historic event. The unprecedented generosity with which the United States has come to the aid of needy nations throughout the world has not been brought home to these nations. The moral authority of the Presidential office has remained uncommitted even in the conflict over the implementation of the constitutional guarantees to all races, an issue equally crucial for the self-respect and domestic peace of America and its standing and influence among the nations.

It stands to reason that the American propaganda efforts have been greatly handicapped by the substantive foreign and domestic policies and attitudes with which the United States has been identified in recent years. The results of these efforts could have, as we have seen, been better than the substantive policies they were called upon to support, and they could also have been worse. They have indeed been worse. For the present Administration has completely misunderstood the nature of information policy and its organic relation to the whole foreign and domestic policies of the United States. It has treated information policy as though it were a self-sufficient technical enterprise, which is but loosely and haphazardly connected with substantive policies. In truth, however, information policy is as intimately connected with the substantive foreign policies pursued by the United States as are, say, diplomacy or military policy.

All foreign policy is an attempt to influence the will of other governments on behalf of interests believed to be of paramount importance. To that end, foreign policy makes use of different media. It may use the medium of diplomatic suasion. It may use the medium of military pressure. It may use the medium of the benefits of aid and trade. Or it may use the medium of propaganda in order to impress not only the governments but also and primarily the man in the street of other nations with the sum total of the qualities of the nation and of its policies.

Propaganda thus conceived is not only an intrinsic part of foreign policy, it is a major part of it. A nation that uses propaganda adroitly, as Germany did in the 1930's and the Soviet Union is doing under

Khrushchev, may win bloodless victories by convincing other nations that its cause is just or its power irresistible. At the very least, it will create a climate of opinion favorable to the pursuit of its objectives by more tangible means than propaganda. Thus the Soviet Union has made propaganda one of the mainstays of its foreign policy, far surpassing traditional diplomacy in both quantity and quality and surpassed only by its military effort. Most of what the Soviet Union does in its relations with other nations is really propaganda in the guise of diplomacy, foreign aid and trade, cultural exchanges, and the like. It is part and parcel of its political policy, coordinated with it to serve its ends.

The picture the propaganda efforts of the United States present is by comparison deficient in both quantity and quality. The operating budget requested by the United States Information Agency for the fiscal year 1960 amounted to somewhat more than $120 million, and this amount has been reduced for the fiscal year 1961 to somewhat less than $106 million. This is, of course, a mere pittance compared with the amounts requested for other purposes of foreign policy. In the years 1950 and 1951, more than $60 million was appropriated to strengthen the Voice of America broadcasting facilities. In the first five years of the Eisenhower Administration not a single additional dollar was allocated for this purpose; instead, some $10 million of the earlier appropriation was diverted to other purposes. In 1953 the present Administration canceled a project initiated under President Truman to build transmitters on American soil powerful enough to increase greatly our ability to overcome Soviet jamming and to reduce our dependence on relay stations vulnerably located in foreign countries. Five years later it quietly sought appropriations to reinstate the same project—and had to admit that the land acquired in 1952 on which to erect these transmitters had been sold in 1956 at a loss of $1.2 million.

It would be an illusion, however, to think that the ills from which our propaganda efforts suffer could be cured by simply appropriating more money for the United States Information Agency. It is our very conception of propaganda that is at fault. By separating the United States Information Agency from the State Department, of which it formerly was a integral part, the present Administration has severed the organic connection that ties information to substantive policy. In consequence, substantive policy is conducted without reference to its effects in terms of propaganda, and propaganda is conducted without reference to the substantive policies it is supposed to serve.

Many pronouncements and moves in foreign policy have been disastrous in view of their psychological effects on other nations, and it is obvious that nobody paid any attention to these foreseeable effects when it was decided to make a certain statement or embark upon a certain policy. Mr. Dulles developed this disregard for propagandistic values into a kind of system. Rollback, liberation, the unleashing of Chiang Kai-shek, massive retaliation, agonizing reappraisal, the declaration that Goa was a province of Portugal, the cancellation of support for the Aswan Dam, and the diplomacy during the Suez crisis come to mind. To cite but one recent example of the same defect: In February, 1960, immediately after a popular revolt in the Dominican Republic was suppressed with a brutality that was publicly condemned by the Catholic hierarchy, units of the American Navy laid anchor in the port of Ciudad Trujillo and gave the sailors shore leave, as if to demonstrate to the Dominican people American support for the hated tyrant. While it is safe to assume that nothing could have been farther from the mind of Navy authorities, they nevertheless conveyed this impression because nobody called their attention to the probable psychological effects of their action.

As substantive policy proceeds without concern for psychological effects, so information policy proceeds without reference to substantive policy. The information policy of the United States is still to an alarming extent conceived as a public relations job that requires primarily praise of one's own product and disparagement of the competitor's. Too many officials of the Information Agency are still selected for service abroad according to criteria that might qualify them as sales representatives of a commercial enterprise but not as interpreters of what America stands for and tries to achieve in the world. This task, subtle and difficult to perform, requires in the official essentially three qualities: awareness of, and dedication to, the experience and aspirations of America at home and abroad; awareness of, and sympathy for, the experience and aspirations of the foreign nation; and the ability to single out those elements of the American experience and aspirations that are relevant to the experience and aspirations of the foreign nation and correlate the two.

Many field officials of the Information Agency possess the first or the second of these qualities or both, but too few have proven themselves capable of achieving the third. All too often our propaganda effort abroad is like a monologue in which we recite to ourselves what we are proud of, especially in the way of material achievements, without asking whether anybody is listening, whether those who do listen know what we are talking about, or, provided they do, whether what we tell them means anything to them. To give just one recent example, which could be duplicated a thousand times: at the beginning of 1960, we were represented at the agricultural fair in New Delhi by an ultra-modern mechanized farm kitchen that is not likely to be found in the homes of many American farmers. What were the barefoot Indian farmers, filing through this exhibit, supposed to think of it? In what way was this exhibit supposed to make friends for the United States? The most charitable assumption is that no American official ever asked questions such as these.

The defects of the information policy of the United States are obvious, and so are the remedies. There are six.

1. We must recognize information policy as a major branch of foreign policy, as important in its way as diplomacy or military policy. We must therefore stop treating it as a stepchild both in terms of the quantity of money we are willing to spend for it and in terms of the quality of the human and material resources we are willing to allocate to it.

2. We must recognize the organic connection between information policy and the substantive policies the United States pursues abroad. We must restore that connection in terms of organization by returning the Information Agency to the Department of State, from which it must receive political direction and to which it must give psychological advice.

3. We must recognize that everything we say and do in relation to other nations will have an impact upon our prestige and influence abroad. Close liaison is therefore needed between the Information Agency and the departments of government that have dealings abroad, such as Defense, in order to enable the latter to choose courses of action in harmony with our information policy.

4. Considering the importance and diverse responsibilities of information policy and the high demands it makes upon the knowledge and judgment of its practitioners, the officials of the Information Agency ought to be selected and trained with much greater care than has been in evidence thus far. What our information policy needs is not well-intentioned nice guys who would like to spend a couple of years abroad, but men of the highest competence, equally at home in the substance of policy and in the techniques of propagating it, who in their persons represent what is best and most attractive in American life.

5. We must more particularly recognize that the medium through which information policy proceeds is language. The gap that exists between ourselves and non-English-speaking peoples must be bridged by our officials, mastering the language of the countries to which

they are assigned, and by enabling as many citizens of those countries as possible to learn English. Officials of the Information Agency who are ignorant of the language of the country to which they are assigned are greatly, if not fatally, handicapped in the performance of their functions. Foreigners who do not know English are by that very fact excluded from that intellectual and emotional intimacy with our culture which only the sharing of that culture's language can give. The United States ought therefore to embark upon a world-wide program of teaching English, covering, as far as possible, the countries behind the Iron Curtain and bringing as many English-speaking foreigners as feasible to the United States in order to give them firsthand experience of American life and culture.

6. We must finally recognize that whatever improvements we might make within our information policy will be of little avail as long as the substance of our foreign policy and our national life as a whole are lacking in the qualities for which America throughout its history has been admired and emulated by other nations. America must rediscover itself and its mission in the world. Only then will the information policy of the United States have something worth informing other nations about, and something other nations are eager to learn.

29

The Impotence of American Power

[November, 1963]

The United States has at its disposal the greatest concentration of material power existing in the world today; in terms of productive capacity and military strength, it is the most powerful nation on earth. Yet the government of that most powerful nation is incapable of making the actions of even the weakest of foreign governments conform to its desires. It is incapable of doing so even with regard to governments that owe their very existence to American support and could not survive for twenty-four hours were that support withdrawn.

South Vietnam, South Korea, and Taiwan are cases in point. None of these governments could exist without the economic and military support of the United States and without the American commitment to go to war in their defense. Yet we have told the Government of South Vietnam that it ought to change its policies and composition, and it has changed neither. We have told the Government of South Korea that it ought to respect at least a minimum of democratic rights, and we have been rebuffed for our "intervention." We have told the Government of Taiwan that it ought not to station some of its best troops on the offshore islands, and these troops are still stationed there.

Within the traditional sphere of influence of the United States, Cuba has been transformed into a military base at the service of a hostile power and into the headquarters for the subversion of the Western Hemisphere, and we have been unable to put a stop to it. In many countries of Latin America, we are unable to forestall the threat to our interests implicit in the polarization of the politics in those nations between the defenders of the *status quo* and the revolutionaries.

The history of our foreign-aid policy is testimony to our inability to achieve our political purposes even with an abundance of material means. So is our economic policy vis-à-vis the Communist bloc; our attempts to wage the Cold War by economic means have been frustrated by the eagerness of our most prosperous allies to make economic gains at the risk of strengthening the common enemy. The Atlantic Alliance, the cornerstone of our foreign and military policies, is crumbling, and we stand watching the process of decay without being able to arrest it. Pakistan is our ally and has received billions in American aid, but we have been unable to dissuade it from making common cause with Communist China against India, a country we support. We tried to transform the army of a neutralist Laos into an instrument of American policy, and Laotian Communism is today stronger and more threatening than before.

We are here in the presence not of isolated failures, which any foreign policy must take in its stride, but of a pattern of impotence that points to organic disabilities in our foreign policy. That so powerful a nation as the United States is so consistently unable to achieve what it sets out to achieve cannot be due to accidents or personal insufficiencies alone. The cause must be sought in certain impediments to the effective exercise of American power, which seem to paralyze even the best makers of policy. Three types of such impediments can be distinguished: the objective conditions under which contemporary foreign policy must be carried on; the moral and intellectual assumptions underlying the American approach to foreign policy; and the anti-Communist tenet of American foreign policy. No single one of these factors can explain the impotence of our power, but together they may well do so.

Two objective conditions of contemporary world politics limit our power, as they do the power of all major nations: the availability of nuclear weapons, and the moral stigma that attaches to colonialism and to the policies traditionally associated with it.

The availability of nuclear weapons limits the freedom of action of the nuclear powers even more than it does that of the non-nuclear ones. The latter may reason that they can afford to threaten another nation with conventional force or actually use force against it, for the risk that one of the nuclear powers will intervene with nuclear weapons on one or the other side is likely to be remote. Nuclear powers in this respect are in a much more precarious situation. If they face each other with the threat or the actuality of conventional force, escalation into nuclear violence is an ever present possibility whose realization depends upon accidents, miscalculations, and, above all, the importance of the stakes. The situation is only somewhat, and not necessarily much, less precarious if a nuclear power threatens force against a non-nuclear one to whose defense another nuclear power is committed.

Since nuclear war, in contrast to conventional force, is recognized by all concerned not as a rational instrument of national policy but as a suicidal absurdity, nuclear powers are extremely reluctant to use any kind of force in support of their respective national interests. Yet in a world of sovereign nations it is impossible to support national interests effectively without the ultimate resort to military force. Thus the impotence of American policy toward Cuba is matched by the impotence of Soviet policy with regard to Berlin.

The example of our policy toward Cuba also points to the other objective condition limiting the use of our power. Twenty years ago, it would still have been a simple matter to remove through the use of force the threat Castro's Cuba constitutes to our interests. The Marines did it before, and they could have done it again. Leaving the problem of nuclear war aside, it would not be impossible to do the same thing even today, but it would not be a simple matter, and for two connected reasons. This is the age of the emancipation of the weak nations from the control of the strong ones. It is not only former colonies that have been emancipated; legally sovereign but actually dependent nations have been emancipated as well. In dealing with these latter, the strong nations can no longer use their power at will without incurring moral reprobation and risking in consequence a loss of prestige and influence. A great power may take these risks if the interests at stake appear important enough. This is what the Soviet Union did when it sent its army against the Hungarian Revolution of 1956, and while the moral reprobation the Russians earned for this move is but an ineffectual memory, the political and military gains have proved to be lasting.

However, the change in the moral climate has also affected the military issue itself. Twenty years ago, the government of Cuba presided over a by and large inert mass of people; it was an old-style dictatorship, and the military problem consisted in the main in removing it and replacing it with one favorable to the interests of the United

States. Today, just as the weak nations have been emancipated from control by the strong ones, so have the populations of the weak nations been emancipated in differing degrees from passive submission to their respective governments. Some of these peoples have become active participants in the process of emancipation, and they now have governments that govern in their name and with their support. Thus, a strong nation intervening with military force may not accomplish its task by removing the government or even by conquering the country. It may also have to subdue the population at large, which may take up arms against it. While these possibilities do not rule out the use of force, they make the powerful nations think twice before resorting to it.

The United States has gone farther in abstaining from the use of its power than is justified by a correct assessment of these two objective factors. It has been paralyzed in the use of its power, military and other, by two moral principles which, it has persuaded itself, have governed its foreign policy in the past and must govern it in the future: equality and nonintervention. In its relations with its allies, the United States has been caught in a dilemma between its responsibilities as the most powerful member of an alliance and the principle of the equality of men and nations, which has guided its judgment, if not its actions, since the beginning of its history. The consistent application of superior American power would have reduced the allies to satellites and would thereby have defeated the very purpose for which these nations had become the allies of America. On the other hand, the successful conduct of an alliance on the basis of the equality of its members presupposes that the identity of interests among the allies and their awareness of this identity are so complete that they will pursue common interests with common measures through spontaneous cooperation. To the degree that reality falls short of this assumption, the alliance cannot operate.

Of these two alternatives, the United States has chosen consistently the latter. The United States has refused to bring its superior power to bear upon its alliances on behalf of common interests that were naturally inchoate and were competing with divergent ones. The result has been disintegration, of which NATO is the prime example, or else the exploitation of American resources by a weak but determined ally. Governments that govern only because the United States maintains them, such as those of Taiwan and South Vietnam, and governments that have no alternative to the American association, such as those of Pakistan in the 1950's and Spain, have been able to play a winning game in which the United States holds all the trumps.

The most potent of these trumps is intervention, through either the withholding of benefits or the inflicting of disadvantages. It is this trump that we have consistently refused to play on moral grounds. Yet regardless of one's moral evaluation of intervention, it is obvious that we are intervening massively and effectively all over the world and that what we have foresworn is not intervention *per se* but only certain kinds of intervention. This position is morally untenable and, as will be shown, politically self-defeating.

To cite the example of South Vietnam, which is but more flagrant and at present more acute than many others, we intervened by putting President Diem into power and supplying him with the implements of power. He owes his authority and power to our continuous political, military, and economic intervention. We intervened by establishing and keeping him in power because we thought that such intervention was in our and his countries' interests. If this kind of intervention is morally justified, where is it written that it is morally indefensible to intervene in order to compel President Diam to pursue the policies for the sake of which we installed and kept him in power, or to remove him from power when he has proved himself incapable of pursuing those policies? The Western tradition of political philosophy justifies revolution against a tyrannical government, and even tyrannicide. Intervention in support of such morally justified undertakings is by the same token morally justified.

The issue here is not really moral but intellectual, and the moral issue is raised only as justification and rationalization of an attitude that shrinks from certain kinds of intervention, not only in the domestic affairs of other nations but in the political *status quo* as such.

We are at home with political actions that are but a repetition of past action and whose results are likely to stabilize things as they are. Yet we dread unprecedented political action because we dread the uncertainties, the risks, and the unknown results that such action is likely to conjure up. Thus we prefer safe routines in support of the *status quo* to innovations that will disturb it. It is only when we are face to face with a clear aand present military threat that we act with bold and innovating zeal. But when we are faced with a political crisis, actual or impending, we are incapable of the foresight, sureness of touch as regards means and ends, and manipulative skill that are the prerequisites of successful political action. We tend to make the political problem manageable again by redefining it in military terms; thus we can act once more with unambiguous simplicity and without regard for those complexities, uncertainties, and risks inherent in the political act. And as concerns the political problem, we wait for something to happen: for de Gaulle to disappear from the political scene, for the Diem regime to straighten itself out, for something to turn up in China. However, short of death and natural catastrophes, nothing can happen but the actions of others, filling the void our paralysis has left.

Hence, the crisis of the Atlantic Alliance, proclaimed but by no means created by de Gaulle in January, 1963, took Washington by surprise. Our government reacted with indignation but not with reflection and political action. Yet the Suez crisis of the fall of 1956 ought to have opened its eyes to the inevitable decline of our alliances due to radically altered objective conditions. Pointing to the forms this decline was likely to take, I wrote in 1957: "While these considerations are admittedly speculative from the vantage point of 1957, they may well reflect the actuality of 1960." However, faced with the actuality of 1963, our government has been able to think of only one remedy: the multilateral seaborne nuclear force, a military device of most dubious value.

A similar pattern of passivity is revealed by our reaction to the crisis in South Vietnam. Knowing that we cannot win the war with Diem but unwilling to replace him, we argue with a patent lack of consistency that since there is no alternative to Diem let us go on with the war. Yet the argument is in the nature of a self-fulfilling prophecy: There is no alternative to Diem because our support of Diem prevents prospective alternative leaders from emerging. Such leaders cannot present themselves to public inspection since they have been exiled, imprisoned, or are under constant close surveillance by the secret police. They can emerge only after Diem is gone.

Finally, our impotence is aggravated and rendered irreparable by our commitment to anti-Communism as the overriding objective of our foreign policy. For most of our allies, anti-Communism is at best incidental to concrete national objectives and at worst irrelevant to them, being a mere device to secure and keep American support. Thus the governments of Taiwan and South Vietnam are not so much anti-Communist on principle as competitors for power with governments that happen to be Communist. Pakistan has allied itself with us in order to be able to fight not Communism but India, and it turned to China as soon as we gave military support to India against the latter.

While the anti-Communism of these and others of our allies is a matter of expediency rather than principle, it is our commitment to an indiscriminate anti-Communism, neglectful of concrete national interests, that enables our allies to deprive us of our freedom of choice. They can counter every move of ours that displeases them with an argument supplied by us: "If you do that, we shall go Communist." And so we stand helplessly by while they have their way.

Our impotence in the fullness of our power is, then, in some measure the result of objective conditions over which we have no control and which restrict the power of other powerful nations as well. In good measure, however, the source of that impotence is in ourselves. We are paralyzed because our moral, intellectual, and political judgment has gone astray. Our judgment must be reformed before we can expect to recover the use of our power, and upon that recovery the improvement of our foreign policies must wait.

30

The Future of Europe

[May, 1964]

In 1963, President de Gaulle, by slamming the door to the Common Market in the face of Great Britain, brought the movement toward the unification of Europe to a halt and opened a new chapter in the history of Europe. The year 1964 is likely to be decisive in the competition among four present conceptions of a unified Europe—the Gaullist, the functional, the American, and the Soviet.

De Gaulle defined his conception of a united Europe for the first time in Volume III of his *War Memoirs*, where, referring to the period immediately following World War II, he wrote: "I intended to persuade the states along the Rhine, the Alps and the Pyrenees to form a political, economic and strategic bloc; to establish this organization as one of the three world powers and, should it become necessary, as the arbiter between the Soviet and Anglo-American camps."

The United Europe de Gaulle seeks is different in its foundations and purposes from what the other proponents of European unity have in mind. "Now what are the realities of Europe? What are the pillars on which it can be built?" de Gaulle asked at his press conference of September 5, 1960. "The states are, in truth, certainly very different from one another, each of which has its own spirit, its own

332

history, its own language, its own misfortunes, glories and ambitions; but these states are the only entities that have the right to order and the authority to act. To imagine that something can be built that would be effective for action and that would be approved by the peoples outside and above the states—this is a dream."

The cornerstones of a Gaullist Europe, then, must be the sovereign nation states, which when united "must not cease to be themselves" and which will build their unity by means of "organized cooperation between states." The Franco-German treaty of January 22, 1963, providing for coordinated measures in foreign policy, defense, education, and cultural exchanges, is a model of the kind of "organized cooperation" through which de Gaulle expected to build a united Europe. It is "an example which may be followed and a framework which may be enlarged."

This united Europe must be an independent force between East and West. Above all, its members must have independent means for their defense. De Gaulle stipulated in his press conference of April 11, 1961, "the right and the duty of the European continental powers to have their own national defense. It is intolerable for a great State to leave its destiny up to the decisions and actions of another State, however friendly it may be. In addition, it happens that, in integration— for it is integration that I mean—the integrated country loses interest in its national defense, since it is not responsible for it." This new Europe would be "balanced between the Atlantic and the Urals," a third world power that would be the equal of the United States and the Soviet Union, "the indispensable condition of the equilibrium of the world."

De Gaulle's conception of a united Europe has been developed in opposition to the school of thought that has dominated the actual processes of European unification since the end of World War II. Its foremost spokesman and statesman has been Jean Monnet, and its monuments are the European communities at present in operation: the European Coal and Steel Community, the European Atomic Energy Community, and the Common Market. Its philosophy is "functional," a term first applied systematically in 1943 by David Mitrany, formerly a professor at the London School of Economics and Political Science, in his book *A Working Peace System*. The functional approach to unification would

> overlay political divisions with a spreading web of international activities and agencies, in which and through which the interests and life of all the nations would be gradually integrated. . . . [It] would help the

growth . . . of common habits and interests, making frontier lines meaningless by overlaying them with a natural growth of common activities and common administrative agencies.

The European Communities try to solve common problems, which none of the member states could have solved by its own efforts, through the coordination of technical functions on a supranational level. To that end, they combine central, supranational direction in the execution of policies with negotiated agreement as to the nature of the policies to be pursued. The recent negotiations among the members of the Common Market, seeking a common agricultural policy, are a case in point. They were negotiations of the traditional international character in that they were predicated upon the equality of all states. Yet once these negotiations have culminated in an agreement, their execution rests in the hands of supranational agencies, which, within still relatively narrow limits, perform vis-à-vis the member states and their citizens the functions of a genuine federal government.

The supporters of the functional approach expect the example of the existing European communities, creating a European community of interests within their limited technical spheres, to spread to other functional fields, such as transport, electricity, and defense. Finally, it is hoped that out of this accumulation of functional units political unity will grow organically. Once all the functional organizations have been established as going concerns, sovereignty will have been transferred in fact to a common European government by gradual steps.

In order to understand the American attitude toward the unification of Europe, especially in view of the acute issues raised by de Gaulle, it is first necessary to point out that we have had throughout our history an emotional preference for federations of states. Thus we welcomed and supported the successive steps toward the functional unification of Europe, which we expected to culminate in a United States of Europe. We took it for granted that a Europe so united would also be closely tied to the United States of America, and we saw in NATO the focal point of such a union, which would accentuate the division of labor between the nuclear deterrent of America and the conventional forces of a united Europe.

De Gaulle's initiative administered a dual shock to our expectations: It called a halt to the organic continuation of functional unification, and it challenged the nuclear monopoly of the United States. Our reaction has been twofold: uncompromising opposition to de Gaulle's design and the proposal of a nuclear "partnership" between the United

States and united Europe, which has taken the provisional practical form of a multilateral seaborne nuclear force (MLF)—that is, surface vessels armed with Polaris missiles and manned by multinational crews. Thus we hoped to isolate France for the time being and to forge closer military cooperation among the nations of Europe and between them and the United States, while at the same time preventing the proliferation of nuclear weapons among an increasing number of individual nations. If this design had succeeded, it would have resulted in at least a temporary split of Europe, and an American-German military axis would for all practical purposes have taken the place of the stalled functional integration and a stillborn Franco-German combination.

The Soviet Union would no doubt officially oppose such a development, but in private it would have to find it more acceptable than some other alternatives. For the Soviet Union, too, has a conception of a united Europe, a Europe in which the unifying force of the United States would be replaced by that of the Soviet Union. The Soviet Union has already unified Eastern Europe under its auspices. The road to the similar unification of all of Europe leads through the fragmentation of Western Europe and its separation from the United States. It is for this reason that the Soviet Union has been consistently opposed to the Marshall Plan, the European Communities, NATO, MLF, and de Gaulle's design for a Franco-German combination.

The Soviet opposition to a Europe united under Western auspices is both strengthened and modified by one concern, overshadowing all others: the fear of Germany. Thus the Soviet Union has looked with particular distaste upon de Gaulle's design, in which it sees a device for delivering Europe into the hands of Germany. If Germany cannot be isolated from Europe and America, the Soviet Union must prefer a German association with the United States, strong and hence capable of exerting restraint, to one with a weak France. However, in the long run the Soviet Union looks forward to the day, whose coming Khrushchev considered inevitable, when an isolated Germany will associate itself in one form or other with the Soviet Union. Once this has happened the rest of Europe will follow suit.

While the Soviet Union is opposed to all Western conceptions of a united Europe, the Western camp itself is split three ways. What the functionalists seek—and here they have the support of the United States—is the exact opposite of de Gaulle's aim. The functionalists want to build a united Europe by transferring, step by step, more and more functions from the national governments to supranational agencies; they want to wear away national sovereignty in order to transfer it. De Gaulle, on the other hand, wants to erect a united Europe on the foundation of unimpaired national sovereignty, strengthened by the acquisition of nuclear weapons, and envisages only in a distant and somewhat hazy future a Europe united by the preponderance of Franco-German power, a process not dissimilar to the unification, a century ago, of Germany through the preponderant power of Prussia.

Yet de Gaulle and the politically influential functionalists see eye to eye on one point, and here they differ from the United States: the emancipation of a united Europe from the nuclear monopoly of the United States. What de Gaulle has proclaimed with brutal frankness, other European leaders have stated in more tactfully subdued terms. A week after de Gaulle at the press conference of January 14, 1963, inveighed against "a colossal Atlantic Community under American dependence and leadership," Prime Minister Macmillan wished for a Europe "great and strong enough to build a more equal and worthy partnership" with the United States. On January 30 he foresaw the end of the alliance if the United States were allowed "for all time the sole authority" over the nuclear deterrent. The German Foreign Minister Schroeder has expressed himself in similar terms.

To which of these four conceptions of a united Europe—Gaullist, functional, American, or Soviet—does the future belong? Which will prove capable of translating the new—and old—realities of international life into viable policies? None of the Western approaches, as now formulated, has a chance to succeed, for the strong points of each are vitiated by weaknesses.

De Gaulle, alone among the Western statesmen, has seen clearly the political core of European unification. De Gaulle has made two valid points: the unreliability of traditional alliances in the nuclear age and the impossibility of moving from functional integration to political unification in a gradual organic fashion. A nation without nuclear weapons, indeed, cannot rely upon an ally armed with such weapons to come to its aid if its interests are threatened by a nuclear power; for no nation can be relied upon to risk its own existence in the interests of another nation. De Gaulle is also right in doubting that nation-states can gradually merge their respective sovereignties into a higher political authority without a deliberate break in the constitutional continuity through the creation of a new center of political decision. That doubt is borne out by the way the European nation-states, especially Germany and Italy in the nineteenth century, were unified. Everywhere a new center of political power emerged, came into conflict with the local centers, and prevailed over them.

Yet while de Gaulle has the insight in the political conditions of unification, he lacks the political power to pursue the policies commensurate with his insight. The independent nuclear deterrent is a dubious instrument of French national policies, for its ability to deter is questionable. The Franco-German combination, which de Gaulle envisaged as a new center of political decision for a united Europe, has remained a dead letter; for Germany, weighing the power of France and the United States in the scales, has not found it hard to decide where the preponderance of power lies. Thus de Gaulle can only proclaim the political truth about European unification but cannot act upon it.

What de Gaulle possesses without being able to use it constructively, the functionalists are lacking: the awareness of the crucial importance of the political factor. The functionalists assume that the political unification of Europe will somehow take care of itself and that this qualitative change in the relations of the European states will result from the quantitative accumulation of functional European communities. Yet this jump from national to European sovereignty must be made by an act of will, it cannot be assumed just to "happen." It requires a political decision that coordinates the divergent interests of individual nations and the policies serving them and creates a political authority capable of keeping recalcitrant members in check.

On the other hand, the functionalists have supplied the indispensable material foundation for the political unification of Europe. They have created common economic and technological interests, protected and promoted by common institutions. These common interests, to be fully realized and to be protected from the ever present threat of disintegration, require common political institutions. The functionalists have provided the incentive for the creation of such institutions, but they have been unable to provide the institutions.

Our position has been characterized by two contradictory impulses, each justified in itself but in combination cancelling each other out. On the one hand, we are opposed to the proliferation of nuclear weapons: We shrink from the international insecurity that such proliferation is likely to call forth. On the other hand, we seek to meet the aspirations of the major European powers to nuclear equality by inviting them to participate in the operation of nuclear weapons through MLF and by offering nuclear "partnership" to a united Europe.

However, this position suffers from the fatal flaw of trying to evade the political issue. MLF seeks to create the illusion of equal participation in the manipulation of nuclear weapons while in truth our monopoly of nuclear decision would remain intact. "Partnership" implies that the decision to use nuclear weapons can be "shared." In truth, however, such a decision is, like sovereignty, indivisible. It rests either in Washington or elsewhere, but it cannot rest in two places at the same time.

De Gaulle's initiative has achieved one result: It has made the *status quo ante* January 14, 1963, untenable. Policies seeking to preserve or restore this *status quo* are doomed. Europe either will go forward toward new forms of political integration or will go backward toward the restored independence of its national units, but it cannot stand still.

Since, as we have seen, none of the Western approaches to European unification has a chance to succeed, hope rests in the combination of what is sound in each of them. Functional integration presents no problem, because everybody is in favor of it. The stumbling block is political, and it must be removed by political means. That stumbling block is the result of the divergence of the interests and policies of the United States from those of its major European allies and of a similar divergence among the major European nations. The trade policies of the United States, Great Britain, and France vis-à-vis the Soviet Union, China, and Cuba are a case in point; so are the policies of France and Germany vis-à-vis the United States.

What we face here is a major task of political reconstruction. That reconstruction must aim at re-creating the identity of interests and coordination of policies that existed in the first decade following World War II not only among the European nations but also between the European nations and the United States. This kind of political harmony will deprive the issue of the nuclear decision of its present political sting. A united Europe would then consider using nuclear weapons for the same purpose as the United States, and vice versa, and the locus of the decision would be of technical but no longer of substantive importance.

The outlook for such a political reconstruction certainly looks bleak if one considers the present disarray of the Atlantic Alliance. Hope, on the other hand, rests on the following factors, which have not yet had a chance to be translated into political action: our proven capacity for pragmatic reorientation when the chips are down; the continuing vitality of the European Communities, as demonstrated in the recent decisions on tariffs on steel and agricultural products; and the vaunted realism of de Gaulle. De Gaulle has shown before, for instance with regard to Algeria, how he adapts himself to circumstances he cannot change. In his press conference of January 31, 1964, he declared: "One does not see how the economic community could live and, *a fortiori*, develop without political cooperation." In his latest New Year address, he moved closer to the American position when he declared the political, military, cultural, and economic union of Europe to be one of the three major tasks of France in the coming year and continued: "Next we must assist our Western Europe, from the time that it is united, in practicing with America a truly concerted political, economic, and strategic entente."

And there is, finally and most importantly, the prospect, dangerous to all the nations of the West, that if Europe is not united on Western terms it will be united on the terms of the Soviet Union, using the unfulfilled aspirations of Germany as an entering wedge. For if we and the nations of Western Europe should fail in this endeavor, the immediate alternative would be the perpetuation and accentuation of what both we and de Gaulle prefer to consider a mere intermediate stage in the process of unification: the restoration of the European nation-state as the ultimate focus of political loyalty and decision. This alternative would signify the end of European unification on Western terms and would greatly increase the chances for the ultimate unification of Europe by the Soviet Union.

31

The Problem of Germany

[September, 1963]

Even in its present truncated stage, Germany is again the foremost economic, military, and political factor on the European continent. It has the highest gross national product and per capita income in Europe and has sufficient surplus resources to give economic and technical aid to scores of underdeveloped nations. Its industrial production in 1960 was 276 per cent above the level of 1936.

The German military establishment, already substantial, is rapidly growing. The German military budget has risen from 11.7 billion marks in 1959 to 19.7 billion in 1963. The German army today is the backbone of the ground forces of NATO. In view of the defection of France and the military weakness of the other European allies, NATO tends to become the organizational superstructure of what is in substance an American-German alliance.

Politically, Germany has become the kingpin of the Atlantic Alliance. It is wooed like a highly desirable but reluctant bride. After de Gaulle and Adenauer had signed in January, 1963, what looked like a marriage contract between Germany and France, President Kennedy had to to go to Germany in June to demonstrate that, regardless of what France and Germany had signed, no one can love Germany more than America, and the President of the United States transformed himself in the process into a German (*"Ich bin ein Berliner"*). President de Gaulle then had to go to Germany in July in order to see and, if possible, to repair what was left of the Franco-German marriage after the passionate American interlude.

The limits of American policy toward the Soviet Union are determined by what is acceptable to the government in Bonn. American policy is not being made in Bonn, but Bonn decides how far Washington can go. We have had but recently an illustration—unbecoming and irrational—of that strange relationship. Although the carefully worded text of the partial test-ban treaty precludes the possibility of even approaching something like recognition of the East German regime, the publication of the treaty created near-hysteria in Bonn. The President of the United States had to write a personal letter to Chancellor Adenauer. The Secretary of State of the United States had to go to Bonn. So did an Assistant Secretary of State and the Secretary of Defense. After the latter had gone to attend the opera in Salzburg, he was summoned back to Bonn by Mr. Adenauer, who lectured him for almost an hour on the dangers of the test-ban treaty without allowing him to put in a word of his own. A hundred years ago, Bismarck wouldn't have dared treat, say, the British Secretary of War like that; nor would the British Secretary of War, for that matter, have allowed himself to be so treated.

Whence does this crucial power of Germany come? It has two main sources. One is the objective circumstances that have dominated the European scene since Bismarck created a unified German state in 1871: The German people are, by dint of their natural endowments, the most numerous, the most industrious, and the most disciplined people of Europe, with the most productive industrial plant on the continent at their disposal. In consequence, if nature were allowed to take its course Germany could make itself the master of Europe. But it is this mastery that the other peoples of Europe have refused to accept and which they have fought two world wars in this century to prevent. It is for this very same reason that both we and de Gaulle, in our different ways and with the support of Adenauer, have endeavored to integrate Germany into a larger whole, be it an Atlantic Community, a federated Europe, or a Europe dominated by a Franco-German combination.

The other source of Germany's strength lies in the circumstances of its present existence. In consequence of the dispositions the allies made toward the end of World War II, Germany finds itself today divided into two states, while the provinces east of the Oder-Neisse line—Silesia, Pomerania, West and East Prussia—have been incorporated by Poland and the Soviet Union into their respective territories. The recovery of these provinces and the unification of the country are the two national objectives to which oft-repeated official declarations and the results of public opinion polls assign the highest priority. When Germany joined NATO in 1954, it did so with the understanding that its allies would support these aspirations, and the United States has consistently done so.

It is, however, obvious to all concerned that, regardless of the opportunities that might have existed in the past and might emerge in a distant future, there is in the foreseeable future no chance for the recovery of the eastern provinces or the unification of the country as long as the Soviet Union is opposed to, and has the power to prevent, either one. While all Germans will admit this in private, most of them —particularly the politicians—are wont to talk in public as though convinced that the achievement of the two objectives not only is indispensable but also can be achieved by Western efforts.

Yet while the West can only talk about unification and the recovery of the eastern provinces, there is one power that could achieve these two German objectives overnight if it wanted to, and that is the Soviet Union. The road to the realization of these objectives, then, leads through a German understanding with the Soviet Union. The U.S. Government knows this, the German government knows it, and— most importantly—Mr. Khrushchev is fully aware of it. He has before his eyes the vision of an eastern orientation of a united Germany. He has hinted at this development in a memorandum submitted to the West German Government in December, 1961, and has mentioned it to many visitors in recent years. "One day," he said to Paul-Henri Spaak in July, 1963, "the Germans will want another Rapallo. It won't happen under Adenauer's successor, nor probably under his successor's successor. Later, perhaps. But the day will come, and we can wait."

What is a pleasant dream in Moscow is a nightmare in Washington and a source of great political strength for Bonn. Bonn and Washington are verbally committed to the illusory proposition that their military alliance is the instrument for unification and the recovery of the eastern territories. Since the alliance is the cornerstone of its European policy, Washington cannot afford to pursue policies that entail the risk of weakening the alliance. It is this consideration that gives Bonn for all practical purposes a veto over the European policies of the United States. More particularly, whenever Washington takes a step, however small and innocuous in itself, that so much as points in the direction of an accommodation with the Soviet Union on the basis of the European *status quo* (i.e., the test-ban treaty), Bonn is likely to call Washington to order.

Such is the power, both natural and circumstantial, of Germany today. What makes us, the outside observers, as well as many Germans, uneasy in its presence? Three unanswered questions provide the key.

1. What is the political significance of the agitation for unification and the recovery of the eastern provinces? The agitation itself is a ubiquitous fact, ever present to the eyes and ears of the visitor. Listening to the radio on my first day in Germany, I was startled to hear a reference to *"Mitteldeutschland"* which formerly was a geographic term like our "Middle West" and now signifies what we call "East Germany"—implying, of course, that the real East Germany lies beyond the Oder-Neisse line. Walking through the streets of the university city of Tübingen, I encountered at every turn big placards in crying red, showing prewar Germany divided into three parts with the legend: "Thrice divided—never!" What does it all mean? The Russians, the Poles, and the Czechs say it can mean only one thing: preparation for a war of revenge. On the other hand, all Germans to whom you put that question will tell you that it means nothing in concrete political terms, that it is a moral commitment, a sentimental aspiration, for the sake of which few would want to sacrifice much and nobody is ready to die.

One can accept that explanation for the present without closing one's eyes to the risks of the future. For it is an inherently unhealthy state of affairs for a political elite to commit itself in public to objectives that it admits in private cannot be realized in the foreseeable future. The moment of truth is bound to come. When it comes, will the leaders be capable of trimming the professed objectives down to the level of the means safely available, or will they embark upon risky policies in order to keep popular favor?

2. What kind of leadership can be expected of Adenauer's heirs? Adenauer's political personality is composed of three basic ingredients: an authoritarianism that uses the procedures of democracy as instruments of personal power, a deep mistrust of the political abilities of the German people and their elected representatives, and a deep commitment to a Western orientation of Germany, primarily as insurance against its self-destructive tendencies. Given these tendencies, Germany in Adenauer's view needs a strong authority, restrained by a democratic ethos rather than by the minutiae of democratic procedures and informed by a wisdom inaccessible to the people and its representatives.

Even if one refuses to judge Adenauer's heirs presumptive—Erhard, Strauss, and Brandt—by these standards, one must admit that each of them has shown weaknesses that put into question his ability to use German power wisely. Erhard gives the impression of a decent, capable technician who has neither ability nor taste for politics. There are many in Bonn, otherwise out of sympathy with Adenauer's views, who share his low opinion of Erhard's political ability. As Chancellor, he will have to cope with two leaders far superior to him in this respect: Erich Mende, a secondary figure who, however, as chairman of the Free Democrats will have great political power, since without the votes of his party Erhard will be unable to govern; and Franz Josef Strauss, the chairman of the Christian Social Union, the Bavarian branch of the Christian Democrats, without whose votes Erhard cannot govern either.

Strauss is without doubt after Adenauer the most gifted German politician. He is ambitious, shrewd, skillful, and a man of real power; he is also ruthless, and there are those who say that he is without scruples as well. His policies, such as the demand for a national nuclear deterrent, appeal to German nationalism rather than Western solidarity. His role in the *Spiegel* affair—the arrest, upon his instigation, of the editors of this very influential weekly, comparable to *Time* magazine, for treason and his initial disavowal of any part in it—leave no doubt about his lack of interest in democratic procedures and cast serious doubts upon his democratic ethos as well.

In comparison with this sharply profiled, formidable personality, Willy Brandt, the Chancellor-designate of the Social Democrats, is a rather shadowy figure. He is attractive and highly emotional in his public utterances, especially when it comes to unification. But what else is he? There are close associates of his in the Social Democratic Party who doubt that he is anything else. Will he be the molder of German opinion rather than the exponent of its innate tendencies?

3. What are the innate tendencies of German opinion? Have they become, if not democratic, then at least rational and self-contained, or are they still dominated by that irrational expansionist urge of which Nazism was the most extreme manifestation? Is the quality of the German mind that gave rise to Nazism dead, or is it only dormant?

This is obviously the crucial one of the three questions we have posed, and the answer we can give to it will in good measure determine the answer to the other two as well. Unfortunately, the answer can only be ambiguous at best. Germany, as it were, still has to make up its mind. On the one hand, there is the revulsion against the outrages and, more particularly, the failures of the Nazi regime; there are the attempts to atone for them; there is the indifference, and even active aversion, to traditional nationalism on the part of large masses of German youth; there is a general retreat into the private sphere, with the satisfaction of private needs taking the place of public concerns.

On the other hand, there is a new national assertiveness as a by-product of newly acquired power and as a reaction to de Gaulle's new nationalism. There is a cynicism about democracy, politicians, and the Bonn regime, which expresses itself in thunderous applause whenever a nightclub comic makes a crack about them. Finally, and most importantly, there is a kind of unnatural emptiness in the German mental landscape, a quiet before momentous events, a great people waiting for a new mission and perhaps a new leader. I watched the people of Frankfurt welcoming President Kennedy, hundreds of thousands of people filling the sidewalks from walls to curb, their eyes wet, their faces transformed in ecstasy, welcoming not so much a foreign statesman on a pragmatic mission as a savior sent from on high especially for them to set things right. Had I ever seen anything like that before? I had indeed, decades ago. Everything then was exactly as it was now: the same ecstasy, the same passion, the same abandonment, the same irrational hopes. Only the recipient of those emotions was different then: He was a little man with hypnotically piercing eyes, a funny mustache, and an outstretched right arm.

What should American policy be in the presence of that new German power and our uneasiness about it? The United States has one fundamental goal: the prevention of a drastic change in the world balance of power through an Eastern orientation of a united Germany. It has made common cause with Germany in maintaining the illusion that Germany's Western orientation will be the instrument for the realization of its national aims. This illusion has created a schizophrenia in the German mind by causing it to set itself objectives that cannot be achieved by the means chosen. America has also created a schizophrenia for itself: Its commitment to the German nonrecognition of the European *status quo* is incompatible with its search for an accommodation with the Soviet Union. The United States has the extremely difficult task to disentangle itself from these two contradictions without impairing its relations with Germany and in the end driving Germany into the waiting arms of the Soviet Union.

No neat and simple formula can show the road to the achievement of that task. What is required is a patient, cautious, and subtle endeavor, unceasingly pursued, of narrowing gradually and unobtrusively the gap that exists today between illusory verbal commitments and the facts of life. This must be done by simultaneously toning down the verbal commitments and trying to restore the human contacts between the two Germanys. The former is indeed one of the preconditions for the latter; for the verbal commitment to the unification of Germany on Western terms and the restoration of the frontiers of 1937 has been one of the main factors in cementing the unity of the Soviet bloc and in making the realization of achievable Western aims impossible.

Paradoxically enough, if the United States should continue to be, in its verbal commitments at least, as intransigent as the most intransigent Germans, it is likely to find itself left behind by a new generation of German leaders who will, in one fashion or other, try to change circumstances rather than declaim against them. Thus American policy must cope with two dangers: the remote one of a new Rapallo, the Eastern orientation of a united Germany, and the more immediate one of losing the initiative in the incipient realignment of positions in Europe. If it goes too far too fast in trying to narrow the gap, it will increase the former danger; if it goes not far enough, and too slowly, it increases the latter. It is the measure of the new power of Germany that such are the difficult and risky choices with which it confronts the most powerful nation on earth.

32

Arguing About the Cold War

[May, 1967]

In the summer of 1965, Mr. Robert M. Hutchins, President of the Center for the Study of Democratic Institutions and former President of the University of Chicago, issued A *Declaration to End the Cold War*, which started thus:

> I propose to ask the President of the United States to make the following statement at the next session of the General Assembly of the United Nations: "I hereby declare the Cold War is over. . . ."

There is something engaging in the neat precision of this proposal: The captain of a football team blows the whistle because he thinks the time has come to quit. However, the practicality of this proposal to end the Cold War is predicated upon a particular assumption concerning its origin. The President of the United States would indeed have it in his power to end the Cold War by unilateral declaration, if the Cold War had been started by such a declaration on his part. Yet nobody would seriously argue that the Cold War was a result of someone's conscious decision. Quite the contrary, it is generally recognized that it grew out of a series of circumstances and policies whose cumula-

347

tive effects imperceptibly brought to the fore those irreconcilable interests and hostile policies associated with "Cold War."

What distinguishes the Cold War from the many hostile confrontations history records (and, hence, justifies its name) are two factors: the impossibility for all concerned, given the interests at stake and the positions taken, of pursuing conciliatory policies that, through the instruments of give and take and compromise, might have led to a settlement of the outstanding issues; and the necessity (following from this impossibility) for all concerned to protect and promote their interests through unilateral direct pressure on the opponent's will by all means available—diplomatic, military, economic, subversive—short of the actual use of force. Thus, we have been in a "war" because the purpose of all concerned was not to accommodate the other side in return for accommodation on its part but rather to compel the other side to yield. "Rollback" and "liberation" are terms of war that imply not an agreed-upon accommodation but unilateral action. The threat of military force should the other side not yield its position in West Berlin partakes of the same characteristic. But while both sides have used the techniques of war rather than diplomacy to achieve their ends, they have been very careful not to resort to force, at least in their relations with each other. Thus we have been in a "war" insofar as unilateral techniques are the instruments of war and not of diplomacy; and the war has been a "cold" one because the use of force upon a major opponent has been excluded from the instruments of unilateral action.

The causes of this state of affairs have recently become the subject of scholarly controversy in the United States. The official and widely held popular version attributes all responsibility for the Cold War to the policies Joseph Stalin pursued during the last year and in the aftermath of World War II. More particularly, the origin of the Cold War is traced to the Soviet violations of the Yalta agreements. At this point, the official and popular version divides into two schools of thought. There are those who see in Stalin a mere exponent of the unalterable attitudes and objectives of Communism; and there are those who concentrate all the blame on Stalin as a person in contrast to Khrushchev and his successors, who are credited with the desire to "make an end to the Cold War." C. B. Marshall's very brief and popular account leans toward the former view, while Marshall Shulman's book, primarily policy-oriented, points in the other direction.*

---

* Charles Burton Marshall, *The Cold War: A Concise History* (New York: Franklin Watts, 1965); Marshall D. Shulman, *Beyond the Cold War* (New Haven, Conn.: Yale University Press, 1966).

Against this view, which has been both a result and an instrument of the Cold War, a twofold reaction has set in. One has been revisionist and polemical, a kind of counterfoil to the view it opposes in trying to show how much the United States is to blame for the Cold War. D. F. Fleming's massive attack upon the official doctrine is in good measure a Cold War polemic in reverse, shifting the principal blame from the Soviet Union to the United States. Gar Alperovitz sets himself the more limited task of showing that the atomic bomb was used against Japan not primarily for military reasons but as a political weapon in the confrontation with the Soviet Union.*

The other reaction transcends the polemics of the Cold War. It lets the diplomatic record speak for itself, as does Martin Herz, or it assesses the merits and demerits of each side's case with an impressive measure of philosophic detachment, as do John Lukacs and Louis Halle.† (The record is made particularly eloquent in Mr. Herz's book through the device of seventy-eight questions and answers summarizing the conclusions to be drawn from the analysis.) Or, it seeks to substitute for the enmities and rivalries of traditional power politics an altogether new type of foreign policy aiming at a world community, as does the Barnet-Raskin volume.‡

Of these books, Louis Halle's is in a class by itself. It not only presents a penetrating account of world politics in the last two decades, but that account is embedded in, and permeated by, a melancholy wisdom that is informed by an awareness of the irremediable folly of mankind, evoking the memory of Thucydides, whom Halle is fond of quoting.

The picture of the origins of the Cold War that emerges from these books was already forshadowed by Walter Lippmann's analysis and by other earlier accounts, based upon primary sources, by Herbert Feis and William H. McNeil.§ It is starkly at variance with the

---

* D. F. Fleming, *The Cold War and Its Origins* (New York: Doubleday, 1961); Gar Alperovitz, *Atomic Diplomacy: Hiroshima and Potsdam* (New York: Simon & Schuster, 1965).

† Martin R. Herz, *Beginnings of the Cold War* (Bloomington, Ind.: Indiana University Press, 1966); John Lukacs, *A New History of the Cold War* (New York: Doubleday, 1966); Louis J. Halle, *The Cold War as History* (New York: Harper & Row, 1967).

‡ Richard J. Barnet and Marcus S. Raskin, *After 20 Years: Alternatives to the Cold War in Europe* (New York: Random House, 1965).

§ Walter Lippmann, *The Cold War: A Study in U.S. Foreign Policy* (New York: Harper & Row, 1947); Herbert Feis, *Churchill, Roosevelt, Stalin: The War They Waged and the Peace They Sought* (Princeton, N.J.: Princeton University Press, 1957); William H. McNeill, *America, Britain and Russia: Their Co-operation and Conflict, 1941–1946* (New York: Johnson Reprints, 1953).

official and popular view. Stalin appears not as the adherent of a "rigid theology," to quote Arthur Schlesinger's summary of that view in his polemic against Alperovitz,* but as a hard-headed realist who thought in the traditional terms of spheres of influence. That conception of the postwar world clashed head-on with Roosevelt's philosophy, most strikingly expressed in his report on the Yalta Conference.†

The incompatibility of these two conceptions of the postwar world came to a head in the controversy over the kind of governments to be established in the nations of Eastern Europe. Stalin insisted that these governments be "friendly." Roosevelt and Churchill conceded that they should be "friendly" to the Soviet Union, but they insisted that they should also be "democratic." Stalin clearly saw the inner contradiction of that position. "A freely elected government in any of these countries," he said, "would be anti-Soviet, and that we cannot allow." Stalin could not help but interpret the Western position as implacable hostility to Russian interests, while the West (mistaking Stalin for Trotsky) saw in the ruthless transformation of the nations of Eastern Europe into Russian satellites empirical proof of the un-limited ambitions of Soviet Communism. Thus the Cold War started. From then on, the issue was no longer whether "spheres of influence" should be abolished or maintained, but how far the sphere of influence of either side should extend. When, in the late 1940's, Europe for all practical purposes had been firmly divided into two spheres of in-fluence congealing into two military blocs, the Cold War centered upon the concrete political issue as to whether the line of mili-tary demarcation of 1945 dividing Germany was to be the definitive boundary between the two spheres, or whether the boundary ought to run farther east or west. That issue has remained unresolved to this day.

In this contest, the Soviet Union had two advantages: The Red Army was in physical possession of most of what the Soviet Union claimed to be its sphere of influence, and the Communist parties of Western Europe were at the beck and call of the Soviet Government to support its policies. The West had nothing with which to oppose the Russian sphere of influence except legal and moral complaints about the violations of the Yalta agreements and the rhetoric of German unification, of "liberation" and "rollback." Against the ex-tension of the Russian sphere it used successfully the weapons of military containment, the Marshall Plan, and the implementation of the Truman Doctrine.

The Cold War changed its character drastically under the impact of

* *The New York Review of Books,* October 20, 1966.
† See above, page 76.

the hot war in Korea. The North Korean aggression was interpreted by the West as the opening shot in Moscow's campaign for the conquest of the world. It seemed to provide the clinching proof of the assumption held by the West since the beginning of the Cold War that Stalin's foreign policy was in line of succession not to the imperialism of the Tsars but to the world-wide Bolshevik aspirations of Lenin and Trotsky. Mr. Halle stresses correctly the erroneous character of this interpretation, and I have gone even farther in pointing to the element of accident in the Soviet acquiescence in the Northern attempt to unify Korea by force of arms.

The misinterpretation of the North Korean aggression as part of a grand design for world conquest originating in and controlled by Moscow resulted in a drastic militarization of the Cold War in the form of a conventional and nuclear armaments race, the frantic search for alliances, and the establishment of military bases. This militarization was both the effect and the cause of the increased expectation that the Cold War might develop into a hot one. That expectation, shared by both sides, in turn increased the likelihood of such a development. As Mr. Halle put it:

> By 1953 the entire foreign policy of the United States . . . was based on the Cold War. It made sense only on the premises on which the Cold War was being fought. Specifically, the policy was based upon the belief that Moscow was determined, by fraud or violence, to establish its ideology, its political system, and its domination over the entire world.

It is against this background that one must judge the import for the Cold War of Khrushchev's ascent to power. The view is widely held—and Mr. Halle reflects it—that, in terms of the conduct of the Cold War, Khrushchev was an improvement over Stalin; for Khrushchev is supposed to have sought the abatement of the Cold War through what he called "relaxation of tensions." I have never shared this view and can only summarize here the arguments I presented a decade ago in order to show that Khrushchev changed the quality and increased the range and intensity of the Cold War but contributed nothing to its abatement. While Stalin conducted a Cold War of position, Khrushchev was the champion of a Cold War of movement. When Khrushchev spoke of relaxation of tensions, he wanted the West to stop challenging the *status quo* of 1945. In order to force the West to do this, he himself challenged the *status quo* of West Berlin at the risk of war. But in order to maintain the *status quo* of the Soviet empire he went to war in Hungary with methods as ruthless as any Stalin had ever used.

However, Khrushchev showed himself as the innovator of the Cold War of movement by making the whole world its theater and by using new methods of waging it. Here he is the heir not of Stalin and the Tsars, but indeed of Lenin and Trotsky. Khrushchev revived the Bolshevik expectation of the communization of the whole world as an immediate goal of Soviet foreign policy and made it the basis for a new policy, which he called "competitive coexistence," tied to support for "wars of national liberation." His aims were the aims of Lenin and Trotsky, and the methods he used to achieve those aims were his original contribution to the Cold War. These methods run the whole gamut from military intervention and threats to diplomatic pressure, foreign aid and trade, support of subversion, and the exploitation of the new technological prestige of the Soviet Union. Thus he threatened war with Great Britain and France over Suez and with the United States over Cuba. He competed with the United States and China for the allegiance of the new and emerging nations, and he transformed Cuba into a political and military outpost of the Soviet Union. This quantitative and qualitative transformation of the Cold War was the work of Khrushchev, not Stalin. It was Stalin, not Khrushchev, who said to Eden that the trouble with Hitler was that he didn't know when to stop: "I know when to stop." Khrushchev did not know it, or he learned only in 1962, when the Cuban missile crisis brought the United States and the Soviet Union as close to nuclear war as they have ever come.

The post-Khrushchev phase of the Cold War is characterized by the extension of movement to the nations of Europe—east and west. In Europe, the aim of Khrushchev's Cold War of movement was identical with that of Stalin's Cold War of position: the stabilization of the political and territorial *status quo* of the immediate postwar period. In these two types of Cold War, two blocs opposed each other as political and military instruments of the two superpowers. Now the two tightly controlled blocs have been replaced by traditional alliances of varying closeness. Across what was once the boundary of the two blocs, whose impenetrable proximity was symbolized by the Iron Curtain, the nations of Eastern and Western Europe move in search of new alignments and configurations, putting into question not only the boundary but even the viability of the spheres of influence of the postwar period.

In the course of these movements, unfettered to an ever increasing degree by the stifling weight of the two superpowers, the natural weights of individual national power have reasserted themselves. Thus West Germany as the second most powerful nation on the European continent exerts a new attraction upon France, on the one hand, and upon countries like Czechoslovakia and Rumania, on the other. In consequence, East Germany, once the western spearhead of the Soviet bloc, might well become an island, precariously placed in a moving sea and maintained in that position only as long as the Soviet Union is able and willing to maintain it.

Do these developments spell the end of the Cold War? There is a tendency to answer that question in the affirmative, not in view of the relevant factors of interests and power in which the Cold War originated and which have kept it going for more than two decades, but in view of a superficial and obsolescent criterion: the degree of hostility exhibited by the United States and the Soviet Union in their relations with each other. From the fact that the U.S. and the U.S.S.R. have not challenged each other openly in recent years in Europe and their diplomatic relations are more nearly normal than they used to be, the conclusion is drawn that there is nothing for them to fight about and that therefore the Cold War has ended. However, the arms race continues, and military bases remain intact. For the Americans and the Russians continue to oppose, and compete with, each other throughout the world. Vietnam, the Middle East, and Somalia are three spectacular cases in point. According to the *Economist* (November 19, 1966),

> The Middle East is one of the parts of the world where Cold War politics are far from dead; Russia and the West have their chosen proteges, and to preserve the balance keep them armed. The resultant arms race is something outsiders ought to get excited, as well as gloomy, about.

In Europe the conflict of interests that has pitted the United States against the Soviet Union since the end of World War II persists, even though it has taken on a new appearance. And the question that the Cold War brought to the fore two decades ago remains unanswered: Which way is Germany going to turn? Khrushchev, as has been mentioned,* saw clearly the crucial importance of that issue and expressed in a number of private conversations his confidence that sooner or later there would be "another Rapallo," *i.e.*, another alignment between the Soviet Union and Germany against the West.

This remains the crucial issue today as it has been for two decades, and it is a matter of secondary importance whether it is going to be fought out through the unilateral methods of the Cold War or

---

* See page 342.

through the traditional methods of diplomacy. The answer to that question depends primarily on the policies to be pursued by the Soviet Union. Thus far it has addressed West Germany in the Cold War language of Stalin and Khrushchev. But how is it going to act? Will it try to protect the remnants of its empire against the attraction of West Germany through the unilateral methods of the Cold War? Or will it try to exchange what is left of that empire for a German-Soviet combination, which might promise to draw all of Europe into its orbit? Or will it use both methods simultaneously, or alternately, as the situation might suggest?

Thus even if the Cold War should come to "an end"—and especially if it should—the diplomacy of the West (and, more particularly, of the United States) will have to deal with issues infinitely more complex, more risky, and also more promising than those it dealt with successfully during the first two periods of the Cold War. Until now, its main task has been to hold the line, and it has held it. It is an open question whether a less rigid Western diplomacy would have had a chance in 1953 and then again in 1956 to push that line farther east. In any event, from now on, the objective conditions of Europe and the policies of the European nations rather than political rhetoric will pose the question as to whether and where that line should be redrawn and whether there will be a line at all.

It testifies to the power of stereotyped modes of thought and action that none of the books under consideration, with the exception of Mr. Shulman's, addresses itself explicitly to this issue. They are all oriented toward "ending the Cold War" as a good in itself. But under present conditions, that issue concerns the techniques of diplomacy, not its substance. For after the Cold War has ended, the struggle for the substance of power will continue.

33

Communism

THE CRISIS OF COMMUNISM

[1965–66]

It is of course obvious that Communism today is in a serious crisis both domestically and internationally. But it is less clear in what this crisis consists and, more particularly, what its results are likely to be for the rest of the world.

In order to understand the nature of this crisis, it is first necessary to consider the nature of Communism itself. For Communism is not just another political philosophy nor is it just another political, social, or economic system. It claims to be, and it acts upon the assumption that it is, the repository of all the truth there is to be had about man and society; that, in other words, it has a monopoly of truth. And the claim on the part of its leaders to govern resides in their inferred monopolistic access to the truth of Communism.

We are here, in other words, in the presence of a system of government which is of a charismatic nature. That is to say, there were certain people—Lenin, Stalin, for a time at least, Khrushchev—who claimed that they stood in a special intellectual and moral relationship to the truth of Communism, and it is this relationship which gave them the right to govern. There exists, then, a quasi-religious re-

355

lationship between a "scientific" or "revealed" truth, "revealed" through the "genius" of Marx and Lenin, on the one hand, and the rulers, on the other—a relationship that establishes the authority of the government. It is a historic turning point in the history of Communism that this authority was challenged first by Yugoslavia in her external relations with the Soviet Union, the "Fatherland of Socialism," and then by Khrushchev through his denigration of Stalin in 1956. Those are the two events that made the crisis of Communism manifest and acute. What we have witnessed recently and what no doubt we are going to witness in the future will be an echo or a future development of those two critical turning points in the history of Communism.

It follows from this special quasi-religious relationship which Communism assumes to exist between its leaders and the truth of Communism that there can be only one authentic source of Communist truth. The monolithic character of Communism, as it existed until the defection of Yugoslavia in 1948, is of the very essence of the Communist system. It is no more possible to recognize two equally authentic sources of revealed religious truth than to accept two equally authentic sources of the so-called scientific truth that Communism presumes to represent. So the dictatorship of the ruling group is not, within the framework of Communism, a deviation or, as it was still in the mind of Marx, a transitional period, but it is of the very essence of Communism as a political philosophy and as a system of government itself.

There has been much debate in the past as to how it came about that the original libertarian aspirations of Marxism were, as it was said, corrupted into first the dictatorship of Lenin and then the tyranny of Stalin. Certain scholars, such as the late Professor Laski, have pinpointed a debate that occurred between Lenin and another socialist philosopher as the event after which Lenin, as it were, went wrong. Present-day Communists have, of course, been at a loss to explain how this scientific system of government could produce, in their own words, such a monster as Stalin. If one accepts Khrushchev's assessment of Stalin as valid, one certainly must raise the question as to how this cult of personality, degenerating into a bloody tyranny, could grow from the pure scientific soil of a Communist system of government.

The truth is, of course, that the root of Communist dictatorship, the root of Stalinist tyranny, and the root of the cult of personality —of which Khrushchev accused Stalin and of which the successors of Khrushchev have accused him—lies in the very nature of Marxism itself. For any system of social and political thought that assumes infallibility, that is, the monopolistic possession of the truth about men and society, is of necessity, by dint of that very claim, precluded from tolerating, as it were, other gods besides itself, other sources of the truth and different kinds of truth.

The very intolerance of dissenting opinion to be found in the personality of Marx, who was continuously engaged in violent debates and squabbles with other socialist leaders, foreshadows similar doctrinal and much more far-reaching disputes of later times, down to our own. The whole history of Marxism is a continuous and frequently acrimonius debate about what the truth of Marxism actually is. From Marx on through a succession of German Socialist parties with their different programs, their different revisions of the original program, to the present split between the Soviet Union and China, we are in the presence of a continuous attempt at squaring historical experience with the Communist claim to infallibility. The cult of personality is inherent in the system, and it is an ironic fact—which is more ironic to us as the outsiders than it must be to the Communists who look at it from the inside—that Khrushchev was accused of the very same crime of the cult of personality of which he accused his predecessor, Stalin.

Why is it that the cult of personality paradoxically is inherent in the very system of philosophy that claims to be completely objective, which claims to have discovered the objective rational laws by which the historical process moves toward its predetermined consummation? The reason for the inevitability of the cult of personality lies exactly in this monopolistic claim to truth which, as we have seen, is the very foundation of the authority of Communist government. Thus a succession of Communist governments in different countries must all claim, for the time being at least, that what they are doing is the mere scientific application of the truth of Communism and that their opponents are revisionists, fascists, saboteurs, bourgeois deviationists, warmongers, and whatnot. Once they have governed, as it were, during their assigned time, once they have used up their reservoir of good will, their political capital, they are replaced by another elite, which denounces its predecessors for having been heretics, tyrants, and cultists of personality. Then they engage in exactly the same practices, not because they are worse, morally speaking, but because they cannot help themselves, considering the philosophic system in the name of which they govern. So there is no doubt that if the present leaders of the Soviet Union should last they will engage in the cult of their own personalities; for here lies the source of their authority, here lies the moral justification for their being in the seat of power.

Thus we see the crises within the government of the Soviet Union, which we have witnessed since the denigration of Stalin in 1956, as a result not of certain historical accidents but of the very nature of

Communism as a philosophic and political system, and I am convinced that we have not seen the last of this yet. For Communism and its leaders could maintain their claim to infallibility only as long as there existed at least a semblance of harmony between their presumptions and the observable empirical reality.

Aside from those crises within the Soviet Union to which I have referred, however, the whole history of Marxism, at least the history of Marxism in the twentieth century, is a story of a continuing conflict between the Marxist assumptions and historical realities. That is to say, time and again at the great turning points of the history of our century, history has denied the empirical claims of Marxism. Thus, step by step, the plausibility of Marxism has been weakened until today, as I shall try to show, it has really disappeared as a living system of political thought.

The first great disappointment Marxism suffered at the hands of history occurred in 1914 at the outbreak of World War I. It had been one of the basic assumptions of Marxism, in both theory and practice, that the solidarity of the international proletariat would transcend the loyalty of individual proletarians and individual proletarian parties to their respective nations and governments. It is for this reason that up to 1914 no socialist party in Europe, for instance, ever voted one cent for military appropriations for their respective governments. This was an article of faith. Thus, Marxists all over the world believed that war had become impossible by virtue of the fact that no proletarian would be willing to fight for his own government—that a kind of international sit-down strike of the proletarian masses would make it impossible for the capitalist governments to fight each other. Now we all know that in August, 1914, the proletarians of the world did not unite but started to kill each other in the name of their respective nations and governments. That is to say, the exact opposite happened from what Marxism had prophesied.

The second great disappointment Marxism suffered at the hands of historical experience occurred at the end and in the aftermath of World War I. The October Revolution of 1917 should not have occurred in Russia at all, according to the strict principles of Marxism. The revolution should have occurred in one of the most advanced industrial countries whose inner contradictions would have made it ripe for the proletarian revolution. But it was utterly unMarxist that it should occur in a backward country, half feudalistic, with an early capitalistic system far from maturity, and without a large mass of an industrial proletariat. But it occurred.

Lenin, again in full accord with Marxist principles, expected the

Russian Revolution to be of necessity followed by revolutions in the most advanced industrial nations, such as Germany, Austria, and Great Britain. He could not conceive of the Russian Revolution as an isolated historical event. He believed that the Russian Revolution could not survive as an isolated event, surrounded as the Soviet Union was by hostile capitalistic nations. In consequence, his foreign policy was bound to aim at stirring up revolutions everywhere, that is to say, to try to make the world ripe for world revolution.

But it became obvious already in Lenin's lifetime that the Russian Revolution was not to be followed by revolutions elsewhere, that it either would have to survive as an isolated event, again in an utterly un-Marxist fashion, or could not survive at all. It is here that Stalin and Trotsky split, for Trotsky continued to try to apply the orthodox Marxist principles to Russia and to the world situation. He was still convinced that socialism could not survive in one country, while Stalin was convinced that it could because it had to. Thus Stalin coined the phrase "socialism in one country," pursuing an extremely cautious foreign policy in order to provide no pretext for the capitalistic enemies of the Soviet Union to attack it while it was still weak. The historical importance of Stalin really consists in that he radically departed from the Marxist assumptions and created a powerful, at least in part, industrially advanced nation where formerly there existed only a backward nation in the form of imperial Russia. The revulsion and the disappointment that large masses of Western idealistic Communists felt in the face of the Stalinist regime is the result of their disappointment at Stalin's radical departure from the Marxist assumptions and his establishment of an isolated nation-state on what were supposed to be Marxist foundations.

The third disappointment occurred with the rise of fascism. The rise of fascism was welcomed by orthodox Marxists as a necessary stage in the decay of capitalism, to be followed by the proletarian revolution. For here seemed to be the ideal situation, which Marx had foreseen, of large masses of the population sinking down into the amorphous masses of the proletariat as a result of the decimation of the middle classes, first by inflation and then by the economic crisis of 1929. Here was the classic juxtaposition between a small group of monopoly capitalists and the great mass of the people, who had become proletarized through the policies of the former.

Yet it is the historical paradox of this situation, which developed most clearly in Germany, that the great masses of the proletarized middle classes, out of protest against their proletarization, went fascist, while, according to Marx, consciousness follows the material conditions and not the other way around. According to Marxist principles, the consciousness of the proletarized middle classes should have reflected their proletarized position. They should have become Marxists. They became the exact opposite, because they sought to close the cleavage between their conscious aspirations and their actual conditions not on the latter's terms, but on the former's. Here is one of the main roots of fascism.

The Marxists reconciled themselves to this situation, in itself utterly un-Marxist, by saying that once fascism had failed, as it was bound to fail, Marxism would take over. Once those proletarized masses had gone through the provisional stage of fascism, they would embrace Communism. Again nothing of the kind occurred. Not only did it not occur, but the implicit alliance that the Soviet Union concluded with Nazi Germany in 1939 was, of course, a death blow to the faith of large masses of Communists who had believed in the inevitable hostility between fascism, as the last defense of a decaying monopoly capitalism, and Marxism.

One must see the present crisis of Communism in the historical context of those successive blows that Marxism suffered at the hands of historical experience. Marxists were already weakened in their faith in the infallibility of Marxism when in 1948 Yugoslavia split with the rest of the Communist movement. This, especially in retrospect, appears as an event of far-reaching historical importance. Stalin, in expelling the Yugoslavs from the Communist camp, was perfectly consistent with the basic assumptions of Marxism. There could not be two authentic sources of Marxist truth; Tito, by claiming a special national road to Communism, branded himself as a heretic who had to be expelled. But while one can debate the respective merits of the positions of Stalin and Tito in an academic fashion, historically it is obvious that Tito succeeded. One can argue that what Tito has created in Yugoslavia is not real Marxism, not real Communism; but one would still have to admit that Tito has created a system of government and of economics that is at least no less effective than the orthodox systems that developed in other Communist countries.

It is interesting to note that it is the Yugoslav experience which has provided the precedent for the Chinese rebellion against the monopolistic position the Soviet Union has occupied in the Communist camp. It is certainly one of the roots of the Chinese revolt. The other root lies in the dethronement of Stalin by Khrushchev in 1956. This is indeed the second great turning point in the recent history of Communism and, of course, a much more dramatic and far-reaching one than the defection of Yugoslavia.

By denigrating Stalin, by declaring him to be a murderous tyrant and not the true representative of Communism, Khrushchev denigrated the Communist system as well. For, as I have said before, the Communists were bound to ask themselves what kind of a system it was—allegedly objective and scientific, allegedly in the possession of a monopoly of truth—that could produce such a bloody tyrant. The internal liberalization of Communism is, of course, the result of the doubt Khrushchev has cast not only upon Stalin's right to govern, but upon the very legitimacy of Communist government itself. One can find an element of Shakespearean tragedy, with a considerable element of comic relief, in the fact that this vulgar and shrewd peasant destroys the reputation of Stalin and thereby destroys his own ability to govern. By destroying the throne upon which Stalin sat, he destroyed the throne upon which he sat as well.

What is called the liberalization of Communist societies is really the raising of the questions and doubts I have raised here, although generally in a much more subdued form. Once the charisma not only of the leader but of the whole system has been put into question, it cannot be restored. In other words, when Khrushchev attacked Stalin, he inflicted a mortal wound upon the political system of Communism itself. The questions that have been raised ever since go back to this attack upon the demigod, as Stalin was bound to be represented to the Communist faithful. For once it is admitted that a great leader who governed for thirty years as the "greatest genius of humanity," the man who won World War II virtually single-handed, the true disciple of Marx and Lenin, was a bloody tyrant, the whole system of Communism is put into question. All the questions that have been raised about Communism in Communist countries and parties since 1956 go back to this massive attack with which Khrushchev destroyed the reputation of Stalin.

This process of internal disintegration of the Communist system, of the plausibility of the claims of Communism, has gone much farther than we are inclined to believe. I have just read the minutes of a session of the Czech Academy of Science in which professors and academicians discussed the causes of the economic distress in which Czechoslovakia finds itself today—with individual statements being attributed to individual professors. And those professors and academicians were unanimous in saying that the economic failure cannot be attributed to individual mistakes or faults in administration and management—they are the result of the system itself. This is a frontal assault upon Communism, an undisguised, unqualified denial of the claims that for a century Communists have accepted as revealed truth.

This process of internal disintegration is, on the one hand, greatly accelerated and aggravated by the external dissensions among Communist nations. On the other hand, the external dissensions are a mere function of the internal disintegration. For once the authority of the government of the Soviet Union as the infallible interpreter and developer of Marxist-Leninist thought has lost its plausibility, the governments of Poland and Czechoslovakia and of China and Rumania must ask themselves: Why should we subordinate our national interests to the interests of Russia—why should we follow the orders of a foreign government whose head is being denigrated as a bloody tyrant and whose successor has been accused of being a cultist of personality? Thus, the national aspirations that have made themselves felt within the Communist camp are the direct result of the decay of the Communist faith and of the belief in the truth of the Communist revelations, as embodied in the Government of the Soviet Union.

This external conflict has come to a head in the form of the Soviet-Chinese split. This split is not a passing tactical disagreement but a fundamental conflict concerning both doctrine and national interest. Mao Tse-tung prevailed in China in a way that was utterly un-Marxist and was opposed–by Stalin. For Stalin, in accordance with orthodox Marxist doctrine, believed that the Chinese Communists should base their policies upon the industrial proletariat of the cities. Here was the source of Marxist strength. But Mao Tse-tung based his operations upon the landless peasants, and he succeeded while Stalin thought that Chiang Kai-shek would win the civil war. So Mao Tse-tung, like Tito, owes nothing, as far as his victory within his own country is concerned, to Russian Communism. Quite to the contrary, his very victory is the result of heretical disregard for the allegedly infallible authority of the Kremlin. The very fact that he was victorious against the Kremlin's advice is a living demonstration of the fallibility of the Soviet government.

Secondly, when Tito split with the Soviet Union and when Stalin's authority was destroyed by Khrushchev, there was only one first-rate Communist leader left who was not tainted by Stalinism and who was not involved in the Titoist heresy. This was Mao Tse-tung. So Mao Tse-tung could and of course did claim that he was the authentic successor of Marx and Lenin, that the mantle of successorship, which Khrushchev had torn from Stalin's tomb, belonged rightfully upon his shoulders. This doctrinal claim was bound to be resisted by Moscow, for with this claim goes supremacy within the world Communist movement. Whoever can make this claim plausible, whoever can demonstrate that he possesses that monopoly of Marxist truth which Marx and Lenin were supposed to have possessed, by that very fact assumes the legitimate authority to rule over world Communism.

Yet the very fact that the two great Communist powers, the Soviet Union and China, compete with each other for this exalted position —which is quite a different matter from the not very serious competition between Tito and Stalin—this very fact damages the claim of both. For many Communists have raised the question: If Moscow claims to be the true successor to Marx and Lenin and if Peking claims the same, could it be that the claim of neither is justified? To make matters worse for Communism, the list of pretenders to the successorship is virtually unlimited; for there are, potentially at least, as many successors as there are Communist parties and governments that can make Communism stick. Here is the root of what we call "polycentrism," that is, the claim that the monopoly of wisdom and virtue in Marxist terms is not located in a particular capital, a particular man, or a particular nation but resides, as it were, in the world Communist movement itself. This is a kind of pantheistic conception in secular political terms, so that there are as many legitimate roads to socialism as there are Communist governments and Communist parties able to travel that road.

Intimately connected with the doctrinal competition between the Soviet Union and China is a great-power competition. One might even argue that the doctrinal competition is simply another aspect of the great-power competition. The split between the Soviet Union and China came into the open when the Soviet Union refused to help China to become a great modern power, that is to say, when it reneged upon the agreement by which it had obligated itself to supply China with the implements of nuclear power. This refusal of the Soviet Union to help China to become a nuclear power was a refusal to help China to become the most powerful nation not only in the Communist camp but in the world. For if one assumes that 800 million Chinese will come into the possession of the instruments of modern technology in the fields of communication, transportation, and weaponry, it follows that China will then have become the most powerful nation on earth, surpassing both the United States and the Soviet Union. It is this specter of a China, which contests today the supremacy of Moscow in the Communist world and which might become tomorrow or the day after the most powerful nation on earth, that has given the Russians pause.

Thirdly, we must consider the age-old rivalries between Russia and China over influence in Asia and over frontiers. China and the Soviet Union compete, for instance, for influence in North Korea and North Vietnam. China lays claim to large parts of Soviet territory in Asia which either China was forced to cede by treaty during the period of its humiliation in the middle of the nineteenth century or which Russia occupied as no man's land, since China exercised no effective control over them. If there should ever be war between the two countries it is most likely to break out over a concrete issue of territorial sovereignty.

What we are witnessing today is perhaps the last or at best the next to the last act of a drama in which a great political philosophy, promising the liberation of man by making an end to his self-alienation, first transforms itself into a political religion, then degenerates into an ideology justifying a bloody tyranny, and finally ends up as a mere verbal ritual in whose truth few believe. One has only to take a look at the formerly great Marxist parties of Western Europe, which are still very numerous in terms of votes but have lost their faith in Marxism. The formerly very influential and powerful socialist parties in Germany and Austria, for instance, have made a concerted effort since the end of World War II to get rid of the last vestiges of Marxism. I remember, and it is is one of the most vivid recollections of my early youth, that I once went with my father, who was a physician, to the house of a worker who was dying of cancer, and he pointed to a very much used pamphlet on his night table, asking my father to put this pamphlet into his coffin after his death. When we came out of the house, I asked my father, "Was this the Bible?" And my father said, "This was his bible, this was the *Communist Manifesto*." One cannot imagine today a worker in Italy or France, let alone Germany or Austria, with the kind of faith in the truth and the liberating force of Marxism that man had more than half a century ago.

Having said this, I must also say that while Marxism in its original form has lost all its plausibility and most of its charismatic power, it has transformed itself into something utterly different, and in that transformed stage it exerts considerable influence; that is, as the primitive justification for dictatorial rule in many underdeveloped nations. It is here that its impact is today felt, especially in its Chinese version. For the Chinese are using a simplified, crude version of Marxism, which has really very little to do with the original Marxist philosophy, as a propagandistic and subversive device by which to gain allegiance in the new and emerging nations of Africa and Latin

America. While Marxism, even in its original form, does not fit at all the conditions of the workers in the highly developed industrial nations, its crude Chinese version meets the psychological and political needs of the new elites and counter-elites in those nations.

So the crisis of Marxism, which has appeared in a spectacular form as the denigration of Stalin and the dismissal of Khrushchev and as a tug-of-war between the Soviet Union and China, has very profound causes. What we read about in the newspapers are merely spectacular surface phenomena of a disintegrating process which has really led, if not to the death of Marxism, at least to its fatal disease.

What, then, are the chances for the survival of the Soviet regime in the face of these difficulties and dilemmas? Four factors militate in its favor.

First, even though the credibility of Marxism and the principle of Soviet legitimacy have been seriously damaged, the creed is still accepted in a general, vague, and unenthusiastic way by large masses of the population. Some Soviet citizens will tell you that they do not believe in specific tenets of Marxism and that they are unconvinced and even repelled by the government's self-serving use of the doctrine; but they will assert that they are Marxists and believe in socialism, though a different kind from that practiced by the government. Skepticism and even cynicism coexist uneasily with a weakened faith that maintains itself precariously against reason and empirical evidence. This contradictory mood has its parallel in Western societies —for example, in attitudes toward religion and democracy.

Second, the tendency to cling to the faith is strengthened by the patent absence of a viable alternative. Where should those disenchanted with Marxism turn for a more meaningful principle of legitimacy? Their dissatisfaction has no opportunity to find a new focus of allegiance, because there is none.

Third, even if there were such a focus, the regime's monopoly over the instruments of coercion would make a politically relevant transfer of allegiance impossible, at least so long as the rulers retain the loyalty of the armed forces and of the police. Given this condition, a modern government can take a good deal of popular dissatisfaction in its stride. What it must guard against is allowing discontent to become so deep and widespread that the military and police forces are themselves infected.

Fourth, and most important, ideological dissatisfaction may lead to grumbling and indifference, but it will not lead to political action as long as the government is able to satisfy the basic aspirations of the population at large. As long as these aspirations are met, it will matter little that segments of the intellectual elite are discontented.

Thus the "end of ideology" in the Soviet Union does not necessarily mean the end of the regime. As long as all or even some of these four factors operate, the Soviet regime has a chance of surviving the erosion of the Marxist principle of legitimacy. Again, Western experience bears out this analysis.

On the other side of the coin, with the ideological basis of its legitimacy destroyed, the Soviet regime is exposed to three basic threatening possibilities.

First, persistent and spectacular failures at home and abroad, for which an elite of uninspiring technicians would be held responsible, could lead to the rise of a new Caesarism, civilian or military, which might base its rule on the charisma of a single leader, combined with promises of economic and social improvements in the name of socialism and with appeals for the patriotic defense and promotion of Russia's interests.

Second, it is conceivable that social and economic interests might become diversified and crystalized as a consequence of decentralization. These interests might press for a direct and institutionalized part in the process of policy formation, competing for political power within the general ideological and institutional framework of the Soviet regime. The result would be a pluralistic system, in which various factions would operate in the name of Marxism. The differences among them would be not ideological but pragmatic. The American party system offers an analogy for such a development. Yet there would be a significant difference in that such a pluralism would still be contained and limited through institutionalized totalitarianism, whereas American pluralism is kept within bounds by spontaneous conformism.

Third, it is possible that the stresses arising under either of the preceding alternatives would cause such a degree of social, political, and moral disintegration that it could not be handled within the institutional framework of the regime. What has happened elsewhere in Asia, Africa, and Latin America might then happen in the Soviet Union: The army—as the best-organized, disciplined, and effective social force, with a claim to legitimacy deriving from its past vital services to the state—might take over the reins of government.

There is no rational basis for speculating as to which of these alternative developments is most likely to materialize. The responsible observer must content himself with being aware of the alternatives and watching for empirical evidence to indicate a trend in one direction or another.

THOUGHTS ON THE OCTOBER REVOLUTION

[November, 1967]

Viewed from the vantage point of 1967, the October Revolution of 1917 appears as the most important political event of the twentieth century. It is an open question whether it will so appear from the vantage point of the year 2000. For it may well be that during the last third of this century its consequences for the world will be overshadowed by the achievements of the Chinese Revolution, provided 800 million Chinese will be able to master the instruments of modern technology. Yet while our judgment of the ultimate place of the Bolshevist Revolution must perforce remain suspended, its accomplishments are clearly visible today. They are three: the modernization of Russia, the establishment of the first totalitarian state, the destruction of Marxism as a living political philosophy.

The Bolshevist Revolution did for Russia under the conditions of a highly developed technology what the Revolution of 1789 did for France under the conditions of primitive capitalism: It destroyed the fetters of a decaying social system and put new productive forces in the hands of a new society. The French Revolution liberated the rising bourgeoisie and established, at least in principle, the individual rights of all men. This soil nurtured both the intellectual thrust and moral force of Marxist thought. What the French Revolution had established in principle Marx set out to achieve through a radical transformation of the economic system, freeing the productive forces of the working masses and thereby restoring their humanity. The Bolshevist Revolution endeavored to put into practice what Marx had taught. It transformed the inert masses of the Russian people, and of the non-Russian nationalities of the Russian empire, into a modern working force. Thus Russia has become a modern state, the other great power in the world today.

The Revolution not only increased the productive capacity and material power of Russia, but it also made Moscow a new Jerusalem, Mecca, and Rome: the fountainhead of Marxist truth and virtue, the visible manifestation of the fulfillment of the Marxist prophecies, the center that would direct and support the transformation of the world in the Marxist image. The Soviet Union did not simply become one great power among others, it became the "Fatherland of Socialism," whose interests were identical with those of humanity and to which all progressive men everywhere owed primary allegiance. That moral attraction drew strength from the material power of the Soviet state; in turn, the state used its power to further its own ends.

In truth, the material transformation of Russia was paid for by the sacrifice of those very libertarian purposes the French Revolution established in principle and Marx tried to put into practice. "The jump from necessity to freedom," in which Marx saw the consummation of the historical process, became a jump from the necessity of wage slavery into the necessity of the utter degradation and helplessness of the individual. While Hegel had postulated history as the "slaughter bank on which the happiness of the individual is sacrificed for the progress of reason," Stalin made the Soviet Union the slaughter bank on which the very existence of the individual was sacrificed for the material progress of Russia. Armed with the pretense of a monopoly of truth and virtue, as well as a monopoly of power derived from and supporting that pretense and enforced by the instruments of modern technology, Stalin developed a new form of government—the totalitarian state. The world had seen bloody tyrannies before, but never before had it witnessed a tyrant who was also the pope of a secular religion and who possessed the technical means to degrade and destroy millions of men on behalf of a material end postulated by that religion.

The end to be achieved determined the means to be employed, and no extraneous restraint was permitted to limit the means deemed necessary to achieve the end. When Lady Astor asked Stalin: "When are you going to stop killing people?" Stalin replied: "When it is no longer necessary." To an English journalist who asked him about the millions of peasants who had died during the collectivization crisis, Stalin countered: "How many died in the Great War?" And he continued, "Over 7,500,000 dead for no purpose at all. Then you must acknowledge that our losses are small, because your war ended in chaos, while we are engaged in a work which will benefit the whole of humanity."

It is both intellectually easy and morally convenient to hold Stalin personally responsible for this terrible perversion of the Marxist intent. This is a kind of "cult of personality" in reverse, the exorcism of the personality that is being blamed for Marxism's having gone astray. There is nothing new in these attempts at saving, as it were, the honor of Marxism by blaming one of its prominent exponents for its failings. The truth is more complex, however, and less reassuring for the honor of Marxism. For the perversion of the Marxist intent in practical application follows inevitably from the nature of Marxism itself.

Marxism-Leninism, pretending to have possession of all the truth about man and society, must also pretend that the answer to any question is not extraneous to itself but is of necessity in the hands of the faithful. The truth is revealed once and for all in the writings of Marx and Lenin; it only needs to be applied to concrete cases. That is the task of the elect few who, by dint of charismatic endowment, speak to the issues of the day in the voices of Marx and Lenin.

Since there can be only a single truth, the one propounded by the official interpreters of Marxism-Leninism, dissent from the official truth is bound to be illegitimate. Since the truth has already been revealed, there can be no room in the marketplace for the dissenter to compete with the official view. The dissenter is an outcast by definition. He is not to be argued with on rational grounds or overruled because he is pragmatically mistaken. He is to be denounced as a saboteur and traitor and ostracized as a "deviationist."

Just as the monopolistic pretense of Marxism-Leninism is of necessity tantamount to a pseudo-religious dogmatism in theory, so this dogmatism calls forth in practice the monolithic structure of Communist society. When the truth of Marxism-Leninism, as officially interpreted, is not accepted voluntarily, political power forces its acceptance, and that power is totalitarian because it exerts monopolistic control over the instruments of modern technology. All regimes laying claim to the Marxist heritage show this pattern of political oppression. To be sure, Stalin's bloody excesses, especially the wanton killing of innocent people, stem from the tyrant's paranoiac personality. Yet political oppression for the sake of maintaining the monolithic rule of the political elite has survived his rule.

The monopolistic possession of the Marxist truth and virtue, then, reveals itself in the last analysis as a function of the monopoly of political power. Stalin became the legitimate interpreter and augmentor of the truth of Marxism-Leninism because he was able to dislodge Trotsky and the other Old Bolsheviks from political power. Trotsky was exposed as a traitor, a deviationist, and a saboteur because he could not keep political power. When in 1956 Khrushchev denounced Stalin as a blood-stained tyrant, the despoiler of the principles of Marxism-Leninism, he performed three interconnected destructive deeds. By destroying the myth of Stalin's infallibility, in Marxist-Leninist terms, he cast doubt upon the legitimacy of any ruler or regime governing in the name of Marxism-Leninism. By doing this, he impaired the monolithic character of Soviet rule within the Soviet Union and destroyed it abroad. And, as pointed out previously,* if a blood-stained tyrant could rule supreme for twenty years in the name of Marxist-Leninist legitimacy, how trustworthy was the test by which the successors of Marx and Lenin were chosen? That question was now bound to be raised with regard not only to Stalin but also to any Communist regime tracing its legitimacy from Marxism-Leninism— including Khrushchev's and all subsequent regimes. The answer is likely to depend less and less upon conformity with the teachings of Marx and Lenin, and more and more upon the pragmatic test of success and the sheer ability to hold on to power.

Khrushchev's attack upon Stalin went to the very heart of Communist legitimacy. By destroying Stalin's reputation, it impaired his ability and that of his successors to govern in the name of Marxism-Leninism. The supporters of Khrushchev and the defenders of Stalin found themselves in the same leaking boat: They could not help but cast doubt upon the validity of a doctrine and the legitimacy of a political system that brought such leaders to the fore. And the doctrine had no plausible argument to dispel that doubt.

Held equally by the governors and the governed, that doubt is the source of what is called the internal "liberalization" of the Soviet regime. It is the peculiar nature of charismatic legitimacy to be particularly vulnerable to failure. A "gift from heaven," it must at the very least guard against the exposure of being of this world. Once it is so exposed, it is emptied of its substance. The governors may continue to govern in its name, and the subjects may still pay obeisance to it, but both will have lost faith in the wisdom, the virtue, the unchallengeable power of the government—and this faith is the vital force of any legitimacy. They may go through the motions of mouthing worn tenets and observing empty rituals, which at best serve the purpose of providing justifications and rationalizations for the actions of the government. However, this is not what makes those actions acceptable to the governed. That acceptance now rests effectively only upon the power of the government to enforce its will, and upon the benefits that the governed receive from it.

This is indeed the essence of the "liberalization" of the Soviet regime. The Soviet Government can no longer impose its will with the same totalitarian ruthlessness that characterized Lenin's and Stalin's rule. It has lost that ability not from a lack of the physical power to impose its will upon a recalcitrant citizenry but because it has ceased

* See above, pages 116 ff., 361.

to believe firmly in the charismatic source of its own legitimacy. It cannot maintain the monolithic character of Soviet society because it is no longer monolithic itself. In short, the Soviet Government has lost the moral conviction of its own legitimacy which could overcome the new moral conviction of the dissenters in its midst.

While the government is morally incapable of suppressing dissent after the fashion of Lenin and Stalin, it must continue to exert a considerable measure of monolithic control to maintain its monopoly of political power. It cannot morally afford to suppress dissent altogether, nor can it politically afford to allow dissent free rein. Thus it vacillates between the reassertion of monolithic control and "liberalization." This dilemma derives from the very nature of totalitarian rule. For if a totalitarian government were to pursue the policy of concessions consistently, it would jeopardize the foundations of its very existence. Totalitarianism and freedom are essentially incompatible, and a full measure of freedom is the very negation of totalitarian rule. Thus a Communist regime, faced with popular disaffection, must seek a compromise between totalitarian rule and freedom, a *modus vivendi* that will allow just as much freedom as is compatible with the preservation of totalitarian rule. Such a compromise and *modus vivendi* is bound to be heavily loaded in favor of totalitarianism and, in view of the unquenchable aspirations for freedom, of an extremely precarious nature.

Viewed from the special perspective of the Soviet Union, this dilemma is a function of the divorcement of political power from the legitimacy that gave birth to it. The monopoly of power in the hands of the Soviet Government is the political expression of the monopolistic pretense of Marxism-Leninism. The monopoly of power has survived the monopolistic pretense. It is power denuded of legitimacy. As such, it is uncertain of itself, indecisive in application, and of dubious longevity.

By denying the legitimacy of Stalin's rule, Khrushchev had implicitly put into question the legitimacy of Soviet rule. The question was from then on to be raised explicitly not only within the Soviet Union but throughout the Communist world. Within the Soviet Union, the negative answer given resulted in the "liberalization" of the Soviet regime. The same negative answer abroad resulted in polycentrism—a variety of Marxist societies and movements denying in theory and practice the Soviet monopoly of truth, virtue, and power.

Thus the Bolshevist Revolution presents a spectacle more awesome and more revealing of the human condition than did the French Revolution. Both, by devouring their own children, showed that truth and virtue enforced are truth and virtue destroyed. Yet the magnitude, permanence, and rational control of that destruction in the Soviet Union mark a qualitative difference from similar destructions in the past. There is an awe-inspiring majesty of Hegelian proportions in the inevitability of the progression from Marx's devotion to the truth and libertarian aspirations to the compulsory modernization of Russia achieved in the name of Marx. The progression moves from mass murder, mass deception, and the slaughter of tens of millions of people to the pragmatism of a totalitarian bureaucracy covered up with the dead ritual of quotes from Marx and Lenin and threatened by the self-same libertarian aspirations which Marx sought to fulfill for all men.

The very freedom Marx strove for and Marxism destroyed in his name now rises against the Marxist state. Thus the Bolshevist Revolution has shown what man can do for man, and what he can do to man if he allows his ends to overwhelm his means. It has also shown what he cannot do to man: He can degrade and kill him, but he cannot still his desire to be free. This is the ultimate lesson the Bolshevist Revolution carries for all of us.

34
Fascism

[February, 1966]

The main difficulty that stands in the way of the theoretical understanding of fascism is of course the intellectual poverty of fascism itself. French and German fascism were in this respect far superior to the other types; while their intellectual equipment was so untenable that it could not withstand an objective philosophic or scientific examination, it at least existed. In contrast, Italian fascism, for instance, consciously avoided doctrine, as Mussolini pointed out in the article on Fascism in the *Encyclopædia Italiana*, and instead emphasized action for its own sake. To grasp the nature of fascism is, then, an infinitely more complex and treacherous task than to understand Marxism; for Marxism has presented us with a great body of authoritative and interpretative material, from which many writers have tried, with more or less success, to construct a coherent intellectual edifice.

A writer who sets himself a similar task for fascism would get nowhere if he were to confine himself to similar authoritative and interpretative material. In order to perform his task he must take into view the whole society from which fascism sprang and which it tried to dominate, the historical events that shaped it and, in turn, were shaped by it, the social and intellectual forces that struggled for the minds of men. In order to understand fascism fully, one must be a sociologist, a historian, and a philosopher at the same time, commanding a thorough knowledge of the forces that shaped the first half of the twentieth century. This is a formidable prerequisite indeed.

Even so, it is a sad comment upon the decline of Western political thought that Nolte's is the first book * to come to terms with what is the great event in the Western political history of the twentieth century: the rise and fall of fascism. Marxists and many liberals as well have completely misunderstood fascism as an extreme rightist reactionary movement. Others have obscured its peculiar characteristics by seeing in it nothing more than a particular manifestation of totalitarianism, a brother under the skin of Bolshevism. Others still have tried to explain it in terms of a particular national character, especially that of Germany, and have searched the historical past for antecedents. It is the great merit of Hannah Arendt's pioneering *The Origins of Totalitarianism* to have shown that fascism cannot be understood through the traditional categories of politics, that it is neither right nor left, neither authoritarian nor democratic, but in truth "a new form of government," trying to stem and reverse the disintegration of modern society.

Professor Nolte is the first to have built upon this basic insight a theoretical structure enabling us to understand fascism as a political phenomenon *sui generis* and to distinguish among its different manifestations and phases of development. This is, then, a book of extraordinary intellectual importance, a true landmark in the history of political thought. It also makes extraordinarily difficult reading. The author's propensity for Hegelian abstractions is a formidable barrier to understanding even in the German original and confronts the translator with a well-nigh insuperable task. Thus the book inevitably reads like a translation from the German, and it is a tribute to the translator's skill that not infrequently the original is clarified through the translation. However, the author's intentions would have been better served if the title had been rendered more closely to the original, as "The Era of Fascism."

It is indeed the author's basic contention that the period from 1919 to 1945 was dominated by fascism in the same decisive way in which, say, the second half of the sixteenth century was dominated by the Counter Reformation. He quotes with approval Thomas Mann, who called fascism "a disease of the time which is at home everywhere and from which no country is free." The author is not primarily interested

---

* Ernst Nolte, *Three Faces of Fascism: Action Française, Italian Fascism, National Socialism* (New York: Holt, Rhinehart & Winston: 1966).

in writing a chronological, coherent history of fascism but rather in developing a typology of fascism through an analysis of the historical material. "The aim of this study is not to present a picture of the era but a concept of it as far as this can be derived from the nature of 'Fascism.' The author finds that nature in the testimony of fascism itself, that is, in the ideas and actions of those who called themselves fascists. He takes fascist "ideology" at face value, not, like so many others, as the rationalization or justification of some hidden political or economic interest and position. What he offers is a typology of the fascist idea as it manifested itself at different places in different periods of history.

Professor Nolte stresses rightly the decisive importance the rise and fall of Marxism has had upon the development of European fascism. For here was a powerful political philosophy and movement that in the heyday of liberal optimism, the middle of the nineteenth century, had with uncanny prophetic insight laid bare the weaknesses of European society, resolving first to aggravate them to the point of disintegration and then to reintegrate European society in the image of the Marxist Utopia. Yet in August, 1914, and during the three years or so immediately following World War I, Marxism was called to the test of historical performance in terms of two of its basic philosophic presuppositions and political prophecies—that the working classes in the capitalist countries would not go to war against each other, and that a successful Marxist revolution in one country would touch off a worldwide revolution—and utterly failed that test.

In consequence, the credibility of Marxism as "the" science of society and as its savior had been impaired if not destroyed. From the ordeal of war and revolution the nation-state emerged, bloodied and tottering, but still as the only force that could keep the European societies together. War and Marxism had weakened the nation but had not destroyed it. Marxism continued to weaken and to threaten it with destruction. Yet the intellectual illusions and political weakness of Marxism having been made manifest, the nation appeared to be the sole alternative to social disintegration and political anarchy. Thus the very threat to the survival of the nation evoked a fanatical determination to save it. It was at this point that the historical hour of fascism struck.

Fascism endeavored to save European society by combining a fanatical appeal to nationalism and social revolution with a totalitarian military organization of society. This dual appeal is expressed in the name of the German fascist party, "the National Socialist German Workers' Party." Thus the author can define fascism correctly as "anti-

Marxism which seeks to destroy the enemy by the evolvement of a radically opposed and yet related ideology and by the use of almost identical and yet typically modified methods, always, however, within the unyielding framework of national self-assertion and autonomy."

It is of course obvious that German Nazism and Italian fascism must be counted among the main types of fascism. It is not as obvious that the French variety represents as distinct a type. First of all, it was historically much less consequential than the other two main types, and its influence was limited to a relatively small section of the French population. Second, and more important, the French variety was very strongly infused with conservative romantic elements. Whether the *Camelots du Roi* were fascist stormtroopers or monarchist rowdies playing soldier is a very open question. This brings me to a general issue, which Nolte's over-all treatment of fascism raises.

That issue is Nolte's emphasis upon the conservative opposition of fascism to the heritage of 1789. This trend was certainly strong in Italian fascism, which made an alliance with the Church and the monarchy for the protection of the *status quo*. Yet even Italian fascism knew a revolutionary, equalitarian tendency which tried to found the regime on the equalitarian consensus of the people at large, destroying the traditional sources of social power in the process. This revolutionary trend was the distinctive and dominant characteristic of German Nazism. Yet this attempt at establishing a direct "democratic" link between the organized people and the elite and the leader has intellectually strong Rousseauist connotations, and politically it can be considered the very confirmation of two of the three main aspirations of 1789: equality and fraternity, for the sake of which liberty is sacrificed. Thus, while on the one hand fascism was opposed to the libertarian aspirations of 1789, on the other it can be considered the consummation of the equalitarian and fraternal tenets of 1789, however much distorted and corrupted they became in the process.

Professor Nolte's analysis makes again strikingly obvious the obsolescence of the traditional juxtaposition of "right" and "left." This discrepancy between the traditional meaning of our political concepts and the underlying political reality shows clearly that there is something wrong not only with our concepts but with our understanding of political reality itself.

35

Czechoslovakia

[September, 1968]

Our reactions to the events in Czechoslovakia are only somewhat less distressing than the events themselves. These reactions result from the same kind of misunderstanding of the character of Soviet foreign policy that has bedeviled our intellectual understanding and foreign policies at least since the Yalta Conference. We continue to attribute to Communism what is more plausibly explained by reference to the traditions of the Russian state. The Soviet invasion of Czechoslovakia is indeed an event of great historical significance. On the one hand, it signifies the final liquidation of the myth that the Soviet Union is "the Fatherland of Socialism." On the other, it reaffirms Western recognition of the Soviet sphere of influence and, hence, the spuriousness of Western dedication to the freedom of the nations of Eastern Europe.

Soviet policy in Eastern Europe since Yalta has been burdened with an inner contradiction: Following in the footsteps of Tsarist imperialism, it sought the establishment of friendly governments, which would serve as a buffer against foreign invasion and keep out Western, particularly German, influence. Yet the Soviet Union was in no position to permit the formation of friendly governments that would be

377

popular too. For, with the exception of Bulgaria and Czechoslovakia, all the nations of Eastern Europe have traditionally perceived Russia, Tsarist or Soviet, as a threat to their national independence, if not as their hereditary enemy.

Stalin, who was a paranoiac tyrant but also a great statesman, saw the contradiction clearly at Yalta when he countered Western demands for friendly and democratic governments in Eastern Europe by pointing to the impossibility of this combination.* The only governments in Eastern Europe that could be expected to be friendly were Communist governments, set up by the Soviet Union and subservient to it. Thus Stalin proceeded to establish such governments. Moscow could rely on them as long as it could maintain control through the instrumentalities of a monolithic Communism.

Once the nationalism of the Communist nations of Eastern Europe reasserted itself, the Soviet Union had to rely for its security upon the convergence of the national interests of those nations with its own. This convergence has existed in the relations of the Soviet Union with some of the nations of Eastern Europe, but by no means with all of them.

Poland, almost extinguished by the German *Drang nach Osten*, seeks protection from the Soviet Union. East Germany, an artificial creation serving the Kremlin's interests, depends for its very life on Soviet support. The need of the other East European nations for Russian assistance, however, is not so clear-cut. They have a freedom of maneuver that is foreclosed to Poland and East Germany. And therein lies the threat to the security of the Soviet Union.

It is an existential fact, which has determined the fate of the nations of Eastern Europe for centuries, that none of them can stand on its own feet but must lean on one or the other of its powerful neighbors. One of these neighbors is Russia; the other, Germany. In the measure that a nation such as Czechoslovakia moves away from the Soviet Union, therefore, it must move closer to Germany. What Stalin said about democratic governments in Eastern Europe, which were bound to the "anti-Soviet," applies here: ". . . that we cannot allow."

For it is another existential fact, which has dominated the fate of Europe, East and West, that Germany—by virtue of its geographic position, size and quality of population, political organization, and industrial potential—is the most powerful nation on the Continent. This is true even of truncated West Germany today. Consequently, Germany exerts a natural attraction upon its weaker neighbors, especially those to the east. While the attraction has been powerfully counter-

---

* See quotation on page 350.

acted by the terror the Nazi armies spread throughout the region, it testifies to its force that it is making itself felt again.

This attraction terrifies the Soviet Union. There is, of course, no doubt that much of the verbal attacks the Soviet Union has launched against West Germany is propaganda and so is not to be taken seriously. But underneath the verbal excesses there is a genuine fear nourished by both the history of a century and the experiences of World War II. Germany provides, by dint of its very existence, the natural alternative to the Russian orientation of the nations of Eastern Europe. The Soviet Union regards this alternative as a threat to its security and the stability of Europe. It is resolved to oppose even the beginnings of the realization of this alternative by all means, fair or foul.

If this interpretation of the Soviet move in Czechoslovakia is correct, then that move constitutes not so much an affirmation of Communism as a denial of some of its basic tenets. It demonstrates, first of all, that Communist governments after the Soviet model are not expressions of the popular will but creatures of an elite monopolizing political power. Secondly, it demonstrates that the Soviet Union is not the "Fatherland of Socialism" tied to other Communist governments and movements by a natural harmony of interests, but that it has been trying to impose its will upon these movements and governments in order to use them for the purposes of the Russian state.

These two revelations are bound to have far-reaching consequences. They discredit once more the Marxist-Leninist philosophy, and to the extent that they do they weaken the political movements and governments whose legitimacy derives from that philosophy. This is especially true of the Government of the Soviet Union both at home and abroad.

The secularization of the Soviet state has taken another big step forward. The Soviet Union now stands revealed as just one state among others, compelled to pursue its aims with particular ruthlessness, since its claim to the spontaneous support of all Socialist peoples has proved to be false. The Soviet rulers, unable to rely upon that support and faced with the hostility of peoples thirsting for freedom, have no recourse other than brute force to keep themselves in power.

But power thus maintained is bound to be precarious. A ruling group armed with the modern technologies of communication, transportation, and warfare can keep itself in power against a rebellious population only if the spirit of freedom does not affect the ruling group itself. It is upon this proviso that the future of Communist government depends.

It is ironic that, while the Russian imperial state stands ideologically naked before the world, we continue to reason not only as though the ideological vestments of the Soviet Union were still intact but also as though their existence could explain the events in Czechoslovakia. Thus we attribute what happened on August 20, 1968, to Communism. Having also attributed what has happened in Vietnam to Communism, we are happy to find confirmation for our actions there in what the Russians are doing in Czechoslovakia. Communism, so the argument runs, has shown its true colors in Czechoslovakia; hence, we are right in opposing it in Vietnam.

While this reasoning, using one superstition to support another, has strengthened our resolve in Vietnam, it cannot strengthen a nonexistent resolve with regard to Czechoslovakia. Our complete passivity gives the lie to our professions of concern for freedom, democracy, and resistance to aggression. What I said in February, 1957, on the occasion of the Hungarian Revolution applies here:

> The events of the fall of 1956 have opened up a gap between our verbal commitment to a policy of liberation and the actual policy we pursued when the opportunity, not to *initiate* liberation but to support it after it had already been achieved, arose in Hungary. These events made obvious what some of us had suspected all along, that the United States was actually pursuing a policy of containment conceived in terms not of liberation but of an implicit and thus far unacknowledged agreement to recognize the existence of spheres of influence.
>
> The American abstention in the face of the German uprising of 1953 and of the Polish and Hungarian revolts of 1956, coupled with the renunciation of force on the latter occasion, has made it perfectly clear that liberation for the United States is a matter of desire and hope, "a consummation devoutly to be wished," but not an objective of policy to be pursued by deliberate action. The United States, far from seeking out or creating opportunities for opening the door to liberation, has proved to be unwilling even to enter the door when a satellite nation kicks it wide open.
>
> The question I am raising here is not whether this is good or bad policy; I raise only the question of what the policy of the United States in regard to the satellite countries has revealed itself actually to be. This policy not only recognizes the special interests of the Soviet Union east of the 1945 line of demarcation, but also pledges non-interference with Soviet policies east of that line. It is tantamount to a unilateral recognition of a Russian sphere of influence wherein the United States concedes, without receiving any concessions in return, what it has consistently refused to concede since Yalta, and what Winston Churchill urged us to concede only in the give and take of a negotiated settlement.
>
> This concession, if it proves to be permanent, profoundly alters not only our judgment of the Cold War as it has been waged during its first

decade, but the objective nature of the Cold War to be waged in the future. It makes the Cold War of the past, insofar as it was fought for more than strict containment, look like a rather quixotic affair fought for the sake of appearances rather than of substance. By the same token, the Cold War of the future will lose its main issue if both sides continue to refrain from trying to change the 1945 line of demarcation.

This diplomatic revolution, this acceptance of the division of the world into two gigantic spheres of influence, with the consequent disappearance of the main issue and justification of the Cold War, conforms to the Stalinist conception of the postwar world. Clio, goddess of history, must savor the irony of a situation which sees Stalin disavowed both in the heritage of his own deeds and in the words and deeds of his Kremlin successors, and yet proven right by his main opponent.

36

The Middle East

[June, 1967]

The actions of states are determined not by moral principles and legal commitments but by considerations of interest and power. Moral principles and legal commitments may be invoked to justify a policy arrived at on other grounds, as in the case of Vietnam; they may strengthen or weaken, depending upon the particular situation, the determination with which a certain policy is pursued; but they do not determine the choice among different courses of action. A rational discussion of the Middle Eastern crisis must start with this basic fact, however unpalatable to our moral sensibilities and law-abiding preferences.

It can be said that in a sense the present crisis has its origins in the neglect of that fact in 1957. Israel had then conquered the Sinai Peninsula and was in control of the Straits of Tiran. It gave up what it gained by force of arms in exchange for the recognition of its right of free access to the Gulf of Aqaba through the Straits of Tiran. I remember very vividly the separate conversations I had at that time with two men prominently involved in the negotiations leading to the settlement of the Suez crisis, one an Israeli diplomat and the other a member of the State Department.

382

I warned the Israeli against giving up a tangible advantage for a mere promise, to be or not to be honored according to circumstances. I reminded him of the United Nations Security Council resolution of September 1, 1951, calling on Egypt to lift its embargo on Israeli shipping through the Suez Canal, which Egypt simply disregarded without evoking any reaction from the members of the Security Council, either collectively or severally. I told my American friend that the United States was selling Israel down the river, as it had Great Britain and France before. Who would enforce freedom of navigation for Israel when the chips were down? Both officials replied that the United States had committed itself unequivocally and could be relied upon to honor its commitments.

To put this expectation to the test, though, it is not necessary to raise any questions concerning the public morality of successive Administrations in Washington. The only relevant question is how they have conceived the interests of the United States in the Middle East. The officials responsible for our Middle Eastern policy have consistently favored a pro-Arab orientation, qualified by consideration of the Jewish vote in this country. They have considered Israel a nuisance, which has made it impossible for the United States to pursue a straightforward policy among the Arabs.

In the light of Washington's 1957 commitments, it is significant that during the more than two weeks preceding the outbreak of the war in 1967, the United States saw no way of enforcing the principle of free navigation through the Straits of Tiran. It was even unable, in concert with other maritime powers, to devise a formula reasserting this principle at least in theory. The statements of the Secretary of State were paradigms of evasive ambiguity. Yet on June 5, the spokesman for the Department of State, in an unprofessional lapse from cant, made the position of the department perfectly clear when he said that the United States was "neutral in thought, word, and deed." It is obviously impossible to be committed to the freedom of navigation through the Straits of Tiran and at the same time to be neutral between those who have violated that freedom and those who are trying to restore it.

It should not be forgotten that the very creation of the State of Israel was not the result of a positive act by the West favoring such a state but the result of two embarrassments that could be most conveniently eliminated by allowing it to come into existence: the breakdown of British rule due to the activities of the Israeli underground and the existence of a couple of hundred thousand Jews whom Hitler had not gotten around to exterminating and whom nobody wanted as permanent residents. By dropping the Palestine question into the United Nations' lap, Great Britain extricated itself from a burdensome responsibility and the West provided a piece of real estate where the ships that had sailed from port to port in search of a place to unload could finally dump their human cargo. When President Truman recognized the State of Israel with precipitate haste, he did so not on the intrinsic merits of the case in view of American foreign interests but for emotional reasons and with an eye to the Presidential election of 1948.

A correct assessment of the Middle East situation and our position with regard to it must take into account the sharp cleavage between official pronouncements and popular sympathies, both largely favorable to Israel, and the actual policies pursued by the United States. In the world of the State Department, the Arab states loom infinitely larger than Israel, in terms of geographic location, economic resources, and influence upon the world balance of power. Egypt can close the Suez Canal, the Arab states can withhold their oil from the West and nationalize or even destroy Western installations, and they can move into the Russian or Chinese camp, carrying other Muslim countries with them. Israel has none of these assets. It has only two trumps to play: It is the strongest military power in the Middle East, and it has wide moral support in the West.

Thus, on the one hand, the United States must protect the Arab states against Israel's superior military power by either preventing its use altogether or, if that proves impossible, by preventing its decisive use. On the other hand, the United States must underwrite the continuing existence of Israel as an independent state and give it the support necessary to hold its own against the Arab states. Consequently, the United States has been engaged in a typical balance-of-power policy, supporting both sides up to a point, extending economic and military aid to both, and presiding over a controlled armaments race—all for one purpose: to maintain the existing distribution of power and thereby preserve the territorial *status quo*.

I shall not raise here the question of whether that policy was sound in the past. I shall rather ask whether it is still sound today and likely to be so tomorrow. In the past, the Arab states could be divided into three groupings: those supporting Egypt, such as Syria and Iraq; those opposed to Egypt, such as Saudi Arabia and Jordan; and those controlled by Great Britain, such as the sheikdoms on the Persian Gulf. In that three-cornered configuration, the United States supported the second of the groupings in order to maintain an intra-Arab balance of power, just as it tried to maintain the balance of power between the Arab states and Israel.

These two complex operations could succeed only as long as all participants were willing to abide by the rules of the game. It is obvious that neither Great Britain nor Nasser's Egypt were willing to do so any longer. Great Britain announced that it would liquidate its position in Southern Arabia in 1968, and its control soon began to disintegrate. The war Nasser waged in Yemen was a token of his determination to move into the vacuum Great Britain left behind. Nasser, who, very much like Mussolini, is a clever and daring tactician but an incompetent national leader, would then have controlled not only a large strategically located land mass but also large economic resources in the form of oil. He would have put his Arab enemies at a hopeless disadvantage and would have been on his way toward making himself the master of the Arabian Peninsula, looking to North and East Africa for a further extension of his influence. To what extent the six-day military disaster reduced Egypt's ambitions remains to be seen.

In any event, Egypt will no longer be uncommitted between East and West, straddling the fence and trying to extract maximum advantage from both. As a matter of fact, Egypt has already left that profitable but uncomfortable position. It has become a full-fledged member of the Russian camp, the recipient of massive economic and military aid and the beneficiary of unqualified diplomatic support. This emergence of the Soviet Union as a potent factor in the Arab camp radically changes the context within which U.S. foreign policy in the Middle East has operated in the past. The emergence is primarily the result of the settlement of the Suez crisis of 1956. That settlement, in turn, was a result of the policies pursued by the United States. As I observed in another journal in December, 1956:

Thus it has come about that of the seven main factors of interest and power present in the Middle East—Egypt, the other Arab countries, France, Great Britain, Israel, the Soviet Union, and the United States—four have combined to destroy the power and jeopardize the interests of Great Britain and France and make Egypt and the Soviet Union the predominant powers in the area. That such an outcome is in the interest of Egypt and the Soviet Union is obvious. That it might be supported by the other Arab nations is understandable. That it is against the vital interests of the United States stands to reason, for by helping to destroy the power and jeopardize the interests of Great Britain and France, the United States destroys the power of its strongest and most reliable supporters in the area and in the world at large. And what does it gain in return? It strengthens the power of its implacable enemies, the Soviet Union and Egypt, and the demonstration of its weakness and lack of policy will alienate whatever good will it might have gained temporarily, by its opposition to Great Britain and France, among other Arab countries.

The settlement of 1957 reflected this configuration of interest, power, and policy. I continued in the same article:

The great issue which the Middle East has presented to the world since the end of the Second World War has been the creation of a viable settlement which, if not acceptable to the parties concerned on its merits, could at least be enforced by unchallengeable power. The United Nations endeavored to define such a settlement which none of the parties concerned saw fit to accept on its merits. Unable to support this settlement with unchallengeable power, the United Nations had to limit itself to pointing with regret to repeated violations of the settlement by all concerned. The survival of the settlement at least in a rudimentary form reposed upon a precarious balance of power between Israel and the Arab countries. The emergence of the Soviet Union as a dominant power in the region using primarily Egypt and Syria for its purposes, and the failure of Great Britain, France, and Israel to redress the balance has dramatically reopened the two basic issues: the substance of a viable settlement, and the distribution of power in support of it.

The contribution of the United States to the solution of these issues has been twofold: cooperation with Egypt and the Soviet Union in the destruction of British and French power in the area, and support for a United Nations police force. The first of these contributions, as already pointed out, runs counter to the interests of the United States, since the United Nations police force. The first of these contributions, as already that of Great Britain and France. The political and military vacuum created by the destruction of British and French power in the area . . . has . . . been filled by the power of the enemies not only of Great Britain and France but of the United States as well: Egypt and the Soviet Union. The substance of the settlement is bound to reflect this fact.

The United Nations police force has nothing decisive to contribute to the twin issues of the distribution of power and the substance of a viable settlement. The successful operation of a police force depends upon the presence of two conditions: a legally defined *status quo* capable of defense and deemed worth defending, and an unchallengeable preponderance of the power of the police and the law-abiding members of society over those opposed to the *status quo*. Neither condition is present in the Middle East. The real issue there has not been how to defend an existing *status quo* but how to create one that can be defended and is deemed worth defending by at least some of the parties concerned. The police are able to protect my property because all concerned know what it is and most accept the law defending it as just. In the Middle East, what one nation claims as its own others claim as well, and the conceptions of justice from which the rival claims derive are irreconcilable.

In the absence of even an approximation to a consensus about the legal order which the United Nations police force could defend, that police force would have to be of such magnitude as to be able to impose a settlement upon the parties concerned even in the face of the active opposition of most or all of them. It is hardly necessary to point out that the United Nations police force, as presently constituted, far from being able to impose a settlement on anybody, is politically and militarily at the mercy of Egypt.

Out of the vague and ill-defined functions assigned to it there emerge two major purposes for its presence in Egypt: to provide a thin and fragile screen of respectability behind which Great Britain, France, and Israel can withdraw their troops from Egyptian territory, and to provide a similar screen with which to mask, on the one hand, the triumph of Egypt and the Soviet Union and, on the other, the diplomatic and military impotence of the United States.

In short, the United Nations police force is supposed to perform hardly any of the functions commonly associated with a police force. In its essence it is a polite gesture on the part of the community of nations, a diplomatic device, an elaborate make-believe through which everybody pretends, for however different reasons, not to have witnessed the embarrassing spectacle of the bankruptcy of the foreign policy of the three great leaders of the West.

The fragility of the 1957 settlement has been made manifest by the events of 1967, and so has the persistence of the configuration of interest, power, and policy from which that settlement arose. Listening to the Security Council debate of June 6, 1967, one could not help being struck by the contrast between the purposeful political orientation of the Soviet delegate, seconded by his Bulgarian echo, and the vague and hypocritical mush of most other statements, the American one included. What the Soviet Union wants is clear: to save as much as possible of the power of the Arab states and of its own prestige among them by rolling back the Israeli armies.

But what does the United States want? It is no answer to the question to say that it wants peace. Everybody wants peace if he can get it on his own terms. What are the terms of the United States? A return to the pattern of 1957, however modified, could but restore the fragility to which I pointed in 1956, and such a settlement would sooner or later dissolve again in war. There appear to be only three viable alternatives, which are being discussed in an ascending order of preference.

One is to accept as inevitable the Cold-War rivalry between the United States and the Soviet Union in the Middle East and to use Israel as the spearhead in that rivalry—that is, to do exactly what Moscow and the Arab states have, without good reason, charged the United States is already doing. Under favorable circumstances, this policy might impose the restraints of the Cold War upon the endemic warfare of the Middle East. More likely, it would impart to the Cold War a new dimension of instability and thereby increase the risk of a general conflagration.

The second alternative is to allow the nations concerned to settle their conflicts on the basis of the existing distribution of military power—in other words, to allow the Middle East to find its own equilibrium. For the main source of instability in the Middle East has been the grotesque discrepancy between the political order imposed from the outside and the actual distribution of military power. The discrepancy has been revealed three times in the arbitrament of war, which has twice been nullified by the imposition of a political order that took no cognizance of it. This alternative is predicated upon a genuine hands-off policy on the part of the superpowers, a policy not likely to be achieved in the present stage of the Cold War.

The third alternative is the imposition of a settlement by the United States and the Soviet Union, which will at least approximate the actual distribution of military power and will take the Middle East out of the competition of the Cold War. As I pointed out elsewhere in March, 1958:

> The United States and the Soviet Union have two interests in common in the Middle East. They are both interested in seeing to it that the Middle East does not strike the spark that might ignite a world conflagration; and they are interested in settling the outstanding issues that might cause such a spark. Both interests can be satisfied only through cooperation and are likely to be jeopardized by military competition.

At the moment of this writing there is no indication which of these three alternatives the United States will choose or whether it will choose any of them. The fuzzy pattern of thought and action we have applied to the Middle East for twenty years, in contrast to the single-minded pursuit of its interests by the Soviet Union, makes one wonder. The mood of wonderment is not relieved by the procedures of the United Nations Security Council, which put a premium on fuzziness and the avoidance of any simple, clear-cut political decisions.

37

The Far East

[1968]

Reflecting on our Asian policy, I am reminded of the statement the great sociologist William Graham Sumner made at the beginning of the century: "The amount of superstition is not much changed, but it now attaches to politics, not to religion." Most of what we hear about foreign policy has very little to do with facts that are empirically ascertainable. Most of what we hear is really superstition or it is ideology, that is to say, a special kind of superstition for the purpose of making things appear different from what they actually are.

So talking about our interests in Asia and our policies with regard to Asia, one has first, as it were, to take leave of the current folklore about our foreign policy, which may or may not be correct, in order to find an objective standard by which one can determine the correctness or incorrectness, the soundness or unsoundness, of our foreign policy. One must start with a discussion of the permanent interests that the United States has pursued throughout the world since the beginning of its history.

For there exists in the life of nations, as there does in the life at least of healthy individuals, a consistency of purpose which sets one nation apart from others, which in a sense determines the individuality of one nation as against the others. Thus when one looks at the history of the United States, one realizes that beneath the differences of political parties, political philosophies, and political personalities, there has always existed an impressive consistency concerning the interests that the United States must protect and promote throughout the world.

It is true that this consistency is more obvious in our relations with Europe than in our relations with Asia. But I think even with regard to Asia, underlying all the changes in policy, ideology, parties, and personalities, there exists a basic purpose, an objective standard by which one can assess the individual policies pursued.

If we take a look at Europe for a moment, we realize that from the beginning of the Republic to this day the United States has had one persistent interest, and that is the maintenance or, if need be, the restoration of the balance of power. For the United States realized from the very beginning that its safety, and afterward its hegemonic position in the Western Hemisphere, was predicated upon a distribution of power among the major European powers that would prevent any one of them from seeking adventures and conquests in the Western Hemisphere.

In other words, in view of the security interests of the United States, there had to be a distribution of power in Europe by which one nation would check another nation so that neither of them would find its hands free to pursue imperialistic policies in the Western Hemisphere. Our intervention in the two world wars was clearly motivated by this basic interest. We opposed Germany twice because Germany threatened to become a hegemonial power on the European continent, and once it had achieved that goal, it would then have been free to look to the Western Hemisphere or elsewhere for new conquests. For exactly the same reason, in the immediate aftermath of World War II, we instigated the policy of containment vis-à-vis the Soviet Union. For it was then the Soviet Union that had replaced Germany as the prospective hegemonial power on the European continent.

To this day our whole European policy is based upon this basic assumption, which has determined our European policies from the beginning of our history—that it is in the vital interest of the United States to contain an imperial power, to prevent it from becoming a hegemonial power by gaining ascendancy over the whole European continent and thereby constituting a direct threat to the security of the United States.

Our interest in Asia in a political and military sense did not start before the turn of the century. The Open-Door policy of Secretary of State Hay was originally a commercial policy. It sought to keep China open for the competitive exploitation of all major powers. It sought to prevent any one European or Asian power from gaining control of the enormous power potential of China, acquiring a monopoly for the exploitation of China. But this Open-Door policy very quickly took on a military and political connotation because it dawned upon the American statesmen that any nation, European or Asian, that would add to its power the enormous power potential of China would thereby make itself the prospective master not only of Asia but of the world. Thus the Open-Door policy was transformed into a balance-of-power policy with regard to Asia.

The first clear manifestations of this perennial goal of our Asian policy were the diplomatic moves Theodore Roosevelt made on the occasion of the liquidation of the war between Japan and Russia in 1905. For when, in consequence of that war, Russia was defeated and Japan emerged as the most powerful nation of Asia, it was the purpose of Theodore Roosevelt to limit the increase in Japanese power and to mitigate the consequences of the defeat for Russia in order to maintain the semblance of a balance of power in Asia.

Without going into detail, let me only say that the Washington Conference for the Limitation of Naval Armaments of 1922, which led to the dissolution of the alliance between Great Britain and Japan and the consequent isolation of Japan, again had as its aim the limitation of the ascendant power of Japan. And clearly, when Japan invaded Manchuria in 1931, embarking upon a policy of hegemonial conquest on the mainland of Asia, the United States opposed Japan first in words and from 1938 onward with deeds.

In 1931, Secretary of State Stimson pronounced a doctrine, which came to be known as the Stimson Doctrine, according to which the United States would refuse to recognize acquisitions of territory effectuated by force. It was, of course, directly aimed at the actual and prospective Japanese conquests in Asia. This policy has been called, I think quite correctly, a policy of making faces, because it did not prevent any Japanese soldier from conquering what he intended to conquer. It was a typically moralistic and legalistic pronouncement which had no consequence in the world of facts. But it is indicative of the direction in which American policy actually moved when the threat of Japanese imperialism became unmistakable and when the Japanese Empire began to spill over into Southeast Asia and began to dominate the whole Western Pacific.

It was indeed in the summer of 1941 when Roosevelt and Hull told the Japanese Government that the United States would not countenance any further aggrandizement of Japan that in a sense Pearl

Harbor became inevitable. This is the kernel of truth that can be found in the revisionist historiography, which explains Pearl Harbor in terms of a devilish intrigue by Roosevelt, goading, as it were, the Japanese into attacking Pearl Harbor. This is the typical demonological interpretation of history, the elaboration of a superstition that attributes historical events to the machinations of one devil or a group of devils located in Washington, Moscow, or Peking, according to the preferences of the believer. But it is true—and this is the important point—that the opposition of the Government of the United States to any further expansion of the Japanese empire confronted the Japanese Government with two alternatives: either to give up the aspirations for a still greater Japanese Empire or to go to war with the United States. And Japan chose the latter alternative.

In anticipation of a new balance of power in Asia, following World War II, the United States envisaged a powerful China checking a defeated Japan. In other words, it sought to prevent the rise of a new Japanese imperialism and thereby maintain a distribution of power in Asia that would prevent repetition of the crisis that occurred in the 1930's in consequence of Japanese expansion. It is a measure of the defeat this policy of ours suffered in the Communization of China that in 1949 this whole conception of an Asian balance of power broke down.

For now it was not Japan but China that had to be checked as a would-be imperialist power. And at least immediately it could not be Japan that would check China, because we had just convinced Japan that it ought to embrace pacifism, and the constitution MacArthur persuaded Japan to adopt prohibits regular military forces. Thus it was psychologically, politically, and even militarily impossible to change the expectations for a new balance of power so radically as to support one scale in the balance rather than the other right away. Thus it fell to the United States to take over the position of the counterbalance to Chinese power, which in the natural course of events one would have expected Japan to occupy.

It is at this point that we must take a look at the position and the prospective policies of China. Here, as you shall see in a moment, I must deviate from the folklore about what Chinese foreign policy is all about. It is, of course, a fact of nature that China, with its independence restored, is the most powerful nation on the Asian continent. This has always been so, and it was this tradition, covering a couple of milleniums, which was interrupted only a little more than a century ago when the period of the humiliations of China and the reduction of China to a semicolonial status began.

That this is not only the way in which we *ought* to look at China from an objective point of view, but that it is also the way Asians actually look at China, was forcefully brought home to me when I first went to Asia in 1955. I had gone, of course, with certain literary conceptions of what Asia was all about, and I had read about the contest between India and China for the mind of Asia. I was taken aback by the complete absence of such a contest. The great secular event, which impressed observers from Tokyo to Karachi, was the restoration of China to the position of at least a prospective great power. This was the great event, which Asians beheld with a mixture of awe and admiration. It is this fact that determines today, and is likely to determine tomorrow, the fate of Asia.

We have made a great deal of what we call Chinese imperialism, and we have been wont to quote extreme statements of Chinese statesmen about their world-wide aims, especially Lin Piao's manifesto of the fall of 1965, a kind of geopolitical absurdity, which we took to be the *Mein Kampf* of the Chinese. The Chinese have indeed talked like madmen, they have made the most extravagant claims, and they have from time to time tried to support them with actual policies throughout the world. But they failed. They have become the verbal champions of what they call wars of national liberation. They believe in—they declare themselves at least to believe in—the inevitability of world revolution, which will destroy capitalism. In other words, they have adopted a simplified version of Marxism-Leninism as an ideology. It is indeed an open question whether if they had the power they would not actually make good upon those claims.

But if one compares those ideological claims with China's actual policies in Asia, one realizes that there exists a striking contrast between the ideological claims and the actual policies pursued. Review for a moment the major moves the Communist Government of China has made in its Asian policy since 1949, and you realize that they all have been based not upon Communist ideology but upon the national interests of China, and that they have been supported by Chiang Kai-shek.

Take the frontier with India. No Chinese Government, Chiang Kai-shek's included, has ever recognized the MacMahon Line as the historical, legitimate frontier between India and China. Both Mao Tse-tung and Chiang Kai-shek have made the point that the MacMahon Line was imposed by the British upon a helpless China and that the historical and legitimate boundary runs much farther south than the Mac-Mahon Line. Take the question of Tibet. Both Mao Tse-tung and Chiang Kai-shek have always held to the proposition that Tibet is an integral part of the Chinese Empire, artificially separated from it in 1921 because of the semicolonial status of China, and no other government has ever recognized Tibet as a sovereign nation. I should also say in passing that Chiang Kai-shek had in his Cabinet a Commissioner for Outer Mongolia and Tibet, visibly making the claim that those two territories were an integral part of the Chinese Empire. Take the question of the Yalu frontier between Korea and China. It was not necessary in 1950 to have technical intelligence as to the intentions of China. One needed only to take a look at the map and another brief look at Chinese history in order to realize that no Chinese government able to help itself would countenance the approach of a potentially hostile army to the Yalu. Or take, finally, the question of Taiwan. Both Mao Tse-tung and Chiang Kai-shek agree that Taiwan is an integral part of China. They disagree upon the minor question of who shall govern China, but on the point of Taiwan they are in full agreement.

I remember very vividly a talk I had during the Korean War, after the Chinese had intervened, with a deputy director of the CIA. He said to me—and the statement startled me at the time—that if Chiang Kai-shek were reigning in Peking we would have the same troubles with China we were having then. Reflecting on this startling statement, I realized that it was entirely correct. In other words, the foreign policies Mao Tse-tung has pursued in Asia since 1949 have been the foreign policies of China, not of Communism, and the support, quite ineffectual, that China has given to revolutionary movements in Africa and Latin America has been a kind of marginal enterprise—you may say a tribute to the ideology but not the result of the permanent aspirations of China.

It is of great relevance for our policies in Southeast Asia that for a thousand years China has not tried to expand its influence and power westward and southwestward by military conquest and annexation. It has, rather, relied upon the natural attraction of Chinese civilization. It has relied, and history has shown it could rely, upon the enormous attractiveness its powerful civilization has had for the border states to the west and the southwest. China has traditionally been satisfied with establishing tributary relationships with an adjacent country, such as Cambodia, in which the political identity of that country remained intact. The King had to recognize the suzerainty of the Emperor of China, as according to Chinese theory the sovereigns of all nations had to, and he had to pay annual tribute to Peking. If the King defaulted in such payments, the Chinese would send an army to the capital to see to it that the tributary relations were being restored, and after that the Chinese army would go back to its own country.

We have here a traditional relationship between China and its neighbors to the west and the southwest, which is infinitely more subtle and more complex than the traditional relationships between a powerful nation and weak neighbors with which we are accustomed from the history of the West. So the idea that, for instance, China is poised to conquer Southeast Asia by physical force certainly has support neither in Chinese history nor in the actions the Chinese Government has put into effect since it came to power in 1949. It is much more likely, in view of its relations with Burma and Cambodia today, that what China wants is essentially what China has always wanted, that is, nations on its western and southwestern borders that retain their political identity —or, as we would say today, remain neutral—but recognize that the predominant power on the Asian mainland is China and adapt their policies to this basic fact.

We have pursued with regard to China since 1950 a policy of non-recognition and what I call peripheral military containment. We have looked at China very much as we failed to look at Hitler Germany— that is to say, as a power bent upon world conquest—and the spokesmen for successive administrations have time and again pointed to the similarity between Mao Tse-tung and Hitler, Munich and Vietnam, and so forth. In truth, as I have tried to point out elsewhere, this analogy is utterly mistaken. And even if it were not mistaken, if it were completely true, the policies we have pursued since 1950 have been only temporarily successful because of the weakness of China. For it is utopian to believe that the policy of peripheral military containment —that is to say, the erection of military strong points at the periphery of the Chinese Empire, from Taiwan to Thailand—will have any effect on Chinese expansionism if one assumes that expansionism to be of the traditional Western variety, once China is strong enough to spill over its present frontiers.

In other words, if one wants to contain China (and I am all in favor of containing China) then one has to anticipate not the weak China of today but a strong China, a China of 800 million people in full possession of modern technology. Such a nation will be not only a strong power but the most powerful nation on earth. This being the case, one has to ask oneself what good it will do to have some tens of thousands of American soldiers in South Korea, the Seventh Fleet in the Straits of Taiwan, airfields in Thailand, and half a million men in South Vietnam, if and when China really becomes powerful and tries to do what we assume it will do—after the model of the Soviet Union or Germany —that is, to conquer Asia. Obviously, the peripheral military measures we have taken will be utterly useless and will be swept away in a matter of days. What then will contain China is exactly the same policy that has contained the Soviet Union. And here I refer to what I regard as the correct historical analogy.

The Soviet Union has been successfully contained since 1945, not by the six divisions we were able to put into West Germany but by the overall power of the United States committed to the containment of the Soviet Union. In other words, the six divisions east of the Rhine were nothing more, and this is very important, than a symbolic token of our determination to go to war with the Soviet Union rather than allow it to conquer the rest of Europe. Exactly the same reasoning applies to China. If one assumes that China is bent, once it is strong enough, on conquering Asia, one has to contain it in exactly the way in which the Soviet Union was successfully contained. That is to say, one has to make clear to China that if it should try to conquer, e.g., India, which I regard as a hypothetical and rather unrealistic assumption, then you would have to commit the overall power of the United States to the containment of such a China, and the present policy would certainly be ineffective.

But if my assumption is correct that China does not seek the physical conquest of additional territories, at least to the west or southwest —I am not speaking here of the large territories Russia occupied more than a hundred years ago, which China might well want to recover sooner or later—then the peripheral military containment of China is not only going to be ineffective but is also going to be provocative. For a strong China is not going to countenance a ring of American military bases from Taiwan to Thailand, regardless of its intrinsic intentions with regard to the rest of Asia.

In other words, our present policy leads directly to a military confrontation with China, and that this confrontation has not yet occurred is due not to the goodness of the Chinese but to their weakness. History has allowed us a temporary breathing space during which we can, if we have a mind to, radically change our policies with regard to China and in Asia in general. If you ask what this policy ought to be, let me refer to the famous speech the then Secretary of State Dean Acheson made to the National Press Club in Washington in January 1950. In this speech he outlined the defense perimeter of the United States with regard to Asia as following the island chain from Japan to the Philippines, leaving the mainland of Asia beyond. And this is, in my view, not only good political policy, it is according to the testimony of Generals MacArthur, Eisenhower, and Ridgway, also good military policy.

Those three generals have warned us against a military commitment on the mainland of Asia, which sooner or later is bound to bring us into direct conflict with China on a terrain favorable to the latter. For the Chinese are predominant on land, where our strength in the air and on the sea is minimized. So, let me say in conclusion, the rationale of our Asian policy remains intact—our vital interest in a distribution of power in Asia that will not allow one nation to gain a hegemonial position in Asia. On the other hand, this basic principle, this basic rationale, has been obscured by policies that, under the impact of the Korean War, have led us astray. We have been engaged in a policy of peripheral military containment which not only does not serve the purpose of containment but also entails the risk of a war with China, fought on terms disadvantageous to us, in which our vital interests would not be involved.

38

Vietnam

JOHNSON'S DILEMMA:
THE ALTERNATIVES IN VIETNAM

[May, 1966]

The events of recent months have brought the Vietnam war to a turning point. They have shattered at two places the wall of myths that thus far has protected us from contact with reality. Through two gaping holes reality stares us in the face, reducing to its true fictional dimensions what we mistakenly took to be the facts.

First of all, there is no such thing as a government in Saigon, and there has not been one since Diem's downfall in November, 1963, that we can be committed to assist and defend. South Vietnam is for all practical purposes divided into four autonomous fiefdoms, coterminous with the four corps areas and governed by their respective military commanders, over which the Saigon government exerts at best only the most tenuous control. In the attempt to restore its control over the First Corps area, the Saigon government had to resort to civil war.

The erosion of central control started with Diem's downfall and has been accentuated under Ky. Charles Mohr reported in *The New York Times* of April 15, 1966, that Ky "had virtually no popular support." He has no support from his subordinates either. When he criticized General Thi on March 3 in Danang in front of his staff, the latter asked: "Should we listen to this little man from Saigon?" General Chuan, appointed by Ky as the successor to Thi, expressed himself in favor of the aims of the antigovernment demonstrations, while mildly opposing in words their occurrence, and was forthwith dismissed. General Chieu, the Secretary-General of the military Directory, was seized in Hue by demonstrators and, in a speech over the radio station, duplicated General Chuan's performance. General Dinh, who was appointed to replace Chuan, is reported to be backing a "revolutionary corps" composed of rebellious troops and students. When the government troops approached Danang on May 14, he fled to the house of General Walt, commander of the US Marines. According to *The New York Times* of May 16, he "was relieved of command because of 'disloyalty to the central government.' He was reported to have fled to Hue to join in open rebellion against the Ky regime. In his place, the government appointed Brig. Gen. Huynh Van Cao. . . . General Cao is the fourth man to hold the First Corps post in a little more than two months."

Junior officers of the First Corps issued a declaration of no confidence in the regime. Soldiers, policemen, civil servants—those who are the government in action—demonstrated in the streets against Ky and his associates. Robert Shaplen reports in *The New Yorker* that "one of the highest ranking leaders in the present government remarked to a friend that he did not know who among the 26 members of the present cabinet 'might be Communists'." C. L. Sulzberger summed it all up when he wrote in *The New York Times* of April 20:

For today the North of this tortured land, comprising the heart of ancient Annam, is almost an autonomous third Vietnam: although it is not controlled by Hanoi, it is but tenuously linked to Saigon. Vietnam once comprised three administrative areas—Tonkin, run from Hanoi; Cochin China, run from Saigon; and Annam, run from Hue. At the moment history repeats itself.

The other myth that has been exploded by recent events is the assumption that we are in Vietnam to protect the freedom of a people who want to be protected by us. The recent disturbances have been marked by widespread anti-Americanism aimed at our presence in South Vietnam. That sentiment was openly expressed by the demonstrators and voiced by high military personnel. Buddhist leaders declared their satisfaction with the prospect of our departure. In his speech of April 18 at Hue, the Buddhist leader, Tri Quang, declared, "We are oppressed by two pressures—the Communists and the Americans. In the face of such monopolization and control, we must regain our right of self-determination." It is significant that General Dinh, mentioned above, invited Tri Quang to repeat this speech in Danang. The missteps of Ky, whom President Johnson had compared to Professor Rexford Tugwell, one of the architects of the New Deal (as he had compared Diem to George Washington), were widely blamed on his "American advisers." Workers on American installations went on strike. American were attacked in the streets, and in consequence several hundred American civilians had to be evacuated from Danang and American soldiers ordered off the streets of Vietnamese cities.

The mythological character of these two assumptions—the existence of a government in Saigon, which we are committed to aid and defend, and the existence of a South Vietnamese people eager to be saved by us from Communism—has, of course, been well known to those observers who were capable of looking at the situation objectively, and there is no lack of printed material pointing to it. (On anti-Americanism, for instance, see Jack Langguth's article in *The New York Times Magazine,* August 8, 1965.) Yet the clash between fiction and reality, revealing the fictions for what they are, has come as a shock to many of those who had lived in a self-created world of what Mark Twain has called "conscience-soothing fantasies." In consequence, there has been a sharpening and a radicalization of policy alternatives. There are those who recommend that we take over the government of South Vietnam and pursue the war with new vigor in the South and, more particularly, in the North. Others, such as Senators John Sherman Cooper, Vance Hartke, Jacob Javits, Richard Russell, John Stennis, and many others who want to maintain their anonymity suggest that we leave Vietnam if a duly-elected government requests us to, and some, such as Senators Russell and Stennis, are identified with both recommendations as alternatives.

The chief victim of this new contact with reality is likely to be President Johnson's moderate policy. The recent escalation of air attacks against the North is likely to be a portent of things to come. The mainstay of that moderate policy has been a two-pronged war, seeking pacification in the South and interdiction of supplies and erosion of the will to wage war in the North. Both policies have failed. Pacification, aside from its incompatibility with a war necessarily waged without discrimination between combatants and civilians, requires a government that can keep pacified areas under its control and command the loyalties of the inhabitants. Yet the Saigon government cannot even control its own officials and its cities, which openly defy it and are honeycombed with Viet Cong agents.

The bombing of the North, strictly limited in terms of targets, suffers from the same inner contradiction that Winston Churchill, on the occasion of the League of Nations' sanctions against Italy during the Ethiopian War, put in the following epigram: "First, the Prime Minister had declared that sanctions meant war; secondly, he was resolved that there must be no war; and thirdly, he decided upon sanctions. It was evidently impossible to comply with these three conditions." Similarly, President Johnson knows that effective bombing of North Vietnam conjures up the risk of a military confrontation with China or the Soviet Union or both; he is resolved that there must be no such confrontation, and he has decided upon the bombing of North Vietnam. Thus, in terms of its objective of bringing the Hanoi government to its knees and isolating it from the South, the bombing of North Vietnam, limited by the risk of a military confrontation with China and the Soviet Union, is of necessity an exercise in futility. It is at this point that the advocates of expanded bombing have logic on their side. If you want to test bombing as an instrument of political warfare, you must hurt the enemy until you have reached the limits of his endurance. Where these limits are is, however, a very open question. The experiences of World War II and of the Korean War cast serious doubt upon the effectiveness of even unlimited bombing as an instrument of political warfare. They suggest that under the impact of continuing attacks from the air, the morale of a government and of a people may stiffen rather than disintegrate.

The main issue raised by the suggestion to lift the restraints upon the bombing of North Vietnam, however, transcends the effectiveness of bombing as an instrument of political warfare. It concerns our relations with China and the Soviet Union. Neither of the two major Communist powers can afford to watch the destruction of a "fraternal Socialist country" without giving aid commensurate with the threat. Their leadership of the world Communist movement and, more particularly, their competition for it compel them to escalate their aid in proportion to our escalation of the damage we inflict upon North Vietnam. For China, that compulsion is compounded by its concern for national security. Where such escalation would stop or whether it could be stopped at all is anybody's guess. One can certainly not exclude the possibility that the Soviet Union and China would supply North Vietnam with "volunteers" and "technicians" on a large scale. The possibility of escalation, therefore, includes the risk of a direct military confrontation between the United States, on the one hand, and China or the Soviet Union or both, on the other.

To the question as to whether we ought to take such a risk, no a priori affirmative or negative answer can be given. Rather the answer depends upon the assessment of the stakes in terms of the national interest of the United States, for which such a confrontation would take place. In other words, we are facing here again the much debated question, why are we in Vietnam? If the stakes in Vietnam are as high as the supporters of the war make them out to be, if indeed the credibility of the United States and its prestige as a great power are at issue, if perhaps even the fate of Asia and of the non-Communist world at large will be decided in Vietnam, then the risk of a direct military confrontation with China and the Soviet Union is worth taking. If, on the other hand, the stakes are minor or as mythological as the commitment to a Saigon government and the eagerness of the people of South Vietnam to be defended by us have already proved to be, then the risks we have been taking have been out of all proportion to the interests involved, and by the same token there is no legitimate reason for increasing drastically these risks. This is indeed what I believe.

The stakes by which our continuing presence in Vietnam and the expansion of the war are justified are, in ascending order of plausibility, resistance to aggression, the containment of China, the containment of Communism, and the prestige of the United States.

We must prove, so the first argument runs, that aggression, especially in the form of "wars of national liberation," does not pay by frustrating it in Vietnam. I shall not raise here again the otherwise relevant question as to whether we are facing in South Vietnam foreign aggression in the true sense of the word, and shall limit myself to pointing out that the argument assumes both a uniform pattern of aggression and a causal nexus among different manifestations of it. In this view, there exist, say, five opportunities for aggression throughout the world. By stamping out number one, one is supposed to have gone a long way toward preventing the others from materializing. This is, of course, an utterly dogmatic view of the world, completely oblivious of the concrete circumstances of time and place that determine the success or failure of political action. From this apolitical and unhistorical vantage point, the political processes appear as a series of litigations, the outcome of which is determined, in the manner of a legal precedent, by the outcome of the first.

In truth, each case of "aggression" is *sui generis*, and except in the rare case of a close political and military connection, the outcome of one can at best have only a remote psychological influence upon the outcome of the others. The success of Soviet "aggression" in Hungary and Cuba did not predetermine the success of aggression elsewhere. Neither the failure of the Bay of Pigs invasion nor the success of the intervention in the Dominican Republic provide a precedent for any-thing. What happened in North Vietnam in 1954 and in Laos since 1958 has had no determining effect upon what happened elsewhere in the world, Southeast Asia included; at best, it was one factor among many. Our stake in thwarting "aggression" in South Vietnam must, then, be judged on its own merits, not in the unreal terms of remote determining effects.

That requirement is answered by the argument that we are in South Vietnam in order to contain China. However, the argument is devoid of factual support on three grounds. First, it assumes that the exten-sion of Hanoi's rule to South Vietnam or the establishment of an inde-pendent South Vietnamese Government of which the Viet Cong are a part would be tantamount to the expansion of Chinese influence into South Vietnam. In truth, however, China is being contained in Vietnam, North and South, even under the present most adverse cir-cumstances, not by our military presence but by the innate national-istic hostility of all of Vietnam to China. The expansion of Chinese influence has been stopped by the nationalism of Vietnam, as it has by that of North Korea.

Our military presence in South Vietnam and our war against the North—and this is the second error—far from serving the cause of China's containment, actually serves its expansion; for it weakens that indigenous nationalism which everywhere in the uncommitted world contains the influence of the great powers. By making war upon the Viet Cong and North Vietnam, we are making war upon the most effec-tive instruments of Vietnamese nationalism, and in the measure that we escalate the war, we force them into unwanted dependence upon China. Thus our policy has results exactly opposite to those intended.

Finally, the result would not be different if we were successful in our aim of destroying the power of the Viet Cong in South Vietnam and establishing and maintaining some sort of anti-Communist govern-ment there. Such a government would from the outset be discredited in the eyes of the Vietnamese people, since it could not maintain itself without massive American support. From whatever angle one approaches the problem, one cannot escape the existential incom-patibility between Vietnamese nationalism and a white military pres-ence, however benevolently conceived.

This being the case, the argument that we must remain in Vietnam in order to contain China blends into the one that we must remain in Vietnam in order to contain Communism, regardless of the prefer-ences of the government and people of South Vietnam. By shifting the argument to an abstract ideological plane, we hope at the same time to avoid entanglement in the concrete issues of Vietnamese politics and to put our policy into the framework of a world-wide anti-Communist design. Yet that shift does not allow us to escape the confrontation with Vietnamese nationalism, which is fatal to that argument, too. It is the polycentric nature of modern Communism, as it reveals itself in the extremely peculiar conditions of Vietnam, that defeats the argument.

The interests and policies of China, the Viet Cong, and the Government of North Vietnam are not identical, although they all embrace Communism. North Vietnam seeks the unification of Vietnam under its own auspices; among the Viet Cong, there are strong anti-Northern tendencies; and China wants to reduce all of Vietnam to the position of a satellite. If we want to contain the Communism of the North, we might want to strengthen the Viet Cong's tendencies toward autonomy. If we want to contain the Communism of the Viet Cong, we thereby weaken one element that could have contained the Communism of the North. And by weakening either, we of course weaken the nationalistic barrier that Vietnamese nationalism interposes against the expansion of Chinese power. Thus a doctrinaire anti-Communism makes a rational foreign policy altogether impossible.

Finally, there is the argument that our prestige requires us to stay in Vietnam. It is really the decisive argument with which our policy stands or falls. It is implicit in all the others that have been advanced —commitment, defense of freedom, opposition to aggression, containment—and it has a measure of merit. Our prestige is indeed engaged in Vietnam. However unwise it might have been to engage it and, more particularly, to escalate that engagement drastically in word and deed, the engagement of our prestige is an undeniable fact. We have committed our power, our resolution, and our wisdom to an outcome of the struggle in Vietnam favorable to the interests of the people of South Vietnam, as we see them, and to our own.

However, this threefold commitment of our prestige shows a fatal flaw. Nobody at home or abroad doubts our power to destroy the Viet Cong, be it even through genocide. Nor can anybody doubt our resolution to do so if this were to serve the interests at stake. What many Americans and an overwhelming majority of foreigners doubt is our wisdom in engaging our power and resolution in behalf of patently fictitious assumptions. Is our prestige better served by proving again and again what requires no further proof—that we have power and resolution—or by correcting policies that so many disinterested observers regard as being politically unwise, militarily unprofitable, and morally dubious? Is it really a boon to the prestige of the most powerful nation on earth to be bogged down in a war that it neither is able to win nor can afford to lose? This is the real issue presented by the argument of prestige.

The rational resolution of that issue is rendered difficult by two factors. On the one hand, it requires the admission that the nation's policies have been mistaken and have fallen short of their goals. On the other hand, it requires the admission that the nation's policy-makers have been mistaken and have fallen short of their tasks. Thus the prestige of the nation is inextricably intertwined with the personal prestige of the policy-makers. Certainly this nation is great and successful enough for its prestige to survive the admission of a misadventure. But those who govern us do not seem to think so; for they are lacking in that measure of confidence in themselves, of inner strength, nay, of greatness, which will give a government the courage to step before the nation and the world and say, We have been mistaken. In the short run, the continuation of bankrupt policies, concealed by fictitious assumptions about the real world, promises an easy way out. In the long run, no government can escape the consequences of its mistakes, and the longer it persists in them, the greater will be the loss both to the substance of the national interest and to national and personal prestige.

The arguments in favor of our staying in Vietnam, then, do not bear objective scrutiny. This has always been so. What is new in the present situation is the opportunity it provides to disengage ourselves honorably and with a minimum loss of prestige from a profitless and risky misadventure. According to present plans, there are supposed soon to be elections in South Vietnam. These elections, if they are held at all, are not going to be representative or "free." First, elections can be held only in that part of Vietnam, comprising at best half of the population, that is firmly under the control of the military. Second, the Viet Cong will not be allowed to participate. Third, since the advocacy of a negotiated settlement is a criminal offense in South Vietnam, one very important segment of opinion will have no legitimate outlet. Finally, Vietnam has no real tradition of fair nationwide elections on national issues. Thus the government that administers the elections is likely to win them. It is in our interest to see to it that elections are actually held, and that through them political elements will come to the fore that will seek to liquidate the war through a negotiated settlement. To that end, we ought to work for the establishment of a broadly based coalition government in which war-weary elements of the South Vietnamese population would have a decisive voice.

These political elements conceive of the issue of the war in different terms from ours. While for us the issue is between Communism and freedom, the South Vietnamese, insofar as they are anti-Communist, see it as a contest between a tryanny that at least can boast of having liberated the country from foreign domination, and a succession of tyrannies considered the tool of yet another foreign domination. These Vietnamese tend to equate the Communists and the Americans, and they would like to get rid of the latter while being confident of being able to fend off the former. Tri Quang's statement quoted above is a faithful expression of that position. We may consider this position to be utterly mistaken and contrary to the best interests of the people of South Vietnam as we see them, but if we are not prepared to impose our conception of their interests upon them by seeing to it that they be rather dead than Red, we must accept it as the point of departure for a new American policy of disengagement.

The implementation of such a policy would be subordinated to the policies of the Government of South Vietnam. We would refrain from imposing our conception of our commitments upon such a government and would leave it to them to interpret it. While the ultimate goal of such a policy would be the phased withdrawal of American forces, they would remain during the period of negotiations as a bargaining counter on behalf of the Government of South Vietnam. This political purpose would be served by the continuing American occupation of the cities and coastal bases, which are today the mainstay of American military power in South Vietnam.

The "enclave" policy I advocated in the *Milwaukee Journal* of June 27, 1965, with which more recently Generals James M. Gavin and Matthew B. Ridgway and others have been identified, here finds a new and productive political purpose. This policy would amount to the temporary acceptance on our part of the existing *de facto* division of South Vietnam into the territories controlled by the Viet Cong and by the South Vietnamese military. It would imply the cessation of search-and-destroy forays and of air attacks and the maintenance of the *status quo* in the cities and the military bases at present under anti–Viet Cong control. Since such an arrangement would be intended to last only for the duration of negotiations, it could be expected, and might even be stipulated, that the Viet Cong would abstain from attacks upon, and acts of sabotage within, these enclaves.

We had the opportunity to embark upon such a policy in June, 1965, when some prominent members of the Quat government tried to move toward a negotiated settlement. It was exactly because of this that the Administration allowed that government to be overthrown by General Ky. Is the Administration readier now to grasp that opportunity, especially after two assumptions upon which our present policy is based have been revealed as fictions? It would be rash to give a positive answer to that question.

There have always been government officials of fairly high position who were in favor of such a policy, and many common citizens, journalists and even hawkish senators, under the impact of recent events, have come to see reality at least partially in its true light. Yet the spokesmen of our government, as by conditioned reflex, endeavor to close the holes in the wall of myths with new fictions in order to keep an unwelcome reality out. One spokesman has dismissed the political disintegration of South Vietnam as "growing pains." Another has welcomed the upsurge of anti-Americanism as a healthy sign of nationalism. In contrast, and in the face of all the evidence to the contrary, a third one has discovered that the recent political turmoil in South Vietnam contained "only a very small overlay of anti-Americanism" and basically was "about the kind of government that can most efficiently carry on the war." These inanities are shown up for what they are by a Saigon dispatch of Charles Mohr in *The New York Times* of April 21, quoting an official source to the effect that "there is a very real war-weariness in this country and the Buddhists represent it politically. I don't think there is any doubt that they will try to find ways to end the war."

The melancholy conclusion is inescapable that governments, like men in general, if they are capable of learning at all, learn from experience rather than from rational arguments. A blister burned on a child's finger is more persuasive than parental warnings. Perhaps we have not yet suffered enough for the lessons of Vietnam to sink in. Thus men must die, women must weep, what nature has provided and man has wrought must be destroyed, because governments, blinded by prejudice and paralyzed by pride, learn too slowly for the good of the governed.

ROOM AT THE TOP

[June, 1966]

Stripped of all pretenses, double-talk, and outright lies, two simple and stark choices face the United States in Vietnam. First, on the assumption that in Vietnam the vital interest in the containment of Communism and, more particularly, the credibility of the United States and its prestige as a great power are irrevocably engaged, the

United States can tolerate only one outcome of the war: victory, and never mind that victory is bound to mean the physical destruction of Vietnam, South and North. The other choice assumes that the war is primarily a civil war owing to local conditions, that its global significance is remote, that, far from containing China and Communism, it opens the gates to both by destroying the social fabric of Vietnamese nationalism which is implicably hostile to China. In consequence, the aim of our policy must be to avoid getting more deeply involved in the war and to extricate ourselves from it while minimizing our losses. We can serve that aim in three ways: through the offer of meaningful negotiations, something we have not yet done, appearances to the contrary notwithstanding; through the establishment of a government in Saigon that will initiate such negotiations; or through the *de facto* division of South Vietnam in consequence of the "enclave" policy.

President Johnson appears to believe that there is a third alternative, that of controlled response, which he has chosen. Time and again, in private and in public, he has tried to disarm the advocates of the second alternative by pointing to the differences between his policy and the first alternative, of which the Joint Chiefs of Staff are the most potent advocates. In truth, however, the difference between the two policies is one of degree and not of kind. Seeking a victory that cannot be obtained with the means employed, the President is compelled by the logic of his position to increase the means in order to achieve the ever elusive end. If on a higher level of commitment the end of victory still eludes him, he must increase the commitment still more in that never-ending pursuit of victory. Thus the President is the prisoner of the goal he has set himself. Since he wants victory through war, he must want the means that promise victory. Since he wants victory, he must want escalation. Thus he is compelled to escalate, albeit he is escalating more slowly than the Joint Chiefs would want him to. The persistent escalation of the war during the last fifteen months bears eloquent witness to that compulsion.

These elementary considerations are occasioned by an extraordinarily strange book* by a former special assistant to Presidents Kennedy and Johnson. Mr. Goodwin was one of the most brilliant and responsible members of Kennedy's intellectual circle. He has written here a highly critical account of our Vietnam policies. Yet this account is marred by one monumental lapse of taste at the begin-

---

* Richard N. Goodwin, *Triumph or Tragedy: Reflections on Vietnam* (New York: Random House, 1966).

ning, one monumental abnegation of political judgment at the end, and a number of contradictions throughout.

The book starts out with a tableau that in its intellectual irrelevance and mawkish sentimentality is the kind of journalism one has come to expect from Mr. Joseph Alsop. The tableau juxtaposes two American soldiers, identified by name, stalking the jungles of Vietnam, with the opening, "Eleven thousand miles away, where the Potomac broadens," of the Vietnam hearings of the Senate Committee on Foreign Relations under the chairmanship of "J. William Fulbright, Senator from Arkansas, foe of civil rights, almost Secretary of State, Rhodes Scholar and backwoods politician, hero to some and demagogue to others." Twenty minutes before the opening of the hearings, "while the first curious arrivals were claiming the scarce seats, a grenade flung anonymously through the jungle-fed night had exploded in their bunker. They were dead."

This beginning astounds by its poor taste. More seriously, the end shocks by its abnegation of political judgment. At the end of the original piece, published in *The New Yorker*, the author raises the question as to how it all will end. On the one hand, the author states, "It is easy, and it would be wrong, to be apocalyptic about a conflict that is still so strictly limited and so full of hopeful possibilities for settlement." On the other hand, he quotes "an important politician" to the effect that "he thought that if large-scale war ever comes, it will come not in a burst of Strangelove madness or a Fail-Safe accident but through a long series of acts and decisions, each seemingly reasonable, but which slowly place the great powers in a situation in which they will find it impossible to back down. It will be no one's fault." In a Postscript, the author adds these reflections: "Comment on the appearance of this essay in its original form revealed the ending to be more confusing than I had intended. 'It will be no one's fault,' but it will be the fault of many—leaders, politicians, journalists, men and women in a hundred different occupations in many lands who failed to see clearly, or act wisely, or speak articulately. There will be no act of madness, no single villain on whom to discharge guilt; just the flow of history." The author obviously believes the second ending to be an improvement over the first. Yet both have in common an unwarranted depersonalization of the historical process. In the first version, responsibility cannot be assessed at all; in the second, it is so widely distributed as to be meaningless. Either it is nobody's fault or it is everybody's fault.

The historical truth, as Mr. Goodwin must know, is different. The President is personally in charge of the war in Vietnam, and he cannot escape either blame or praise for what we are doing there. Furthermore, we can pinpoint the sources of advice upon which the President has based certain fateful decisions. We know, for instance, who, from the beginning of President Johnson's tenure in office, has consistently urged the bombing of North Vietnam as a means of bringing the war to a quick, victorious conclusion. We know that this man is today one of the President's principal advisers. We know that if the Secretary of Defense had been as consistently wrong in his calculations as president of the Ford Motor Company as he has been in the conduct of the war in Vietnam, either the Ford Motor Company would have gone broke or he would have been fired.

Hand in hand with this refusal to place political responsibility where it historically belongs goes a tendency to exempt specifically the President from political responsibility. Time and again, the President is quoted approvingly. He gets high marks for having spoken, "with clearer insight," of "the confused nature of this conflict," which after all is not too startling an observation. He gets even higher marks for the "painful, consistent Presidential desire to prevent defeat while resisting proposals to enlarge the conflict beyond what the present seemed to demand." Mr. Goodwin here throws caution to the winds, for the problematical character of the President's policies is wrapped up in the phrase "what the present seemed to demand." What indeed does the present demand? Does it demand escalation, however slowly applied, or does it demand disengagement? Mr. Johnson has given one answer to that question, his critics have given another. In spite of the evidence of ineluctable escalation, Mr. Goodwin finds it "significant, and heartening, that the President has not called for armed triumph. . . . I hope, and I believe, that the President will resist such pressure [for enlargement of the war in the North], for no one is more painfully aware than he of the immense hazards of enlarging the war in the North."

While President Johnson thus emerges as a kind of hero from Mr. Goodwin's analysis and while others, such as the Secretary of Defense, General Maxwell Taylor, Mr. McGeorge Bundy, come in for a fair share of criticism, the villain in Mr. Goodwin's piece is the Secretary of State. I have retained a great affection for Mr. Rusk, and there was a time when I had reason to admire his civic courage and political judgment. I am constrained to find his conduct of affairs as Secretary of State far from admirable; but I find it also inadmissible, in view of the historical evidence, to burden him with a responsibility that is not his. It is true that Mr. Rusk has gotten into the habit of talking in a mechanical, legalistic, and moralistic vein, reminiscent of Mr. Dulles in his weaker moments. It is also true that Mr. Rusk is far from carrying the same responsibility for the actual formation of policy that Dulles carried under Eisenhower. To exonerate the President and blame Rusk is simply to reverse the actual historical roles.

The strangeness of this book is most clearly revealed in its discussion of the substance of our Vietnamese policies. Mr. Goodwin strongly favors the local containment of China on the mainland of Asia. While conceding that "geography is important," he is particularly hostile to the idea that China, like other nations in other continents, might have a legitimate sphere of influence in Asia, from which another power could try to exclude it only at the risk of war. This is of course the Administration position pure and simple, and Mr. Goodwin marshals with considerable skill and eloquence arguments in support of it. At the same time, he demolishes the more extravagant legal claims and historical analogies of the Department of State.

I am here concerned not with the merits of the Administration's and Mr. Goodwin's position but with the inner consistency of Mr. Goodwin's arguments. The military policies that successive Administrations have pursued around the periphery of China derive from the basic position Mr. Goodwin shares with the Administration. The war in Vietnam, seeking to contain Communism and, through it, China, forms an integral part of these military policies. Seeking to contain China and denying it a sphere of influence on the Asian mainland, the Administration is consistent in waging war in Vietnam. Mr. Goodwin, however, is not consistent. After advocating the containment of China and denying it a sphere of influence on the Asian mainland, he concludes that "the bedrock vital interest of the United States . . . is to establish that American military power, once committed to defend another nation, cannot be driven from the field. It is not to guarantee South Vietnam forever against the possibility of a Communist takeover." In consequence, he argues forcefully against "victory" as the objective of the war and calls instead for limited objectives defined as "standoff." These objectives, he thinks, "have largely been accomplished." It is consistent with this definition of our military objectives that Mr. Goodwin opposes a further escalation of the war in the North and even favors "to slow down or halt the present bombing of the North."

Thus Mr. Goodwin, while embracing the basic philosophy of the Administration, ends up advocating the policies of the opposition. Yet, by doing so, he involves himself in two further contradictions. On the one hand, he opposes the pursuit of victory and the extension of the war in the North. On the other hand, he favors the continuation of the war in the South much as the Administration does. He sounds very much like a spokesman for the Administration when he says,

> We are under attack, and withdrawal is impossible and unwise. Here we must commit the forces needed to hold our positions, erode the enemy ranks, and clear guerrillas from the countryside. The objective, however, should be not to crush the Viet Cong in pursuit of an unlikely surrender but slowly to retake key areas of the country, mile by painful mile. Neither manpower nor money nor energy should be spared in the top-priority program of pacification.

It remains a mystery how such an outcome, which is a limited victory rather than a standoff, could be achieved by limiting the war to the South, without stopping the supply of men and materiel coming from the North.

Mr. Goodwin, in accord with the Administration, foresees "a long, bloody, inconclusive war of attrition, until returning sanity brings a political settlement." What form would a political settlement take? Here we are in the presence of still another contradiction. Mr. Goodwin is convinced that no such settlement is possible without the active and independent participation of the Viet Cong. As to the content of such a settlement, he deems it "unlikely we will permit any government to come to power which would inflict on us what some would see as the 'humiliation' of requesting our withdrawal." In the Postscript, however, he sees a chance

> that a new government, while continuing the battle, will begin to make contact and carry on discussions with the leaders of the Viet Cong, preparing the ground for their own negotiated solution. It would be well if we supported a government stable and self-confident enough to carry on this process. If there is to be a negotiated peace, it is more likely to be shaped between Vietnamese on both sides, than among the United States, North Vietnam, and China. Such a result would flow from the almost forgotten truth that this is, or at least should be, an Asian war whose course and resolution is determined by Asians.

If this be the nature of a negotiated settlement, it is virtually inconceivable that the withdrawal of our military forces would not be part of it.

What can account for these contradictions, surprising in an author so superbly equipped? They are the result, so it seems to me, of the author's ambiguous political position. If the author were a detached intellectual he could have written either a straightforward critique or defense of our policies in Vietnam. If the author were a member of the Administration he could have written a straightforward defense of these policies. Yet Mr. Goodwin is neither. On the one hand, he is a former member of this Administration, residually loyal to it, and he may well be a member of another Administration to come. On the other hand, he is an intellectual with a critical mind of his own. The combination of these two positions is bound to be psychologically revealing but politically calamitous.

WHAT SHOULD WE DO NOW?

[August, 1966]

President Johnson is wont to ask the critics of his Vietnam policy, "What would you do if you were in my place?" This is a legitimate question, and it deserves an answer. Having been a consistent critic of our Vietnam policies for more than five years, I have tried to answer that question before and am glad to do so again.

Mr. President, I would say, you must choose between two alternative policies. You can start with the assumption that in Vietnam the credibility of the United States and its prestige as a great power are irrevocably engaged; that the war in Vietnam is a test case for all "wars of national liberation"; and that in consequence, the fate of Asia, and perhaps even of the non-Communist world at large, might well be decided in Vietnam. If you believe this, then you must see the war through to victory. That is to say, you must escalate the war both in the South and in the North by committing what will amount (according to authoritative estimates) to a million American combat troops and by bombing, without restrictions, the industrial and population centers of North Vietnam. By doing this, you will destroy Vietnam, North and South, and risk a military confrontation with China or the Soviet Union or both. Yet these risks are justified by the magnitude of the issues at stake.

This is the policy that the Joint Chiefs of Staff have been advocating and that you have pursued since February, 1965, even though you have been anxious to differentiate your policy from that of the Joint Chiefs. In truth, the difference between the two has been one not of kind but rather of degree. You have been escalating the war at a slower pace than the Joint Chiefs recommended. But escalate you did, and you will continue escalating because the assumptions from which you have started leave you no choice.

There is another policy, Mr. President, which you could and, in my view, should have pursued. This policy assumes that the war is primarily a civil war; that its global significance is remote; that, far from containing China and Communism, it opens the gates to both by destroying the social fabric of Vietnamese nationalism, which is implacably hostile to China; and that, in consequence, the risks we are taking in the pursuit of victory are out of all proportion to the interests at stake.

We should never have gotten involved in this war, but we are deeply involved in it. The aim of our policy must be to avoid getting more deeply involved in it and to extricate ourselves from it while minimizing our losses. Recent events in Vietnam offer us the opportunity of initiating such a new policy of disengagement. These events have clearly demonstrated two facts. The Saigon government is hardly worthy of the name, and the great mass of the people of South Vietnam prefer an end to the war rather than a fight to the finish with the Viet Cong. The two main arguments with which our involvement has been justified have thus been demolished: that we have a commitment to the government of Saigon to assist it in the fight against the Viet Cong; and that the people of South Vietnam want to be saved by us from the Viet Cong—even at the risk of their own destruction. The prospect of elections to be held in South Vietnam provides us with the chance to use these new facts for the initiation of a new policy of disengagement. Such a policy would proceed on two fronts, the political and the military.

Politically, we ought to work for the achievement of four goals.

1. We must promote the establishment of a broadly based government in which the elements seeking an end to the war would have decisive influence. This government would have the task of organizing elections for a constituent assembly and a legislature at an early date. It must be recognized that such elections will be neither representative nor "free." The group that organizes them is likely to win them. Hence, the crucial importance of the composition of the government presiding over the elections.

2. We must see to it that the government that emerges from these elections will negotiate with the Viet Cong for a *modus vivendi*. Such a settlement would no doubt increase the risk of a complete takeover by the Viet Cong. However, it is quite possible to visualize a coalition government under which different sections of the country, after

the model of the Laotian settlement, would be governed by different factions. One can even visualize a South Vietnamese Government that would be anxious to maintain its independence vis-à-vis the North.

3. We should put United States military forces stationed in South Vietnam at the disposal of the government that emerges from the elections, to be used as bargaining counters in negotiations with the Viet Cong. In other words, we would honor our commitments and would leave it to the South Vietnamese Government to interpret them in order to bring the war to an end.

4. Our ultimate goal would be the withdrawal of our armed forces from South Vietnam. Such a withdrawal would be coordinated with the progress of negotiations between the Government of South Vietnam and the Viet Cong. Our military forces would be gradually withdrawn, and our military presence would always by commensurate with the political purposes it is intended to serve.

Pending such withdrawal, our military policy would come in three parts:

1. We would stop both the bombing of North Vietnam and the search-and-destroy operations in South Vietnam that seek to kill the Viet Cong and occupy territory controlled by them. For the continuation of such operations in the North and South is compatible only with a policy aiming at victory, not with one seeking a negotiated settlement among the Vietnamese factions.

2. We would hold the cities and coastal enclaves that we and the South Vietnamese military now control. That is to say, we would be satisfied with a *de facto* division of South Vietnam.

3. We would expect the Viet Cong to reciprocate by ceasing attacks upon the perimeter of our positions and by stopping sabotage within them. It can be assumed that we and the Viet Cong have a reciprocal interest in maintaining the military *status quo* pending negotiations.

The policy here advocated, Mr. President, is anathema to the men who advise you. Yet it has always been supported by officials fairly high in your Administration. It now has the support of a number of senators who in the past have been "hawks" rather than "doves." You, Mr. President, will have to decide whether the present policy—morally dubious, militarily hopeless and risky, politically aimless and counterproductive—shall be continued or whether a better policy shall take its place. You aspire to be a great President. Whether you remain the prisoner of past mistakes or have the courage to correct them will be the test of your greatness.

THE DOCTRINE OF WAR WITHOUT END

[November, 1968]

It has become fashionable among scholars, retired public officials, and politicians to admit that our involvement in Vietnam has not been a success. It has also become fashionable to turn from this admission of failure to the post-Vietnam future without pausing to ask what accounts for that failure. It is more important, so it is argued, to end the war than to discover what led us into it. To bury the past and get ready for the future is taken as a manifestation of both positive and patriotic thinking. In many cases this attitude is no doubt self-serving, for the Vietnam ship is obviously sinking, and in consequence many members of the crew jump overboard and frantically swim to shore, making it appear that either they were never aboard or were only doubting and unwilling mates. Yet on closer examination this attitude reveals itself as an organic element in the political pathology that is responsible for the disaster of Vietnam.

When a government composed of intelligent and responsible men embarks upon a course of action that is utterly at variance with what the national interest requires and is bound to end in failure, it is impossible to attribute such persistence in error to an accident of personality or circumstances. Nor is it possible to make such an attribution when the preponderant weight of public opinion—political, expert, and lay—for years supports such a mistaken course of action. When a nation allows itself to be misgoverned in such a flagrant fashion, there must be something essentially wrong in its intellectual, moral, and political constitution. To lay bare what is wrong is not an idle exercise in ex post facto fault-finding. Rather it is an act of public purification and rectification. If it is not performed and accepted by government and people alike, faults, undiscovered and uncorrected, are bound to call forth new disasters, likely to be different from the one in Vietnam but just as detrimental.

Such an examination of the roots of the disaster promises to be particularly illuminating when the call either to win the war or to lift its burden emanates from men of such eminence as General Maxwell Taylor, former Chief of Staff of the United States Army and Chairman of the Joint Chiefs of Staff, former Ambassador to South Vietnam, and special consultant to a succession of Presidents, and Mr. Mc-

George Bundy, one of the chief architects of our Vietnam policy.

General Taylor's book, *Responsibility and Response,** presents a telling example of what one might call "the Wheeler Syndrome." A few years ago, a high official of our government told me that whenever he called the attention of General Wheeler, Chairman of the Joint Chiefs of Staff, to the new polycentric character of the Communist world he would agree, but that there was no trace of that recognition to be found in his policy recommendations.

General Taylor is one of the most brilliant and learned men the armed services of the United States have produced. *The Uncertain Trumpet* was indeed an important contribution to military theory; it paved the way for the Kennedy-McNamara strategy of flexible response. This book, however, will be remembered only as an embarrassment. For its reasoning is casual, vague, and contradictory; its task, to transform the lessons of Vietnam into a doctrine of countering "wars of liberation," remains unachieved.

The author sets out to reconcile the dogma of Communist aggression with the realities of the contemporary world. The first sentence sets the intellectual tone for the whole book: "One of the most significant political developments in this decade has been the progressive dissolution of the bipolar nuclear confrontation of the United States and its allies with the Sino-Soviet Communist bloc and its replacement by a multipolar power relationship." Two disparate phenomena are here obviously confused: nuclear bipolarity, which still exists and continues to cast its shadow over world politics, and the transformation of the two monolithic blocs into polycentric associations.

The concept of "multipolarity" is General Taylor's tribute to the reality of polycentrism. General Taylor goes so far as to admit that "Peking and Moscow are not the only troublemakers capable of interfering with the pursuit of American objectives about the world" and that "the purposes of the leadership in Hanoi are not always identical with those of Peking," and he assigns to Castro's Cuba a permanent place "on our list of potential troublemakers." Defining the "troublemakers," he states that "most of them are presently Communist, but this is not an essential characteristic."

Yet once these concessions to empirical reality have been made, the author proceeds as though they did not exist. What General Taylor has in mind is not the dissolution of the Communist bloc into its national components but rather its splitting up into "the Soviet bloc

* Maxwell D. Taylor, *Responsibility and Response* (New York: Harper & Row, 1967).

and the Chinese bloc." We are confronted not with individual nations, to be dealt with on their merits, but with two blocs instead of one. From page seven onward, we hear of nothing but "Communist expansion," "Communist intention," "Communist attitude," and so forth. All cases of what the author calls "subversive aggression" show the same pattern attributable to Communism. "We recognized it [the guerrilla war in South Vietnam] as the same tactic employed in the civil war in Greece, in the Huk insurrection in the Philippines, in the guerrilla warfare in Malaya, and during parts of the Chinese civil war." Thus the dogma of Communist uniformity, which is at the very least a blood relation of the Communist monolith, if not just a particular aspect of it, obliterates the awareness of empirical diversities.

General Taylor assigns to the United States the task of frustrating "wars of liberation." He recognizes that such a war

> is essentially a threat to weak governments and thrives on poverty, social injustice, and all similar conditions which encourage popular discontent. Since these are conditions present in many if not most of the emerging countries, we are evidently talking about a very large number of possible target countries where a "War of Liberation" may be undertaken under conditions favorable to its success.

As far as the author is concerned, the ubiquity of these conditions conducive to revolution casts no doubt upon the dogmatic assumption that these revolutions must be attributed to the ubiquity of the Communist conspiracy. However, the author draws another conclusion from this empirical statement: "We need to be selective in opposing these revolutions. That selectivity should be based upon an enlightened appreciation of the nature of our essential interests." Here are some of the standards we ought to apply:

> There may be good reasons to use our resources to resist a troublemaking power which commits aggression against a weak and friendly state if the subversion of that state would be a significant gain to the troublemaker or a significant loss to us. Even then, we should have a reasonably accurate and encouraging estimate of the chances of success before we act. We cannot afford to stake our world standing on a lost cause or on one with unduly high risks of failure.
>
> This thought leads to a third lesson, the degree to which the effectiveness of the United States in opposing a troublemaker is limited by the character of the local government which we wish to assist. We have learned from our Vietnam experience how great a disadvantage it is to work with an ineffective local government unable to utilize much of our assistance. . . .

The obvious lesson of this experience, I believe, is the need to take careful account of the political situation within a country before the United States commits itself to assist it. We must be sure that there are reasonably able leaders with whom we can work, who are cooperative, and who have an attitude like our own toward the problems which we are to resolve in common. We should be slow to rush into situations where there is no likelihood of governmental stability for the indefinite future. Some of the emerging countries we have been considering, in Africa for example, are in such a state of ferment that it is unreasonable to expect a leadership to emerge in the short run which will be capable of staying in power long enough to use effectively such aid as we might be inclined to provide. We must be philosophical and recognize that turbulence will be a rule for a long time in a large number of these new countries and be slow to back individuals and parties which, at best, are poor bets in the short term.

It seems to follow inevitably from this empirical analysis, if it is as sound as I think it is, that our intervention in Vietnam does not meet these standards. However, this is not General Taylor's conclusion.

At this point, I have often been asked whether, in the light of the demonstrated political weakness of South Vietnam, I now thought that the United States had made a mistake in 1954 in becoming involved in the defense of that country and in continuing to support it in the subsequent years. I have no hesitancy in saying that I believe our government did the right thing.

We must remain involved in South Vietnam "until we have exposed the myth of the invincibility of the 'War of Liberation' and have assured the independence of South Vietnam." If the principle of selectivity supports our intervention in Vietnam, is there any intervention against a "war of national liberation" that could not be so supported? Thus dogma triumphs again over reality, and selective intervention becomes identical with indiscriminate intervention.

This conflict between dogma and reality not only spoils General Taylor's arguments, it also impairs his understanding of reality and involves him in blatant contradictions and incongruities. In defense of the bombing of North Vietnam, General Taylor can say on page twenty-six: "The South Vietnamese have no illusions as to who is hurting them—it is Hanoi and the Hanoi leadership." Here we are in the presence of the dogma of "Communist subversive aggression." On page thirty-eight, he can argue against the advocates of all-out bombing of North Vietnam in these realistic terms:

That is the opposite of the get-out alternative and I would say almost equally unacceptable. I often ask the proponents of this alternative what would happen if Hanoi were suddenly to disappear. Suppose everything of value in the North were destroyed; we would still have over 200,000 armed guerrillas in South Vietnam who would still have to be accounted for in some way. For food they could live off the land without supplies from the North. If they avoided contact with large military forces, they could husband their weapons and ammunition stocks and maintain for a long time a low level of sustained depredations and terrorist activity. If they were determined to carry on the war, if their morale did not collapse at this disaster in the North, they could conceivably remain in action for the next ten years, or the next twenty years, and we might still be tied down by this vast guerrilla force.

Finally, dogma triumphs without any reference to reality with this dismissal of the risk of escalation:

I personally have never felt that this danger of possible escalation is something that should make us timid or reluctant to do the right things. There seems to be a conclusion, borne out in our past relations with the Communist world, that one never provokes Communists to do anything—they will do what suits their purpose in their own time, when it is to their interest. They will not withhold doing us a bad turn because we are nice to them. Hence, when one expresses concern about attacks by the Viet Cong on our shipping at Saigon if we mine the port of Haiphong, it carries no weight with me, because the Viet Cong have been trying to damage the port of Saigon for years and have recurrently attacked shipping there. They will continue to do so regardless of what we do to Haiphong.

There is nothing unpleasant in the South that the Viet Cong can do which they have not already done. They have no reserve bag of dirty tricks which they are holding back. As time goes on, they may find ways to do worse things to us, but their action will not be delayed because they have had any reluctance to use all their resources against us. Hence, I would not worry too much about "provoking" them.

Here the dogma conceives of the enemy no longer as a human being reacting psychologically as you and I would react, but as a kind of static monster doing evil to the full, like a dragon spewing fire, regardless of what we are doing. What is disturbing is not that such things can be said but that a man of real substance can say them without being aware of their absurdity.

Mr. Bundy's address of October 12, 1968, at DePauw University is distinguished from other "revisionist" documents by the characteristic self-assurance with which it defends the decisions of 1965 to enter the war in full force while asking for their revision now. Mr. Bundy offers us ten basic propositions:

1. The avoidance of defeat in Southeast Asia justifies the 1965 decision "to stand and fight in South Vietnam."
2. This decision has been "validated" by events in the area.
3. We do not need to lose what we have gained by a new course of action.
4. "The right goal now is to lift the burden of this war as we now know it."
5. We cannot "continue with annual costs of $30 billion and an annual rate of sacrifice of more than 10,000 American lives," for this burden prevents us from moving "forward effectively with other great national tasks," nor can we "accept the increasing bitterness and polarization of our people."
6. "It is not right for Asia that it [the war] should go on as it is going, and the people of our own country simply will not support the current level of cost and sacrifice for another period of years."
7. We cannot expect a military solution, since the American forces have been able to "prevent defeat" but not to "produce victory." Thus only two alternatives are left: a negotiated settlement or "a gradual but substantial reduction in the level of our own military effort there."
8. "We should be ready for a compromise well short of victory in which the eventual outcome would remain to be settled by the people of South Vietnam." In the absence of such a compromise, our government "must decide that it will steadily, systematically and substantially reduce the number of American casualties, the number of Americans in Vietnam, and the dollar cost of the war." But we will "keep at least 100,000 troops in place for years." These changes are "possible" and will not jeopardize "the basic purpose of our forces in Vietnam—the purpose of preventing defeat."
9. The reduced American effort "can stimulate increased self-reliance" among the determined anti-Communists in South Vietnam.
10. This program offers a "way down—but not surely the way out. . . . Now we should cut back—but we need not and should not give up."

For the Administrations Mr. Bundy has served, the crucial issue has always been: Who shall govern South Vietnam, the Communists or their opponents? This issue can be interpreted in two different ways, one narrow and short-range, the other broad and long-range. It can mean the prevention of a Communist takeover, or it can mean, in the words of President Johnson, favorably quoted by Mr. Bundy on another occasion, "the independence of South Vietnam and its freedom from attack," that is, the defeat of the Viet Cong and of North Vietnam. If one takes the former interpretation as the measure of our success or failure, then the United States has been successful; for it has prevented the Communist takeover of the Government of South Vietnam, which appeared to be imminent at the beginning of 1965. Judged by the latter interpretation, the United States has failed; for South Vietnam's "freedom from attack" has not been achieved, and its "independence" can be maintained only through the presence of half a million American troops. In other words, the distribution of military and political power that threatened the existence of the Saigon government at the beginning of 1965 still threatens it today. If we were to reduce our military presence to the level of four years ago, the Saigon government could not maintain itself in power. Our massive intervention has not decisively affected the over-all distribution of military and political power unfavorable to the Saigon government, which distribution our intervention was intended to reverse.

By espousing the narrow interpretation of our goal, Mr. Bundy can justify our intervention and claim success for it. But by doing this, he cannot justify the kind of war we choose to fight, and at the same time advocate the reduction of our armed presence to a minimum of 100,000 men. For if 100,000 men will be sufficient to keep the Saigon government in power in the near future, why weren't they sufficient at the beginning of 1965 when hardly any organized units of Either we have wasted, during the last four years, our human and material resources on a monstrous scale in order to achieve a result that could have been achieved much more cheaply, or the 100,000 men whose presence Mr. Bundy ultimately envisages in South Vietnam will not be sufficient to keep the Saigon government in power. Mr. Bundy's argument either damns the war as we fought it as an appalling extravaganza or prepares us for defeat.

In truth, it is not only Mr. Bundy's logic that is at fault, but also his historical recollection. The whole conduct of the war—search and destroy, pacification, the massive bombing of Vietnam, North and South—is of course intelligible only if one assumes the broad interpretation of our goal. That interpretation was indeed the one supported by our policy-makers, Mr. Bundy included, who in 1965 spoke of "victory" and not the mere prevention of defeat, before the inevitability of failure had become obvious, albeit not acceptable, even to President Johnson. What the Administration wanted until recently, and sacrificed annually 10,000 American lives (and uncounted Vietnamese lives) and spent $30 billion a year to get, was not to keep the Saigon government just barely in power but to win the civil war for the Saigon government by destroying the Viet Cong as an organized political and military force. By now making it appear that what we wanted all along was nothing more than the avoidance of defeat, one can offer the avoidance of defeat as the equivalent of victory.

Mr. Bundy's position is also vulnerable to pragmatic considerations. The gradual reduction of the American presence to a minimum of 100,000 men is predicated upon two assumptions, both dubious in the extreme: that the Vietnamese, North and South, will not take advantage of our greatly weakened military and political position in order to expel the hated foreigner from the national soil, and that the Saigon government can substitute its own strength for that to be withdrawn by the United States. The later expectation has been the mirage we have followed into the Vietnamese jungles since 1965, however obvious it should have been from the outset that a government overwhelmingly composed of men who sided with the French against their own people, supported in the main by the landowners and the urban middle class, infiltrated on a massive scale by the Viet Cong, and able to govern only with the bayonets of a foreign army of occupation, simply cannot compete with Ho Chi Minh and the Viet Cong for the allegiance of the people of South Vietnam. No amount of American advice, money, and weapons has been able to overcome that handicap, and none is likely to do so.

But regardless of these prospects, will the Viet Cong and the North Vietnamese, committed as they are to national liberation, allow an American army of 100,000 men to install itself in South Vietnam in virtual permanence, withholding control of military bases and major cities from them? If they do not and we don't escalate our military effort again, either, at best, the war will go on indefinitely and South Vietnam will become an American Ireland, or, at worst, America will be defeated. Even under the best of circumstances, the wound that the Vietnam war has opened in the body politic of America will then not be closed but only narrowed; the life blood of America will continue to flow out of it, but in smaller driblets; and the infection of the body politic will spread more slowly, but as inexorably as before. Mr. Bundy's design stands in the same relation to President Johnson's conduct of the war as that conduct does to

Goldwater's plans of 1964. As Johnson did more gradually what Goldwater wanted to do, till the futility of the enterprise became obvious
to all, so—in the teeth of the obviousness of that futility—Mr.
Bundy suggests doing on a lower level of military effort what Johnson
has been doing. In other words, he approaches the future with the
same modes of thought and action that proved so disastrous in the
past; only he does so in a lower key.

What worries Mr. Bundy really is not the futility of the war but
its cost and the unwillingness of the American people to continue
bearing that cost. It is primarily for this reason that he advocates the
de-escalation of the war. That argument raises a fundamental philosophic issue. If our waging war in Vietnam serves a vital national interest, as Mr. Bundy still maintains, is it permissible to support this
interest with less than wholehearted effort, let alone jeopardize it,
in order to satisfy the aspirations for reform and mollify popular moods
at home? These reforms will avail us nothing and the popularity of
the government will be short-lived if in consequence of the de-escalation of the war the security of the United States is imperiled. If
the people are unwilling to bear the burdens the security of the country demands and if the government is unable to impose them, then
America will not, and ought not to, remain a great power. A nation
that refuses to accept the primacy of foreign policy over domestic
politics has doomed itself.

This is the conclusion to which Mr. Bundy should have been led
by his premise, and that was indeed the conclusion he drew in January, 1967, when he wrote that "retreat in Vietnam is not the
road forward at home." He now maintains that partial retreat in
Vietnam—from victory to the defense of the Saigon government—is
the road forward at home. Let me say bluntly that it is the road to
disaster on the installment plan at home and abroad. At best, it will
not liquidate the war but only draw it out indefinitely on a lower
level of military effort. In consequence, it will do nothing to relieve
the malaise at home but will only deepen it by calling forth expectations sure to be disappointed. Mr. Bundy now neglects what he once
perfectly understood and put into practice, viz., that the narrow and
broad interpretations of the American objective in Vietnam—the prevention of defeat and victory—are interconnected: In the long run
the former cannot be had without the latter, and decreasing our
military effort without complimentary efforts on the part of our friends
and enemies must greatly diminish the chances for preventing defeat.

Mr. Bundy's plan suffers from the same disability that frustrated
the policies pursued by the Administration of which he was a mem-

ber: to try to gain a national objective without taking the risks and bringing the sacrifices necessary to achieve it, to will an end without willing the means. From 1965 to March 31, 1968, we wanted to defeat the Viet Cong, but not at the risk of war with the Soviet Union or China nor through the commitment of a million American men, which military authorities then deemed necessary to achieve that purpose. What Mr. Bundy now proposes partakes of the same defective mode of thought, compounded by an even greater disproportion between means and ends. Instead of preventing the Communists from taking over the Government of South Vietnam by defeating them, we are told that we shall achieve that goal by defending the Saigon government with a drastically reduced military effort. What Mr. Bundy has never understood and what he cannot now admit without discrediting the policies he devised and supported so prominently and defended so strongly in the past is the untenability of the basic premise upon which our Vietnam policy, past and present, as well as Mr. Bundy's proposal, rest: that our military intervention was justified in 1965 because a vital national interest was at stake. If you believe that you cannot liquidate the war without victory, then you cannot liquidate it at all, since victory is not in sight. If, on the other hand, you believe that our military intervention in 1965 was a blunder and that, once the blunder had been committed, the issue before us was not how to continue the war to victory but how to liquidate it as quickly and advantageously as possible, then you have no real problem in liquidating it now. You will simply see to it that a genuinely civilian government is established in Saigon, which inevitably will make it its first order of business to come to an understanding with the Viet Cong. That government would use the presence of our troops as a bargaining counter in the negotiations, after the completion of which it would thank us for our assistance and bid us farewell. The terms of settlement would be none of our business, and we could not be blamed for them.

Things are naturally more complicated for men who bear the responsibility for this misadventure and the evils, domestic and international, attendant to it. They cannot be expected to liquidate the war, nor is their counsel, so false in the past, worth listening to now. The best they can do for the country that they have served so ill is to allow wiser men to try to repair the damage they have caused. That is also the best they can do for themselves. As a latin proverb has it: *Si tacuisses, philosophus mansisses*, which, very freely translated, would read: If you had only kept silent, you might still pass for a statesman.

39

The Rhetoric of Nixon's Foreign Policy

[March, 1970]

When I approached the 119 single-spaced pages, containing 40,000 words, of *United States Foreign Policy for the 1970's*, the President's report to Congress on the state of the world, I expected the kind of *tour d'horizon*, taking up one country after the other in geographic sequence, with which the foreign ministers of Great Britain and France annually bore their parliaments. Long stretches of this document are boring, all right, but in a different way. It resembles nothing so much as those lesser papal encyclicals that pronounce a series of unexceptionable abstract principles, leaving practical judgment and action where they found them. There is, however, one difference: The Pope quotes Scripture and the pronouncements of his predecessors in support of these principles; Mr. Nixon quotes himself thirty-one times directly, if my count is correct, and innumerable times by reference to a previous statement. The tone is one of magisterial authority and imperial decisiveness. It conjures up the image of the great leader fully informed, unfailing in judgment, acting and ready to act again. It begins with "When I took office . . ." and the first person singular appears at frequent intervals ("I have often reflected on the meaning of 'peace' . . ."); it ends with a repetition in full of

426

the lengthy toast Mr. Nixon offered to the Acting President of India on July 31, 1969. It is far from modest in defining its task: "This first annual report on U.S. foreign policy is more than a record of one year. It is this Administration's statement of a new approach to foreign policy, to match a new era of international relations."

This byzantinism, individual and collective, the product of the invisible hand of the public relations expert, must put the reader off. So does the excessive vagueness and blandness of the document. In a certain measure, these faults are inevitable in a document of this sort; for in foreign policy, as in other spheres of human action, there is a gap between general principles and concrete issues, which cannot be filled by abstract reasoning but only by concrete action informed by those principles. More particularly, a philosophy that retreats from the grandiose and global into a more restrained and cautious stance is hard put to express itself in slogans equal in flamboyance, say, to "rollback," "liberation," "massive retaliation," the world-wide "Great Society." Even so, there is more vagueness here than appears to be inevitable.

Take the "concept of partnership" that "guides our relations with all friendly nations" and is more specifically applied to our relations with the nations of Asia and Europe. This concept, which was first used by John F. Kennedy in this context, does not elucidate the issues of our relations with our allies; it rather evades them by glossing them over with an attractive phrase. If two partners see eye to eye on the issues concerning them, there is no problem. If they don't, invocation of their partnership will not help them. Partnership is predicated upon the identity of interests and policies; without such identity there can be no partnership. If the interests and policies of France and the United States were identical, we would be partners in fact. In the measure that such identity is lacking, there is no partnership, and it cannot be restored by invoking its name. It can be restored only through a political effort seeking to harmonize divergent interests and policies.

If the concept of partnership evades the political issues, the "Nixon Doctrine" buries them, both in the obvious and in evasive ambiguity. "This is the message," the document announces grandly "of the doctrine I announced at Guam—the 'Nixon Doctrine.' Its central thesis is that the United States will participate in the defense and development of allies and friends, but that America cannot—and will not— conceive *all* the plans, design *all* the programs, execute *all* the decisions and undertake *all* the defense of the free nations of the world. We will help where it makes a real difference and is considered in our interest."

The first sentence states what has been the policy of the United States all along. The United States has never conceived "*all* the plans,"

designed *"all* the programs," executed *"all* the decisions," and undertaken *"all* the defense of the free nations of the world." Messrs. Diem
and Thieu, to give only one example, have had their share, for better
or for worse, in planning, designing, executing, and defending. That
we should do everything has never been the issue. The real issue is,
under what conditions shall we intervene with military force? Mr.
Nixon announces, "where it makes a real difference and is considered
in our interest." That statement covers Vietnam and Laos. And it
would cover Cuba and Brazil, as well as any other country one can
think of. Nobody, not even Mr. Dulles, or Mr. Nixon in 1954, has ever
suggested that we ought to intervene where intervention would make
"no real difference" and would not be considered "in our interest."
The crucial question raised by the experience of Vietnam—Where do
our real interests lie when it comes to military intervention?—is here
not so much answered as assumed to be answered by restating it in
assertive form.

This evasive ambiguity carries over into the discussion of our commitments. It has been argued that the United States is overcommitted
and must pare down its commitments to the level of its power and
interests. But is this Mr. Nixon's view? On the one hand, Mr. Nixon
declares that we must "maintain our commitments," and he comes
out against "giving up our friends or letting down our allies." On the
other hand, he finds it

> misleading, moreover, to pose the fundamental question so largely in
> terms of commitments. Our objective, in the first instance, is to support
> our *interests* over the long run with a sound foreign policy. The more
> that policy is based on a realistic assessment of our and others' interests,
> the more effective our role in the world can be. We are not involved in
> the world because we have commitments; we have commitments because
> we are involved. Our interests must shape our commitments, rather than
> the other way around.

The syllogism is patently specious. "Involved" is here obviously a
synonym for "having interests." Nobody will deny that we ought to
support our "involvements," that is, our "interests" with commitments
appropriate to them. But what about "commitments" entered into
without being appropriately grounded in our "interests," which then
create "involvements" of their own? This is the issue to which Vietnam
has given rise, but the document does not address itself to it.

While we must keep our present commitments, "we will view new
commitments in the light of a careful assessment of our own national

interests and those of other countries, of the specific threats to those interests and of our capacity to counter those threats at an acceptable risk and cost." This is sound thinking indeed, but it does not answer the question why it should not apply to present commitments as well.

What is first of all remarkable in a positive sense about this document is its tone and general philosophy. The world has indeed changed since John Foster Dulles was Secretary of State and Richard M. Nixon Vice President, and so has America's outlook upon the world. The ideological polemic, which still set the tone of official pronouncements on foreign policy in the 1960's, has virtually disappeared: "Then, the slogans formed in the past century were the ideological accessories of the intellectual debate. Today, the 'isms' have lost their vitality—indeed the restlessness of youth on both sides of the dividing line testifies to the need for a new idealism and deeper purposes."

What there is polemical in this document is subdued and presented almost by indirection. Thus, after recognizing the polycentric character of Communism, manifesting itself not only in diversity but also in hostility within the Communist camp, it scores, by way of illustration, a telling polemic point: "The only times the Soviet Union has used the Red Army since World War II have been against its own allies —in East Germany in 1953, in Hungary in 1956, and in Czechoslovakia in 1968." As concerns the Middle East, it mitigates its warning to the Soviet Union by couching what is an established fact in conditional terms: "But the United States would view any effort by the Soviet Union to seek predominance in the Middle East as a matter of grave concern."

When it deals with the concrete issues of American foreign policy, the document is curiously uneven. Sometimes, it is brilliant, penetrating, and informative. The National Security Council system, the Middle East, and arms control deserve to be singled out. The discussion of the National Security Council system presents an impressive picture of a division of labor in order to achieve competent determination of facts and systematic planning on the interagency level. It is the intended result to make the President aware of a full range of options and thus to enable him to render a responsible decision. That method of Presidential decision-making deviates drastically from that of Mr. Nixon's three immediate predecessors, and there is in the document more than a trace of implied criticism of Mr. Eisenhower's committee system:

I do not believe that Presidential leadership consists merely in ratifying a consensus reached among departments and agencies. The President bears the constitutional responsibility of making the judgments and decisions that form our policy. . . . I refuse to be confronted with a bureaucratic consensus that leaves me no options but acceptance or rejection and that gives me no way of knowing what alternatives exist.

The discussion of the Middle East provides an excellent analysis of the respective positions of the parties, pointing to their irreconcilable differences as well as to the choices open to the involved outside powers. What the document has to say about arms control avoids the confusions between arms control and disarmament and between conventional and nuclear arms control and disarmament that have marred Mr. Nixon's statements on the subject in the past. It provides, to the best of my knowledge for the first time, an intelligible account of the purpose of the preliminary SALT talks that took place in Helsinki in November and December of last year. Instead of agreeing within the government upon a position to be presented to the other side for the purpose of negotiations, the Administration

laid out preliminary models of possible strategic-arms-limitation agreements. We compared these both with each other and with the situation most likely to prevail in the absence of an agreement. . . . And this process had several advantages. We were not tied to a single position; instead we had building blocks for several different positions depending on our decisions and what might prove negotiable. Opening talks with the Soviets could concentrate on the principles and objectives underlying any type of strategic-arms agreement.

On the other hand, the discussion of our Latin American policy is trivial: "We were determined to reflect the forces of change in our approach and in our actions." But what does that mean when the chips are down, that is, when you have to choose between an unviable *status quo* and revolution? Are we to continue to come down on the side of the *status quo*, or are we going to join the progressive wing of the Catholic Church in supporting radical reform and even revolution, or at least are we going to keep our hands off in the contest between radical change and the *status quo*? Upon the answers we give to these questions our future Latin American policy will depend. But the document does not even pose the questions.

To give just another example of insufficiency: The document repeats all the arguments Mr. Nixon has presented before in support of his policy of Vietnamization, which is tantamount to the indefinite continuation of the war with reduced American casualties. But neither here nor elsewhere has Mr. Nixon ever raised the crucial question as to what he is going to do if and when Vietnamization should fail. He will then be faced with two choices, both painful and politically risky: either to disengage completely and openly admit defeat or re-escalate the war to the point where the complete destruction of the South Vietnamese countryside will dispose once and for all of the issue of who shall govern it. If it is true that the President has thus far refused to face the possibility that he might have to make such a choice, it is not surprising that the document keeps silent on the possibility of avoiding this dilemma by seeing to it that a truly civilian government is established in Saigon, which would have a vital interest not in continuing the war but in negotiating a peaceful settlement with the Viet Cong.

It is more surprising that the document has nothing to say about Laos; about the potential, inherent in the new East European policy of West Germany, for a radical change in the military and political alignments in Europe; and about MIRV's, the multiple independently targetable re-entry vehicles whose further development might well jeopardize the SALT talks.

Yet whatever the merits and defects of this document are, they can have only a tenuous relation to the foreign policy actually pursued by the Nixon Administration. Such a document performs two major functions: It tells the American people what they are supposed to like hearing, and it presents the Administration's assumed modes of thought and action in a most favorable light. In these respects, it is very much like the prospectus or annual report of a corporation.

To what extent the document actually reflects the future conduct of American foreign policy it is impossible to say. First of all, many of the pronouncements, as pointed out above, are so vague as to lend themselves to the support of virtually any foreign policy upon which the Administration would like to embark. Furthermore, the evidence provided by the first year of the Nixon Administration points to clever political manipulation rather than changes in the substance of foreign policy. The Administration's innovation's have dealt with the politics of foreign policy—and have done so quite successfully—rather than with foreign policy itself. The defusing of the Vietnam war as a domestic political issue, in step with its indefinite continuation, is a case in point. There is only one point at which the document and the assumed new foreign policy of the Nixon Administration coincide: the lack of ideological fervor and the avoidance of flamboyant rhetoric in general. What this change in tone portends for the future, only the future can tell.

Epilogue

If one must admit the failure of these essays, insofar as they had an immediate political purpose, to influence political action, one cannot help noticing either that the experience of their futility is not a private, personal matter but coincides with a collective experience of futility that pits American youth not only against American politics and society but against the modern world itself. And that American revolt, in turn, is but a national manifestation of a world-wide revulsion against the world as it is. The student revolt, expressing itself positively in attempts at creating a new culture and negatively in aimless destructiveness and revolutionary tantrums, has its most profound roots in the seeming meaninglessness of life as it is led throughout the world and, more particularly, in the United States. What does a man live for? What is his purpose in life? What is the meaning of death, which appears to wipe out that life as though it had never existed? What, in one word, is the truth about the human condition?

Man has always had to ask such questions, and in the past religion, reason, and science have endeavored to lay his questioning to rest. Yet the different systems of truth provided by these three methods of comprehending man and his world have tended to cancel each other out. Religion did not pass the test of reason, science discredited the metaphysical systems engendered by reason, and science has given us mastery over a monstrous world that needs religion and reason to give it meaning. That world is doubly monstrous because it sacrifices human ends to technological means, as well as the needs of the many to the enrichment and power of the few, and thereby diminishes the stature of man and threatens his very existence.

The universities have provided us with that mastery over nature, but they have been unable to give it meaning and harness it to human purposes. They claim to be dedicated to the disinterested search for truth about man, society, and the universe. But they have transformed themselves, through the very dynamics of their undertakings, into gigantic and indispensable service stations for the powers-that-be, both private and public. They serve society but do not sit in judgment on it. The student who enters the university with those questions about man and the universe on his lips finds himself in the presence of an institution that, to paraphrase Tolstoy, is like a deaf man answering questions nobody has asked. The university pretends to be the mouth-piece of the truth, the whole truth and nothing but the truth. But in actuality, insofar as what it presents as the truth is really true, it is largely irrelevant to what concerns man, young and old, and much of what it presents as truth is either not truth at all or truth only by accident, arrived at because it furnishes the powers-that-be with ideo-logical rationalizations and justifications for the *status quo*.

When the student turns from the university as the pretended source of truth and experiences it as one social institution among many, he comes face to face with another gap between pretense and reality. Social institutions pretend to serve the individual, and the university even pretends to do so *in loco parentis*. However, for whatever services they render, they exact a price, which, in turn, impairs or even negates the services themselves. Social institutions, in the measure that they are mechanized and bureaucratized, diminish the individual, who must rely upon others rather than himself for the satisfaction of his wants, from the necessities of life to his spiritual and philosophic longings. What he once controlled himself others now control, and in the measure that they do, they diminish his freedom.

Thus, modern society suffers from a profound ambivalence. It pre-tends to take care of needs that formerly the individual himself had to struggle to take care of, and to a high degree it lives up to that pretense. Yet the institution that takes care of man's needs also has the power to withhold that care. If it does, the individual's needs are left without care, insofar as he has no alternative means to satisfy them through his own individual efforts; and the sphere in which such individual efforts can be effective has been reduced by the mechanization and bureaucra-

tization of social institutions below the minimum necessary for the satisfaction of the individual's elemental needs. In one word, the individual,
to a high and unprecedented degree, is at the mercy of the institutions
established for the purpose of meeting his needs.

When the student turns to the economic sphere, he faces a contradiction between the objective conditions conducive to an economy of
abundance and economic practices carried over from the traditional
economy of scarcity. On the one hand, he is surrounded and well-nigh
engulfed by the hedonism of the *status quo* as the prevailing economic
attitude, the *status quo* being synonymous with the continuing increase
of material wealth enjoyed by a substantial majority of the people.
An ever greater national product, ever higher personal incomes, ever
more extensive social benefits, ever more amenities of life, an ever
greater variety of novelties, and change for its own sake of the cogs
and bolts of a hardly moving social machine—such are the goals in
which the purpose of America seems to exhaust itself. As I pointed out
in 1960 in *The Purpose of American Politics:*

> The unrestrained and self-sufficient hedonism of contemporary society
> has brought in its wake what must be called a society of waste. For where
> the productivity of the nation feeds, as it were, upon itself and does not
> serve as a mean to transcendant ends that select and assign the goods to
> be produced, waste necessarily ensues. Production, engendered by the
> needs of life and carried forward by the desire to make life easier, more
> attractive, and more nearly complete, becomes like a cancerous growth,
> multiplying and creating with elaborate and costly artificiality demands
> that can be called rational only in view of the goal of producing more
> and more goods. This system of production is irrational because it rejects
> human needs and genuine human desires as determining factors, replac-
> ing them with quantity of production for its own sake. . . . This system
> of production is irrational not only because it performs no positive
> economic or other social function, but also because it is wasteful of the
> resources of the nation. . . . This waste is a result of artificially induced
> competition and obsolescence. Essentially identical products compete
> with one another for a greater share of the market. They are essentially
> identical because the needs they serve are identical and must in the
> nature of things be satisfied by identical products. Competition among
> products of this kind can be justified neither in terms of price nor of
> quality, since both are essentially identical.

The enormous, wasteful proliferation of virtually identical products for
competitive purposes, sometimes even within the same company, calls for
the artificial creation and ever renewed and increased stimulation of demand. These wants are created, stimulated, and satisfied by artificial or
imaginary obsolescence, advertising, and marketing. These efforts, as

wasteful as the proliferation of products of which they are the inevitable result, add nothing to the substance of the product but serve exclusively the purpose of selling a maximum quantity of the product to people who would otherwise feel no need for it.

Not only American youth is repelled by this conspicuous irrationality. At a conference on "Culture and Society" held in Belgrade in the winter of 1969, one participant expressed dismay at a similar prospect for his society: "If the social development is not directed energetically toward a radical change of the social role and importance of the intellectual and cultural factors, I doubt whether it will be possible to achieve on our soil anything more important than a belated Balkan variant of modern technological-consumer civilization." In America that intellectual dismay becomes moral outrage. For while the orgy of wasteful production and distribution devours the resources of the nation, society appears to be unable to relieve hunger and stamp out poverty. While in 1967 the Bureau of the Census classified more than 25 million Americans as poor and, hence, in want of food, farmers are allowed to burn potatoes in order to get higher prices, and the government pays farmers for not producing. As school lunches for the poor tend to be perverted into subsidies for middle-class children* and farmers, so the agricultural support program tends to make the rich farmer richer and leave the poor farmer poor.† The regulatory agencies intended to protect the consumer have become the protectors of the economic forces they were created to regulate. The traditional liberal remedies have turned out to be not only unsuccessful but irrelevant to the issues at hand.

These experiences of a gap between pretense and performance culminate in the political sphere. The student has been told that his is a government of the people, by the people, for the people. Yet three basic experiences contradict that statement. First, the experience of the bureaucratization and mechanization of social life and the consequent diminution of the human person, to which we have referred before, is particularly pronounced in the political sphere. For the very political relationship—that is, one man imposing his will upon another —of necessity diminishes the latter's stature as a person. Yet contemporary political relationships are marked by an unprecedented discrepancy in power between the weilder of power and its object. That power overwhelms the individual not only by its irresistibility,

* See Robert Sherrill, "Why Can't We Just Give Them Food?" *The New York Times Magazine*, March 22, 1970, pp. 29, 91–103.
† See "Farm Policy Helps Make the Rural Rich Richer," by William Robbins, *The New York Times*, April 5, pp. 1, 56.

but also, because of its mechanized and bureaucratized nature, by its unfathomable anonymity. He lives in something approaching a Kafkaesque world, insignificant and at the mercy of unchallengeable and invisible forces.

Furthermore, the student not only feels helpless in the face of the powers-that-be but also appears incapable of influencing them. Students have demonstrated for freedom of speech in totalitarian countries; they have demonstrated against the Vietnam war and in support of racial justice in the United States and elsewhere. But what has been the result of all their demonstrations? Totalitarian governments still allow freedom of speech only to the rulers, the Vietnam war is still going on, and racial justice is still a postulate rather than a fact. The Chicago Democratic Convention of 1968 was experienced as the epitome of the sham of democracy.

This experience of futility is powerfully reinforced and made definitive by a third factor: the lack of a viable alternative to the dominant philosophy, regime, and policies. That is as true of the Soviet Union as it is of France, as true of Japan as it is of the United States. What difference does it make for whom one votes, when the policies of different persons and parties are virtually interchangeable?

Take the classic case of the 1964 presidential elections. Most of us thought that it was as clear-cut a case of two different personalities, two different political philosophies, and two different political programs as one could wish. But those who voted for the loser were pleasantly surprised to find that his political program, at least on the international scene, was in good measure executed by the victor who had opposed that political program in the election campaign. As Senator Goldwater put it in the fall of 1969, when asked how he felt about President Johnson's executing his program: "Well, he did it after he had read my speeches."

Thus the world into which the student is born, and into which he is supposed to fit himself to find his life's fulfillment, must appear to him as a world of make-believe, a gigantic hoax where nothing is as it appears to be and upon which what he feels, thinks, aspires to, and does has no effect except to provide inducements for harassment and repression. All the while, that meaningless and unbending world carries on under the shadow of an atomic cloud, which, if present trends continue, is likely to make an end to all of us. The virtual assurance of atomic destruction under present conditions compounds in the long run the senselessness of human existence that the practices of society bring home every day. The reaction of the activist youth has been threefold. It attacks universities as the weakest and most easily accessible outpost of the "establishment." It challenges the "establishment" at its fringes, as in the draft and the windows, furniture, and offices of public and corporate buildings. It tries to create a new culture in which man will come into his own, satisfying his emotions and expanding his consciousness.

However, while the destruction of a university is easy—a couple of hundred determined students can do it—it is also irrelevant to the distribution of power in society. One can even assert that insofar as the university has been faithful to its mission to speak truth to power, it has been a thorn in the side of the powers-that-be. Thus the destruction of the university may for a fleeting moment satisfy the emotions of the destroyers, but it performs no useful political or social function. The same conclusion applies to challenging the "establishment" at its fringes. The fringes are expendable and easily repaired. The demonstrated futility, in terms of the distribution of power in society, of the attacks upon the university and upon the fringes of the "establishment" by the very same token reveals for all to see the "establishment's" unchallengeable power.

It is a different matter with respect to the attempts at creating a subculture different from, and opposed to, the prevailing culture. If such a subculture were able to impose a new system of values and new modes of thought and action upon the material conditions of society, it would indeed thereby create a new society. Yet as far as one can see, what the proponents of a subculture seek is not to make rational and humane use of those material conditions but either to destroy them or to escape from them. Isofar as they do the latter— returning to a state of nature both physical and emotional—they may at best save themselves as individuals. But they do nothing—except set an example for some—for society at large.

Thus far we have spoken of what youth can do to society. However, given the weakness, both in terms of power and purpose, of youth, it is much more important to ask, given its unchallengeable power, what society may do to youth and the rest of us. Society has essentially two choices: It can face the issues its own dynamics has created by perverting and faulting its original purpose of equality in freedom, to which it is still rhetorically committed, and thereby renew itself, or it can try to maintain the *status quo* with all means at its disposal, even at the expense of its original purpose. The preservation of the *status quo* then becomes the ultimate purpose.

There can be no doubt, in view of the record, that American society has chosen the latter alternative. Regardless of the libertarian and reformatory rhetoric, its policies, both at home and abroad, have served the defense of the *status quo*. Abroad, the United States has become the antirevolutionary power *par excellence*, because our fear of Communism has smothered our rational insight into the inevitability of radical change in the Third World. Our interventions in Indochina and the Dominican Republic are monuments to that fear. At home, our commitment to making all Americans equal in freedom has been at war with our fear of change and our conformist subservience to the powers-that-be.

Our commitment to the American purpose of equality in freedom has won a battle in enforcing the rights of the black Americans at least in certain respects, a step forward that appears rather big as compared with the conditions of twenty years ago and rather insignificant as compared with the present conditions of the blacks in education, employment, and housing. What the change in the status of the blacks amounts to is the willingness of the powers-that-be to coopt blacks in such numbers and such conditions as not to endanger the over-all distribution of power within American society. When the powers-that-be perceive, rightly or wrongly, that the danger point is being approached, they call a halt to change and man the bastions of the *status quo*. Thus, the American purpose is about to lose the war, because the powers-that-be will allow the *status quo* to be dented, but not endangered.

The extent of the repression in store for the dissenters will depend upon the subjective estimate of the seriousness the powers-that-be place upon the threat to the *status quo*. Considering the thus far marginal nature of the threat, society will need only resort to marginally totalitarian methods. The dissenters will people our prisons, our graveyards, our Bohemias or—as utter cynics—our positions of power. Those last will not be unlike the Marxist-Leninists of the Soviet Union: They will mouth a litany of slogans which they not only do not believe in but which they also despise. Such a society can carry on for a while, like a body without a soul, but sooner or later it must either recover its soul—that is, the purpose that has given it life—or disintegrate from within. Perhaps, then, a new society, with a new purpose, will be built upon the ruins of the old; or perhaps nothing will be left but ruins for later generations to behold.

Index